RESTLESS SECULARISM

RESTLESS SECULARISM

Modernism and the Religious Inheritance

Matthew Mutter

Yale
UNIVERSITY
PRESS
New Haven & London

Published with assistance from the foundation established in memory of William McKean Brown. Copyright © 2017 by Yale University. All rights reserved. This book may not be reproduced, in whole or in part, including illustrations, in any form (beyond that copying permitted by Sections 107 and 108 of the U.S. Copyright Law and except by reviewers for the public press), without written permission from the publishers.

Yale University Press books may be purchased in quantity for educational, business, or promotional use. For information, please e-mail sales.press@yale.edu (U.S. office) or sales@yaleup.co.uk (U.K. office).

Set in Electra and Trajan types by IDS Infotech Ltd.
Printed in the United States of America.

Library of Congress Control Number: 2016960136
ISBN: 978-0-300-22173-2 (hardcover : alk. paper)

A catalogue record for this book is available from the British Library.

This paper meets the requirements of ANSI/NISO Z39.48-1992 (Permanence of Paper).

10 9 8 7 6 5 4 3 2 1

CONTENTS

ACKNOWLEDGMENTS

Study and writing are solitary enterprises, but this book would have been considerably weaker without a number of guides and friends who engaged my ideas along the way.

This book had an earlier incarnation as a dissertation. David Bromwich and Pericles Lewis, who advised my project, were tireless readers and advocates. Pericles's work on religion and the modernist novel was crucial for the development of my ideas, and I can only hope that the spirit of moral seriousness in David's criticism, which has long been a model for my own, has found its way into this book. I am also grateful to Amy Hungerford, who provided sharp and generous feedback for this project, and Michael Warner, whose seminar "Secularism and Anti-Secularism" at the Cornell School for Criticism and Theory helped me crystallize my own understanding of secularity. Other faculty at Yale—Wai Chee Dimock, Katie Trumpener, Ruth Yeazell, and Paul Grimstad—read or aided this project along the way.

The Institute for Advanced Studies in Culture at the University of Virginia provided a generous postdoctoral fellowship that allowed me to rework and expand the book in an extraordinary interdisciplinary setting. I would especially like to thank James Davison Hunter, the director of IASC, who has supported me since I was a young man, full of imagination but (at the time) little intellectual discipline. I had important conversations there with Matthew Crawford, Joe Davis, Jennifer Geddes, Regina Schwartz, Chad Wellmon, and Josh Yates. Charles Mathewes generously read an earlier version of my introduction and made sure that its theological claims were relatively sound.

Bard College has been a wonderful place to think and write. I am grateful to the Literature Program for granting me leave to finish this book, and I would like to thank my colleagues who read portions of my manuscript: Maria Cecire, Bruce Chilton, Deirdre D'Albertis, Liz Frank, Nancy Leonard, and Marina van Zuylen. Beyond Bard, I would like particularly to thank Jeffrey Perl, who has supported my work for many years and who provided painfully astute comments on a draft of the introduction, and Michael Levenson, whose detailed remarks on my entire book manuscript helped me say everything I was trying to say better.

The most stringent thinking and unconstrained argument happen in informal settings, and I thus owe a debt of gratitude to my long-time intellectual companions. Patrick Redding read much of this book at earlier stages, and my long conversations and arguments with him about religion, secularity, and modernist literature, which began our first semester of graduate school and continue to the present day, have sharpened and complicated my own convictions. Kathryn Reklis, a theologian and scholar of religion, was an important interlocutor for me as I developed my understanding of religion and aesthetics. Together they have been two of my most faithful friends. Kevin Seidel has been an immensely supportive advocate, and I owe many insights to our fifteen-year friendship. His comments on my manuscript, and his own work on similar theoretical problems in a different literary context, have been invaluable. Siobhan Phillips's masterful knowledge of modern poetry and carefulness as a scholar have consistently inspired me, and she has always read my work in exquisite detail, down to the notes.

Jennifer Banks and Heather Gold at Yale University Press have been remarkable editors, and they have helped me navigate the publishing of my first book with great patience and generosity of spirit. And I could not have pulled everything together without Anna Hadfield's editorial rigor. Anna is already, at a young age, a powerful cultural and social critic.

My greatest debt, however, is owed to my wife, Sarah Mahurin: "What you do / Still betters what is done." She and I have been discussing our own religious inheritances for almost ten years. Her extraordinary teaching and witness have shown me a different way of being an intellectual; I can only hope, one day, to have the impact on my students that she has on hers. She has read through this manuscript in its various iterations countless times and always made it better, though I cannot match the eloquence of her writing. She carried me through a long, long illness during which it seemed that a book like this would never be possible. Without her it wouldn't have been. Her energy and joy are contagious. So is that of our daughter, June, who has heaped delight upon delight on our lives. It is up to us, now, to provide a religious inheritance for her and to imbue her with the restlessness that will inevitably complicate it. "To my one son the hunger": that is the last of R. S. Thomas's "gifts" to his family. I would give the same to June.

Abbreviations

A	*The Collected Works of W. B. Yeats*, vol. 3, *Autobiographies*
AV	W. B. Yeats, *A Vision*
CP	Wallace Stevens, *Collected Poetry and Prose*
CPA	W. H. Auden, *Collected Poems*
CPY	*The Collected Poems of W. B. Yeats*
DH	W. H. Auden, *The Dyer's Hand*
EA	*The English Auden: Poems, Essays, and Dramatic Writings, 1927–1939*
EE	*The Collected Works of W. B. Yeats*, vol. 4, *Early Essays*
L	*The Letters of Wallace Stevens*
LE	*The Collected Works of W. B. Yeats*, vol. 5, *Later Essays*
LY	*The Collected Letters of W. B. Yeats*
MD	Virginia Woolf, *Mrs. Dalloway*
P	W. H. Auden, *Collected Prose* (3 vols.)
TL	Virginia Woolf, *To the Lighthouse*
TP	*The Collected Works of W. B. Yeats*, vol. 2, *The Plays*
TW	Virginia Woolf, *The Waves*

INTRODUCTION: MODERNIST SECULARISM
AND ITS DISCONTENTS

There is a famous passage in Virginia Woolf's *To the Lighthouse* where Mrs. Ramsay, knitting in solitude after her children have gone to bed, accesses a "self" beneath her social identity. She calls this self "a wedge-shaped core of darkness."[1] Its fluidity and obscurity allow her to ignore the boundaries that establish discrete identities and separate things from one another. In this darkness there is no "personality" that confronts the world as a series of competing objects to be placated, mastered, or managed; rather, there is a "summoning together" of all things in a complete "rest" outside "the fret, the hurry," and "the stir." As Mrs. Ramsay watches the stroke of the lighthouse on the horizon, "she bec[omes] the thing she looked at" (*TL*, 63). In the hypnotic aura of "this peace, this rest, this eternity," the light she has become "lift[s] up some little phrase or other . . . lying in her mind." Initially it lifts the apparently trivial saying on which she reflected before her moment of solitude—"Children don't forget, children don't forget"—but the speech continues: "It will end. It will end, she said. It will come, it will come, when suddenly she added, We are in the hands of the Lord" (63).

Mrs. Ramsay is immediately "annoyed with herself for saying that." "Who had said it?" she thinks: "Not she; she had been trapped into saying something she did not mean" (63). But who or what has trapped her? The novel doesn't provide a clear answer. It is tempting to read her instinctive turn to theological language as unwelcome interference by her cultural unconscious; this is what Mrs. Ramsay herself believes. The phrase was, she insists, a moment of "insincerity," a linguistic contamination of the "truths" she attained in the silence of her deep self.[2] In order to defend this claim she appeals to her avowed beliefs. When she asks for a second time "[w]hat brought her to say that," she rehearses

Victorian agnostic arguments concerning the impossibility of reconciling a good creator God, the ostensible source of "reason, order," and "justice," with the reality of the world's "treachery": "suffering, death, the poor" (64).

The appeal does not answer her question. Mrs. Ramsay's is a distinctively modernist problem: there is a gap between her secular "belief" and the continuing inner authority of emotions, along with the interpretations of the world embedded in them,[3] that have been bound historically to religious language. "We are in the hands of the Lord" is not merely an obsolete phrase thrown at experiences to which it no longer belongs. The language seems built into the nature of the experience; she moves toward it almost irresistibly. She has intuited a noumenal domain of "rest," "peace," and "eternity" beyond the phenomenal world, and before she is "trapped"—the word suggests that the path of her experience has conspired against her, offering only one outlet—she has already sensed an eschatological reality enclosed in that domain. "Children never forget," a phrase that conjures the painful layering of memory on a ceaselessly accumulating yet immutable past, yields to lines that imagine a future where this accumulation is folded into the eternity beneath things: "It will end . . . it will come." The trap has been set before the offending phrase arrives.

This is a book about the intricacies of the modernist relation to secularism.[4] Collectively these intricacies reveal a profound ambivalence in modernism over the nature and consequences of secularization.[5] This ambivalence is sometimes configured along the lines of Mrs. Ramsay's problem: writers are "trapped" between attractive religious paradigms for thought and feeling and a secularism that disavows the language and metaphysics that makes these paradigms intelligible. The ambivalence is exacerbated by another problem: many modernist writers display a heightened awareness concerning the dependence of secular conceptions of subjectivity, language, and world on the religious sources they are meant to displace. Nietzsche famously announced the death of God, but his principal challenge to post-religious consciousness—a challenge internalized by modernism—was to dispel what he called God's "shadows," the theological ideas and values that had migrated to, but still remained operative in, secular territory.[6] The modernist writers this book examines—Wallace Stevens, Virginia Woolf, W. B. Yeats, and W. H. Auden—call these secular revisions of religion into question. For these writers there is a growing suspicion that conceptual and ethical worlds are not interchangeable.

Secularization is often narrated by means of what the philosopher Charles Taylor has called a "subtraction story."[7] Once, the story goes, we believed in certain objects and forces in the world—gods, spirits, mana, providential agency. Now that the world is "disenchanted," those objects and forces are simply removed from the landscape. Nothing else changes; what remains is simply things as they are. Our perception of these things, sharpened by the discipline of a disengaged epistemology, is finally unencumbered by any extraneous ontological furniture. Writers like Taylor and the anthropologist Talal Asad, however, have been describing a secularism that does not merely discover a true world scrubbed of illusion or a transparent human nature beneath its religious augmentations but actively constructs both.[8] The world that secularism knows is the achievement of a particular kind of knower, who carries a set of values to the activity of knowing and whose self-understanding is confirmed by that activity. Religious history was a time, as Wallace Stevens writes, "[b]efore we were wholly human and knew ourselves" (*CP*, 280). The implicit achievement of secularism, then, is at once epistemological and existential: secular knowledge is indistinguishable from accurate *self*-knowledge, and to chart the "human" is simultaneously to become more fully or completely— "wholly"—human. The methods of secular knowledge are thus inextricable from a veneration of what this knowledge discloses: a self that is, as Stevens writes in another poem, "unsponsored, free" (56). The various claims of secular metaphysics, epistemology, and anthropology are embedded in and sustained by historically contingent and contestable ethical and aesthetic evaluations concerning what sort of person it is good or beautiful to be. Secularism has, in other words, a distinct imaginary.

I have chosen these writers because of their sustained ambivalence toward both religious and secular imaginaries.[9] This ambivalence throws the contested imaginaries into relief by dramatizing the tensions between them; indeed, the very power of their writing often depends on the articulation of such tensions. They make literature out of the conflict between religious and secular emotions (the desire for transcendence and the desire for pure immanence in Stevens), between religious and secular ideas (theological beauty and a secular sublime in Woolf), between religious emotions and secular ideas (the ego's fantasy of magical omnipotence and the realities of disenchantment in Auden), and between religious emotions and religious ideas (the aggressive, pagan "passions" and the Christian imperatives of self-exposure, repentance, and justice in Yeats). I have also chosen them because each is concerned with the implications of competing secular and religious imaginaries for a particular field of experience: language (Stevens), aesthetics (Woolf), emotion (Yeats), and the body and material life (Auden). That these writers link the struggle between religion and secularity to these fields means that the central religious problem for modernism is not explicit belief or disbelief in God but the entire fabric of thought and feeling implicit in the religious or secular imaginaries where belief situates itself.[10]

A focus on belief has often prompted scholars to talk about secularization in modern literature as if its consequences were primarily psychological. The decline of faith is marked by disorientation and anomie, a sense of meaningless-ness, and a search for alternate consolations. Art responds by reoccupying the deserted psychological ground. As one study puts it: "Individuals transfer [to art] the psychic energy formerly reserved for religion in which they seek the same gratifications, and often the same forms and rituals, as previously afforded by religion."[11] It is true that critics like Matthew Arnold, Clive Bell, and I. A. Richards thought that the form-giving and emotion-stimulating capacities of literature were analogous to religious belief and might be employed to organize human emotion in a secular age.[12] And many modernist writers (like many Romantics and Victorians before them) were drawn to the rhetoric of a "reli-gion of art." But this narrative depends on an essentialized and functionalist understanding of religion. It asks us to imagine two structurally identical vessels (religion and art) and a neutral content ("psychic energy") that is being trans-ferred from one to the other without any apparent modification ("they seek the same gratifications"). Religion and secularism (obscured by its proxy, "art") are not conceived as different paradigms for modeling reality or subjectivity but as vehicles for satisfying emotional needs that are unaffected by shifts in these paradigms. The "religion of art" narrative is meaningful only when "religion" has been distilled into a thin abstraction. Clive Bell maintained that both religion and art were "expression[s]" of "the emotional significance of the universe,"[13] but that formulation tells us nothing about the details of these expressions or how conflicts between them are adjudicated in literature.[14]

By focusing on religious and secular imaginaries rather than on belief or the psychological function of religion, I hope to show how comprehensively modernism confronted the challenge of secularization. One of the major efforts of modernist writing is the construction of new imaginaries to replace those understood to be in disrepair.[15] Such imaginaries explore how metaphysical and ontological frames resonate in everyday moral and aesthetic life, and how, in turn, valuations implicit in that life sustain the viability of the frames. Wallace Stevens's early poem "A High-Toned Old Christian Woman" is a representative investigation of these interrelations:

> Poetry is the supreme fiction, madame.
> Take the moral law and make a nave of it
> And from the nave build haunted heaven. Thus,
> The conscience is converted into palms,
> Like windy citherns hankering for hymns.
> We agree in principle. That's clear. But take

The opposing law and make a peristyle,
And from the peristyle project a masque
Beyond the planets. Thus, our bawdiness,
Unpurged by epitaph, indulged at last,
Is equally converted into palms,
Squiggling like saxophones. And palm for palm,
Madame, we are where we began. Allow,
Therefore, that in the planetary scene
Your disaffected flagellants, well-stuffed,
Smacking their muzzy bellies in parade,
Proud of such novelties of the sublime,
Such tink and tank and tunk-a-tunk-tunk,
May, merely may, madame, whip from themselves
A jovial hullabaloo among the spheres.
This will make widows wince. But fictive things
Wink as they will. Wink most when widows wince.

(CP, 47)

The poem irreverently explores how moral experience becomes aesthetic experience, how together they become comprehensive frames for the world ("supreme fictions"), and how reconfigurations of the frame may reconfigure experience. The imaginative architecture of Christianity is built when the original intuition of a "moral law" is "converted"—Stevens appropriates and transvalues that religious word—into an aesthetic place (the "nave" of a cathedral). This place, in turn, is expanded into a comprehensive metaphysical setting ("haunted heaven") that seems, retrospectively, the origin and source of the world's order. The power of the moral law is aestheticized and objectified so comprehensively that it becomes a cosmos. This is what it means for "the conscience" to be "converted into palms"—the palms are Stevens's name for the ability of an image to make an interior experience an exterior, sensuous element, or a *world*.

Particular kinds of aesthetic experience are sustained in such a cosmos: here it is (Stevens's version of) Kant's version of the "sublime." Kant's sublime was an experience of the "moral law" as the transcendent reality of human being. In Kant's theory, the feeling of being overwhelmed and terrified belongs to our vulnerability as sensuous, embodied creatures. But the pleasure it gives as the experience unfolds is linked to the disclosure of a "supersensible vocation," a sense of the self as a rational, moral, and finally religious aptitude that transcends nature.[16] Kant famously said that what moved him most was "the starry heavens above me and the moral law within me."[17] Kant, whose moral theory is ascetic, could easily be one of the poem's "disaffected flagellants . . . / Proud of such novelties of the sublime." The implication is that the manner in which the sublime is produced depends on the values—including the religious values—that the subject holds most dear; Kant's particular experience of the starry heavens as sublime requires his prior exaltation of moral freedom and a religious picture of the world that makes this moral freedom intelligible.

The speaker proposes that if one began with a different tone of experience—"bawdiness"—one could make it into a pagan "peristyle" rather than a Christian "nave," and from it "project" that experience into a "masque / Beyond the planets." What is important is that, here too, these three stages all reinforce one another. The immediate experience or value (bawdiness or morality) has a correlative architectural space (peristyle or nave), which in turn has an imaginative architecture, or cosmos (masque or heaven). Because they reinforce one another, the projection moves in multiple directions. The nave, with its vaulted arches and its hymns, is a place where the religious sublime is cultivated. The peristyle, with its pagan gods and jazz ("squiggling saxophones"), cultivates its own disposition: bawdiness. The broader imaginative architecture—the world-picture or cosmos—confirms the smaller spaces and concrete experiences.

The poem suggests, moreover, that looking at the same experiences in a different light, or lodging them in a different imaginative architecture, will transform the experiences themselves. This is what happens (or "may" happen) to the "disaffected flagellants" at the end of the poem. If seen from the perspective of bawdiness, their "sublime" and their asceticism are transformed. In Kant's sublime, the sensuous experience initially undermines the desire to find a rational order in the world because it defeats the faculties of understanding and imagination. Because of Kant's theological vision of the world, however, the self overcomes that defeat in the knowledge of its transcendent moral vocation. In the poem's alternate vision, the first stage of the sublime (the defeat of the understanding) is the only stage. But this cognitive confusion is experienced not as defeat but as a pleasurable intimation of the nonsensicality of the world. If the understanding has been overwhelmed, this is only because the cosmos has become a "masque beyond the planets." Stevens turns the confusion of faculties into an affirmation of cosmic indeterminacy (in the sense of "mask") and cosmic play (in the sense of "masque"). His nonsense syllables ("tunk-a-tunk-tunk") and excessive alliteration ("May, merely may, madame") suggest that the incomprehension characterizing sublimity is an occasion not for the self's transcendence of its sensuous condition but for worldly gusto (a capacity to dwell in the gaiety of sounds that resist the determinations of meaning). Even the flagellants' ascetic practices—whipping themselves—betray a "jovial hullabaloo." Their flagellation has been refigured as the "smacking" of "their muzzy bellies." What look like religious practices are recast as secular merely by a shift in metaphysical presupposition and interpretation (a new "supreme fiction") yoked to the sensuous resources of language.

Stevens's poem wryly envisions the comprehensive revision of moral, aesthetic, linguistic, and cosmological registers. It constructs a new secular imaginary to compete with the unsatisfying religious one. Preserving any one feature of religious experience or thought is impossible; a tug on a particular thread (moral, aesthetic, or cosmological) reveals that it is woven into all the others. Stevens's project is therefore representative of a strain in modernism that cannot comfortably be called "post-secular." That term tends to invoke the emergence of heterodox, hybrid, and private (noninstitutional) religious modes within a frame that remains broadly secular. The best recent books on twentieth-century literature and religion—Pericles Lewis's *Religious Experience and the Modernist Novel*, Amy Hungerford's *Postmodern Belief: American Literature and Religion after 1960*, and John McClure's *Partial Faiths: Postsecular Fiction in the Age of Pynchon and Morrison*—all tend, even if they do not use the term, to conceive of the persistence or reemergence of religion along the lines of the "post-secular."[18] Lewis's book challenges the secularization thesis and explores the alternate forms of the sacred developed by modernist novelists in conversation with emerging social scientific accounts of religious experience; Hungerford argues that post–World War II American novelists constructed a "belief" without "content" that focuses its energies not on metaphysical meanings but on the mystical, non-semantic aspects of language; McClure sees the postmodern novel as replete with a progressive, "weakened" religiosity that is comfortably suspended in "ideologically mixed . . . middle zones" that playfully challenge both secular conceptions of the real and fundamentalist reactions to those conceptions.[19]

From another perspective, however, these reconfigured religious forms can be understood as versions of the secular.[20] As we will see, secularization often involved the modification, redistribution, and privatization of religious ideas rather than their eradication. Hungerford's book documents the migration of religious energies into the domain of literature; properties of God become aspects of literary form. She acknowledges the Romantic and Victorian origins of this practice of transference; McClure, too, observes that his "post-secular" reaches back to Romanticism and American Transcendentalism. Lewis notes that the modernist novel's "characteristic concerns are sociological or anthropological rather than spiritual"; they thus seek a "satisfying *explanation* of . . . spiritual phenomena."[21] But early twentieth-century social science was itself a powerful secularizing agent; its accounts of religion tended to redescribe it from distinctly secular premises, according to which the "real" origin and orientation of religion was society contemplating itself (Durkheim) or psychic disorder and need (Freud). Thus modernist fiction's characteristic secularizing mode is what Lewis, adapting M. H. Abrams's Romantic "natural supernaturalism," calls "social supernaturalism"; religion was displaced onto the social rather than nature.[22]

By focusing on secularism rather than religion, this book investigates not post-secular religious experience but the secular frames that alter the coordinates of all experience, religious or other. The post-secular is, as McClure and Hungerford suggest, part of the Romantic inheritance. But the modernists in this study are suspicious of the Romantic strategies of either naturalizing or "socializing" religious thought, experience, and moral culture. A good deal of modernist rhetoric was expended in disavowing the Romantic legacy. I want to view that debate from a fresh perspective: it is a quarrel over modes of cultural secularization. I thus take T. E. Hulme's famous formulation at face value: Romanticism can be understood as "spilt religion."[23] But the implications of this apparently casual figure stretch well beyond the rhetorical interests of those working to establish a rival "classicist" sensibility. The writers in this study want to know, "palm for palm," as Stevens says, what kind of anthropology is appropriate to a new, secular cosmology (even if, as for Auden, the legitimacy of the secular is underwritten by God's transcendence). They want to disentangle the religious from the secular and see what each entails for language, aesthetics, emotion, ethics, and the body.

THREE MODELS FOR THE SECULAR

Stevens knew that comprehensive secular revision was difficult, for Western secularism was entangled in the Christian and Platonic legacies that it sought to displace.[24] In a 1940 letter to his friend Henry Church, he reflected:

> The major poetic idea in the world is and always has been the idea of God. One of the visible movements of the modern imagination is the movement away from the idea of God. The poetry that created the idea of God will either adapt it to our different intelligence, or create a substitute for it, or make it unnecessary. These alternatives probably mean the same thing.[25]

Secularization is often conceived as the replacement of religious belief with knowledge drawn from the domains of natural and social science (which Stevens calls "our different intelligence"). This passage, however, argues that "the movement away from the idea of God" is both difficult and complex: difficult because it will not simply vanish (it "*is*" the "major poetic idea"), complex because the transition can take several forms. Indeed, Stevens delineates three models: adaptation, substitution, and elimination. He collapses his distinctions by suggesting that these three alternatives "probably mean the same thing." This book will insist, on the contrary, that they do not, and that recognizing these models and their limitations is the key to understanding modernist encounters with religion.

ADAPTATION

The first option Stevens mentions, adaptation, is a revisionist strategy. It entails a reinterpretation or translation of religious concepts into a "naturalized" idiom. Jewish and Christian eschatological doctrines, for instance, which look forward to the transformation and perfection of all things, may be modified into modern doctrines of historical progress.[26] The doctrine of the Fall, too, has been naturalized in modernity by being recast as the alienation of subject from object (Coleridge and Marx), a fall into self-consciousness (Hegel and Emerson), a fall out of benevolent instinct into civilization (Rousseau), or even, in the case of Nietzsche, an enemy of Christian theology, a fall from aristocratic, heroic nonchalance into the moral obsessions of the "ascetic ideal."[27] Naturalization was a common procedure, as M. H. Abrams argued, in Romantic poetics and philosophy:

> It is a historical commonplace that the course of Western thought since the Renaissance has been one of progressive secularization, but it is easy to mistake the way in which that process took place. . . . The process . . . has not been the deletion and replacement of religious ideas but rather the assimilation and reinterpretation of religious ideas, as constitutive elements in a world view founded on secular premises.[28]

Stanley Cavell is thinking of a similar tendency when he calls Romanticism an "alternative process of secularization"; it avoided the hostility toward religion and anticlericalism of a particular strand of Enlightenment thought through the assimilation and reinterpretation of religious ideas.[29]

SUBSTITUTION

The second alternative, substitution, overlaps with adaptation but has a different logic. Substitution shifts attention from the content of a religious idea to the psychological needs and desires that generated it. If these needs are intractable, one seeks other agents or structures to satisfy them. According to this logic, it is possible that humans have a "need" for socially unifying beliefs, or to atone for guilt, or to gather their fragmented experiences into a metaphysical narrative. If these needs produced religious ideas and those ideas are now obsolete, one might satisfy the needs with new objects, ideals, and cultural goods. This conviction is at the heart, for instance, of Stevens's concern with the "supreme fiction,"[30] of the attempt by Auguste Comte to establish a new church based in positivist science, and of Matthew Arnold's desire to invest "culture" with the agency to govern the emotional and moral worlds once ordered by religion.[31]

An offshoot of the substitutionary logic that Stevens and the early Auden sometimes found attractive is the claim, first articulated by Ludwig Feuerbach, that theology is really anthropology. Feuerbach argued that God was the self-alienation of humanity (an inversion of Hegel, for whom humanity is the self-alienation of God): "Man—this is the mystery of religion—projects his being into objectivity, and then again makes himself an object to this projected image of himself thus converted into a subject; he thinks of himself not as an object to himself, but as the object of an object, of another being than himself."[32] This insight claims to demystify religion. Humans lose control of their proper imaginative capacities—the projection of being into objectivity—by subjecting themselves to their own imagined objects. But Feuerbach's insight also makes religion a source of true human knowledge. Not only is human "being" the content projected, but the objectification itself is an aid to self-understanding, for it allows us to observe our own desired perfections. Theology is anthropology because it articulates the idea of the human; religion is thus a necessary detour to secular self-knowledge. Stevens makes a similar claim when he argues, in his essay "Two or Three Ideas," that "the gods are the definition of perfection in ideal creatures. . . . [T]hey have fulfilled us," he writes: "they are us but purified, magnified, in an expansion" (CP, 847). In Yeats, too, the gods are imaginative paradigms for human passion and action: the hero "copies their gestures and acts."[33] For the later Auden, the pagan gods make visible forces that, though they belong to human agents, seem to determine and transcend them: "To believe in Aphrodite and Ares merely means that one believes the poetic myths about them do justice to the forces of sex and aggression as human beings experience them in nature and in their own lives."[34] In this model, secularization does not necessitate the expulsion of religious content, only its re-articulation outside mythic categories. Hans Blumenberg refers to this re-articulation as the "extraction of the anthropological core" from theology, a reclamation of the human from the more than human.[35]

ELIMINATION

The last strategy, elimination, challenges the assumptions of both the adaptive and substitutionary models. Elimination does not look for substitute *satisfactions* but uproots the very needs, desires, and moral assumptions that were a part of the religious framework. As Nietzsche wrote in *Human, All Too Human,*

> But in the end one also has to understand that the needs which religion has satisfied . . . are not immutable; they can be *weakened* and *exterminated.* Consider, for example, that Christian distress of mind that comes from sighing over one's inner depravity and care for one's salvation—all conceptions originating in nothing but errors of reason and deserving, not satisfaction, but obliteration.[36]

Needs and desires did not just create a religious order; rather, the religious order helped constitute those needs and desires. Elimination, then, would not only discard the idea of God but would also discard all of the ancillary ideas and dispositions that accompanied that idea: Nature, Man, the self, grammar.[37] Michel Foucault and Jean-Luc Nancy have been two of the most influential proponents of this basically Nietzschean position, as when Foucault claims that modern psychoanalysis merely reproduces pernicious Christian themes of inwardness and confession, or when Nancy suspects that the very sense of our "modernity" is beholden to a monotheistic understanding of the world as a project.[38]

THE MODERNIST IMPASSE

Why are these models important for modernism? Modernism has become critically aware of the Romantic methods of naturalizing and adapting religious concepts. The method has become a *problem,* and the confrontation with this problem is a major theme in modernist writing. The writers this book investigates—both religious and secular—are no longer satisfied with a literature saturated by Hulme's "spilt religion."[39] The problem with the adaptive strategy—a problem that modernists, as late, self-critical Romantics came increasingly to see—is that it tends to disfigure the original concepts to the point where they are no longer recognizable. Adaptation raises questions of legitimacy and coherence that force one to ask whether originally religious ideas remain intelligible in an alien framework. For the post-religious, it leaves the logic and power of religious categories intact; for the religious, it betrays the difference of distinctly theological ways of thinking and feeling. Thus while modernists continue to pursue adaptation and substitution, they are haunted by

the challenge of elimination. George Santayana, the Spanish-American philosopher, novelist, and interlocutor for Stevens, Eliot, Pound, and others, repri-
manded Idealists and Romantics for their

> tendency to retain, for whatever changed views it may put forward, the names
> of former beliefs. God, freedom, and immortality, for instance, may eventually
> be transformed into their opposites, since the oracle of faith is internal; but
> their names may be kept, together with a feeling that what will now bear those
> names is much more satisfying than what they originally stood for. If it should
> seem that God came nearest to us, and dwelt within us, in the form of vital
> energy, if freedom should turn out really to mean personality, if immortality,
> in the end, should prove identical with the endlessness of human progress, and
> if these new thoughts should satisfy and encourage us as the evanescent ideas
> of God, freedom, and immortality satisfied and encouraged our fathers, why
> should we not use these consecrated names for our new conceptions, and thus
> indicate the continuity of religion amid the flux of science?[40]

Santayana thought, like Arnold before him, that religion was a form of poetry.
But this identification meant precisely that religious ideas did not need to be
naturalized—to become "vital energy," "personality," or "progress"—when they
entered the domain of poetry, for they retained their subjective, imaginative
power even if they did not capture anything empirically or materially true about
the world.

Santayana was an atheist, but the hybridity of the dominant secularisms
bothered religious writers as well. T. S. Eliot, who became a Christian, also
questioned their incoherence. In an essay on religion and "humanism" (a
descendant of the Enlightenment version of secularism), Eliot wrote,

> Humanism depends very heavily, I believe, upon the tergiversations of the
> word "human"; and in general, upon implying clear and distinct philosophical
> ideas which are never there. My objection is that the humanist makes use, in
> his separation of the "human" from the "natural," of that "supernatural" which
> he denies. For I am convinced that if this "supernatural" is suppressed (I avoid
> the term "spiritual" because it can mean almost anything), the *dualism* of man
> and nature collapses at once. Man is man because he can recognize super-
> natural realities, not because he can invent them. Either everything in man
> can be traced as a development from below, or something must come from
> above. There is no avoiding the dilemma: you must be either a naturalist or a
> supernaturalist. If you remove from the word "human" all the belief in the
> supernatural has given to man, you can view him finally as no more than an
> extremely clever, adaptable, and mischievous little animal.[41]

For Eliot, in other words, there can be no such thing as what Abrams called "natural supernaturalism." A thoroughgoing naturalism would also erase, Eliot argues, elements of the "human" historically tied to religious tradition, for these elements can only be seen, in that view, as particularly inventive strategies to accomplish the aims pursued by everything else in nature: adaptation and survival. Eliot has as little patience with naturalized theology as Nietzsche, but his attack comes from the position of belief rather than purified unbelief.[42]

The modernists were not without their vehement adapters. The program of Auden's early prose, beginning with "Psychology and Art Today" and "The Good Life" (both 1935) and culminating in 1939's *The Prolific and the Devourer* (a book of *pensées* modeled after Pascal and Blake's *The Marriage of Heaven and Hell*), was to unify the claims of Christianity, psychoanalysis, and Marxism. All three, Auden writes, begin with an implicit claim—"Man is an organism with certain desires existing in an environment which fails to satisfy them fully"—and proceed to elaborate a theory of "reconciliation."[43] Auden resituates Christian doctrines ("The Fall of Man," "The Kingdom of Heaven," "Paradise," and "the forgiveness of sins") and the sayings of Jesus within the discourse of modern psychology, material science, and economics.[44] Yet Auden abandoned *The Prolific and the Devourer* around the time he entered the Anglican Communion, and the shift in his later work demanded a renunciation of the practice of secular assimilation. The censorial attitude the later Auden adopted toward some of his most powerful early poetry is really a product of this renunciation. A line from "September 1939"—"We must love one another or die" (*EA*, 246)—provoked the most famous of these judgments: that phrase, and indeed the whole poem, he wrote, "was infected with an incurable dishonesty."[45]

The source of this dishonesty was the rhetorical association of love with a biological imperative. In *Prolific*, written just months before the poem, Auden says of Jesus's command, "Thou shalt love thy neighbor as thyself": "Again Jesus bases love on the most primitive instinct of all, self-preservation."[46] A few years before, he had written that Jesus's "call to enter the Kingdom is an immediate one, not a reference to something that may take place after death," and this Kingdom was imminently available because "[t]he driving force in living things is a *libido*," which is "unconscious and creative," inconceivable "apart from matter," and "always without error" (*EA*, 345). These naturalizations of Christian love transformed it from gift and ethical task into a quasi-physiological drive that would move its vehicle toward perfection were it not impeded by neurosis. But Auden came to distrust this conceptual alchemy. The refusal to love was not a strangulation of the life-instinct but an ethical failure irrelevant to our physiological fortunes: "we must love one another," Auden said the line should have read, *"and* die."[47] Though the early Auden was an adapter, the very fault lines of his career were forged out of a growing suspicion, visible in modernism more broadly, that religious and secular anthropologies were not interchangeable. "If," the early Auden wrote, "one chooses to call our knowledge of existence knowledge of God, to call Essence the Father, Form the Son, and Motion the Holy Ghost, I don't mind. Nomenclature is purely a matter of convenience."[48] But for the later Auden, "nomenclature" matters; adaptation is neither truly secular nor truly religious, but a "dishonest" blend of incongruous categories.

Modernists understood their moment and work as transitional. Pound said that the Christian era ended definitively with the publication of *Ulysses;*[49] Woolf famously claimed that human character changed "on or about December 1910";[50] Yeats envisioned, in certain moods, that a post-Christian "Second Coming" was at hand; and Stevens insisted that "the imagination" always arrives "at the end of an era" (*CP*, 656). While critics have rightly suggested that this internal account was exaggerated,[51] modernism, I believe, *is* the first sustained moment in the long secularization of Western intellectual culture where writers begin to imagine a comprehensively post-Christian culture, and where secularism becomes, out of necessity, an object of reflection. This position allows it to interrogate the strategies of intellectual and cultural secularization characteristic of eighteenth- and nineteenth-century writers that, to the modernist eye, still lean too heavily on the theological paradigms that preceded them.[52] It also allows modernists to ask whether experience can conform to a secularism purified of those paradigms.

I have been using the term "secularization" to describe a method that generates a content. But when we approach the question of content, the term seems, at first glance, to fit modernism poorly. If secularism means the inheritance of Enlightenment rationalism, with its emphasis on "self-assertion" and reason's potential mastery of nature and history,[53] modernism shares Romanticism's protest against that vision and adds its own accents of impotence and exposure. (In Eliot's "Gerontion," "History" has "many cunning passages, contrived corridors / And issues"; Stevens imagines receiving the "force that destroys us" with the "politest helplessness.") If secularization is synonymous with "disenchantment," and the agent of disenchantment the form of reason that resolves experience into its constitutive material causes, there too modernism dissents.[54] For Stevens, dedication to a "reality" divested of spiritual causation and intrinsic meaning does not mean that what is available to the mind is merely empirical:

> We seek
> Nothing beyond reality. Within it,

Everything, the spirit's alchemicana
Included, the spirit that goes roundabout
And through included, not merely the visible,

The solid, but the movable, the moment,
The coming on of feasts and the habits of saints,
The pattern of the heavens and high, night air.

(CP, 402)

"Spirit" for Stevens may have lost its theological or Idealist grounding, but it is still resolutely a part of the real, and contains its own enchantments. A still more metaphysically comprehensive enchantment is evident in the poetry of Baudelaire, Mallarmé, Rilke, Yeats, H.D., and Pound, which is replete with the imagination of occult energies, magical patterns, and spiritual arrangements.

As an ontology and an ethos, secularism is often taken to entail a series of affirmations: the life of immanence over transcendence; mutability over stasis; the impassioned body over ascetic discipline; the luminosity of everyday experience and material detail over metaphysical revelation; and self-determination over submission to traditional religious and cultural norms or a presumption that human capacities are disfigured by sin. Such affirmations are prominent in modernism; Stevens's polemically anti-Christian poem "Sunday Morning" contains perhaps all of them. But they often depend on binaries that secular rhetoric establishes to articulate its difference. These binaries depend, in turn, on a caricature of Christianity as otherworldly, hostile toward the body, and obsessed with human powerlessness. Moreover, many secular affirmations began as theological ones. Charles Taylor has argued that "the affirmation of the ordinary" was a prominent feature of Reformation piety; Caroline Walker Bynum has shown that ancient and medieval Christian understandings of the self were thoroughly somatic and particularly attuned to the importunate but disagreeable nonsexual dimensions of embodiment such as digestion, defecation, and putrefaction; and Thomas Pfau has claimed that secular modernity has witnessed a contraction rather than expansion of vocabularies for human will and agency.[55] Indeed, there is a significant tension between the moral ethos of secularism, which emphasizes self-determination, and the accounts of causation characteristic of modern science (the authoritative mode of secular knowledge), which emphasize the manifold material and social determinations that constitute the ostensibly self-determining subject. Freud, whose work is so important to modernism, is representative of this tension: one finds in his writing a rhetoric of metaphysical independence juxtaposed to a vision of the self as overwhelmed by forces operating below and beyond consciousness or will.[56]

The various configurations of secularism, moreover, have not always generated such affirmations. As Weber showed in *The Protestant Ethic and the Spirit of Capitalism*, "this-worldly asceticism" in the economic domain was inaugurated by Lutheran understandings of vocation (*Beruf*) and Calvinist anxieties over signs of election, but it soon escaped those theological origins to become a generalized secular ethos. And Weber's own vision of the "vocation" of the secular scholar—the echo of Luther is deliberate—demands another kind of asceticism: the rigorous "eliminat[ion]" of the "personal point of view" from all scientific inquiry, a determination not to allow considerations of value to encroach on the investigations of facts.[57] For Yeats, by contrast, the man of science is still a passive, empty ascetic, no different from "Saint Anthony in his cavern." The questions, "'Do I realize my own nothingness before God?'" and "'Have my experiments and observations excluded the personal factor with sufficient rigor?'" are at bottom, for Yeats, the same. The aim of both scientist and ascetic, he writes, is "to hollow their hearts till they are void and without form."[58]

MODERNIST SECULARISM AS PAGANISM

As with Yeats, who finds an unhappy analogy between Christian and scientific asceticism, many modernist writers looking to construct a viable secular ethos contest those modes of secularism that remain dependent on Christianity. These are writers who incline toward the "eliminationist" model I have described. That leaves in question, however, the positive content—the aesthetics, ethics, and images of and for experience—that might replace both the Christian ethos and its secular analogues. These writers look toward what I want to call paganism.[59] Yeats and Lawrence, for instance, are decidedly post-Christian, but they resist secularism in its humanist mode; Stevens later said of "Sunday Morning" that it was "simply an expression of paganism" (*L*, 250). A major fault line in modernism within the broader tension between the religious and the secular is really a divide between paganism and what Nietzsche called "ascetic ideals."[60]

By paganism I do not mean what Stephen Dedalus derides, in reaction to Buck Mulligan's call to "Hellenise" Ireland, as "new paganism . . . *omphalos*."[61] It is neither humanist neoclassicalism nor the sensual aestheticism of the Decadents. (Joyce, in an essay on Oscar Wilde, doubted what he called "the good news of neo-paganism," a gospel aiming to "bring back the Golden Age.")[62] This modernist paganism disavows both the humanistic equipoise characteristic of what Matthew Arnold called "Hellenism" and those aspects of the decadent sensibility that preserved close ties to Catholicism's ritualism and spiritualized sensuality. While there are traces of aestheticist neopaganism in the early poetry of Yeats and Stevens (as tragic beauty in the former and as hedonism in the latter), both writers developed a more exacting, antihumanist, *metaphysical* paganism that emphasized not rational or aesthetic order but submersion in the world's immanent flow. Stevens's "The River of Rivers in Connecticut" expounds this vision:

> In that river, far this side of Stygia,
> The mere flowing of the water is a gayety,
> Flashing and flashing in the sun. On its banks,
>
> No shadow walks. The river is fateful,
> Like the last one. But there is no ferryman.
> He could not bend against its propelling force.
>
> It is not to be seen beneath the appearances
> That tell of it. The steeple at Farmington
> Stands glistening and Haddam shines and sways.
>
> (*CP*, 451)

The poem appropriates the chthonic and "fateful" features of the pagan underworld but renders them secular (in the sense of this-worldly): the river of rivers, or the force of becoming that drives all things, is "far this side of Stygia." Yet there is finally neither near nor far in this world, for it is a "mere" flowing. That word evokes a singularity so copious, an abstraction so concrete, that it does not need depths to be profound: it cannot "be seen beneath the appearances / That tell of it" and there is no "shadow" on its banks. It is like the God who is both everywhere and nowhere, but its "propelling force" is immanent rather than transcendent; it is not anchored in an eternity outside time but coincident with time itself. The river is dangerous ("fateful") from the perspective of any being that would "bend against" it to establish a position of stability or control, but this danger is simultaneously a "gayety." (Stevens uses "gaiety" elsewhere; the archaic spelling suggests the antiquity of the force.) The church that appears in the poem does not have to be disavowed: the steeple "stands glistening" because it is merely, to add a sense of diminishment to the poem's use of the word, one more flash in a world of "flashing." It too is all surface.

This is a river, the last line of the poem reads, "that flows nowhere." The affirmation of this figure—the will to call it a "gayety"—is effortful in Stevens, for elsewhere he could write of "our sense of evil," "our sense that time has been / Like water running in a gutter / Through an alley to nowhere" (*CP*, 593). Stevens's pagan flow is thus an affirmation of a world indescribable in Christian eschatological or secular progressive terms, which are able to frame evil from the vantage point of eternity or a historical telos. The "sense of evil" is trans-valued into a sense of abundance painful only to the individualized nodes of identity propelled yet ultimately destroyed by it. What makes this post-Christian pagan affirmation different from pre-Christian paganism is, as Bernard Williams says, precisely that it has passed through Christianity.[63] It takes the overwhelming force of the world, seen in Homer's pagan world as an intransigent background impervious to questions such as "Why is it like this?" or "Where is it going?" — Auden writes that in "Homer's world" the earth "alone is seriously *there*"[64] — and adds an element of the biblical "it was good." This affirmation is made not in spite of the world's dangerous, impersonal force but because of the flash, shine, and gaiety it brings in its train.

Modernist paganism is thus a mode of what Charles Taylor has called the "immanent counter-Enlightenment," a current of secular thought and feeling that turned against Enlightenment humanism. This current resists "the standard form of modern anthropocentrism" and operates instead along a "tragic axis" that "reject[s] the too-harmonized picture of life, in which suffering, evil and violence have been painted out."[65] So Woolf, like Yeats, looks to Homer and the Greek tragedians to help us learn how to place the pleasures of immanence back on the tragic axis:

> With the sound of the sea in their ears, vines, meadows, rivulets about them, they are even more aware than we are of a ruthless fate. There is a sadness at the back of life which they do not attempt to mitigate. Entirely aware of their own standing in the shadow, and yet alive to every tremor and gleam of existence, there they endure, and it is to the Greeks that we turn when we are sick of the vagueness, of the confusion, of the Christianity and its consolations, of our own age.[66]

"Fate," Woolf suggests, is not a meaningful category for either Christianity, with its consoling redemption, or secular humanism, with its consoling projects of world amelioration and its stance of self-assertion rather than "endur[ance]."[67] "Fatal Ananke," Stevens writes, "is the common god" (*CP*, 161). Like Woolf, who would attend to every "gleam of existence," he links secular everydayness (his god is not uncommon) to the force of necessity.

The moral ethos of modernist paganism often rejects the Christian ethic of agape and de-emphasizes the secular ethic of sympathy and benevolence; it gives, Taylor writes, "positive significance to the irrational, amoral, even violent forces within us." These forces "cannot simply be condemned or uprooted, because our existence . . . vitality, creativity," and "strength depend on them."[68] Thus modernist paganism's values are often, to use the terms popularized by

Karl Jaspers and recently rehabilitated by numerous scholars, "pre-Axial" rather than "Axial."[69] Instead of Axial Age dedications to transcendent ethical criticism, ascetic self-regulation, and universalizing theory, modernist paganism posits a creative but dangerous and amoral cosmos that generates intensity rather than goodness, a self whose constitutive energies cannot be ascetically organized from a vantage point beyond the world,[70] and a form of nontheoretical thinking that does not generalize about phenomena but pursues what Lawrence calls a "state of feeling-awareness" that (like Stevens's river) "get[s] nowhere" because its aim is mythic participation in the world rather than knowledge about it.[71]

The reemergence of paganism is a major theme in Max Weber's "Science as a Vocation," the source of the famous concept *Entzauberung* ("disenchantment"). The essay, which describes the ubiquitous rationalization of modern institutions, models for knowledge, and what Weber calls the "conduct of life," has received significant critical attention in recent years, much of it framed as dissent from Weber's bleak diagnosis of the intractable conditions of modern secularism.[72] But disenchantment is not the most salient category in Weber's essay. The ambiguities of that term recede before his description of what he calls, with audible unease, "polytheism." He elaborates:

> [W]e realize again today that something can be sacred not only in spite of its not being beautiful, but rather because and insofar as it is not beautiful. . . . And, since Nietzsche, we realize that something can be beautiful, not only in spite of the aspect in which it is not good, but rather in that very aspect. . . . It is commonplace to observe that something may be true although it is not beautiful and not holy and not good. Indeed it may be true in precisely those aspects.[73]

Polytheism, then, is a condition in which the fundamental domains of value are not only plural but incommensurable or actively hostile.[74] Christianity and Platonism affirm the ontological unity of the true, the good, and the beautiful.[75] But in Weber's vision of the secular condition, one may only enjoy one part of being, and such enjoyment frames no transparent window onto life, for it is by definition besieged by other authoritative values in conspiracy against it. This is the case in the "Time Passes" section of *To the Lighthouse*, where the "strange intimation" generated by aesthetic experience—"that good triumphs, happiness prevails, order rules" (*TL*, 132)—is continuously and implacably brought to grief; or in Jean Toomer's *Cane*, which asks, "What's beauty anyway but ugliness if it hurts you? God, he doesn't exist, but nevertheless he is ugly."[76]

Modernist paganism depends, then, on a view of the world as impersonal, intractable conflict.[77] Yeats affirms, "It was Discord or War that Heraclitus called 'The God of all and the Father of all'"; and his post-Christian counter-annunciation ("Leda and the Swan") comes from the recognition that "Love and War came from the eggs of Leda."[78] "Why should we never believe," he asks, "that religion can never bring round its antithesis,"[79] and concord be exchanged for discord, Christ for Oedipus? George Santayana sees a world in which there is an unbridgeable gap "between existence and justice," where "conflicts are whole-hearted on every side, and universal Will has no qualms about contradicting and thwarting itself. That is its business. War is the father of all things that actually arise, since they arise by the confluence of forces; and universal Will has no prior purpose but lives only in the perpetual result."[80] For Stevens, "there is a war between the mind / And sky"—"a war that never ends"—and the poet's task is to distill praise out of this conflict: "To live in war, to live at war, / To chop the sullen psaltry" (*CP*, 351, 142). Though Woolf does not, like Yeats, aspire to develop a pagan ethos (or, like Auden, to resist the reemergence of such an ethos), her characters "deplore" the irresistible impression that "strife, divisions," and "prejudices" are "twisted into the very fiber of being" and consistently struggle to combat what they call, variously, the "illimitable chaos," "formless imbecility," or "undifferentiated forces" of "life" (*TW*, 226, 249, 255).[81] In Lawrence's *The Man Who Died*, the embodied self only escapes the banality of the "personal" when it is mythically absorbed into the "greater life" of what the book variously calls the "seethe of phenomena," "the blue flood of invisible desire," and the "vast invisible sea of strength."[82]

For Weber, secularism may involve the attempt to preserve a religious ethos while abandoning the religious metaphysic from which it is derived. It may also involve the ascendancy of rationalizing forces unwittingly set into motion by ascetic religion, which struggled to organize the natural plurality of passions and impulses into a singular ethical project. From this perspective, Western secularism is a "late" Christian phenomenon, indelibly marked by the theology out of which it developed. But in another sense, secularism is pre-Christian. "We live as the ancients did," Weber writes, "when their world was not yet disenchanted of its gods and demons, only we live in a different sense."[83] This different sense is "disenchantment"—the accounts of causation have changed, the impressions of the world as infused with *logos* have been altered—and yet the underlying ontology has resurfaced. That ontology, for Weber as for Yeats, Stevens, and Woolf, is at bottom agonistic: "different gods struggle with one another, now and for all times to come." These gods "take the form of impersonal forces," but they are just as implacable, relentless, and hostile.[84] And because these forces will war "for all times to come," this type of secularism eschews the eschatological vision so crucial to Judaism and Christianity, which various secularisms appropriated in their liberal-progressivist and Marxist modes.

When the world is best described as heterogeneous, impersonal force, personhood appears, for some modernists, an ontological anomaly and anthropocentric illusion.[85] And because this world is superior in intensity, the self that desires attunement with it may divest itself of features associated with personhood: narrative continuity and coherence, durable identity formed in the matrix of intersubjectivity, and even agency. Mrs. Ramsay's "wedge of darkness" is beneath "personality"; Septimus's suicide is understood by Clarissa Dalloway as an attempt to "reac[h]" a "centre" that eluded his attempts to "communicate" with other persons. Stevens calls the "impersonal" his "ultimate inamorata."[86] For Yeats, the "Incarnation," that conversion of transcendent reality into a person, created "modern science and modern efficiency and also the modern lyric feeling which give body to the most spiritual emotions. It produced a solidification of all things that grew from the individual will."[87] To circumvent the subjective consequences of this Christian anthropocentrism, Yeats seeks not "oneself" but one's "opposite," a "mask," not an "identity." Auden's poetry, meanwhile, is a sustained attempt to preserve a sense of the secular that does not re-enchant impersonal force and also to protect the domain of personhood (the "face") from those secular descriptions that reduce it through a science of behavior and statistic.

Because, as Stevens writes, "It is the human that is the alien, / The human that has no cousin in the moon" (*CP*, 288), many modernists can no longer confidently affirm, as Emerson did, that "Nature is a symbol of spirit," for that claim presumes that the world is metaphysically disposed to unfold itself in human meaning.[88] They cannot "[p]roclaim," like Wordsworth, "how exquisitely the individual Mind . . . to the external World / Is fitted" and "how exquisitely, too . . . The external world is fitted to the Mind."[89] These Idealist, secularizing solutions to the decentering of the human subject allowed that subject to operate as if the world were still a "creation," a place that, because it originated in something analogous to human mind (*logos*) or spirit, was still reflective of and responsive to human language and desire. As Georges Poulet argued, the Romantics were convinced of "the essentially religious nature of human centrality": "situating the non-self, or nature, at the periphery, and the self at the center, it confers a value to the circle not only more human, but more subjective; for at bottom, if the center is the self, this self, that is human consciousness, reigns over the circle."[90] Stevens insists, on the contrary, that the world "is not our own and, much more, not ourselves" (332). Yeats asserts that "warring opposites"—rather than "thought"—"created the world."[91] In other words, at the very moment modernists are exploring the depths of consciousness, that consciousness is simultaneously seen by many as *ontologically* marginal and epiphenomenal. Thus the "sublime"—we will see this in Woolf—becomes less an encounter with the numinous or a sign of one's "supersensible destiny" (Kant) and more a disclosure of Being's indifference to the self. The imagination is no longer the "repetition in the finite mind of the eternal act of creation of the infinite I AM" (Coleridge)[92] but rather an embattled faculty trying to order a fundamentally chaotic exterior, an energy that does not grant access to, but rather resists, the aggressive "pressure" of reality (Stevens).[93] A disenchanted ontology complicates those models of subjectivity for which the world is a mirror of the self.

THE STRUCTURE OF THE BOOK

The chapters of this study are arranged as a series of case studies meant to clarify the implications of the conflict between religious and secular imaginaries for certain categories of thought and experience: language (Stevens), aesthetics (Woolf), the body and materiality (Auden), and emotion (Yeats). There are a number of overlapping concerns that reemerge in each chapter. All four writers labor against the secular critique of anthropomorphism, which maintained that the basis of religious thinking was the human tendency to project its own features and desires onto the world.[94] In Stevens this critique threatens the validity of poetic analogy; in Woolf it challenges attempts to predicate the "beauty" of the world; in Auden it undermines the logic of a magical thinking that would subjugate the otherness of the world; and in Yeats it becomes a full-scale revolt against the emotions associated with a "personalized" human subject. Because the critique questions the legitimacy of investing the world with moral features, and because the world is no longer (for any of these writers except Auden) grounded in a moral source (God), the problem of anthropomorphism opens onto the interpretation of evil. In "Esthétique du Mal" Stevens is more concerned with "The death of Satan" than the death of God. The problem of beauty in Woolf is closely linked to the aesthetic dimensions of theodicy. Auden worries that attempts to re-enchant the world lead to a sacralization of force and to the elimination of the distinctly "historical" element proper to human beings, which is a domain of moral freedom rather than sacred violence. And Auden's reflections on these matters arise from a resistance to the influence of Yeats, who juxtaposes the amoral "passions" to the responsible, remorseful, ascetic self.

What the chapter arrangements make visible, I hope, is the extensive impact that a shift in the religious landscape has on concerns that might initially seem unrelated to specific beliefs. That Stevens's poetry repeatedly returns to the death of God as a condition of existential vertigo is a scholarly commonplace,[95] but my chapter argues that for Stevens, language itself harbors a dangerous bias toward transcendence. Stevens is mistrustful of the way metaphor slides into metaphysics, the way an analogical worldview becomes a theological one, and the ways in which signs and symbols tend to refer solid, immanent things to supersensible narratives or "meanings." In the face of this danger, he develops a poetics of tautology meant to divest language of such bias. Yet later in his career he returns to analogy as a mode of transcendence-in-immanence and establishes a concept of "description without place" in which imagined goods, which have no immanent existence, correspond to details of a particular scene. Stevens is, in other words, working out a version of Nietzsche's famous claim that we are not rid of God until we are rid of grammar while simultaneously harnessing the religious possibilities of language.

The chapter on Woolf turns to the uncertain link between metaphysics and aesthetics. There has been a small movement among recent critics and philosophers to rehabilitate the reputation of beauty, which suffered under the modernist fascination with ugliness, Romantic and postmodern prejudice in favor of the sublime, and political criticism of beauty as elitist, inefficacious, and complicit with injustice.[96] This chapter seeks to reframe these debates by examining the link between beauty and religious ontologies. Weber, following Nietzsche, insisted that secular modernity had broken sympathetic relations between beauty and goodness, but in Woolf's novels the beautiful cannot shed its theological aura: its promise of reconciliation, peace, and divine benevolence. Woolf's famous conception of "the world as a work of art"—which has, nevertheless, no "creator"—remains entangled in the aesthetic theodicies she repudiates. Her novels struggle to conceptualize secular, mundane models of beauty while simultaneously clinging to intimations of a metaphysical and moral order implicit in aesthetic experience. Beauty is, in her writing, the last and most intractable stronghold of mystical feeling. If Nietzsche's post-religious challenge to Stevens was to eliminate grammar, for Woolf it is the temptation toward what Nietzsche called "aesthetic anthropomorphisms," and she can decide neither for nor against them.

Chapter 3 investigates the consequences of post-Christian thinking for the emotions. There has been a resurgence of contemporary literary and theoretical interest in the status of emotion and affect, just as there has been in the status of beauty.[97] The example of Yeats suggests that the discourse surrounding emotion must take into account the religious and secular paradigms within which emotion is evaluated. I argue that Yeats rejected the cultural authority of what he called "spiritual emotion," "vague propagandistic emotion," and "modern lyric feeling"—all inheritances, for him, of the inward, ascetic Christian self and its "affections"—and sought to replace them with the pagan "passions." These passions—anger, lust, grief, and joy—are what Philip Fisher has called "monarchical states of being."[98] They assent to the singular, despotic nature of the will's claims on the world and refuse to be subjugated to therapeutic or moral ends. They are equally martial states; they welcome conflict as the condition of their amplification. Yeats's account of the passions depends, in fact, on his view of the world as a terrain of "warring opposites." His ontology of conflict—a conscious break with Christian and Platonic doctrines of creation—and his view of the passions are symmetrical and mutually reinforcing. But in his treatment of "joy," which he understands as the energy underwriting all manifestations of passion, Yeats "vacillates" between Christian models of the receptivity, gratuitousness, and communal reciprocity of joy and pagan models where joy is an achievement of the victorious "will." Many of Yeats's major poems, moreover, dramatize a tension between his pagan ontology of sacred conflict and an ethical recoil from particularized scenes of violence that seem to obey that same ontology. Yeats, in other words, can never fully assent to the de-ethicized, anti-ascetic ethos established by his own rhetoric.

Both Yeats's occultism and paganism and Stevens's tautological poetics form the backdrop against which much of Auden's mature poetry is written. Chapter 4 examines Auden's vision of the body and the broader material character of existence by elaborating his critique of "magical thinking," which for him marks an attempt to subsume the material otherness of the world into human subjectivity. Secularism, for Auden, is caught in a dilemma. As an ethos it is generally understood as a dedication to "this" world rather than any other, but as a method of description it has alienated the very world it means to claim by emphasizing the mechanical, nonhuman character of its animating processes. As a late modernist, Auden is writing against what he takes to be two distorted modernist responses to this dilemma: magic, which disavows the gap between subject and object, and pagan immanence, which identifies with and seeks to resacralize the very inhumanness of the world's material energy. Auden, rather, accepts the secular disenchantment of the world, which for him uncovers a new possibility: an ethical relation to material life, including the life of one's own body, as the nonhuman other. But he simultaneously preserves a Christian, nonreductive vision of the human world as a domain of responsibility, original action, and transcendent aspiration. He thus develops what I call a nonhierarchical "affirmative dualism," a vision of two distinct orders given equal standing. If there is an ongoing tension in Stevens and Woolf between secular and religious desire, and in Yeats between a pagan ethos and both Christian and secular asceticism, in Auden these relations are not so much oppositional as complementary. While secular rhetoric has often pilloried Christianity as an "ascetic ideal" hostile toward the body and the material conditions of existence, for Auden a Christian secularism is necessary to preserve both the integrity of materiality from domination by subjectivity and the integrity of subjectivity from either alienation from or pure identification with materiality.

A NOTE ON METHOD

In 1995, the American literary scholar Jenny Franchot issued a challenge to her discipline. The secular prejudice of critical culture had implicitly invalidated religion "as a serious subject of inquiry."[99] What Paul Ricoeur calls the "hermeneutics of suspicion" had come to dominate the critical perspective so that "religion" had become "that which inhibits, transmutes, or enables political change but is hardly ever an achievement whose priorities take precedence over the social" (834). Religion had been treated as entirely epiphenomenal: there was always some "secular" cause or motive animating it. Scholars, she said, "[a]re everywhere quietly expected to perform precisely this act of translation or 'demystification' to avoid being seen in the wrong light; they must resituate a particular sacred or an individual's interior life into an understanding of culture that denies transcendence" (840).

Given the "turn" to religion in literary and cultural studies (a turn that has been less noticeable in modernism than in broader Americanist scholarship), Franchot's criticisms have in some sense been heard. But there are indications that her concerns about method have not. A good deal of current literary scholarship is still shaped by a functionalist approach to religion. This approach is subtler and less ideologically dismissive toward religion than previous ones, but it is nonetheless marked by a different kind of reductionism and an evasion of normative engagement.

I have already registered my reservations about both the "post-secular" and accounts of how, in a secular age, art supplants the psychological function of religion. But there is another model gaining traction in literary criticism: "lived religion," a sociological movement that focuses on the concrete applications of popular religious practice rather than on the theological frameworks that animate them. Robert Orsi, the most prominent figure in this movement, rejects an understanding of religion (articulated most powerfully by Clifford

Geertz) as "a medium for explaining, understanding, or modeling reality."[100] He proposes instead an account of religion as "relationship." These relationships, he writes, "have all the complexities—all the hopes, evasions, love, fear, projections, misunderstandings, and so on—of relationships between humans" (2). Lived religion thus focuses on how individuals and groups "live in, with, through, and against the religious idioms available to them in culture" rather than the religious idioms themselves.[101]

A number of distinguished literary scholars have appealed to this model as a way forward in literary investigations of religion.[102] Lived religion, according to Lawrence Buell, is a way out of an impasse:

> [L]iterature specialists in search of appropriate critical idioms and analytical registers for talking about literature's religious valences are still having to contend against the constraints of assumptions such as that a text's religious dimension must reside chiefly in some sort of thesis or idea structure, and/or that religious motives are to be decoded in terms of such secular motives as political resistance or cultural survival, whether on the view that these are the kinds of motives that *really* matter or on the view that there is no such thing as a religious motive.[103]

Buell shares—quite rightly—Franchot's dissent from the tactic of translating religious motives into political ones. But the implication here is that both of these "constraints" are different faces of the same excessive intellectualism: on the one hand, the religious dimension of a text is to be found in its governing theological *ideas*; on the other, its governing theological *ideology*. The first merely describes the ideas; the second demystifies them and replaces them with more accurate ones. The lived religion emphasis on practice, however, ostensibly probes deeper than idea or worldview.

The lived religion model may be a powerful sociological tool for investigating the imaginative worlds of everyday religious believers. But it cannot provide an adequate frame for the kind of literature—exemplified by the modernists in this book—that is dedicated to exploring the metaphysical resonances of experience and the experiential resonances of metaphysics. For Buell, if literary criticism is to follow the road of "lived religion," it has to privilege "cultural practices" over "the life-and-text informing beliefs that imbue discursive forms" and to take "the records of religious *experience* as its primary site of inquiry over against canonical scripture."[104] But if the modernist poet is, as Stevens says, "a metaphysician in the dark," no clear distinction between discursive forms and experience is possible. The "poem," Stevens writes, has "not always had / To find: the scene was set; it repeated what / Was in the script"

(*CP*, 218–219). For Stevens, premodern poets wrote, as Orsi puts it in a much different context, "in, with, through, and against the religious idioms available to them in culture." By contrast, the modern poet has to develop new idioms or, in Stevens's image, to both write the script and perform variations on it. She is remodeling the discursive forms and testing their adequacy for experience, or testing experience to measure its commensurability with what seems uncontestable in the new discourse. When Mrs. Ramsay cannot disentangle her experience from the discursive forms that frame it ("we are in the hands of the Lord"), both the experience and the language are open to revision. In Yeats, the authority and intensity of experience can itself generate new myth: "Who thought Cuchulain till it seemed / He stood where they had stood?"[105]

A literary-critical version of lived religion also evades the normative questions central to modernism. It presumes that "human" emotional experience is constituted prior to the involvement of that experience with religious or any other language. One of the mystifications of a certain strand of secular ideology is the assumption that "the human," once stripped of all its metaphysical augmentations, is self-evident. This ideology can be present in modernism itself, as when Stevens (as I noted earlier) writes of the pre-secular world as a time "before we were wholly human and knew ourselves" (*CP*, 280); it is also the ideology Eliot impugns for its unconscious "tergiversations of the word 'human.'" Orsi says that religion-as-relationship has "all the hopes, evasions, love, fear, projections, misunderstandings, and so on — of relationships between humans." Yet what counts as "hope" or "love" or "misunderstanding" or "evasion" is not self-evident but must refer back, at least implicitly, to the larger, normative "understandings" and "explanations" that Orsi rejects in his definition of religion. These words only become intelligible within deeper frameworks of and for human personhood. Is "hope" a confidence in the power of things unseen or a psychological strategy for coping with unhappiness? Is "love" Freud's libidinal energy or, as Shelley claims, "a going out of our own nature, and an identification of ourselves with the beautiful which exists in thought, action, or person not our own"?[106] The answer to these questions depends on what Charles Taylor has called our "strong evaluations" and the sources from which these valuations derive.[107] These sources include both religious and secular modes of imagining the world.

Because it dismisses religion's capacity to model reality and establish normative valuations for moral (and other) experience, lived religion and its affiliated literary-critical attitudes still enact the sorts of reductions they are trying to avoid. They seem exclusively interested in how religious idioms are *used*, and the aim of such use is always something like survival, coping, and comfort, or transgression, subversion, and empowerment. What makes these practices valuable or interesting is how they facilitate "resistance," or how they create consolatory "meanings," or how they provide "tools" for coping with pain, loss, or oppression. Religion, in these accounts, is used "instrumentally" or "strategically."[108] The "contemporary cultural studies understanding of religion," one scholar affirms, views religion as "a venue for creative and political agency."[109] Religion is thus understood as a featureless stage (a "venue") on which the subject performs motives describable primarily in terms of secular sociology and psychology. Agency, and the desires and aims that animate agency, are fully formed before the appropriation of religious language even occurs.[110] Religion cannot describe itself, for it should not be conceived, as Orsi writes, as "a medium for explaining, understanding, or modeling reality." Yet he observes that explaining and understanding is precisely his prerogative as a social scientist: "The point of all these experiments and all this critical attention . . . is to clarify and to understand particular religious ways of living and thinking." Modeling and understanding have not disappeared; social science merely usurps this agency from religion.[111]

The subtle functionalism of this approach is evident in modernist studies, where much of the recent discussion of religion has centered on occultism. Whereas occultism was once a minor embarrassment for critics, recent criticism focuses on—and often celebrates the revolutionary possibilities of—spiritualism, the occult, and magical thinking.[112] But because it remains difficult to take the normative metaphysical and ontological claims of occultism seriously, its significance is understood to reside in something other than its explicit religious activity or language. It is now seen as an act of resistance to the devitalizing, imperialist legacy of the Enlightenment: secular, instrumental reason. In Helen Sword's *Ghostwriting Modernism*, for example, the culture of spiritual mediums is remarkable for its "empowering" agency, its "subversive celebrations of the alternate, often feminine, modes of writing; its transgressions of the traditional divide between high and low culture; and its . . . tendency to privilege form over content."[113] Gauri Viswanathan argues that

> [O]ccult practices . . . permitted colonial relations to be imagined outside a
> hierarchical framework, just as occult doctrines of cyclical evolution of life
> forms from asexuality and hermaphroditism to sexual differentiation chal
> lenged normative conceptions of sexuality. . . . [T]he relevance of occultism
> is precisely that, as a response to the crisis of knowledge it challenged the
> received developmental narratives of Western knowledge and salvaged oblit
> erated histories, cultures, and beliefs.[114]

The content of occult "knowledge"—which is almost certainly alien to the critical rationality of the scholars who affirm it—is praised insofar as it can be mapped onto attractive political dispositions. It is "subversive" and "transgressive" of hierarchies we dislike: high and low culture, male and female, reason and instinct. Here again, religious motives are translated into political or social ones even as they are being celebrated.[15] But while Viswanathan is right that occultism offers a powerful challenge to "the developmental narratives of Western knowledge," how much of that knowledge can be sacrificed? What if modernist occultism were neither an absurd, desperate, reactionary attempt to halt the march of an enlightened secular reason nor a subversive, courageous response to a repressive, colonialist secular reason? What if its aspirations disclose crucial deficiencies in secular modernity but at the same time refuse the irrevocable insights of secularism? In asking these questions, my chapter on Auden takes the metaphysics of occultism seriously by both learning from and criticizing it; it also takes Auden's secularism (the lessons of Marx and Freud) and his Christian theology seriously by assuming that both are powerful vantage points from which to approach the material world.

"What is generally lacking" in literary criticism, Franchot wrote, "is a willingness to engage intensively with the religious questions of the topic at hand *as religious questions*," because religion is not considered "a form of knowledge" (839, 835). This book considers both religion and secularism, in their various configurations, to be forms of knowledge. It is not explicitly concerned with theological inquiry as such, but tries to show how the normative questions both religious and secular forms of thought put to the world are pervasively inscribed in the fields of experience they touch. The work of Yeats, Stevens, Woolf, and Auden reveals secularization to be an invariably complex matter. They recognize that our imaginative pictures of the world and the religious or secular presuppositions that orient them matter for the varieties of experience in the world. Yet these writers remain restless because their worldviews and the experiences configured in their writing are often at odds, or because they sense a gap between what their imaginations desire and what they take to be real. In this they are like the Santayana—an atheistic materialist living his last days in a Catholic convent—that Stevens eulogizes in "To an Old Philosopher in Rome": "alive / Yet living in two worlds, impenitent / As to one, and, as to one, most penitent" (*CP*, 433).

1

"THE WORLD WAS PARADISE MALFORMED": POETIC LANGUAGE, ANTHROPOMORPHISM, AND SECULARISM IN WALLACE STEVENS

Scholars of Wallace Stevens have long recognized that his poetics is bound up with the loss of religious faith. The standard critical picture is that, like many Victorians before him, Stevens gave up certain consolatory beliefs in the "super-natural" and looked to poetry to fill the vacuum of "meaning." Stevens himself wrote bluntly in a letter of mid-career: "[I]t is a habit of mind with me to be thinking of some substitute for religion" (*L*, 348). Critics have usually proceeded, however, as if the terms of Stevens's secularism were self-evident and the transi-tional movement between religion and poetry—"substitution"—is a straightfor-ward process. Secularism is not, for these critics, a distinct and contestable account of the world or mode of inhabiting it. It is merely what we call our awareness of the "real" world that emerged once we abandoned our metaphys-ical illusions. It is, to adopt a phrase from Stevens, "[t]he plain sense of things" (*CP*, 428).

Helen Vendler, for instance, argues that Stevens reorients his "desire" from a "transcendent world" to a "secular" one. Her synonym for "secular" is "actual": this Stevens "shifts the locus of attention away from the transcendent to the actual."[1] Vendler's secular is that which incontrovertibly exists; in this pairing "transcendent" can only mean "unactual." Jahan Ramazani betrays similar assumptions in his eloquent discussion of Stevens's elegy for George Santayana. Stevens, he writes, does not "reach beyond the secular in his version of elegiac apotheosis." Ramazani, too, supposes that the "secular" is our commonsense world, a place or state opposed to the "supernatural." He supposes something further: that one can take a religious idea—"apotheosis"—and "secularize" it merely by refusing it supernatural reference.[2] Robert Rehder adds yet another

30

dimension to this problem. Stevens, he says, made a habit of "advocating poetic solutions in the place of religious ones."[3] But Rehder does not consider that the problems toward which these solutions are aimed might derive from distinctly religious or secular perspectives. Stevens, who understood this, often wants us to relinquish the hold that certain questions have on our imaginations precisely because they are no longer intelligible *as questions* outside of a religious cosmology: "The particular answer to the particular question / Is not in point— the question is in point" (*CP*, 369). He knew that a secular world is not simply what is "left over" after the gods depart, but a new imaginary that competes with an older one.

In the introduction I examined the various strategies—adaptation, substitution, elimination—that Stevens articulated when contemplating a transition from a religious to secular imaginary. His early poem "Lions in Sweden" (1934), a light poem on a serious theme, is exemplary of the difficulties involved in this transition.[4] The central claim of the poem is that one cannot simply discard the idea of the soul without discarding the whole economy of which the soul was a part:

> No more phrases, Swenson: I was once
> A hunter of those sovereigns of the soul
> And savings banks, Fides, the sculptor's prize,
> All eyes and size, and galled Justitia,
> Trained to poise the tables of the law,
> Patientia forever soothing wounds
> And mighty Fortitudo, frantic bass.
> But these shall not adorn my souvenirs,
> These lions, these majestic images.
> If the fault is with the soul, the sovereigns
> Of the soul must likewise be at fault, and first.
> If the fault is with the souvenirs, yet these
> Are the soul itself. And the whole of the soul, Swenson,
> As every man in Sweden will concede,
> Still hankers after lions, or, to shift,
> Still hankers after sovereign images.
> If the fault is with the lions, send them back
> To Monsieur Dufy's Hamburg whence they came.
> The vegetation still abounds with forms.

> (*CP*, 102)

The economic metaphors of the poem are devices for examining religious and secular economies. Sovereigns here are both coins and "sovereign images," the latter denoting the regulating religious ideals (like Faith, Justice, Patience, and Fortitude) that once composed the moral imagination. The sovereign as currency, or token of exchange value, raises the question of whether these virtues are, quite literally, fungible. Can they be translated from a religious to a secular idiom, just as currency is exchanged? The sovereign as a governing *image*, however, suggests that the virtues depend on an imaginative world-picture that orients life. They can't simply be transplanted into a different world-picture. The religious gold that backs the moral and existential currency (the doctrinal framework) and the banks that housed them (the churches) are dwindling, and Stevens wonders what becomes of the currency when that which insures it dissipates.

The speaker tells the metaphysical banker that he no longer hunts sovereigns of the soul. But why, then, does the soul still "hanker" after sovereign images when it has rejected them? It could be that humans have an inexorable need for sovereign images as such, or it could be because the soul *as soul* is constituted by these sovereign images; it does not exist apart from them, and as long as one still harbors the needs and desires proper to the soul's particular logic, it will desire sovereign images. Yet when we try to locate which parts of the self, which desires, are responsible for the metaphysical distortions and thus need uprooting, they are difficult to isolate. Fault cannot be ascribed to one particular agent because it permeates the whole religious economy:

> If the fault is with the soul, the sovereigns
> Of the soul must likewise be at fault, and first.
> If the fault is with the souvenirs, yet these
> Are the soul itself.
>
> (CP, 102)

It is impossible to isolate the needs and desires of the soul from the soul's sovereign images, for those images helped constitute the needs and desires in the first place. Is the fault in the soul? In its sovereign images? In the souvenirs, the identity-forming memories that will no longer be adorned by the religious logic of faith, justice, patience, and fortitude? These memories have habituated the self to religious accounts of the world and religious expectations regarding the meanings of life. But if the soul *is* these memories, how can one evade it? Substitution doesn't seem to work here, because every term in the religious economy of self is implicated in all the others; you can't change one without changing them all. It would seem that a secular economy of self requires the elimination of the religious one altogether. No translation, or exchange, is possible. Yet the speaker insists that the "whole of the soul" still "hankers" after "sovereign images," and makes no apology for this. He apparently wants to satisfy, rather than eliminate, this hankering. None of Stevens's paradigms can be unconditionally adopted, but neither can they be dismissed.

This chapter argues that, for Stevens, the secular engagement with the religious inheritance, and the impact of this engagement on poetry, turns on two key conceptual axes. The first is the critique of religious anthropomorphism and the significance of this critique for the poetic imagination, which is also, according to Stevens, anthropomorphic at its origin. Stevens vacillates between a conviction that poetry must relinquish its tendencies to humanize what he calls the "not ourselves" and a suspicion that poetry is a form of newly self-conscious or avowed anthropomorphism, and so takes over the role of humanizing the world *from* religion. The second involves Stevens's concern that poetic language—in particular analogy, metaphor, and symbol—inclines toward religious conceptions of the world, because through it the immanent, immediate, material world is linguistically referred to an order of desire that transcends it. Stevens experiments with what I call a poetics of "tautology" as a secular employment of language that intensifies rather than displaces immediate experience of the world. I argue, however, that later in his career this tautological poetics gives way to a religious conception of poetry as a mode of transcendence-in-immanence that nonetheless remains anchored in the physical world.

POETRY, RELIGION, AND THE PROBLEM OF ANTHROPOMORPHISM

One of the central concepts for understanding the link between theology and secular self-understanding is anthropomorphism. From the middle of the nineteenth century, anthropomorphism constituted one of the most influential explanations and criticisms of religion. Although the criticism can be found as far back as Lucretius[5] and was rehabilitated in Hume's *Natural History of Religion*,[6] it owed its prestige in the nineteenth and early twentieth century to the ascendency of materialist science and the diffusion of its mechanistic understanding of the world into philosophy and the social sciences. The core of the criticism was that attempts to describe the world using the resources of human experience—analogies derived from personhood, consciousness, or agency—invariably falsified it, for human experience was epiphenomenal when seen from the perspective of the impersonal material processes that constituted the world. According to the argument, the religious imagination—from primitive "animism" to the more "complex" monotheistic conception—could be explained as a desire to make a world indifferent to the fate of humans seem amenable to human aspiration.

Religious interpretations of reality involved, therefore, the transfiguration of the cosmos into a human image. They were the manifestation of an intractable, subconscious egoism responsible for the presumption that human destiny occupied a central place in the career of the universe.

Stevens was persuaded by this critique. He went so far as to suggest that "egotism"—by which he means the tendency toward anthropomorphism rather than moral selfishness—should have the same anthropological centrality that sexuality had come to enjoy in the wake of modern psychoanalysis: "If some really acute observer made as much of egotism as Freud has made out of sex, people would forget a good deal about sex and find the explanation for everything in egotism" (*L*, 305–306). Religion was, moreover, the most expansive form of such egotism: "An anthropomorphic god is simply a projection of itself by a race of egoists, which it is natural for them to treat as sacred" (349). Or, as he wryly suggests in "Like Decorations in a Nigger Cemetery," people ascribe to their gods attributes that reflect their parochial concerns: "God of the sausage makers, sacred guild, / Or possibly, the merest patron saint, / Ennobled as in a mirror to sanctity" (*CP*, 127).[7]

The claim that anthropomorphism—and the anthropocentrism both generated and confirmed by it—was the psychological origin of religion found a home in worldviews that differed widely. In addition to rationalist philosophers, one finds it in the writings of Nietzsche, for whom anthropomorphism involved a tendency to interpret natural phenomena morally, and in Freud, for whom it was a form of psychological consolation, the metaphysical parallel to the child's need for a caring father.[8] Anthropomorphism was a central explanatory hypothesis for early anthropologists of religion like E. B. Tylor and James Frazer as well. They understood it as the primitive philosophical method that generated what Tylor first called "animism," which he believed to be the universal basis of religion. These anthropologists thought that anthropomorphic procedures were a form of early science—attempts to account for environmental causation that lay outside the human purview. Causation made no sense apart from agency, and agency required subjects akin to persons, so the phenomena of the world were invested with spirits whose motivations were both familiar and able to be engaged. Magic and religion were forms of primitive science because they were, like modern empirical science, explanatory and instrumental in function.[9]

Stevens was almost certainly aware of these arguments, and certain poems evidence reflection on their implications. Tylor, for instance, argued (as Lucretius had millennia before) that animistic interpretations derived from the metaphysical confusions produced by dream life.[10] The experience of a second self in dreams generated a theory of soul in which the life of a person exceeded embodied consciousness. Frazer contended something similar: "The soul of a sleeper is supposed to wander away from his body and actually to visit the places, to see the persons, and to perform the acts of which he dreams." In waking life this soul could be discerned in a person's shadow or reflection: "Often he regards his shadow or reflection as his soul, or at all events as a vital part of himself, and as such it is necessarily a source of danger to him."[11]

Stevens alludes to these anthropological accounts of dreams and shadows in "A Word with José Rodriguez-Feo," where he objects to the line of thinking in which "night" discloses "the nature of man's interior world":

> Why should
> We say that it is man's interior world
>
> Or seeing the spent, unconscious shapes of night,
> Pretend they are shapes of another consciousness?
> The grotesque is not a visitation. It is
> Not apparition but appearance. . . .
>
> (CP, 293)

In dreams, the poem insists, we find mere "relaxations of the known," not intimations of the unknown or selves only accessible as religious mysteries. Indeed, the poem suggests that for Stevens, the critique of anthropomorphism has not gone far enough: the religious myth of the deeper, unknown self that is somehow more real (and so the subject of truer desires) than the self that resides on the surface of life has been preserved in modern psychoanalysis, which continues to look for this hidden self in dream life.

The entire idea of a hidden self is, in other words, a religious anachronism. It depends on a false binary, as Nietzsche would say, of surfaces and depths, in which the former obscure the greater truth and profundity of the latter.[12] In the poem's terms, the visitations are "appearance" rather than "apparition"—they are simply manifestations of the embodied life among surfaces rather than hauntings of something beneath or beyond them. Stevens often employs pejoratively a number of interrelated images—"shadow," "night," "sleep"—as evocations of the ostensibly "deep" realm in which religious fantasies take shape. In "Chocorua," for instance, "shadow" is "an eminence, / But of nothing, trash of sleep that will disappear / With the special things of night, / Little by little, in day's constellation" (CP, 267). "Day," by contrast, names a mode of existence that is satisfied by the surfaces of the world, in which desire does not chase the impossible satisfactions of religion. The anthropomorphic imagination postulated a "gold self aloft," "one's shadow magnified" until it became the "magnificence" of a god ("The Man with the Blue Guitar," 144). Much of Stevens's poetry is concerned, as Nietzsche was, with dispelling this shadow or creating a self "Without shadows, without magnificence, / The flesh, the bone, the dirt, the stone" (144).[13]

Thinkers more sympathetic to religion expressed ambivalence toward the anthropomorphic critique. At the end of *The Varieties of Religious Experience*, William James considers the objections of those who hold what he calls the "survival-theory" of religion. These critics felt that religion was a stubborn remainder of the primitive mind that somehow continued to infiltrate modern culture, an "anachronism for which deanthropomorphization of the memory is the remedy required."[14] James agreed that religion involved an intractable elevation of the personal dimension, but he did not think that this should count against it:

> The pivot round which the religious life, as we have traced it, revolves, is the interest of the individual in his private personal destiny. Religion, in short, is a monumental chapter in the history of human egotism. The gods believed in—whether by crude savages or by men disciplined intellectually—agree with each other in recognizing personal calls. Religious thought is carried on in terms of personality, this being, in the world of religion, the one fundamental fact. To-day, quite as much as at any previous age, the religious individual tells you that the divine meets him on the basis of his personal concerns. (534)

James believed that the "real" was nearly synonymous with the personal and individual, which are in turn synonymous with feeling. Since the "recesses of feeling . . . are the only places in the world in which we catch real fact in the making," it followed for him that the "personal" interpretation of phenomena— i.e., religion—was an incontrovertible value even if it tended toward egotism. Moreover, in defending this aspect of religious consciousness, James identified his conception of it with an attentiveness to "the aesthetic and dramatic aspect of existence," existence in its "human suggestiveness" (539). Indeed, religion is for him almost a codification of the pathetic fallacy: "the terror and beauty of phenomena, the 'promise' of the thunder, the 'gentleness' of the summer rain, the 'sublimity' of the stars, and not the physical laws which these things follow," are the things "by which the religious mind still continues to be impressed."[15]

It was just this coalescence of religious and aesthetic anthropomorphism that concerned Nietzsche, who suspected that the latter was a way of surreptitiously preserving the former. In *The Gay Science* he writes,

> Let us beware of thinking that the world is a living being. Where should it expand? On what should it feed? How could it grow and multiply? . . . Let us

beware of positing generally and everywhere anything as elegant as the cyclical movements of our neighboring stars; even a glance at the Milky Way
raises doubts whether there are not far coarser and more contradictory movements there. . . . The total character of the world, however, is in all eternity
chaos—in the sense not of a lack of necessity but of a lack of order, arrangement, form, beauty, wisdom, and whatever other names there are for our
aesthetic anthropomorphisms . . . Let us beware of attributing to it heartless-
ness and unreason or their opposites: it is neither perfect nor beautiful, nor
noble, nor wish to become any of these things; it does not by any means
strive to imitate man. None of our aesthetic and moral judgments apply to
it. . . . Once you know that there are no purposes, you also know that there is
no accident; for it is only beside a world of "purposes" that the world "accident" has meaning. Let us beware of saying that death is opposed to life. The
living is merely a type of what is dead, and a very rare type. . . . When will all
these shadows of God cease to darken our minds? When will we complete
our de-deification of nature? When may we begin to "*naturalize*" humanity
in terms of a pure, newly discovered, newly redeemed nature?[16]

For Nietzsche, the world as a whole eludes any analogy drawn from the realm of
human experience; it has no "order, arrangement, form, beauty, wisdom." Yet
even the late-Victorian agnostic or atheist's characteristic distress before a hostile
universe is subverted here: the world can be no more "heartless" than it could
be generous. (Stevens, working through this problem in "The Auroras of
Autumn," will call the world "innocent.") The complete "de-deification" of
nature requires the end of aesthetic anthropomorphisms as much as the end
of the more conspicuous religious ones.

We can see why, then, the critique of anthropomorphism left a problem
for poetry and poetry's relation to religion. The very conditions that generate
anthropomorphic projection are also, according to Stevens, the conditions in
which poetry itself arises:

From this the poem springs: that we live in a place
That is not our own and, much more, not ourselves
And hard it is in spite of blazoned days.

(CP, 333)

Poetry, like religion, is produced by the conviction that the world is not amenable
to anthropomorphic interpretation. The world is *not ourselves*. This insight,
however, yokes poetry to religion, for they stem from the same act of imagination
and the same existential problematic.[17] Should poetry resist anthropomorphism,
and so distance itself from religion, or should poetry, after religion's demise, take

up the mantle of a demythologized, self-conscious anthropomorphism? This tension never disappears from Stevens's work. As he puts it in "Notes Toward a Supreme Fiction," "Eve made air a mirror of herself" and thus humans "found themselves / In heaven as a glass; a second earth." We know now that "the air is not a mirror but a blank board" (331–332). But the secular self is potentially even more narcissistic: the Feuerbachian revelation that the true referent of religious worship was the idealized human meant that the unconscious narcissism of the old religion became the conscious narcissism of the new secular humanism. Thus Stevens writes, in "Cuisine Bourgeoise," that in "these days" of religious "disinheritance," we "feed on human heads"—we make ourselves the bread and wine of our own Eucharist. When Eve's "mirror," which was for her a window, reverts to being simply a mirror, the imagination's self-projections approach cannibalism: "Who, then, are they, seated here? / Is the table a mirror in which they sit and look? / Are they men eating reflections of themselves?" (209).

Stevens refuses to make the world a mirror. In one of his earliest collected poems, "Nuances of a Theme by Williams," he imagines poetry as a work of praise for things that elude the circumference of human desire. The speaker exhorts a star:

I

Shine alone, shine nakedly, shine like bronze,
that reflects neither my face nor any inner part
of my being, shine like fire, that mirrors nothing.

II

Lend no part to any humanity that suffuses
You in its own light.
Be not chimera of morning,
Half-man, half-star.
Be not an intelligence,
Like a widow's bird
Or an old horse.

(14–15)

"Be not" revises the impulse to say "be thou." In "Notes," Stevens travesties the Shelleyan "thou"s of "Ode to the West Wind": "Bethou me ... Bethou him, you / And you, bethou him and bethou" (340). Too many "bethous compose a heavenly gong," but "It is / A sound like any other. It will end." The integrity of the natural object resides in its imperviousness to anthropomorphic interference.

The very work of analogy—a problem I dwell on later in this chapter—sometimes seems to Stevens a form of egotism: "Narcissism itself is merely an evidence of the operation of the principle that we expect to find pleasure in resemblances" (*CP*, 692). Yet when he writes, late in his career, of the "faithfulness of reality"—a perspective in which "morning and evening are like promises kept" ("Ordinary Evening," 403)—he approaches James's "religious mind." At times, Stevens requires of the "insatiable egotist" that he forsake "the last distortion of romance," which might be thought of as an adventure in anthropomorphism (24). But at other times, the business of both poetry and religion is "to transmute incoherence into romance."[18] What is clear is that both religion and poetry begin for Stevens in an encounter with the "not ourselves," the recalcitrant, enigmatic world resistant to the ego.

Stevens may have adopted this phrase from Matthew Arnold, who argued in *Literature and Dogma* that both religious and poetic feeling was a response to and appropriation of the "not ourselves": "The not ourselves, which is in us and in the world round us, has almost everywhere, as far as we can see, struck the minds of men, as they awoke to consciousness, and has inspired them with awe."[19] Arnold understood the "not ourselves" as the primordial phenomenological experience that eventually underwrites the "sacred" or the "holy." In his essay on Marianne Moore, Stevens summarizes and approves a similar claim he found in an essay by the philosopher of art H. D. Lewis: the "affinity" between art and religion is found in the fact that "both have to mediate for us a reality not ourselves" (*CP*, 703). Stevens, however, was more insistent than Arnold that the "not ourselves" was fundamentally impersonal rather than enigmatically other. He has a paradoxical tendency, moreover, to affirm religious impulses as responses to the "not ourselves" while simultaneously insisting that religion consequentially domesticates this reality through the sentiment of design. So in "Extracts from Addresses to the Academy of Fine Ideas," he says of the "lean cats of the arches of the churches" who savor "a sense of their design": "They bear brightly the little beyond / Themselves" (230). The "lean cats," like T. S. Eliot, have a diminished sense of what is irreducibly other.[20]

The pursuit of this "reality not ourselves" is a mode of secular piety; in "An Ordinary Evening in New Haven," the "search for reality" displaces the "search for god" but also appropriates the intensity of the former enterprise. Together the two searches have a further analogue: "the philosopher's search / For an interior made exterior / And the poet's search for the same exterior made interior" (410). Stevens commends the latter. In this he follows George Santayana's critique of German idealism in *Egotism in German Philosophy* (1916).[21] For Santayana, the pseudo-religious (or incompletely secularized) self of Romantic philosophy consumed the world and reproduced it in its own image—made "the interior exterior." But for Santayana, "The best things that come into a man's consciousness are the things that take him out of it . . . things that are independent of his personal perception and of his personal existence."²² Stevens, who was influenced by Santayana while a student at Harvard, shares Santayana's suspicion of the anthropomorphic operation—making the interior exterior—in religious and Idealist thought. In the 1930s Stevens copied a sentence from a minor work of Christian philosophy—*The Divine Origin of Christianity Indicated by Its Historical Effects*—into his commonplace book: "The philosopher could not love the indefinite and the impersonal principle of order pervading the universe, any more than he could love atmospheres and oceans."²³ Stevens comments: "For myself, the indefinite, the impersonal, atmospheres and oceans, and, above all, the principle of order are precisely what I love; and I don't see why, for a philosopher, they should not be the ultimate inamorata. The premise of [the author] is that the universe is explicable only in terms of humanity."²⁴

Stevens dissents from this premise. The poet's work is to render the exterior interior. This work is consequential in Stevens; in many poems it expands into a comprehensive reconceptualization of the human as constitutively inhuman. To affirm the ontological priority of the exterior is to find the "inhuman of our features," to reorient desire toward "the inhuman more" ("The Sail of Ulysses," *CP*, 467). When the impersonal is "the ultimate inamorata," the value and urgency of personhood recedes. As a poet of "reality," Stevens "fears" "the hierophant Omega"—the religious spirit that "kneels always on the edge of space" and occupies himself with purposeful "end[s]" rather than "beginning[s]"— precisely for his "prolongations of the human" ("Ordinary Evening," 400).²⁵

This high valuation of the inhuman is the backdrop against which Stevens's brief romance with "secular humanism" unravels. When pushed to its limits, the critique of anthropomorphism eventually undermines not only religion, but human nature as well. The first stage of the critique elevates human dignity because it is accompanied by an expanded sense of human responsibility. As Stevens wrote in a letter, glossing a poem from his second collection, *Ideas of Order:* "In A FADING OF THE SUN the point is that, instead of crying for help to God or to one of the gods, we should look to ourselves for help. The exaltation of human nature should take the place of its abasement" (*L*, 295). A similar attitude can be found in any number of critics of anthropomorphism; Freud and Nietzsche are influential examples. If anthropomorphism engendered human dependence and metaphysical consolation, the overcoming of it required that human beings take hold of their own destiny. Secular humanism adopted just this ethos.

The second stage of the critique of anthropomorphism, however, finally threatens to undermine the stance adopted by the first. When the critique is coupled with an imperative to embrace the world in its impersonal otherness, a feeling emerges that the self can cement this embrace by relinquishing the human difference that is so often figured in Stevens as a principle of alienation ("It is the human that is the alien, / The human that has no cousin in the moon" [*CP*, 288]). In the first stage of the critique, human beings appropriate what were once the prerogatives of God—redemptive rationality and ethical perfect-ibility—for these prerogatives were theirs until they divested themselves of them through their own divinizing projections. But in the second stage there arises a suspicion that God is not so much another name for human possibility as for a constellation of values that corresponds to nothing in material existence. Thus the attributes of God that secular humanism has appropriated, and which are said to be the very essence of human distinctiveness, need to be eliminated in order for the human to experience "the inhuman" of its features.

Thus the later Stevens sometimes writes poems like "The Region November," in which the experience of the impersonality of the world leads to a critique not only of God but also of "human nature":

> It is hard to hear the north wind again,
> And to watch the treetops, as they sway.
>
> They sway, deeply and loudly, in an effort,
> So much less than feeling, so much less than speech,
>
> Saying and saying, the way things say
> On the level of that which is not yet knowledge:
>
> A revelation not yet intended.
> It is like a critic of God, the world,
>
> And human nature, pensively seated
> On the waste throne of his wilderness.
>
> Deeplier, deeplier, loudlier, loudlier,
> The trees are swaying, swaying, swaying.
>
> (472–473)

The poem is about the irresistible desire to approach the world as a locus of revelation—to approach it anthropomorphically—even though we know that it cannot be said to *communicate* anything. The swaying of the treetops seems to be a kind of speech but can't be: it is a "saying" that is "so much less than speech." It is a saying below not only "knowledge" but "feeling" as well—it is not received by Romantic intuition. (In "The Course of a Particular," a related poem, the "cry" of "the leaves . . . is not a cry of divine attention, / Nor the smoke-drift of puffed out heroes, nor human cry. / It is the cry of leaves that do not transcend themselves" [460].) It is a revelation without "intention," and so no revelation at all. If pressed to formulate what it says, the poet writes that "[i]t is like a critic of God, the world, / And human nature." It is a critic of intelligibility, a critic of all of the categories by which human beings want to organize the world anthropomorphically. The criticism is so absolute that it includes not only "God" and the "human nature" that has appropriated God's attributes in modernity, but also the "world" itself—the "force" that, for Stevens, opposes so many aspirations toward transcendence. The irony of which the poem is thoroughly aware, however, is that this criticism of anthropomorphism can only be imagined anthropomorphically: the trees become a king, "seated / On the waste throne of his wilderness." The world's harsh revelation of impersonality is only made possible by imagining the revealer as a type of person.[26]

STEVENS AND THE SECULARIZATION OF LANGUAGE: THE PROBLEM OF METAPHOR, ANALOGY, AND SYMBOLISM

There are many areas of concern affected by the critique of anthropomorphism, but one of the most urgent for Stevens involves the ways in which poets (and humans in general) employ the tropes of language and what those figures suggest about how one understands the ends of life. When thinking about what words are and do, Stevens is almost always working against paradigms that he considers religious.[27] There is a constant suspicion in Stevens's poetry that language cannot rid itself of a kind of theological suggestiveness, that there is something "religious" about certain figures of language native to poetry: analogy, metaphor, signs, and symbols. Stevens is mistrustful of the way metaphor slides into metaphysics, the way an analogical worldview has been associated with a theological one, and how signs and symbols tend to refer solid, immanent things to supersensible narratives or "meanings." At the same time, Stevens suggests, the elimination of poetry's theological indiscretions might mean the end of poetry itself.

One of the central poetic strategies Stevens employs to circumvent this problem is the use of tautology, a mode of encountering and describing the world that operates as a resistance to the habits of transcendence and dualism Stevens associates with religion. Tautology is connected, moreover, to an approach to perception that is entirely sensory, and within which human desire is satisfied with the immediately available—with the worldly, the physical, the immanent. In particular, the antidote to religious ideation is often taken to involve a reliance on visual or spatial perception that opposes itself to the hermeneutical activities that aim at finding "meaning." The world does not *have* a sense but *is* sense. "The consolations of space," Stevens says, "are nameless things" (*CP*, 412).[28] His feeling about these matters is formed against the intellectual backdrop of the Symbolist movement, which had a mystical agenda; early anthropology of religion, which had a good deal to say about the religious functions of symbolic and associative (analogical and metonymical) thinking; and Romantic and twentieth-century philosophy.[29]

Stevens's early poetry has often been associated with French Symbolism,[30] and while that influence is not insignificant, Stevens came to dissent from its ontological premises, which are fundamentally religious. As Arthur Symons wrote,

> It is all an attempt to spiritualise literature, to evade the old bondage of rhetoric, the old bondage of exteriority. . . . Here then, in this revolt against exteriority, against rhetoric, against a materialistic tradition; in this endeavour to disengage the ultimate essence, the soul, of whatever exists and can be realised by the consciousness; in this dutiful waiting upon every symbol by which the soul of things can be made visible; literature, bowed down by so many burdens, may at last attain liberty, and its authentic speech. In attaining this liberty, it accepts a heavier burden; for in speaking to us so intimately, so solemnly, as only a religion had hitherto spoken to us, it becomes itself a kind of religion, with all the duties and responsibilities of the sacred ritual.[31]

What Stevens rejects is precisely this "substitutionary" logic in the sense I have been using the term. He does not revolt against exteriority but celebrates it; the inhuman otherness of the world is his "ultimate inamorata."[32] For Symons, the symbol is the invisible made visible, but Stevens desired to "make the visible a little hard / To see" (*CP*, 275). The Symbolist also presupposes a possible world of correspondences between spiritual interior and material exterior. Baudelaire's famous "Correspondences," often considered the first Symbolist poem, makes just this claim. Stevens, in contrast, often spoke of the relation between external and internal as antagonistic: "There is a war between the mind / And sky," he writes (351). The mind is, he says, "a violence from within that protects us from a violence without" (665). His is not a world of correspondences between spiritual significance and physical fact or transcendent and immanent experience.

The Symbolists assumed that the immanent world was not adequate to the spiritual aspirations concealed in the aspirations of language. Stevens's ambition to make language tautological with the experience of the world in its immanence is an ambition to overturn this prejudice against the world, to experience it as something "complete," "sufficient," "adequate," or "enough." These words appear in Stevens's poetry again and again. To experience the world as sufficient, even as a plenitude, is to repudiate the intuition he, following William James, thought the beginning of religious consciousness—namely, that there is "real wrongness in the world," and that our difficulty here means we must refer our discontented desire to something "beyond" in order to render it intelligible and relieve our misery.[33]

Stevens, therefore, often adopts what the German philosopher Odo Marquard has called a "dietetics of meaning," a discipline through which one takes "a step into profane existence" by eliminating certain religious needs and expectations. According to Marquard, "The experience of meaning deficits does not always have to be due to lack of meaning; it can also result from excessive expectations of meaning. In that case it is not that meaning is lacking, but that the demand for meaning is immoderate."[34] Stevens looks to the sensory because it ends with itself, is satisfied with itself, asks nothing beyond itself. The visual imperative in Stevens can therefore be understood as an attempt to overcome the uneasiness toward the visual in monotheistic religions, with their proscriptions of idolatry and their preference for the interior or the inward. Stevens follows Nietzsche's project of collapsing religious binaries like those between surface and depth, appearance and truth, and their moral correlatives, like those between intention and performance.[35]

"On the Road Home" is a poem that promotes this elevation of the visual against dimensions relating to meaning or understanding. The poem is structured as a dialogue between two anonymous speakers. It meditates on an imperative: "The world must be measured by eye." That declaration, moreover, follows syllogistically from a previous negation: "Words are not forms of a single word" (*CP*, 186). There is not, then, a supernatural or transcendent ground of language, no world pregnant with a Word of God that unifies disparate speech and makes of the world a text. The world cannot be approached hermeneutically. One cannot move from the relational indeterminacy of words to the feeling that, as the hermeneutical philosophers argue, there is an "indeterminate totality of meaning that is implicitly present in the spoken word."[36] Stevens dissents from a religious philosophy of language as conceived by a counter-Enlightenment, Christian Pietist thinker like Johann Georg Hamann, who thought that in a prelapsarian world,

> Every phenomenon of nature was a word,—the sign, symbol and pledge of a new, mysterious, inexpressible but all the more intimate union, participation

and community of divine energies and ideas. Everything the human being heard from the beginning, saw with its eyes, looked upon and touched with its hands was a living word; for God was the word.[37]

Here the seen and overflowing signification are one; in Stevens they are at odds. The Symbolists had tried to preserve something similar, even if more private and heterodox, in their theories of correspondence and their accounts of the world as a hieroglyph of the soul (or as raw material for transcendence). But for Stevens experience at its most authentic is spatial rather than hermeneutic: the world must be measured by eye.[38] Sight is tautological: it discloses the intensity of the unmediated, non-linguistically-altered being of the world. This is why, in "Esthétique du Mal," Stevens wants a tautologous state—"to see what one sees"—to be experienced not as a "poverty" or as a "los[s]" of "sensibility" but "[a]s if sight had . . . its own miraculous thrift" (*CP*, 282).

The possibilities for sight in "On the Road Home" emerge as the other partner in the dialogue broaches the problem of idolatry and truth, the correlatives of vision and word:

It was when you said,
"The idols have seen lots of poverty,
Snakes and gold and lice,
But not the truth";

It was at that time, that the silence was largest
And longest, the night was roundest,
The fragrance of autumn warmest,
Closest and strongest.

(186)

Stevens is playing here with the idea of idolatry, or the attempt to make divine truth visible. The speaker seems to be accepting, but is actually inverting, the monotheistic critique of idolatry: if the idols have never "seen" the truth, this is not because truth is a transcendent unity inaccessible to the senses. It is because "the truth," which would gather up the details of the visible world and convert them into a single meaning, is not something to which sight aspires. For Stevens, the monotheistic duality enforced between idolatry (the visible) and truth (the spoken and understood) has devalued the world of sight, made of it something sordid ("snakes" and "lice") or avaricious ("gold"). As the poem closes, the reestablishment of sight outside the boundaries of religious truth has produced a robust spatial world (it is "round" and "close") that yields sensory pleasure (it is "warm" and "strong") in an absence of language (a large, long "silence").

Sensory secularization has been accomplished. A problem Stevens leaves the reader with, however, and of which he is certainly aware, is that this has been accomplished by the internalization of declarative, truth-asserting propositions. The whole poem takes the form of a dialogue that would not be out of place in Plato or the Gospels, and its movement depends on the back and forth of "It was when I said . . . It was when you said." It is a discussion that seems to aim at what is being denied—"the truth." What is more, the outcome of the discussion—a silent sensory bliss—has been generated precisely by the activity of truthful, dialogical speech. The world has been "measured" by words as much as by "eye."

The ontology of "On the Road Home," like the ontology of much of the collection in which it is found, *Parts of a World*, is characterized by plurality and incommensurability. The different parts of the world do not form a whole. This conviction, however, creates a problem for Stevens, for poetry seems bound to analogy, the discovery of similitude in dissimilitude. Shelley's "Defense of Poetry"—a text Stevens cared for—implies that the heart of poetry is analogy; poets discover "the before unapprehended relations of things."[39] Poetic language illuminates the participation of one thing in another. Because our understanding of an object increases with the proliferation of the analogies by which we encounter it, an object is never simply itself, never self-identical. It exists always in relation to other objects. As Paul Ricoeur has written, "analogical predication" is grounded in "an ontology of participation," in which all things "have partially what another possesses or is fully."[40] Because of this ontology of participation, analogy has tended to become theological when turned into a worldview. Finite entities participate in each other, and together they participate in the infinite unity complete in its having and being: God. In Emerson, "the inexplicable continuity of this web of God" ensures that thought is "nothing but the finding of analogy . . . in the most remote parts."[41] The intimation of analogy seems to be "tremulous with the intimation of a world-order," with "the weight of cosmological significance."[42] Whatever one thinks of such an intimation, it is, as Kenneth Burke puts it, in the nature of words that they "may be used analogically, to designate a further dimension, the 'supernatural.' Whether or not there is a realm of the supernatural, there are words for it." This is why, for Stevens, words have a tendency toward metaphysical irresponsibility. But this is the case, Burke asserts, because language can already be thought of as a mode of "transcendence." "There is a sense," he writes, "in which language is not just 'natural,' but really does add a 'new dimension' to the things of nature (an observation that would be the logological equivalent of the theological statement that grace perfects nature)."[43]

Because language adds this new dimension to natural things, it makes possible a proliferation of new desires that have a vexed relation to the material order. So, writes Burke,

> [L]anguages make it impossible for men to be content with sheer *bodily* purpose. And insofar as men "cannot live by bread alone" they are moved by doctrine, which is to say, they derive purposes from language, which tells them what they "ought" to want to do, tells them how to do it, and in the telling goads them with great threats and promises, even unto the gates of heaven and hell. . . . With language, a whole new realm of purpose arises, endless in scope, as contrasted with the few rudimentary purposes we derive from our bodies, the needs of food, drink, shelter, and sex in their physical simplicity.[44]

This is precisely the quality of language that makes Stevens uncomfortable: language has the capacity to create desires and purposes that do not, in a strictly naturalistic sense, have clear or easily achieved ends. It gestures toward a transcendent order of satisfaction but seems unable to deliver this order. And this difficulty is why, in a poem like "Credences of Summer," the imperative to "exile desire / For *what is not*" (emphasis added) can only be accomplished in a world that ceases to be regarded as a text or sign of anything. In this poem, if we can employ a language at all it is the "[p]ure rhetoric of a language without words" (*CP*, 324). There is no analogical order; the "old man" of the poem "reads no book" (323). The speaker calls the world a "rock," "but it is not / A hermit's truth nor symbol in hermitage" (324). Neither the world nor the objects in the world should be rendered symbolic, because symbols generate the possibility of a transcendence that must be refused.

Because of these associations, Stevens strives to secularize analogy or to eliminate it altogether in tautology. In the late poem "An Ordinary Evening in New Haven," analogy is associated with what Stevens calls the "instinct for heaven." By that point in his career, he no longer thinks such an instinct can be expunged, but he nonetheless prefers its secular "counterpart," the "instinct for earth," characterized as "[t]he gay tournamonde as of a single world / In which he is and as and is are one" (406). This secular world is single, univocal—a world in which the comparative "as" collapses into the self-identical "is." The same problem arises in the earlier "Connoisseur of Chaos":

> After all the pretty contrast of life and death
> Proves that these opposite things partake of one,
> At least that was the theory, when bishops' books
> Resolved the world. We cannot go back to that.

> The squirming facts exceed the squamous mind,
> If one may say so. And yet relation appears,
> A small relation expanding like the shade
> Of a cloud on sand, a shape on the side of a hill.
>   (195)

That two things can "partake of one," that disunity is not absolute but grounded in unity, that all things can be understood in "relation" to one another, analogously—these, according to Stevens, were the postulates of "bishops' books." There was behind the chaos of phenomena, if not an actual intelligibility, at least a presumption of intelligibility. Such intelligibility occurred by virtue of the participation of the world (of "creation") in God. For Stevens, "we cannot go back to that." Our world must be secular. But he follows this inflexible declaration with an "and yet." "And yet relation appears": relation, the property that seems to render the world intelligible. One of Stevens's refrains is that "mind" is not at home in the world. Yet the appearance of relation, the discovery of kinship and affinity, seems to suggest that the mind is not simply at the margins of the world, that knowing and being are not helplessly estranged.[45] At the same time, Stevens marks the difficulty of affirming post-religious "relation" precisely by embedding the tentative affirmation *of* relation *in* a relation—a simile—that is hard for the mind to assimilate. For a "relation," which is something abstract and invisible, is here rendered material and spatial, and thus unthinkable. How is a relation like an expanding "shape" or "shade," when strictly speaking it only exists between or among shapes and shades? The poem itself dramatizes the difficulty of dwelling in the merely visible.

The scribbling academic persona in "Connoisseur" claims that "an old order is a violent one"—it does not do justice to the variety and complexity of "facts." He cannot, however, say this without adding yet another qualifying conjunction: "But suppose the disorder of truths should ever come / To an order, most Plantagenet, most fixed . . ." (*CP*, 195). Stevens's appeal to the Plantagenet (the dynasty that ruled England and parts of France) returns us explicitly to that medieval (analogical, hierarchical, fixed) theological world, and yet the ellipses make the line trail off as if in ambivalent nostalgia. The poem closes with an aphorism. "The pensive man," it tells us, is able to perceive the "eagle float / For which the intricate Alps are a single nest." In the earlier "Comedian as the Letter C," the musician-poet must be "[o]blivious to the Aztec almanacs"— texts that document the occult relation between spiritual forces and physical phenomena—in order to "make the intricate Sierras scan" (31). To make mountains scan might be to suppose that the world *is* infused with a kind of poetic *logos* that one can read, but in both passages relation no longer exists in the world, only in the pensive man's poem.

Because he suspects that his recalcitrant desire for analogical order is corrupted by this sort of nostalgia, Stevens's secularizing strategy often turns to the rejection of relation altogether in tautology, a rhetorical formula in which A = A. Tautology is more than a refusal of analogy. It is also a refusal of signs and symbols. The last canto of "The Man with the Blue Guitar," for instance, concludes with the tautological hope that "[t]he bread / Will be our bread," not the bread of the Christian Eucharist (151). In the poem "Evening without Angels," "Air is air, / Its vacancy glitters around us everywhere." Once again, however, there is a paradox that in the rejection of symbolism symbols are slyly reproduced; air is air, but this "vacancy" is a symbol of negation, a refusal of any religious anthropomorphism, as when, in the past, "Sad men made angels of the sun, and of / The moon they made their own attendant ghosts" (137).[46] The anxiety attending tautology is that the plenitude it discloses is indistinguishable from emptiness.

Stevens also uses his tautologies to renounce the religious insistence that special states of consciousness must be developed in order to ensure the proper experience of the world. So in a passage in "Description without Place" that prunes the Gospel of John ("The thesis of the plentifullest John"), Stevens speaks of "[a] text we should be born that we might read" (301). The self does not need to be born *again*, as in the New Testament gospel, but only "born"; the imperative "should be," which normally indicates a state of possibility transcending what merely exists, is deliberately undermined, for being "born," of course, is not a state to which an already existing person could aspire. Anyone who would "read," it is safe to say, has by definition achieved the state of being born.

Similarly, Stevens's tautologies reduce the objects or experiences under consideration to that which is most basic about them: their physical givenness. The most that can be said about these things is that they "are," or, in a temporal register, that they "occur." Stevens returns to the language of "occurrence," inflected by a tone of exasperated distaste for the mechanized repetition implicit in the term and the reality behind it, again and again in a poem like "The Sense of the Sleight-of-Hand Man":

One's grand flights, one's Sunday baths,
One's tootings at the weddings of the soul
Occur as they occur. So bluish clouds
Occurred above the empty house and the leaves
Of the rhododendrons rattled their gold . . .

(205)

The poem thus impishly reduces these ostensibly religious (or romantic) moments in the life of the "soul" to almost mechanical events. To say that they "occur as they occur" gives the reader no new information. We cannot say anything about them other than that they have come to pass. We cannot read them: they are beyond interpretation because they are not situated in a web of significance, metaphysical or otherwise. The meaning of their "occurrence" cannot be distinguished from the appearance of natural phenomena such as clouds or leaves. The poem continues:

> Could you have said the bluejay suddenly
> Would swoop to earth? It is a wheel, the rays
> Around the sun. The wheel survives the myths.
> The fire eye in the clouds survives the gods.
> To think of a dove with an eye of grenadine
> And pines that are cornets, so it occurs . . .
>
> (205)

What survives the myths and the gods—which for Stevens are obsolete cultural modes of explaining phenomena—is simply the endurance of the world in all its "sudden," inexplicable motion. Even associative, poetic thought—thought that brings images from disparate areas of life into relation, the very work of thought that constitutes this poem—is subsumed into an "it" that merely happens.

The poem cannot so reduce itself, however. This truth is acknowledged in the title's suggestion that the achievement of a "sense" before the obsolete modifications of religious language requires a "sleight-of-hand." For in what sense does the identification of "pines" with "cornets," or the discovery that a "dove" has "an eye of grenadine," *merely* occur? The poet's search for a mechanistic image that resists religious interpretation is still an image, and so provides a value-laden picture of the world. The vital energies that animate the world are a "wheel"—they don't occur indiscriminately, but as a cycle. Even as the speaker wants to find images to capture bare "occurrence," he finally returns to the language of religion (perhaps to the Vedas, where the "wheel of time" image may have arisen, or to pagan religious cultures that held cyclical conceptions of time). The speaker claims a religious image can "survive" the theology (the "myths" and "gods") in which it was originally intelligible. He attempts to convert religious images into poetic ones by insisting, as he employs them, that the truth about the world's life cannot be expressed outside the rhetoric of tautology. But this is, precisely, a "sleight-of-hand." The secularization of religious language seems to require a kind of magical manipulation, in which the perception of the origin and significance of a word or image has been obscured. The "ignorant man's" work of "sense"—his immediate experience of the world—is really a work of magic. Moreover, the tautologous desire the speaker leaves us with—"to mate his life with life"—is complicated in the realization that a tautological state is by definition something that cannot be achieved (205). A desire by its very nature requires an awareness of a gap between what one is (an incomplete, individual human "life") and what one would like to be ("life" as such). The desire is, finally, to participate in "life" rather than to be identical with "life," or else life could not, strictly speaking, be desired. And participation, as I have argued, is analogical rather than tautological.

Stevens continues the debate within himself as to the desirability of analogical thinking and experience in "On the Adequacy of Landscape" and "Les Plus Belles Pages," poems I believe are deliberately paired in *Parts of a World*. The pairing of the two poems helps us to further understand the problems of analogical or metaphorical relation as, in Stevens's mind, religious problems. "Adequacy" is a pagan poem engaged in Stevens's ongoing project of declaring, as the title suggests, the adequacy of the world as a realm of experience that requires no justification or meaning beyond its own sheer existence. Stevens's interest in what is "adequate," "enough," or "sufficient" is in the largest perspective an exertion of rhetorical pressure to forget the desire to "justify" the world as a whole, because justification is at bottom a religious project of theodicy. In more local perspective the language of adequacy pressures the self to encounter individual objects without requiring that they bear any significance deriving from their placement in a symbolic matrix. The poem gives us a vision of "being" as this sort of sheer existence. People, the poem suggests, tend to avoid the "hap-hallow hallow-ho / Of central things," things that are characterized merely "by being there." ("[H]ap-hallow hallow-ho" suggests that the encounter with "central things" is best expressed by energetic, non-semantic *sound* rather than hermeneutical meaning.) These people are "insensible" to the "blood-red redness of the sun," shrinking instead to an "oblivion / Beyond the keenest diamond day." The diamond day, however, in which people are at the center because they are "sensible to pain," is a world in which cocks wake animated by a desire "merely to be again." The people open to sensory experience "turn toward" the strength of the day and trees and light, "as if these / Were what they are" (CP, 221–222). In other words, to achieve this heightened yet ordinary state we must experience the objects of our environment (landscape) as self-identical, as being exactly and nothing but themselves. They become tautologous: they cannot be described and thereby displaced, metaphorically, symbolically, or allegorically. "The extent of what they are" can only be felt within a "sensible range." Something similar happens in "The Latest Freed Man," for whom "the morning is color and mist, which is enough" (204). The visible "overtak[es] the doctrine of this landscape." Everything is more real in simply "seeing it."

Yet the following poem, "Les Plus Belles Pages," expresses uncertainty that things can be merely "what they are." Whereas the day in "Adequacy" is nothing but what it is, in this poem "the moonlight / Was less than moonlight. Nothing exists by itself." The moonlight cannot be experienced outside of its relations. The presence of the milkman who "came in the moonlight" suggests that the identity of either only emerges in the analogical interval between them. That this is associated in Stevens's mind with theological problems becomes evident in the surprising appearance of Aquinas in the poem:

> He spoke,
> Kept speaking of God. I changed the word to man.
> The automaton, in logic self-contained,
> Existed by itself. Or did the saint survive?
> Did several spirits assume a single shape?
>
> Theology after breakfast sticks to the eye.
>
> (222)

These lines are obscure. In a note on the poem, Stevens wrote, "What it really means is that the interrelation between things is what makes them fecund" (867). The organicist appeal to fecundity affirms analogy without permitting a transcendent register. In the same note Stevens calls Aquinas a "chance example," but this seems unlikely, and he concludes his commentary on the poem without mentioning his discussion of the automaton and his replacement of the word God with man. Though Aquinas was a famous proponent of "the analogy of being," Stevens seems to think of the doctrine of God's self-subsistence ("in logic self-contained") as a tyrannically monistic conception of being (he seems to have forgotten about the doctrine of the Trinity). And we see how Stevens is uncertain as to the meaning of the secular translation (changing the word) from God to man. If God was an automaton, do we transfer that conception to humans, or do we see the human as dependent on the material energies that constitute it? Does the saint's feeling of "absolute dependence"—which Friedrich Schleiermacher considered the most basic of religious attitudes—"survive" in the feeling of analogical relatedness? And can we affirm, therefore, a unity-in-plurality ("several spirits" assuming "a single shape") so that, as in the theological idea of analogy, the difference of beings does not either undergo violence or have that difference effaced in relation to a transcendent unity? All that we can say for sure is that "theology after breakfast sticks to the eye," that our speech about God is speech about humans, and therefore the secular fate of theological claims has consequences for the claims about ourselves.

If, for Stevens, analogy threatened to slip into a specious sense of world-order, metaphor seemed dangerously close to metaphysics. There is one strand of modernist thought, following Emerson and Nietzsche, which took metaphor, if acknowledged as such, to be an antidote to a theological or metaphysical world-view. If taken as provisional and fluid, metaphor could operate as a mode of representation that evaded the absolutist truth claims of such a worldview. After a recognition that truth itself was, as Nietzsche wrote, merely a "mobile army of metaphors, metonyms, and anthropomorphisms," metaphor could be reclaimed as a tool of thinking proper to the immanence and temporality of existence.[47] Stevens describes this feeling in famous poems like "The Motive for Metaphor," in which, instead of being what you are, you seek a place "[w]here you yourself were never quite yourself, / And did not want nor have to be" (CP, 257). The "motive for metaphor" is a "shrinking from the weight of primary noon," the very gesture of avoidance that was derided in "On the Adequacy of Landscape" as the practice of a people who are "frightened" of the "sharpest sun" and the "keenest diamond day." Metaphor in this light construes the divisions that language produces between a creature and its self-expression as a kind of freedom.[48]

Yet Stevens also harbors a different perspective on metaphor, animated by an anxiety that metaphor still bears the residue of a theological conception that devalues the world as world.[49] One finds this suspicion in Martin Heidegger, a thinker Stevens admired from afar. Heidegger argued, "The metaphorical exists only within metaphysics."[50] As Paul Ricoeur has commented,

> This saying suggests that the trans-gression of meta-phor and that of meta-physics are but one and the same transfer. Several things are implied here: first, that the ontology implicit in the entire rhetorical tradition is that of Western "metaphysics" of the Platonic or neo-Platonic type, where the soul is transported from the visible world to the invisible world; second, that meta-phorical means transfer from the proper sense to the figurative sense; finally, that both transfers constitute one and the same *Über-tragung.*[51]

In this account, metaphor is "transferred sense." This is problematic for Stevens because "sense" is the term he uses most often to denote the register of experience that is most in "touch" with the world. Sense is immediate, and Stevens tends to identify the immediate with the authentic.[52] The problem with the signifying function of language, or with *re*-presentation as such, is that the ostensibly primitive, immediate relation between word and object is now mediated. In "Bouquet of Roses in Sunlight," the speaker comes upon flowers that are "[t]oo much as they are to be changed by metaphor." The poem continues, "Our sense of these things changes and they change / Not as in metaphor, but in our sense / Of them. So sense exceeds all metaphor" (CP, 370).

Accordingly, we sometimes find in Stevens a longing for an animalistic "language" that would be a pure expression of instinctual energies and their relation to their environment. His early poem, "Anecdote of Men by the Thousand," begins with a secular revision: "The soul, he said, is composed / Of the external world." The articulation of such a "soul" would have a bodily immediacy resistant to the spiritualizations of language: "There are men whose words / Are as natural sounds / Of their places / As the cackle of Toucans / In the place of toucans" (41). In the later "Notes Toward a Supreme Fiction," Stevens is less convinced that human speech can operate like a toucan's cackle. There, while the "lion roars at the enraging desert," the "elephant breaches the darkness of Ceylon with blares," and the "bear . . . snarls in his mountain," the human ephebe, who has only a "rented piano," lies in "silence": "You writhe and press / A bitter utterance from your writhing, dumb, / Yet voluble dumb violence" (332). The noise of animals is continuous with their life of sense. But our music is "rented"—it does not belong to us. Our language is somehow at odds with our nature. There is an antagonism between language and the life of sense that we share with animals. The "speech" of animals is triumphant and self-assertive, an audible manifestation of what they are. For humans, however, language is evidence of an unknown or incomplete nature. It is a confused violence and ultimately a poor substitute for sense.

In "The Pure Good of Theory," Stevens discusses what might be called a fall into metaphor. The poem is evidence of Stevens's interest in formulating a genealogy of religious belief. Its argument is something of an amalgam of Keats's celebrated comparison of the imagination to Adam's dream ("he awoke and found it truth") and Nietzsche's more deconstructive account of the way metaphor ossified into metaphysical belief. As with so many other aspects of Stevens's thinking, his solutions to the problems of metaphor and belief are dialectical. On the one hand, there is Stevens's well-known conviction that post-religious belief must be a sort of avowed illusion, fully aware of its meta-phoricity and provisionality. (Stevens calls this "the nicer knowledge of / Belief, that what it believes in is not true" (291). On the other hand, there is the conviction, which I think is less critically understood, that metaphor is an illegitimate abstraction from sensory experience:[53]

> We knew one parent must have been divine,
> Adam of beau regard, from fat Elysia,
> Whose mind malformed this morning metaphor,
>
> While all the leaves leaked gold. His mind made morning,
> As he slept. He woke in a metaphor: this
> Was a metamorphosis of paradise,
>
> Malformed, this world was paradise malformed . . .
>
> (291)

These lines owe something to the early anthropological speculation that religion was born of an attempt to understand the dreamworld as *another* real world that made equal claims upon the self. The genetic account seems to go like this: The experience of diurnal waking is such that it is associated with birth. The relation between waking from sleep at the sun's daily "birth" and actual, physical birth is then confused (the antecedent lines read, "Man, that is not born of woman but of air, / That comes here in the solar chariot . . ."). Meanwhile, the pleasure of the freshness of morning ("the leaves leaked gold"), which is now felt to be a kind of rebirth, becomes confused in the imagination, and the idea of an original state of morning—paradise—develops, in which our birth, as after sleep, came from the sun. Because the metaphor is more compelling, its sensory base begins to feel like a distortion of the metaphor rather than the reverse. The diurnal repetition of the sacred origin feels like a dilution of that origin, and because the world is not always a fresh morning, the morning has become a reminder of when the paradisal world *was* fresh. And so the world, which enabled the metaphor of paradise, becomes "paradise malformed." The metaphorical translation becomes, almost irresistibly, the root of religious dualisms and the theological concept of the Fall.

The impasse of the poem is exemplary of the larger problems Stevens faces when trying to secularize poetry, problems that are the concern of this chapter. Stevens wants to discard the doctrine of the Fall. As he famously writes in "The Poems of Our Climate," "The imperfect is our paradise" (179). Yet as "The Pure Good of Theory" shows, the Fall is reinscribed in the very account of how we came to think of ourselves as fallen.[54] Even if we did not eat the fruit, the illusory concept of the Fall was produced by a very real fall into metaphor, a fall, moreover, that the poet least of anyone has evaded. The secular immediacy

Stevens seeks—the sense of being "at home" in the world—is thwarted by the very poetry through which he strives to obtain it.

THE RETURN TO ANALOGY AND THE DIVINITY
OF DESCRIPTION

Indeed, there comes a point in Stevens's career in which he begins to conclude that language, and so the poetic imagination as such, is an intractably religious element in which certain kinds of desires are created that are not simply "immanent." It is impossible to pinpoint when this transition took place. I do not want to suggest that the new perspective is absolute, or that it does not continue to be assaulted by the desire for a language of immanence. Yet after a long ambivalence toward the work of analogy, one finds in Stevens's essay "The Effects of Analogy" (1948) a celebration of it precisely as an agent of transcendence. Though the essay opens by announcing the obsolescence of the "supreme example of analogy" in English, the explicitly Christian *Pilgrim's Progress*, it closes by commending the man who lives a life of "transcendence"— a surprising value to find in Stevens, the poet of "the cry of leaves that do not transcend themselves" (*CP*, 460)—expressly by dwelling in an analogy:

> Take the case of a man for whom reality is enough, as, at the end of his life, he returns to it like a man returning from Nowhere to his village and to everything there that is tangible and visible, which he has come to cherish and wants to be near. He sees without images. But is he not seeing a clarified reality of his own? Does he not dwell in an analogy? His imageless world is, after all, of the same sort as a world full of the obvious analogies of happiness or unhappiness, innocence or tragedy, thoughtlessness or heaviness of the mind. In any case, these are the pictorializations of men, for whom the world exists as a world and for whom life exists as life, the objects of their passions, the objects before which they come and speak, with intense choosing, words that we remember and make our own. Their words have made a world that transcends the world and a life livable in that transcendence. It is transcendence achieved by means of the minor effects of figurations and the major effects of the poet's sense of the world. . . . [P]oetry becomes and is a transcendent analogue. (722–723)

This is a remarkable passage. On the one hand, Stevens is still fiercely holding on to the basic conception of the world as immanent: this is still a man for whom "reality is enough," a man dedicated to the "tangible" and the "visible." On the other hand, this very at-home-ness in the world, this intimacy with its features, is not a contact with the world in its sheer material, pre-linguistic splendor. Rather, the sense of immanence is constructed *within* a life of transcendence made possible by the language of analogy. It is a fiction of tautology lived within an analogy that has become so completely internalized that it no longer seems to bear any religious dualism. This is a man "for whom the world exists as a world and for whom life exists as life": the tautologous description implies that the desire for "more" is still being disciplined. The world and life are not instinct with hidden meanings and symbolic correspondences that would point to a mode of existence fulfilled in something other than themselves. They are still ends. Yet this world is, nonetheless, "a world that transcends the world."[55]

Stevens's strategy for this vision of poetic transcendence that is, nonetheless, at the service of a life of immanence, is to think about poetic language as a form of "description" that one can inhabit. The virtue of description is that it is faithful to the surfaces of the material world. The idea of description, unlike the idea of symbol or even metaphor, is that it implies a deep attentiveness to the contours of actual life. Description does not point beyond the thing at hand toward some larger "meaning." Nonetheless, Stevens will claim, in "Ordinary Evening," "it comes in the end to that: / The description that makes it divinity" (405).

This is a peculiar idea, for why should the description of anything bear on its divinity? The theory behind it is formulated in a poem from *Transport to Summer*, "Description without Place" (1945). In that poem, too, "description is revelation." The shift in Stevens's mind can be clarified by juxtaposing "The Latest Freed Man" (1938) to "Description without Place," written seven years later. In the earlier poem, "description" is tyrannical, tantamount to a constriction of "doctrine" (*CP*, 187). There "freedom" is a capacity "[t]o be *without* a description of to be" (187, emphasis added). This is a condition of animal potency and autotelic desire ("being an ox"), a condition of pure visuality as opposed to hermeneutic discovery: "the importance of the trees outdoors, / The freshness of the oak-leaves, not so much / That they were oak-leaves, as the way they looked." In that poem, knowledge ("not so much / that they were oak leaves") and style ("the way they looked") were at odds. The immanence of visuality is more important than the understanding generated by the linguistic act of naming.

In "Description without Place," however, "[d]escription is revelation" (301). In this poem, the "knowledge of Spain" and the "style" of the "hidalgo" are one. The poem inverts that earlier conception of freedom. Now "it is possible that to seem — it is to be," and this seeming is produced by a mode of description that has become so internalized that it operates as an objective reality. Yet the work of description is peculiar in this poem precisely because it is "without place." To describe without place is to give an account of what is in terms of what is not, which in turn serves to remake that place. This is something remarkable in Stevens, for whom the desire for "what is not" is generally disciplined by a focus on the adequacy of what is.

The poem articulates a process in which desire becomes knowledge, and knowledge becomes incarnated in sense:

> If seeming is description without place,
> The spirit's universe, then a summer's day,
>
> Even the seeming of a summer's day,
> Is description without place. It is a sense
>
> To which we refer experience, a knowledge
> Incognito, the column in the desert,
>
> On which the dove alights. Description is
> Composed of a sight indifferent to the eye.
>
> (300)

We find here not the pure visuality that Stevens so often opposes to religious modes of encountering the world but something beyond visuality, "a sight indifferent to the eye." "The column in the desert / On which the dove alights" is an allusion to St. Simeon Stylites, the fifth-century desert father who lived atop such a column for much of his life. (The dove is, as in traditional iconography, the Holy Spirit visiting the saint.) The anonymous allusion involves a play on "Stylites," which means pillar in Greek, and also evokes an instrument for writing (stylus) and the meaning that Stevens will give "style" at the end of the poem. The ascetic is he who bears a "style of life." Description becomes a whole "sense" in which, as Santayana says, we make of "experience" something other than itself.

Description *without place*, therefore, takes poetic consciousness out of the material present and designates it as a work of transcendence that nonetheless serves to remake that present. Such description provides an account of where the present came from and where it is going, transforming it through that imaginative account. "It is," the poem says, "an expectation, a desire, / A palm that rises up beyond the sea. . . . The future is description without place, the categorical predicate, the arc" (300). Description takes the future-oriented character of desire and renders it an expectation by making it a firm piece of eschatological knowledge (a "categorical predicate"), to the extent that it becomes not simply wishfulness but "just anticipation / Of the appropriate creatures" (301). (That the creatures are "appropriate" means that they have conformed their lives to this anticipation: their lives are *suited* to it.) Eschatology, so often problematic for Stevens in its implication that things might one day be "redeemed," is here reborn such that humans can make the future conform to the good they desire for themselves, but which currently eludes them. Description is "the book of reconciliation" (301).

As in "The Pure Good of Theory," Stevens provides in this poem a genealogy of how religious imagination develops out of the experience of description. There it was the idea of Eden or paradise; here it is eschatology, an account of the expectation and inauguration of that paradise. The poet pictures Lenin sitting on a bench by a lake:

> Lenin on a bench beside a lake disturbed
> The swans. He was not the man for swans.
>
> The slouch of his body and his look were not
> In suavest keeping. The shoes, the clothes, the hat
>
> Suited the decadence of those silences,
> In which he sat. All chariots were drowned. The swans
>
> Moved on the buried water where they lay.
> Lenin took bread from his pocket, scattered it—
>
> The swans fled outward to remoter reaches,
> As if they knew of distant beaches; and were
>
> Dissolved. The distances of space and time
> Were one and swans far off were swans to come.
>
> The eye of Lenin kept the far-off shapes.
> His mind raised up, down-drowned, the chariots.
>
> And reaches, beaches, tomorrow's regions became
> One thinking of apocalyptic legions.
>
> (299–300)

This scene modifies a similar one in the "It Must Change" section of "Notes Toward a Supreme Fiction" (1942), written about three years before, in which an anonymous man (perhaps the poet himself) also sits on a bench looking at swans. In that scene, too, the swans on the lake become something else— "seraphs," "saints," and "changing essences" (again there is an association between the work of metaphor and the religious imagination). But because the activity on that earlier bench, which takes place in a "Theatre of Trope," is described as "his catalepsy" (343)—a condition in which the body is completely unresponsive to external stimuli—there is something profoundly ambivalent about it, for "Notes" is a poem that refuses a "more than sensual mode" (344).

In this scene, however, the rigid conceptual division between sensuous reality and metaphor as an almost schizophrenic evasion of that reality is broken down. The canto emphasizes the way Lenin's bearing and costume — his style — "suit[s]" his desire, in both the literal and figurative senses. It equally performs and incarnates his desire to the extent that the distinction between interior metaphor and exterior surface is erased. This suggestion that radical politics has a style, and thus a poetics, is unexpected in Stevens. In "Esthétique du Mal," a poem written only two years earlier, we also find a Russian revolutionary positioned by a lake. There the emphasis falls on Konstantinov's sensory indigence: "Konstantinov," "the lunatic of one idea / In a world of ideas," "would not be aware of the lake," just as "he would not be aware of the clouds" (286). In "Description without Place," Stevens's deadpan tone suggests a similar assessment — Lenin "was not the man for swans" — yet the poem characterizes Lenin as a man of imagination who does not ignore but rather transfigures his sensory input. The series proceeds to describe the process by which Lenin, in his desire for what is not, turns his immediate sensory perceptions into an imagination of eschatological possibility or apocalypse. The proposition with which Lenin begins — "all chariots were drowned" — suggests two things. The chariot in Stevens's imaginary is an apparatus of the gods (e.g., the "solar chariot" of Phoebus Apollo); to say that they are drowned is to say, as "The Pure Good of Theory" does, that they are obsolete "junk." At the same time, the drowned chariots evoke the closing of the Red Sea on Pharaoh's forces as the Israelites are fleeing Egypt, and so this is an image not of the death but of the victory of God. The swans, which "move on the buried water" where the chariots "lay," are immediate and sensory and have displaced the distant theological imaginary with their immediacy. Yet in Lenin's contemplation of the future, which we experience as "description without place," he reproduces, or translates, that very theological imaginary into Marxist eschatology. The pure present, experienced visually and spatially in terms of distance, is through desire's work of description confused with temporal distance; as the swans become physically remote they become an eschatological possibility: "The distances of space and time / Were one and swans far off were swans to come." The swans that had displaced the drowned chariots become chariots once again, and Lenin's mind assumes the agency of God in raising up and drowning the chariots (which now operate as images of political tyranny rather than religious myth) that will mark the communist inauguration of justice. Merely through redescribing what is seen through metaphor and analogy, and turning that present into an imaginary scene, the whole experience of the present is transformed: it is now the beginning of what is desired. The future is seen theologically, complete with a translated sense of providence—"The intentions of a mind as yet unknown"—and hope—"an expectation."[56]

All this is to say, as the poem does, "description is revelation." Traditionally, revelation was a disclosure of meaning that was hidden or by nature inaccessible, so it required a reconception or revaluation of experience in light of the unknown becoming known. Here the same reconception and revaluation occur not through access to hidden knowledge but through the implementation of an imaginative paradigm that is implicit in our account of what is before us. Description generates "the double of our lives," but this double life is not dualistic, not a truth applied to experience but experience that is shaped into a truth. Desire does not so much seek a better, second world; rather, it *makes* what Stevens calls elsewhere the "single world" into a desired place. Revelation is not news from some other place but the human capacity to remake ourselves into that which we wish ourselves to be through the discipline of language. As Wittgenstein says in his critique of Frazer's anthropology of religion, "The description of a wish is, *eo ipso*, the description of its fulfillment."[57] Description is the "thesis of the plentifullest John" because, as in that Gospel, "It is the theory of the word for those / For whom the word is the making of the world." Stevens does not reject John's claim that "through the Word all things were made" but radicalizes it. The refusal to textualize the world that I described above has been relinquished. As I noted earlier, those who would read the text are not born again but merely "born"—all they have to do is exist, which they already do—but we see here that tautology has been incorporated into a revised understanding of religious language.

At the end of his career, then, Stevens has reconceived religion as a work of transforming, but not transcending, the recalcitrant world through language. Religion is, in a sense, the performance of an imagined good or an ideal that has been forged out of what we would like to be. Stevens has fundamentally assented to the Feuerbachian idea that religion was created by projecting our own imagined perfections onto a transcendent source. Theology has become, for Stevens, an imaginative anthropology. For Feuerbach, as I argued earlier, this meant that secularization did not require a purgation of religious ideas but the discovery that religious ideas were *our* ideas, and that they were ideas *about ourselves*. It is through this lens that we can understand some of the claims of Stevens's late essay, "Two or Three Ideas" (1951). When Stevens says, in that essay, that "the gods are expressions of delight" and that "the gods are the definition of perfection in ideal creatures," he is taking up the Feuerbachian project (CP, 843, 847). As "expressions of delight" the gods objectify human desire. As "definitions" of perfection, the gods are the means through which identity is

constituted in language. They are also the means through which language
becomes narrative image—the means through which, as Stevens says in his late
poem "The Rock," the "poem" becomes an "icon"—and so something that we
can imitate and toward which we can aspire. As definitions of "perfection," the
gods objectify but also judge desire. They discipline it and give it a goal.

The syllogism Stevens sets out to prove in the essay is this: if "it might be true
that the style of the poem and the gods themselves are one," and also that "the
style of the gods and the style of men are one," then, "As my poem is, so are my
gods and so am I" (844–845). To be a god, Stevens argues, is to have perfectly
integrated language and life, to have achieved what he calls a "style" in which
life has become the performance of the ideals created in speech. What makes a
god a god, he claims, is not freedom from the material limits characteristic of
human life but the total integration of interior and exterior, or *style*, "something
inherent, something that permeates": "What matters is their manner, their
style, which tells us at once that they are as we wished them to be, that they have
fulfilled us, that they are us but purified, magnified, in an expansion. It is their
style that makes them gods, not merely privileged beings" (847). Poetry is the
means through which this style can be achieved. Ideally, it achieves a religious
reconciliation between who one is and what one does. Gods are the perfections
toward which we aspire, and the poem and the gods are one. Living life as a
poem—"the theory / Of poetry," after all, "is the theory of life" (415)—is the
means by which we can live our imagined good and so become the "gods" we
wish to be. This divinization has nothing to do with fantasies of self-creation or
material power. Human finitude is unchanged. But life has been so integrated
into the language of desire that it becomes a *sense*: a supreme sense, so that the
experience of the world as the desired place feels almost unmediated.

Near the end of his life, then, Stevens begins to look to the imagination as the
faculty that preserves religious aspiration while resisting a dualistic ontology: "If
the imagination is the faculty by which we import the unreal into what is real, its
value is the value of the way of thinking by which we project the idea of God into
the idea of man" (735–736). Stevens is still relying on secular assumptions
concerning what is real and what is unreal, but he assumes that a meaningful
anthropology is going to have reference to the idea of God. Stevens will never
become totally disengaged from the determinations of material life, but he nonetheless permits an "enlargement" of that life. In the late poetry we find Stevens
loosening what Henry James called the cable attached to the balloon of experience, and so opening itself to those things that cannot be "known," but can only
"reach us through the beautiful circuit and subterfuge of our thought and our
desire."[58] But he never cuts it, as James thought the writer of romance must.

We see this in "To an Old Philosopher in Rome," Stevens's poem for the philosopher George Santayana, who was spending his last days in a convent in Rome. There, "The extreme of the unknown" always remains in the "presence" of "the extreme of the known":

Things dark on the horizons of perception,
Become accompaniments of fortune, but
Of the fortune of the spirit, beyond the eye,
Not of its sphere, and yet not far beyond

. . . .
It is a kind of total grandeur at the end,
With every visible thing enlarged and yet
No more than a bed, a chair and moving nuns,
The immensest theatre, the pillared porch,
The book and candle in your ambered room . . .

(CP, 432, 434)

These "yets" chasten the supposition that transcendence might be a place rather than a performance of language. Rather, the religious imagination, which provides Santayana the logic of "absolution" and "penitence"—strange words in a Stevens poem—is precisely a "theatre" in which practices like these make sense. Santayana's world in this poem is not a departure from everyday life: "The life of the city never lets go, nor do you / Ever want it to." But it is nonetheless a world created by what "Description without Place" calls the "thesis of the plentifullest John," as the last lines of the poem indicate:

He stops upon this threshold,
As if the design of all his words takes form
And frame from thinking and is realized.

(434)

Santayana here is one of "those / For whom the word is the making of the world" (301). The resistance of the world to the desires forged and performed in language no longer is the focus. Santayana has taken upon himself the prerogative of the Christian God by becoming the Word through whom the world is made. He has "projected the idea of God into the idea of man." In "Less and Less Human, O Savage Spirit," the speaker insisted, "If there must be a god in the house. . . . He must be incapable of speaking" (288), because a speaking god leads to the false assumption that the world might reciprocate our speech. But here the "idea of God" has become precisely the idea of speech, the idea of a world created by the Word. In "The Bed of Old John Zeller," Stevens criticized the religious logic of his ancestors—the "habit of wishing" that "the structure of ideas" was "the structure of things"—and commended the courage to "accept the structure / Of things as the structure of ideas" (287). But Santayana's world is, precisely, the "design of all his words," a structure of ideas, or "thinking," realized *as a world.*

This is all qualified by Stevens's well-known "as if." Religious language in Stevens never becomes a fabric of knowledge. It is a "supreme fiction." But this fiction has come after years of wrestling with the religious indiscretions of poetic language. It is as if Stevens came to accept that speech inevitably takes on a religious dimension. For whatever the truth of its metaphysical claims, religion has always been, as Kenneth Burke noted, a mode of language. Stevens's late poem "Final Soliloquy of the Interior Paramour" includes the line "We say God and the imagination are one" (CP, 444). The "we say" is an essential part of the proposition: maybe, Stevens suggests, it is precisely in what we say, in the linguistic response to and transformation of being, that the religious dimension unfolds. The "we say" is both hesitant—the proposition that follows is not an incontrovertible fact but something proposed—and a suggestion that the aspirations of language may point toward a unity that only seems implausible.

2

"TANGLED IN A GOLDEN MESH": VIRGINIA WOOLF AND THE "DECEPTIVENESS" OF BEAUTY

For Wallace Stevens, the most dangerous residue of religion for aesthetics lay in the tendency of poetic language to generate religious metaphors and anthropomorphisms. The fiction of Virginia Woolf discloses another danger for aesthetics: the propensity of modern experiences of beauty and sublimity to engender religious modes of thought and desire that are no longer intelligible within a secular conception of the world. For Woolf's characters, the beautiful (and its modern cousin, the sublime) is suspended in the uncertain space between religious and secular ontologies. The intensity of experiences of beauty *among* her characters is matched only by the suspicion these experiences produce *in* her characters—a suspicion that the characteristic attitudes issuing from aesthetic consciousness too easily become religious. Beauty in Woolf unwittingly radiates an eschatological suggestiveness—a promise of order, reconciliation, and renovation—and it is just this promise that Woolf rejects as incommensurable with fidelity to the fluid, immanent, secular process she calls "life." At other times, Woolf strives to imagine beauty as the category through which immanent life is affirmed in a mode of secular pantheism. In Dostoevsky's *The Brothers Karamazov*—a novel Woolf admired—Dmitri maintains that "beauty is the battlefield" where "the devil is struggling with God."[1] The contention of this chapter is that beauty is the field on which religious and secular conceptions of reality struggle for authority in Woolf's fiction.[2]

Woolf's reflections on the beautiful and the sublime take place against a modern background in which the transcendental unity of beauty, truth, and goodness has been dissociated. Max Weber argued that the dissociation of beauty, truth, and goodness was a definitive mark of secular modernity. "Today," he wrote, "[w]e realize again . . . that something can be sacred not only in spite of its not being beautiful, but rather because and in so far as it is not beautiful. . . . And, since Nietzsche, we realize that something can be beautiful, not only in spite of the aspect in which it is not good, but rather in that very aspect."[3] Nietzsche, to whom Weber appeals, expands on this idea in the notebooks collected as *The Will to Power*:

> For a philosopher to say, "the good and the beautiful are one," is infamy; if he goes on to add, "also the true," one ought to thrash him. Truth is ugly. . . . [T]he judgment of beauty is shortsighted, it sees only the immediate consequences . . . it lavishes upon the object that inspires it a magic conditioned by the association of various beauty judgments—that are quite alien to the nature of that object. To experience a thing as beautiful means: to experience it necessarily wrongly.[4]

Beauty, for Nietzsche, is not a property inherent in the world. It is merely a name for the subjective imposition of value on the mechanistic neutrality ("truth") of that world. Nietzsche calls this imposition "magic"—an enchanting anthropomorphic mistake.[5]

Recent commentators on the status of beauty in modernity have told a similar story. For J. M. Bernstein, "In modernity beauty is not only alienated from truth, but grieves its loss; modernity is the site of beauty bereaved—bereaved of truth."[6] Alexander Nehamas writes, "[T]he sense that a higher authority—reason or God—secured that alignment [of beauty and goodness] was gradually lost and the picture gradually faded, only the dangers of beauty remaining in the traces it left behind. The desires beauty sparks and the pleasures it promises began to seem dubious. . . . Beauty itself was often taken to be the seductive face of evil, a delightful appearance masking the horrid skull beneath the skin."[7] Woolf recognized this sentiment: "When one gave up seeing the beauty that clothed things," thinks Mrs. Ambrose in Woolf's *The Voyage Out*, "this was the skeleton beneath."[8] Romantic philosophy—which was, for many modernists, insufficiently secularized—could insist, as Hegel did, that beauty was the sensible manifestation of freedom, a true appearance of the undetermined, transcendent life possible for human beings.[9] In his notebooks, Coleridge writes, "[T]he intuition of the *Beautiful!*—This too is *spiritual*—and [by] the Goodness of God this is the shorthand, Hieroglyphic of Truth—the mediator between Truth and Feeling. . . . The Sense of Beauty is *implicit* knowledge."[10]

By the turn of the twentieth century, however, even beauty's sympathetic theorists insisted that it had no metaphysical jurisdiction. George Santayana's *The Sense of Beauty*, which develops what Arthur Danto has called the first truly "secular" account of beauty, insists that its reality is only physiological and psychological; he dismisses the Idealist proposition that beauty is the "sensible manifestation of the good" or that it bears any relation to truth. Beauty is, rather, "pleasure regarded as the quality of a thing."[11] Charles Mauron, whose *The Nature of Beauty in Art and Literature* Roger Fry translated and the Woolfs published, rejected "dubious metaphysics" when exploring the complex "empirical" phenomenon of beauty and the "sensation" that accompanied it.[12] And G. E. Moore, whose philosophy exerted considerable influence on the Bloomsbury group, draws an analogy between moral and aesthetic feeling, but because both exist exclusively in states of consciousness rather than in features of the world, they only supervene upon that world and "lack the power to bring about changes in [it]." Moore could only preserve beauty and goodness from the encroachments of naturalistic explanation by confining them to subjective experience.[13]

Woolf was capable of writing, "Beauty is everywhere, and beauty is only two finger's-breadth from goodness."[14] That finger's breadth, however, is space enough for a fissure; like Weber and Nietzsche, Woolf felt that the connection of beauty to other values had been compromised in modernity. In "The Narrow Bridge of Art" she consistently returns to the incommensurability of aesthetic and moral emotions in modern life, particularly as they bear on large ontological questions: "The mind is full of monstrous, hybrid, unmanageable emotions. That the age of the earth is 3,000,000,000 years; that human life lasts but a second; that the capacity of the human mind is nevertheless boundless; that life is infinitely beautiful yet repulsive; that one's fellow creatures are adorable but disgusting." When she imagines a representative modern person, she emphasizes the contradictions latent in his sensorium: "[H]e is extremely alive to everything—to ugliness, sordidity, beauty, amusement . . . things that have no apparent connection are associated in the mind. Feelings which used to come simple and separate do so no longer. Beauty is part ugliness; amusement part disgust; pleasure part pain." Woolf compares Keats's Romantic attitude toward beauty with that of the "modern" poet (an anonymous T. S. Eliot) by making a remarkable distinction between the "shadow" of beauty and its "opposite." The latter is distinctly modern: "In [Keats's] poem sorrow is the shadow which accompanies beauty. In the modern mind beauty is accompanied not by its shadow but by its opposite. The modern poet talks of the nightingale who sings 'jug jug to dirty ears.' There trips along by the side of our modern beauty some mocking spirit which sneers at beauty for being beautiful; which turns the looking glass and shows us that the other side of her cheek is pitted and deformed."[15] Woolf's reflections on the fate of beauty in modernity do not solely aim to widen the perceptual scope of art—they are not, or not only, a challenge to the modernist artist to engage the non-poetic.[16] Rather, she registers puzzlement as to the metaphysical significance of the admixture of beauty and deformity. The entanglement of beauty and ugliness, moreover, is linked to the innate aspirations of the human mind (it is "boundless") and the apparent truth of its ontological insignificance (the world will exist for billions of years before and after it). These antagonisms have become so severe that one is tempted to "sneer" at beauty for its inability to disclose anything true about the world.

In certain moods Woolf characterizes beauty as a feature of surfaces processed by the eye rather than the mind. In "Street Haunting," the "eye" that perceives beauty, and which is "content with surfaces only," is "not a miner, not a diver, not a seeker after buried treasure. It floats us smoothly down a stream, resting, pausing, the brain sleeps perhaps as it looks." And after a "prolonged diet" of the eye's "simple, sugary fare, of beauty pure and uncomposed, we become conscious of satiety."[17] But beauty only appears superficial and saccharine because of the suffering and 'deformity' that stall the eye: the essay takes a disorienting turn by asking, "What, then, is it like to be a dwarf?" and imagines the pain of a little person whose feet are "beautiful" yet who wishes her entire form might be so. In Woolf's early sketch "Holburn Viaduct," she presents three scenes of arresting beauty: "The kitchen table, with its yellow loaf, white aprons and pots of jam, is rooted to the heart of the world." Here, too, however, each scene is scandalized by suffering: "Then why, wretched boy, do you run across the street with your arm crooked against the wind? . . . Then why does blood-smeared paper drift down the pavement?" But the conflict here is not between beauty (as sensuous surface) and the suffering it masks. The questions — "then why?" — register an awareness of a painful ontological incongruity: this beauty appears securely anchored ("rooted") in being; it is a sign of the world's comprehensive hospitality and benevolence — "*All's* nodding and waving." The observer protests each calamity by appealing to yet more beauty: "Still, still, through the bars of the railings there are caves of redness. . . . Surely, surely, with the fire-light upon the terrier's hind legs."[18] These aesthetic phenomena are marshaled as evidence; they testify to a quality in being that should render violence and deformity impossible, but somehow does not. Beauty is ontologically impotent, but it is suffering, not beauty itself, that appears anomalous ("then why?") in the light of its radiance.

Woolf is the lone novelist in this study. Yet Woolf understood modern fiction as a hybrid genre. She hoped that it would "take over . . . some of the duties which were once discharged by poetry." She claimed, moreover, that this new prose-poetry would yield insight into the very problem of this chapter: the metaphysical status of beauty. Poetry had "always," Woolf writes, "been overwhelmingly on the side of beauty," but the novel has unique access to the "discord" and "incongruity" that characterize "life."[19] Fiction, Woolf believes, can help us see "life" before it is distilled into poetry. I argue, moreover, that her subtle attention to character yields insight into the *psychology* that attends particular efforts of secularization. Charles Taylor has shown in compelling detail how the epistemological claims of secular modernity are inextricable from the values projected onto and asserted by the ostensibly neutral subject of knowledge. As a poetic *novelist*, Woolf is able to illuminate this crucial link between a given philosophical attitude and the psychic needs the attitude satisfies, or the self-image it enables.

This chapter seeks to understand the ambivalent religiosity of beauty in Woolf's fiction. I discuss multiple Woolf novels but focus on two in particular: *Mrs. Dalloway* and *To the Lighthouse*. In *Mrs. Dalloway*, I argue, we find an attempt to subsume the ugly and the painful into an expanded concept of beauty and so affirm the beauty of being as a whole in spite of hostile local configurations. In doing so the novel imagines a secular pantheism in which the world is celebrated aesthetically as an amoral, erotic, undifferentiated process of fecund movement. It accepts the secular rift between beauty and goodness that Weber observed while struggling, nonetheless, to sustain a mystical experience of life as a beautiful whole. Yet this affirmation is complicated by an explicitly religious vision of aesthetic experience: Septimus's theology of beauty, which preserves the religious connection between beauty and goodness but is, finally, oblivious to the "truth" Nietzsche insisted on, and so indistinguishable from madness. Clarissa Dalloway's experience of beauty can be read, I argue, as a mystical compromise with a religious ontology of beauty that for Woolf is no longer sustainable.

This vision of *Mrs. Dalloway*—the affirmation of the exuberant beauty of the world irrespective of its relation to goodness—is displaced by a more suspicious account of the beautiful in *To the Lighthouse*. In the latter novel, beauty becomes not a name for the erotic encounter with the world but the suspension of that encounter in a vision of peace and reconciliation. In the perception of this sort of beauty, the ecstatic agon with life gives way to an intimation of transcendent "goodness." But this aesthetics of peace is felt to be ontologically illegitimate and untruthful precisely because it is associated with a specious, ironized "divine goodness." Like religious eschatology, beauty seems to be a "lure" and a "consolation."[20] Lily Briscoe thinks, "Was it wisdom? Was it knowledge? Was it, once more, the deceptiveness of beauty, so that all one's perceptions, half-way to truth, were tangled in a golden mesh?" (*TL*, 50). The reconciliatory agency of the beautiful—its power to draw things into what Bernard in *The Waves* calls "one beauty"—is felt to be an evasive unity, unfaithful to the contradictions and incongruities of experience.[21] Beauty's radiance is an epistemological trap, closer to illusion than religious revelation. Furthermore, this religious intimation of beauty is undermined by an atheistic vision of the sublime, the aesthetic experience that has characteristically displaced beauty in modernity. And yet, to further complicate this picture, Woolf ironizes this secular, atheistic sublime because of its association with a masculine emphasis on the dignity of the will's confrontation with a dangerous, godless world. Woolf cannot, finally, rest in either a theological beauty or a secular sublime.

In this chapter, "beauty" signifies a general and elastic aesthetic property of being. It is a name for the radiance of certain arrangements of objects and persons in the world that evoke desire, consent, and, at times, an experience of what Woolf calls "peace" and "eternity" (*TL*, 63). Woolf is not the only modernist occupied with radiance. James Joyce, both in his early notebooks and in the character of Stephen Dedalus, argued that "radiance" was the most puzzling element of beauty. Radiance is Aquinas's *claritas*, the third constitutive principle of beauty after "wholeness and harmony" (*integritas, consonantia, claritas*). Stephen argues that radiance (*claritas*) should be understood as the revelation of *quidditas*, the "*whatness* of a thing."[22] In *Stephen Hero*, moreover, radiance is the sine qua non of "epiphany," for it "is just in this epiphany that I find the third, the supreme quality of beauty":

> This is the moment which I call epiphany. First we recognize that the object is *one* integral thing, then we recognize that it is an organized composite structure, a *thing* in fact: finally, when the relation of the parts is exquisite, when the parts are adjusted to the special point, we recognise that it is *that* thing which it is. Its soul, its whatness, leaps to us from the vestment of its appearance. The soul of the commonest object, the structure of which is so adjusted, seems to us radiant. The object achieves its epiphany.[23]

The experience of epiphany—"a sudden spiritual manifestation"[24]—is simultaneously religious and aesthetic. In Woolf, but not in Joyce,[25] it may also be erotic: in *Mrs. Dalloway*, "the religious feeling" generated by Sally Steton's kiss is figured as "the radiance" of a covered diamond "burn[ing] through" its packaging" (*MD*, 36). Epiphany in both Joyce and Woolf is an experience of what Jacques Maritain calls "transcendental beauty": "radiance" as "*splendour formae*, the splendor of form," or "the splendor of the secrets of being radiating into intelligence."[26]

For Woolf's work,[27] this revelatory, nonsubjective character of beauty as "radiance" is essential. Just as Stephen insists that "the commonest object" may become radiant—his example in *Stephen Hero* is "the clock of the Ballast Office"—in Woolf radiance attends objects of no particular aesthetic distinction. Thus Lily Briscoe aspires "to feel simply that's a chair, that's a table, and yet at the same time, It's a miracle, it's an ecstasy" (*TL*, 202). Woolf therefore dissents, at least in certain moods, from the broad tendency of Bloomsbury aesthetics, which privileged the art-object over the beauty found in life precisely because the world had nothing to reveal. Roger Fry, whose 1909 "Essay in Aesthetics" influenced the group, insisted that "aesthetic judgment proper" belonged only to the human artifact, for "we have no guarantee that in nature the emotional elements will be combined appropriately with the demands of the imaginative life."[28] In his study *Art*, Clive Bell argued that the beauty of "significant form" was "unrelated to the significance of life."[29] Christine Froula has recently emphasized Bloomsbury's dependence on Kantian aesthetics, which affirm "the artwork's purely formal beauty, apart from content, truth claims, and external rule," as well as the subjective "freedom" implicit in disinterested contemplation.[30] Woolf's aesthetic attention is unquestionably marked by this disinterestedness, to the point where the ego recedes into a state of impersonality in which objects may impress a beholder uncontaminated by subjective demands. (In this sense, as Froula notes, disinterested aesthetic contemplation is already for Bloomsbury a moral project of selflessness that "mediates sociability and community.")[31] Beauty in Woolf, however, is often unrelated to any exquisiteness of "form."[32]

Moreover, while Kant's aesthetics of the artwork is formalistic, he maintained that natural beauty harbored a metaphysical sign that nature was hospitable to moral life. As Gadamer puts it, for Kant "[i]t is certainly not without significance that we find nature beautiful, for it is an ethical experience bordering on the miraculous that beauty should manifest itself in all the fecund power of nature as if she displayed her beauties for us. In Kant a creationist theology stands behind this unique human capacity to encounter natural beauty."[33] Woolf still seeks these signs in beauty—not only in "natural" beauty narrowly construed but also in configurations of objects, persons, and events *found* rather than *made* by the self. Her fiction is thus saturated with experiences of beauty that challenge the scope of the dominant Bloomsbury aesthetic. Fry maintained that natural beauty was impoverished because the world was "heartlessly indifferent to the needs of the imaginative life; God causes his rain to fall on the just and the unjust."[34] But in exceptional moments the world does, in Woolf, meet these needs, and this confluence is linked precisely to a sentiment of justice. These experiences of beauty depend on an intimation of harmonious order or pattern in the world that emanates from them. As James

Wood has argued, Woolf tends to look "not so much for the aesthetic pattern behind reality as for a further metaphysical pattern behind the aesthetic pattern."[35] I would amend this by saying that Woolf often wants to look *through* the aesthetic pattern to find, implicit in it, a metaphysical pattern. Beautiful particulars are therefore often referred to a larger whole. For G. E. Moore, "to say that a thing is beautiful is to say, not indeed that it is *itself* good, but that it is a necessary element in something which is: to prove that a thing is truly beautiful is to prove that a whole, to which it bears a particular relation as a part, is truly good."[36] Moore never imagined that a "whole" could escape the arrangements of consciousness and circumscribe the entirety of being. But in Woolf, beauty makes just this demand: its reality signals its participation in a comprehensive good that nevertheless cannot be affirmed. The world is, as Mrs. Ramsay says, full of "treachery" (*TL*, 64); to affirm its goodness is to smuggle in a theological claim—a "metaphysical pattern"—that Woolf cannot accept on the level of avowed belief.

While Woolf's novels and essays are replete with the term "beauty," she never provides a succinct definition.[37] There are two main reasons for this. The first is that beauty is characteristically indefinable; as Kant said, it cannot be subsumed under a concept.[38] The feeling evoked by beauty is more than sensory pleasure yet less than knowledge. At the same time—and this is precisely what creates difficulties for Woolf—beauty is a "stimulus" to the understanding (*TL*, 134); it seems to contain an elusive metaphysical or theological message that the understanding can never quite decode. It opens onto religious questions and expectations that are not answered but will not subside. It is, as Borges writes, the "imminence of a revelation which does not occur."[39]

The second reason Woolf never provides a succinct definition of beauty is that her own use of the term, while abundant, is often hesitant and uncertain. It arises in contexts far removed from the familiar aesthetic occasions. In *Orlando*, "beauty" names an experience that begins in something more like pain and has little to do with the aesthetic arrangement of objects. Near the end of the novel, the protagonist approaches what Woolf calls a "moment of being":

> Here she forced herself by a great effort, to stop by the carpenter's shop, and to stand stock-still watching Joe Stubbs fashion a cart wheel. She was standing with her eye fixed on his hand when the quarter struck. It hurtled through her like a meteor, so hot that no fingers can hold it. She saw with disgusting vividness that the thumb on Joe's right hand was without a finger nail and there was a raised saucer of pink flesh where the nail should have been. The sight was so repulsive that she felt faint for a moment, but in that moment's darkness, when her eyelids flickered, she was relieved of the pressure of the

present. There was something strange in the shadow that the flicker of her eyes cast, something which (as anyone can test for himself by looking now at the sky) is always absent from the present—whence its terror, its nondescript character—something one trembles to pin through the body with a name and call beauty, for it has no body, is as a shadow without substance or quality of its own, yet has the power to change whatever it adds itself to. This shadow now while she flickered her eye in her faintness in the carpenter's shop stole out, and attaching itself to the innumerable sights she had been receiving, composed them into something tolerable, comprehensible. Yes, she thought, heaving a deep sigh of relief, as she turned from the carpenter's shop to climb the hill, I can begin to live again. I am by the Serpentine, she thought, the little boat is climbing through the white arch of a thousand deaths. I am about to understand. . . .[40]

Orlando's experience is constituted by elements (such as terror) traditionally a part of the vocabulary of the sublime (discussed later in the chapter). Indeed, Woolf uses the term "beauty" with some hesitancy: it is a concept assigned with trembling and even violence, as one pins a butterfly "through the body." It begins with an experience not of harmony but of disgust and pain. It is here that the ambivalent religiosity in Woolf's language of beauty is most apparent. The missing nail is an image of evil in miniature: it suggests that there is something awry in the world, some distortion or fall. There is nothing—no nail—where something "should have been." But the negation isn't final; it is, as Jacques Maritain writes, "*that kind* of imperfection through which infinity wounds the finite."[41] The pain casts a "shadow," an incorporeal presence ("it has no body") that nonetheless has the power (unlike in G. E. Moore) to "change" things. Orlando calls this shadow "beauty," because the very experience of pain creates a distance—figured as shadow—between the self and the tyranny of the material present. Simone Weil writes that "distance is the soul of beauty,"[42] and this is what we find: the fact that this distance can be conceived as beautiful means that the gap between what is and what should be is not unbridgeable. Beauty implies an eschatological awareness that things might be different, a faith that allows one, as Orlando thinks, to "live again." It becomes the radiance of a possibility for the future—it is "absent from the present"—that is nonetheless obscured in shadow. Beauty is the intimation of an order: the world becomes, through its agency, something "composed" and "comprehensible," equally aesthetic and rational.

Woolf's "moments of being" are characterized by a similar dialectic of pain and beauty. In one of these early "moments," Woolf suddenly, in a revelation of "hopeless sadness," ceases to fight her brother and lets him continue to "pummel" her with his fists. In another, she connects the "horror" of the suicide of a man staying at St. Ives with an apple tree: "I stood there looking at the grey-green creases of the bark—it was a moonlit night—in a trance of horror." These are moments of despair. Yet in others, she has a sense of the interconnectedness of all things that ends in a satisfactory sense of the whole: "I was looking at the flower bed by the front door; 'That is the whole,' I said. I was looking at a plant with a spread of leaves; and it seemed suddenly plain that the flower itself was a part of the earth; that a ring enclosed what was the flower; and that was the real flower; part earth, part flower."[43]

The most peculiar and rarely discussed aspect of these "moments of being" is their connection to pain. For why should pain yield intimations of "being" rather than "non-being," which might be characterized as the privational dimension of evil? Even more remarkable is, as in the passage from *Orlando*, the connection of *beauty* with pain.[44] The "philosophy" that unfolds from these moments of being is charged, therefore, with resolving the incongruity between beauty and pain into a higher congruity, or finding a harmonious pattern that answers for Woolf's "then why?" In "A Sketch of the Past," the figure of the apple tree illuminated in the moonlight is, perhaps, a figure of beauty; beauty's connection with the suicide is a source of horror, for it seems to reinforce the Weberian thesis that the beautiful and the good are mutual antagonists. (This moment is similar to the moment in *Mrs. Dalloway*, discussed later, when Clarissa says that Septimus's suicide "made her feel the beauty.")[45] But ultimately, both beautiful and horrible particulars are subsumed into a participation in the "whole," which is an object of desire and contentment because it is, precisely, experienced as beautiful, or as an order whose intelligibility is found in harmonious pattern.

Woolf articulates this aesthetic response to the whole as she examines the final philosophical implications of her "moments of being":

> I feel that I have had a blow; but it is not, as I thought as a child, simply a
> blow from an enemy hidden behind the cotton wool of daily life; it is or will
> become a revelation of some order; it is a token of some real thing behind
> appearances, and I make it real by putting it into words. It is only by putting
> it into words that I make it whole; this wholeness means that it has lost its
> power to hurt me; it gives me, perhaps because by doing so I take away the
> pain, a great delight to put the severed parts together. Perhaps this is the
> strongest pleasure known to me. . . . From this I reach what I might call a
> philosophy . . . that behind the cotton wool is hidden a pattern; that we—I
> mean all human beings—are connected with this; that the whole world is
> a work of art; that we are parts of the work of art. *Hamlet* or a Beethoven

quartet is the truth about this vast mass that we call the world. But there is no Shakespeare, there is no Beethoven; certainly and emphatically there is no God; we are the words; we are the music; we are the thing itself. And I see this when I have a shock.[46]

The pain of the world—the sense that the world is a hostile "enemy"—is such that it distances the self from the immediacy of material life. It undermines our native trust in being; it incites Woolf to make a classically theological distinction between reality ("some real thing") and "appearanc[e]"—the very distinction that Stevens, like Nietzsche before him, dismissed as insufficiently secular. The sense of the beauty of the whole—of the "world" as "a work of art"—finally operates as a kind of secular theodicy and so restores this trust. Yet this translation of a doctrine of creation into a doctrine of the world as a work of art is precarious. Woolf immediately observes that her analogy fails. A work of art has a creator; if the world is a work of art, it, too, should have a creator. Indeed, this very analogy is at the heart of the theological argument that begins with the "design" seemingly found in the world, an argument famously criticized by Hume, Kant, and Darwin.[47] Yet Woolf insists "certainly and emphatically" that "there is no God," no Beethoven or Shakespeare arranging things in the background. She wants the world to have anthropomorphic aesthetic properties (which are also moral properties, as they mitigate the pain of human exigency), but without any anthropomorphic agent to create them.

It would be misleading, however, to say that this order is only achieved and imposed by human works of art. For she speaks of these moments as revelations that disclose a "*truth* about this vast mass we call the world." Human subjectivity and language are necessary for the formulation of this truth in art, and they may amplify its reality, but this truth is already *there*. It seems, she writes, "given to me, not made by me."[48] These moments leave her "exposed to a whole avalanche of meaning that had heaped itself up and discharged itself upon me."[49] Because the best philosophical work on Woolf centers on epistemological concerns, it seems unable to account for those moments in her work where the subject is susceptible rather than constructive, passive rather than active. In her extraordinary study *The Phantom Table*, for example, Ann Banfield contends that Woolf, like Leslie Stephen, G. E. Moore, and Bertrand Russell, conceives of "reality" as "fundamentally external, inhuman," or, put differently, "*neutral and impersonal*."[50] Her Woolf is a writer for whom human "design . . . oppose[s] beauty and life"; this life is "particular, atomized, accidental, formless."[51] And this is indeed one side of Woolf: a writer who, as a child of her secular milieu, assumes a disengaged model of self and world, wherein, as Charles Taylor writes, "The knowledge of reality as neutral fact comes before our attributing to it various 'values' and relevances." But there is another Woolf at loggerheads with the former, for whom being is a source of meaning that precedes, "expose[s]," and overwhelms the self.[52] For this Woolf, but not for Bertrand Russell or Leslie Stephen, Lily Briscoe's questions—"what is the meaning of life?" or "Why is one sitting here, after all?"—are intelligible, if unanswerable. This Woolf can insist that "human beings" not only organize and arrange but "show the light through," and she can ask, "[W]hat is the light?"[53] Thus "the world" as "work of art"—which reveals *itself* as a beautiful, ordered whole— cannot simply be understood, as it often is in Wallace Stevens, as a product of an ordering human imagination projecting its desire onto the chaos of material becoming. This beauty is something distinct from what art achieves through its sorting and excising. The whole does not admit the sorts of selective exclusions necessary to art.[54]

Woolf's instincts concerning the world as a work of art, then, are character- ized by an ambivalent secular translation, in which a property of the world that was once theological is preserved in secular perspective. In previous chapters I noted that Nietzsche is the post-Christian figure who tirelessly advocates the elimination, rather than the translation or naturalization, of theological catego- ries. Nietzsche criticized just the sort of "aesthetic anthropomorphism" that Woolf continues to find so attractive in her conception of the world as a work of art. To think of the world as an aesthetic harmony—to predicate "beauty" of the world—is to smuggle a concept of God back into the picture. The passage is worth quoting again:

> Let us beware of positing generally and everywhere anything as elegant
> as the cyclical movements of our neighboring stars; even a glance at the
> Milky Way raises doubts whether there are not far coarser and more contra-
> dictory movements there. . . . The total character of the world, however, is
> in all eternity chaos—in the sense not of a lack of necessity but of a lack
> of order, arrangement, form, beauty, wisdom, and whatever other names
> there are for our aesthetic anthropomorphisms. . . . Let us beware of attribut-
> ing to it heartlessness and unreason or their opposites: it is neither perfect
> nor beautiful, nor noble, nor wishes to become any of these things; it does
> not by any means strive to imitate man. None of our aesthetic and moral
> judgments apply to it. . . . Once you know that there are no purposes, you
> also know that there is no accident; for it is only beside a world of "purposes"
> that the word "accident" has meaning. Let us beware of saying that death
> is opposed to life. The living is merely a type of what is dead, and a very
> rare type. . . . When will all these shadows of God cease to darken our
> minds? When will we complete our de-deification of nature? When may we

begin to *"naturalize"* humanity in terms of a pure, newly discovered, newly redeemed nature?[55]

For Nietzsche, aesthetic anthropomorphisms are simultaneously moral anthropomorphisms, for religious models of the world (a *cosmos* rather than mere nature) presume that moral and aesthetic order are one. To think of the world as "beautiful," Nietzsche argues, is to think of it as "perfect," or as a manifestation of "wisdom" and "purpose."[56] While Woolf was not directly influenced by Nietzsche, she understood and internalized this criticism. It was generated by the pressure of what she took to be the ontological consequences of an inescapable atheism. Her novels see characters and narrators bringing something like this criticism against the mystical experiences of beauty they continue to find so compelling. This is what creates the fundamental ambivalence of beauty in Woolf: it seems irresistibly to create a sense or promise of transcendent order that must nevertheless be rejected.[57]

I have said that Woolf's understanding of the world as a work of art operates as a secular theodicy in the sense that it subsumes the pain of the world into a higher, mystical pattern. Theodicy is aesthetic insofar as it suggests that ugliness and evil are only local "appearance"; the deeper historical or metaphysical pattern of which the details are a part is beautiful because the whole is purposeful and harmonious. In theodicy the actual is the metaphysically necessary; the beautiful is a sign that necessity is not just brute—the way things have to be—but a manifestation of the good. Thus Adorno calls Hegel's aesthetics a "theodicy of the real": "Because the idea can take no other form than that in which it is realized, its first appearance or 'first natural form' is 'suitable' and therefore beautiful."[58]

The danger of theodicy is that (in certain modes) it prematurely reconciles us to the violence of the world. By suggesting that there is a deeper, obscure harmony behind disagreeable appearances, one may seem to justify violence and pain by subsuming them into a larger beauty. Theodicy can become, to use a word that Woolf employs with a great deal of ambivalence and often hostility, a form of "consolation." Indeed, the theodicy of aesthetic harmony that so attracts her comes under scrutiny in numerous places in her writing. In *Between the Acts*, for instance, Mrs. Swithin, the naïve Christian presence in the novel, thinks that discord in nature and history is merely local; if we could see the whole, we would understand that the larger architecture is harmonious:

> Mrs. Swithin caressed her cross. She gazed vaguely at the view. She was off, they guessed, on a circular tour of the imagination—one-making. Sheep, cows, grass, trees, ourselves—all are one. If discordant, producing harmony—if

not to us, to a gigantic ear attached to a gigantic head. And thus—she was smiling benignly—the agony of the particular sheep, cow or human being is necessary; and so—she was beaming seraphically at the gilt vane in the distance—we reach the conclusion that *all* is harmony, could we hear it. And we shall. Her eyes now rested on the white summit of a cloud.[59]

The narrator's relation to Mrs. Swithin's conception is unclear (this is actually what William and Isa suspect she is thinking). But her theological imagination is unquestionably ironized. The description of her face as benign and seraphic is acrimonious (as such she is sweetly oblivious to the truth of suffering) as is the characterization of her God as grossly anthropomorphic (a gigantic ear attached to the gigantic head that hears the harmony we cannot). In Woolf's essay on T. J. Cobden-Sanderson—entitled "The Cosmos," a term that conjures a premodern moral and aesthetic order displaced in secular modernity by a neutral "nature"—she wryly delineates the ethical dangers of the unified whole:

> For there was a unity of the whole in which the virtues or even the vices of mankind were caught up and put to their proper uses. Once attain to that vision, and all things fell into their places. From that vantage ground the white butterfly caught in the spider's net was "all in the world's plan" and Englishmen and Germans blowing each other's heads off in the trenches were "brothers not enemies" conspiring to "create the great emotions which in turn create the greater creation." ... [W]e are left asking, "But Mr. Sanderson, how does one 'fly to the great Rhythm'? What is the extraordinary ring of harmony within harmony that encircles us; what reason is there to suppose that a mountain wishes us well or that a lake has a profound moral meaning to impart?"

Woolf writes here as a critic of aesthetic anthropomorphisms; the Romantic idea of nature as a moral source is reduced to personified mountains and lakes.[60]

The problem, however, is that Woolf's own intimation of harmony—of the world as a work of art, as she says in "A Sketch of the Past"—is not easily distinguished from Mrs. Swithin's or Cobden-Sanderson's. Her critique of the latter ("the extraordinary ring of harmony") borrows from her own vocabulary: in "A Sketch of the Past," "a ring enclosed what was the flower," and Woolf is impressed by her mother's "constant sense of the mystery that encircled" those around her. Woolf proposes that "we are the music," just as Mrs. Swithin thinks that all is harmony "if we could hear it." Indeed, the aesthetic hope hazarded in *Between the Acts* is precisely that a large-scale, if provisional, harmony is created by the play and the gramophone: "The gramophone was affirming in tones there was no denying, triumphant yet valedictory: *Dispersed are we; who have come together. But,* the gramophone asserted, *let us retain whatever made that harmony.*"⁶¹ As in Woolf's description of the world as a work of art, agency ("whatever made") is inscrutable but somehow active. In the drama, *beauty itself* seems to have this agency: "Each still acted the unacted part conferred on them by their clothes. Beauty was on them. Beauty revealed them. Was it the light that did it?"⁶² This harmony, however, is questioned by anonymous commentators after the play who speculate on its "meaning." One of the objections to the aesthetic pantheism implicit in the pageant's affirmation is that it does not include the violence of history: "Also, why leave out the Army, as my husband was saying, if it's history? And if one spirit animates the whole, what about the aeroplanes?"⁶³ As the play is being performed German airplanes are bombing England; it isn't clear that such discord can be subsumed into aesthetic affirmation.

Because Woolf is suspicious of her own religious tendency to affirm the beauty of the whole, she experiments with a relation to beauty that is purely immanent. One finds among several of her characters a secular aestheticism that resists any form of transcendence: either transcendence sought by moving beyond the particular toward the whole or the transcendence sought in moving beyond the present moment toward a redeemed future. As in Stevens, one finds in Woolf a desire to experience what is "enough"; and here, too, the reach of "enough" is ambiguous. It is often unclear whether the affirmation is an attempt to praise life in its immanence or a provisional effort to discover a limited, momentary, personal satisfaction within the larger scope of life.

In the passage from *Orlando* discussed earlier, beauty emerged when Orlando distanced herself from the present moment. This gave beauty an eschatological dimension: it marked a promise of new life and a revelation that made possible a new "understanding."⁶⁴ In the mood cultivated by secular aestheticism, on the contrary, the present moment is absolutely sufficient. In *The Waves,* Neville embodies this mood. An early passage from the novel is characteristic of his mind-set:

> "In a world which contains the present moment," said Neville, "why dis-
> criminate? Nothing should be named lest by doing so we change it. Let it
> exist, this bank, this beauty, and I, for one instant, steeped in pleasure. The
> sun is hot. I see the river. I see trees specked and burnt in the autumn sun-
> light. Boats float past, through the red, through the green. Far away a bell
> tolls, but not for death. There are bells that ring for life. A leaf falls, from joy.
> Oh, I am in love with life! . . . They are tossing the skins of bananas, which
> then sink eel-like, into the river. All they do is beautiful. There are cruels

behind them and ornaments; their rooms are full of oars and oleographs but they have turned all to beauty." (*TW*, 81–82)

Here, as in certain moments in Stevens, the world is enough and language ("naming") would only be a distortion of the sensory encounter with it. It is not "enough" in the sense that the whole is justified; Neville's aesthetic attachment to what is immediately before him is so complete that the question of justification cannot even arise. Language only need describe: "The sun is hot. I see . . . I see . . . Boats float past." Beauty is a phenomenon of the saturated present; it does not promise anything beyond itself. It is, as Santayana argued, pleasure "objectified," "pleasure regarded as the quality of a thing."[65]

Neville opposes this aestheticism to the religious mode of being that Nietzsche called "the ascetic ideal." He refuses what he takes to be an attempt to reunite the satisfactions of beauty with the good, which he sees in Louis and Rhoda's desire to find a moral logic—a "plot" or "reason"—in the aesthetic scene:

> But then Rhoda, or it may be Louis, some fasting and anguished spirit, passes through and out again. They want a plot, do they? They want a reason? It is not enough for them, this ordinary scene. It is not enough to wait for the thing to be said as if it were written; to see the sentence lay this dab of clay precisely in the right place, making character; to perceive, suddenly, some group in outline against the sky. Yet if they want violence, I have seen death and murder and suicide all in one room. (*TW*, 197)

Neville wants to affirm the "ordinary scene" over against any transcendent reality characterized by *logos* ("reason") and the narrative coherence ("plot") of Providence. He recognizes that "violence" is precisely what thwarts the aesthetics of immediacy and precipitates the religious desire to find such a plot. Louis, the character in *The Waves* most attracted to traditional Christianity, acknowledges as much:

> This moment of reconciliation, when we meet together united, this evening moment, with its wine and shaking leaves, and youth coming up from the river in white flannels, carrying cushions, is to me black with the shadows of dungeons and the tortures and infamies practiced by man upon man. So imperfect are my senses that they never blot out with one purple the serious charge that my reason adds and adds against us, even as we sit here. What is the solution, I ask myself, and the bridge? How can I reduce these dazzling, these dancing apparitions to one line capable of linking all in one? (219)

Louis associates the harmony of beauty with moral "reconciliation"; "the shaking leaves" and the "white flannel" are the aesthetic signs of social concord. Louis supposes—wryly—that if his senses were "perfect," they would "blot out" evil in an aesthetic intuition impossible to distinguish from the sense of color. But the problem of evil intervenes and asks for what amounts to a theology: a "bridge" that will reveal the moral unity beneath "dazzling . . . apparition." Neville seeks pleasure, not reconciliation or unification.

Neville cannot always sustain his aesthetics of immediacy. It cannot withstand the discontent generated by living in time and, much more, in history. Later in life, after Percival, his pagan hero, has died (a casualty of empire), Neville will shift from an understanding of beauty as the intense quality of a passing moment to beauty as that which must be created by a will to impose proportion and harmony on the "depravity of the world": "We must oppose the waste and deformity of the world, its crowds eddying round and round disgorged and trampling. One must slip paper-knives, even, exactly through the pages of novels, and tie up packets of letters neatly with green silk, and brush up the cinders with a hearth broom. Everything must be done to rebuke the horror of deformity" (180).[66] This feeling marks a serious attenuation of his former aesthetic excitement. Yet the vision of evil in the new aesthetic dispensation is not so much a rebuke to the earlier naïveté as a desperate response to the vacuum its dissolution has left. The earlier aestheticism endorsed a picture of glorious "waste"—the nonutilitarian, anti-capitalistic dimension of aestheticism and *l'art pour l'art*. But here "waste" has become moral ugliness. When his vision of aesthetic abundance subsides, Neville can only invert his sense of beauty. Aestheticism has become Manichaeism, a battle between the artistic will, which can tie up letters with green silk, and the world's depravity. Yet the will's reach is diminished; aesthetic resistance is a matter of private, domestic minutiae—tidying books, letters, and the hearth.

The only character in *The Waves* who can truly sustain a purely immanent experience of beauty is Jinny. For Jinny, unlike Neville, this sensory, aesthetic encounter with the world is entirely instinctive and unselfconscious. In Jinny's experience, "[b]eauty rides our brows"—it is a phenomenon of the material eye (141). For Orlando beauty emerged in "shadow," the figure of the distance between the self and the immediate present of material life. But for Jinny, "all is firm without shadow or illusion." The comment is illuminated by the narratorial interlude at midday, which captures the world at its brightest:

> *Everything was without shadow. A jar was so green that the eye seemed sucked up through a funnel by its intensity and stuck to it like a limpet. Then shapes took on mass and edge. Here was the boss of a chair; here the*

bulk of a cupboard. And as the light increased, flocks of shadow were driven before it and conglomerated and hung in many-pleated folds in the background. (110)

The beautiful here is the intensity of the visible without remainder. There is no distance between the eye and color. Shadow is not the place of mystery, the dimension of beauty in which possibilities are hidden; it is dominated ("driven") by the visible and made to arrange itself according to the eye's desire. Just so, Jinny's beauty is made up of irreducibly discrete phenomena: she does not understand the attempt to make things into a pantheistic whole or "one substance": "I see rocks in bright sunshine. I cannot take these facts into some cave and, shading my eyes, grade their yellows, blues, umbers into one substance" (176).

Near the end of the novel Bernard will think of Jinny in a way that recalls Neville's own attempt to remain within the immediate experience of sensory beauty: "She made the willows dance, but not with illusion; for she saw nothing that was not there. It was a tree; there was the river; it was afternoon; here we were; I in my serge suit; she in green. There was no past, no future; merely the moment in its ring of light, and our bodies; and the inevitable climax, the ecstasy" (252). The recourse to the language of "illusion" when discussing Jinny's life of immanence underscores Woolf's uncertain relation to the language of secular materialism. Anything beyond the sensory, material present is in danger of becoming an illusion (a category into which religion often fell in the late nineteenth and early twentieth century). Jinny's completely embodied life therefore has about it the glow of secular authenticity. She "saw," like Stevens's Snow-Man, but in a different mood, "nothing that was not there."[67]

"BEAUTY ANYHOW": AESTHETIC PANTHEISM AND THE UGLY IN *MRS. DALLOWAY*

I have been arguing that Woolf's characters vacillate between experiencing beauty, on the one hand, as an almost religious phenomenon that discloses a present or future truth about the goodness of being and, on the other, as a purely immanent phenomenon to be received by the senses as pleasure. The question behind these experiences is this: if the world cannot be simultaneously beautiful and good—or if, indeed, there is an antagonism between these values—what is the existential significance of beauty? Further, if one of the missions of secularism, over against religious asceticism, is to affirm life in the world, then how, if recourse to aesthetic theodicies is not an option, does one assimilate beauty to the harshness of life?

I want to look again at Nietzsche's thought for an example of how this problem has been confronted. In another passage from *The Gay Science*, Nietzsche amends his criticism of "aesthetic anthropomorphisms." Though beauty is not something that inheres in being, it is something that can be *willed*:

> I want to learn more and more to see as beautiful what is necessary in things; then I shall be one of those who make things beautiful. *Amor fati:* let that be my love henceforth! I do not want to wage war against what is ugly. I do not want to accuse; I do not even want to accuse those who accuse. *Looking away* shall be my only negation. And all in all and on the whole: some day I wish to be only a Yes-sayer.[68]

For Nietzsche, to affirm life, to be a "Yes-sayer," is to assent to what is "necessary" in things rather than to wish that they were otherwise. What transforms mere acceptance into full assent is the capacity to see the necessary as "beautiful."

Clarissa Dalloway is a character that sees as beautiful what is necessary in things. She is also, as Nietzsche wished to be, "one of those who make things beautiful." Her *amor fati* spills over into a desire to arrange things—flowers and parties—so as to increase and unify life. Like Nietzsche, Clarissa senses that it is "very, very dangerous to live even one day" (*MD*, 8), but this dangerous quality of life—its threat to human subjectivity—is encountered in its aesthetic dimension: a beauty that is no longer "harmony" but incongruous tumult somehow experienced as an incandescent unity. And this is where Clarissa and the novel's broader vision depart from Nietzsche's strictly post-religious will to beauty. Like Woolf in her "moments of being," Clarissa tends toward an aesthetic pantheism in which she emphasizes the interconnectedness of all things in what she calls a "divine vitality" (8). Peter Walsh dismissively calls this her "transcendental theory" and thinks, like a strict late-Victorian anthropologist of religion or Freudian critic of theology, that because it makes possible a kind of "survival" in other things after the end of individual life, it derives from her "fear of death" (153). The novel makes it clear, however, that it emerges from her sense of the aesthetic vitality of both life and death.

In fact, Peter shares Clarissa's aesthetic vision more than either he or she acknowledges. Early in the novel Clarissa suspects that Peter has no taste for the "divine vitality" disclosed in beauty: "But Peter—however beautiful the day might be, and the trees and the grass, and that little girl in pink—Peter never saw a thing of all that" (8). But the novel's most extensive meditation on beauty is Peter's

> Beauty anyhow. Not the crude beauty of the eye. It was not beauty pure and simple—Bedford Place leading into Russell Square. It was straightness and

emptiness of course; the symmetry of a corridor; but it was also windows lit
up, a piano, a gramophone sounding; a sense of pleasure-making hidden,
but now and again emerging when, through the uncurtained window, the
window left open, one saw parties sitting over tables, young people slowly
circling, conversations between men and women, maids idly looking out
(a strange comment theirs, when work was done), stockings drying on top
ledges, a parrot, a few plants. Absorbing, mysterious, of infinite richness, this
life. And in the large square where the cabs shot and swerved so quick, there
were loitering couples, dallying, embracing, shrunk up under the shower of
a tree; that was moving; so silent, so absorbed, that one passed, discreetly,
timidly, as if in the presence of some sacred ceremony to interrupt which
would have been impious. That was interesting. And so on into the flare and
glare. (163)

The passage discloses the metaphysical expansiveness of Woolf's sense of beauty.
It is a phenomenon that leads beyond sight—the "crude beauty of the eye"—
and beyond the material properties of objective form ("straightness," "symmetry")
that have been the focus of empirical accounts of beauty. It is "beauty *anyhow.*"
Woolf plays with that casual term by rendering it ontological: it is beauty *in all
cases, in all events,* and yet haphazardly. Symmetry does create beauty ("of
course"), but there is another kind of beauty that is deeper, almost "hidden,"
and characterized by sheer vitality. One finds it in the incongruous cacophony
of being, in limp stockings and idleness as well as in the pleasure of conversation and music. It characterizes persons, artifacts, and natural objects. "Life"
itself, regardless of its configurations, is beautiful, and this beauty is "mysterious," "sacred." The passage's conclusion, with the words "flare and glare,"
provides a sort of aesthetic microcosm: "flare" is positive in its vitalistic sense of
a burst of light or energy; "glare" is negative in that it implies something harsh,
an assault on the eyes. But the rhyme brings the aesthetic oppositions they
contain back into a final unity.[69]
    Peter sees here what Clarissa has been seeing throughout the novel. In the
book's first pages, for instance, Clarissa experiences London's energy:

Heaven only knows why one loves it so, how one sees it so, making it
up, building it round one, tumbling it, creating it every moment afresh;
but the veriest frumps, the most dejected of miseries sitting on doorsteps
(drink their downfall) do the same; can't be dealt with, she felt positive, by
Acts of Parliament for that very reason: they love life. In people's eyes, in the
swing, tramp, and trudge; in the bellow and the uproar; the carriages, motor
cars, omnibuses, vans, sandwich men shuffling and swinging; brass bands;
barrel organs; in the triumph and the jingle and the strange high singing of

some aeroplane overhead was what she loved; life; London; this moment of June. (4)

The passage evokes the sheer vitality of being. Clarissa's aesthetic feeling for the scene is characterized by the *eros* (she is in "love" with life) with which Plato thought one pursues beauty. But unlike Plato, Clarissa doesn't move from immediate occasions of beauty to an abstract, transcendent value; she stays with the local manifestations. Transcendence is typically articulated in spatial metaphors, and there is no hierarchy here between higher and lower, no distinction between the "aeroplane" and the "tramp and trudge." Clarissa goes beneath rather than beyond, to the undifferentiated energy that animates life as a whole.

Yet as in Woolf's image of the world as a work of art, it is impossible to decide whether this whole, this aesthetic unity, is something given or made, whether it is a property of being or something that the artist (in the largest sense of the word, inclusive of someone like Clarissa) "build[s] . . . round one."[70] As in "A Sketch of the Past," where Woolf proposes a sense of creation without a creator, Clarissa has sentiments of gratitude without an agent to receive them. This paradox creates a complexly secularized religious language. Beautiful scenes appear to "blosso[m] for her eyes only . . . but not for a moment did she believe in God; but all the more, she thought . . . must one repay in daily life to servants, yes, to dogs and canaries . . . one must pay back from this secret deposit of exquisite moments . . ." (29). Here she intuits something like what Christians call grace, as well as the sense of dependence and desire for ethical reciprocity that grace stimulates. Later Clarissa refers to her response—her parties—as "offerings," gifts returned to God or the gods. Yet here, too, she resists the idea of a giver: "And it was an offering; to combine, to create; but to whom? . . . An offering for the sake of an offering, perhaps" (122).[71] These lines echo Woolf's 1919 essay "Reading," which closes with a reflection on the "strange, serene confidence" and the "desire to impart" that "beauty . . . inspires in us": "Some offering we must make; some act we must dedicate."[72] The novel is aware, then, of the difficulty that arises when religious feelings no longer have recourse to religious cosmologies. That Clarissa, like Woolf (and, later, Mrs. Ramsay), after giving an account of a feeling that seems wedded to a religious vocabulary, must immediately protest that the experience does not lead to theism, indicates the difficulty of secular translation.[73]

The majority of the characters in the novel are evaluated by their ability or incapacity to intuit this sort of beauty. It is characteristic of the puritanical Doris Kilman that she fails to find the thread of beauty in the urban cacophony that Clarissa loves. For her, incongruity is disabling. There is a moment in a cafe when she is confronted with a scene that is structurally identical to the many scenes in which Clarissa has rejoiced during the course of the day. Because she is an example of what Nietzsche considered the truth about Christian *ressentiment* (she approaches caricature), she is too busy hating Clarissa for her worldly success to find beauty in chaotic plurality:

> So she sat. She got up, blundered off among the little tables, rocking slightly from side to side, and somebody came after her with her petticoat, and she lost her way, and was hemmed in by trunks specially prepared for taking to India; next got among the accouchment sets, and baby linen; through all the commodities of the stationary, variously smelling, now sweet, now sour she lurched; saw herself thus lurching with her hat askew, very red in the face, full length in a looking glass; and at last came out into the street. (133)

All the incommensurable objects—the tables, the trunks, the baby linen, the opposing smells—and her inability (evident in the parataxis with which she registers them) to orient her relation to them, creates in Miss Kilman a kind of nausea. She can only "lurch" through them toward some sort of stability. That stability turns out to be a church. After she reaches the street, she sees Westminster Cathedral and thinks, "in the midst of the traffic, there was the habitation of God" (133). Clarissa finds beauty in "traffic"—"the swing, tramp, and trudge"—Miss Kilman in the unyielding religious edifice that relieves the world of its unpredictable motion.

There is a significant difficulty, however, that arises from the dissociation of the beautiful and the good implied in Clarissa's (and perhaps Peter's) secular, aesthetic "pantheism." Clarissa responds to the beauty that radiates from life with a faith in life that subsumes pain and ugliness into a larger beauty: "she survived, Peter survived, lived in each other, she being part, she was positive, of the trees at home; of the house there, ugly, rambling all to bits and pieces as it was" (9). The beautiful whole is only fully beautiful *as* a whole; its particulars can be ugly. More importantly, however, the beautiful whole is not necessarily a good whole. This becomes clear in the aesthetic vision of Septimus, whom Woolf referred to as Clarissa's "double." Septimus and Clarissa are both acutely receptive to beauty. But in Septimus's mind, the beautiful is still linked to the good. This is important for two reasons. First, unlike Clarissa, Septimus has suffered an evil that, as Auden would say, cannot be subsumed into the "natural," temporal forces that extinguish life. As a veteran of the Great War, he has experienced "life" in a way that is not readily describable as a part of a larger aesthetic affirmation (like that of Cobden-Sanderson); it is unlikely that he would accept the conditions of Nietzsche's *amor fati*. Secondly, his "madness" is closely associated with his very desire, created by his experience of evil, to see the beautiful as a sign of the good. It is born both of his desperation and of the fact that this desperation presses him to cling to what is, for Woolf, an obsolete consolation — a religious cosmology in which the beautiful, the good, and the true are united.[74]

Like Clarissa, Septimus finds in the unharmonious a "queer harmony." Confusion and disorder are reconciled in this perspective, to the point where the perspective is not an act of imagination but takes on the density of immediate experience:

> Music began clanging against the rocks up here. It is a motor horn down in the street, he muttered; but up here it cannoned from rock to rock, divided, met in shocks of sound which rose in smooth columns (that music should be visible was a discovery) and became an anthem, an anthem twined round now by a shepherd's boy piping. . . . and as, before waking, the voices of birds and the sound of wheels chime and chatter in a queer harmony, grow louder and louder and the sleeper feels himself drawing to the shores of life, so he felt himself drawing towards life . . . (68–69)

The noise of motor horns becomes music, and music becomes anthem.[75] Like Clarissa, too, he has a sense of the "divine vitality" of the world; the divinity of the vitality is what gives the disparate phenomena the appearance of a pattern:

> But they beckoned; leaves were alive; trees were alive. And the leaves being connected by millions of fibres with his own body, there on the seat, fanned it up and down; when the branch stretched he, too, made that statement. The sparrows fluttering, rising, and falling in jagged fountains were part of the pattern; the white and blue, barred with black branches. Sounds made harmonies with premeditation; the spaces between them were as significant as sounds. A child cried. Rightly far away a horn sounded. All taken together meant the birth of a new religion — (22–23)

Septimus has here the sense of interconnectedness so central to Woolf's world as a work of art: the "fibres" of his body are fibers of the leaves. Indeed, it is almost as if he has "bridged," through the "[p]erfection" of his senses, the disparity between aesthetic harmony and evil that will plague Louis in *The Waves*. This "new religion" is not just the credo of a mentally ill man (the scientific vocabulary for such illness is eviscerated in the novel). It shares much with the old religion — it is, in many ways, an aestheticized version of providential Christianity.

The central difference between Clarissa and Septimus's interpretation of beauty is that Clarissa affirms the world as it is, in all its recalcitrant ugliness and pain, whereas Septimus senses in beauty an eschatological promise. The *"aesthetic-utopian meaning"* of "beauty," writes Ernst Bloch, is that of "an existence for Objects which has not yet become, of thoroughly formed world without external chance, without unessentiality, unrenderedness"; it is the "appearance" of eschatological "pre-appearance," of the world "perfected without . . . being exploded and apocalyptically vanishing."[76] The world for Septimus is comprehensively *rendered*; it manifests "premeditation" (23). While Stevens insisted that to experience the world purely one must refuse to think of it as a text, beauty *speaks* to Septimus: it is a language in which one might read the *logos* of the world that is equally truth and wisdom, and therefore goodness. Beauty for him discloses the "reason" or "plot" that Neville will associate in *The Waves* with "fasting and anguished spirit[s]" (197). Early in the novel an airplane writing letters in the sky is the occasion for this intuition:

> So, thought Septimus, looking up, they are signaling to me. Not indeed in actual words; that is, he could not read the language yet; but it was plain enough, this beauty, this exquisite beauty, and tears filled his eyes as he looked at the smoke words languishing and melting in the sky and bestowing upon him in their inexhaustible charity and laughing goodness one shape after another of unimaginable beauty and signaling their intention to provide him, for nothing, for ever, for looking merely, with beauty, more beauty! Tears ran down his cheeks. (MD, 21–22)

"Inexhaustible charity and laughing goodness" are, for Septimus, the truth about the beautiful. As for Clarissa, beauty discloses a world to be received as a gift ("for nothing") and within which mere perception ("looking") is piety. Unlike for Clarissa, however, this is an abundance that points beyond its own exuberance. The world *intends* something toward him, and beauty is the sign of this intention. (Clarissa consistently resists the sentiment of intention that arises when she feels that beauty "blossomed for her eyes only" [29].) This is not the Nietzschean affirmation of the world, which Clarissa so often approaches, in which the incommensurate and the ugly dissolve in an act of atheistic will or pantheistic intuition. This beauty evokes a "laughing goodness," not the joyful, Dionysian laughter that quickened Yeats's imagination. Beauty as laughing goodness reveals an ontology of peace, not primordial tumult, a peace that may be obscured by the world's current state but which is, somehow, the final truth about things.

Later in the novel the beauty of the world speaks clearly to Septimus:

> The trees waved, brandished. We welcome, the world seemed to say; we accept; we create. Beauty, the world seemed to say. And as if to prove it (scientifically) wherever he looked at the houses, at the railings, at the antelopes

stretching over the palings, beauty sprang instantly. . . . all of this, calm and reasonable as it was, made out of ordinary things as it was, was the truth now; beauty, that was the truth now. Beauty was everywhere. (69)

Here Septimus's religious ontology of peace becomes even clearer: beauty welcomes. Beauty "says," at it does for Kant, that the world is hospitable to human being.[77] As for Keats's urn, it is the "truth" about the world.[78] As Septimus reflects further on the revelation he finds a theological affirmation—"There is a God"—and ethical imperatives: "Men must not cut down trees. . . . No one kills from hatred." The bird's song tells him, "there is no crime" (25).

These affirmations begin to look like illusions. People do kill from hatred; there is crime. The ethical aura of the beautiful becomes something not eschatological but present, immediate, almost empirical. Beauty springs from material reality "as if to prove it (scientifically)"; even in his "madness" Septimus is trying to validate his illusions using the secular authority of science. The plane that he saw writing letters in the sky was of course an advertisement for toffee, not God's speech. His religious ontology of beauty seems an illusion generated by, or perhaps synonymous with, his mental illness. Beauty as truth begins to sound like wishfulness; the lessons of the empirical world suggest otherwise.

The reader's sympathy for Septimus, however, calls the easy dismissal of his religious aesthetic into question, for the binary between madness and reason is itself contested. The psychiatrists Bradshaw and Holmes, enemies of Septimus, Clarissa, and Woolf herself, are those who emphasize the positivist, instrumental rationality that characterizes certain excesses of secular reason. When the "unseen" bids Septimus, Dr. Holmes tells Rezia, Septimus's wife, "to make him notice real things," "reality" being ostensibly synonymous with the seen (25). Secular cultural authority has often resided in the prestige of empirical science, for which the criteria of truth is empirical testability, and here Woolf dramatizes the limits of this authority. Bradshaw is called, paradoxically, "the priest of science." He worships "proportion, divine proportion," an aesthetic of emotional balance, where nothing is felt or pursued to excess. (He is "so interested in art.") Bradshaw's aesthetic of proportion is not one in which the exuberantly incongruous is finally experienced as a (queerly) harmonious whole but where secular subjectivity disciplines the influx of phenomena. This proportion is an enervated version of the classic empirical aspects of beauty—proportion, balance, and symmetry. Here their reach is not metaphysical; rather, they are applied to a picture of the well-ordered psyche.

Septimus's religious experience of beauty, then, is finally untenable, not because it diverges from Bradshaw's distinctly secular aesthetic but because it tries to retain the connection of the beautiful with the good and the true.

Clarissa's vision of beauty as the aesthetic harmony of the whole, irrespective of its moral content, is what remains. But that vision comes at a severe cost: the affirmation of the suicide of Septimus. Just as the young Woolf connected the beauty of the apple tree to the horror of Mr. Valpy's suicide, an insight that made possible her vision of the world as a work of art, Clarissa affirms Septimus's suicide by subsuming it into a larger aesthetic vision of life. She is initially outraged that the Bradshaws mention his suicide during her party because it seems to disrupt the aesthetic unity, the reconciliatory offering, that she is trying to create: "And the Bradshaws talked of it at her party!" (184). If the aesthetic whole is also a moral whole—if the beauty of being is also the goodness of being—it does not *fit*. But Clarissa is finally able to see the suicide as an aspect of the beauty she is trying to reveal and to create: "She felt glad he had done it; thrown it away. . . . He made her feel the beauty; made her feel the fun" (186).

This is easily the most startling sentiment in the novel. Woolf is, I think, experimenting with the limits of affirming the whole as beautiful when it is no longer good. The association of "beauty" with "fun" is a deliberate provocation. Clarissa has discarded her moral anthropomorphisms by refusing, like Nietzsche, to think of death as something opposed to life. The exuberant lines of the novel's first page—"What a lark! What a plunge!" (3)—are meant to comprehend Septimus's "plunge": "had he plunged holding his treasure?" (184). The suicide is, for Clarissa, the ultimate act of excess in a world whose beauty depends on excess. It is a sacrifice that parallels her "offerings," the kind of sacrifice that, in George Bataille's vision, puts one back into "continuity" with a life that had subordinated the sacred to a need for instrumental "duration" or self-preservation.[79] She appeals to a mystical language in which death is an attempt to "communicate," to reach the "centre" of things (184). Death is the final stage of an absolute "impersonality." But Clarissa's perspective can only subsume this evil into an aesthetic affirmation by evading the historical particularity of its evil. The novel itself, moreover, seems to confirm and endorse this affirmation by the structure of its final episodes. When Clarissa receives the news of Septimus's suicide, she withdraws from the bustle of the party into isolation, within which she encounters the "mystery" of the old woman in the building opposite (discussed further below) and meditates on Septimus's death. We might be tempted to think of this withdrawal as exuberant beauty facing its other—death, the inviolable "privacy" of the old woman—as something outside the scope of the party, something inassimilable. But Clarissa *returns* to the party, and, in the final sentences, Peter encounters her as a presence that has absorbed this other: "What is this terror? what is this ecstasy? he thought to himself. What is it that fills me with extraordinary excitement? . . . It is Clarissa, he said. . . .

For there she was" (194). The almost tautological, sheerly denotative (yet extraordinary) final line reveals, as in Stevens's tautology, an abundance that need not appeal to anything outside of itself for metaphysical justification. Her radiant eros is the principle both of the "terror" of death and otherness and of the ecstasy of sensuous beauty. "[I]n the middle of my party, here's death," thinks Clarissa (179), and this is where it remains at the novel's end. The party, the figure both of exuberant beauty and of the offering such beauty demands, comprehends death rather than being scandalized by it.

Yet (if one can speak of the novel's events as if they were separable from the novel's rhetoric) Septimus's suicide is not just a "defiance" of the Bradshaws of the world who make "life intolerable"—an attempt, in other words, to reclaim life from its abusers by refusing them access to that life (184, 185). It is an act of despair that stems from his experience in a war where death was not mere natural return from personal individuation into an undifferentiated whole. And it stems, further, from the refusal of the world to conform to his unified vision of beauty and goodness, a vision in which beauty is the sign, as Simone Weil says, that the evil of necessity is not final. In other words, Clarissa's affirmation comes at the expense of the very theological aesthetic through which Septimus hoped to find redemption. His inability to sustain it, and the fact that it is finally, in secular epistemological terms, an illusion of madness, is part of what kills him. All Clarissa can rescue from his vision is the sense of the beautiful whole, not the connection to a transcendent good (or God) through which beauty might generate more than an affirmation of life irrespective of its violence. Woolf sees this, which is why she often foregrounds the suspicions of characters in later books, like Louis, who will never permit the voice of moral reason (the "serious charge")—and the desire for a theological reason this voice generates—to accept an aesthetic reconciliation at the expense of "shadows of dungeons" and "tortures" and "infamies." Louis will only have the beautiful with the good; he will have neither apart from the other. *Mrs. Dalloway* suspects that their unity can only be sustained in a state of madness or obliviousness to the truth of the secular world. Both Clarissa and the novel challenge us to see the world, through a doctrine of creation without God, as a work of art, fully aware of the fate of a Septimus. But the novel leaves us with a deep ambivalence as to what this entails.

TO THE LIGHTHOUSE: BEAUTY AGAINST LIFE

If *Mrs. Dalloway* is a book that experiments with what it might mean to affirm the undifferentiated flux of life and death as "beautiful," *To the Lighthouse*, published just two years later, is a book where the value of beauty and the value of what Woolf calls "life" seem incompatible. The difficult peace Clarissa Dalloway makes with beauty's indifference to the good is broken. The tumult, heterogeneity, and amoral exuberance that characterize "life" in *To the Lighthouse* resist qualities of reconciliation and harmonization that are the sign of beauty. Beauty in *To the Lighthouse* tends to be associated with "stillness," "peace," and "eternity," or what Simone Weil calls the sense of "finality" in necessity that infuses the beautiful with the mystery of God. It seems to be, therefore, as in "Time Passes," the radiance of "divine goodness" (127) or the "toke[n] of divine bounty" (133). For Woolf, however, there is no such token. "Life" therefore becomes precisely the element that undermines the experience of the beautiful, insofar as the beautiful seems to irresistibly generate expectations of a fulfillment of life guaranteed by divinity. Auden writes in an early poem, "This lunar beauty / Has no history / Is complete and early."[80] Just so, Lily Briscoe thinks, "Beauty had this penalty—it came too readily, too completely; it stilled life—froze it" (*TL*, 177). The early Joyce, still influenced by an Aristotelean and Thomistic framework in which movement is a sign of "imperfection," insists that the aesthetic phenomenon is a "spiritual state" of "luminous silent stasis."[81] In *To the Lighthouse*, however, this static quality of beauty speaks against it; beauty generates an atmosphere of peaceful eternity that is unfaithful both to the flux of life and to life's consistent "treachery" (the word is Mrs. Ramsay's). Because beauty in the novel is inexorably saturated with this eternity, it often appears as something specious, an aura of unfounded hope. Goodness is not a property of being, and since beauty seems to promise that being *is* good, it obscures the truth of life. It is, Lily thinks, an epistemological trap: "Was it wisdom? Was it knowledge? Was it, once more, the deceptiveness of beauty, so that all one's perceptions, half-way to truth, were tangled in a golden mesh?" (50). Septimus thought that beauty was wisdom and knowledge. In *To the Lighthouse*, too, Septimus's religious ontology of beauty is attractive but illusory; however, Clarissa's compromise—aesthetic unity without goodness—is no longer possible.

This is not to say that the harmonizing agency of beauty cannot be found in the practice of art. It can: Lily has her vision. Her painter's "brush" is "the one dependable thing in a world of strife, ruin, and chaos" (150). This means, however, that the artist is now tasked with the work of reconciliation that was once the prerogative of God, a reconciliation that could be known in the world—the creation of God—through the sign of beauty. It is much less clear in *To the Lighthouse* that the *world*, however, is a work of art. Moreover, the harmonizing beauty created by the artist is highly provisional and knowingly artificial. The stillness of beauty, its aura of peace, emerges at the expense of "life." Lily Briscoe thinks of painting as the creation of a stillness to oppose the "fluidity" and "quiver" of life: "she exchanged the fluidity of life for the concentration of painting" (158). The rhythm of painting permits her a precarious harmonization which is little more than a lifeboat, "so that while her hand quivered with life, this rhythm was strong enough to bear her along with it on its current" (159). In a book like *Mrs. Dalloway*, to quiver with life *is* beauty. But in *To the Lighthouse* the quiver is not enough; it must be mastered in art.

Yet the novel remains preoccupied with the beauty of the world. This beauty remains ambiguously religious insofar as it harbors a promise of reconciliation — a promise that art does not have to achieve in opposition to life. Mrs. Ramsay experiences this ambiguity early in the novel. During her walk to town with Charles Tansley, the "great plateful of water" strikes her in such a way that she cannot help but exclaim, "Oh, how beautiful" (12). Soon after, when she has returned to the house, the aesthetic rhythm of the waves produces in her two very different feelings:

> [T]he monotonous fall of the waves on the beach, which for the most part beat a measured and soothing tattoo to her thoughts and seemed consolingly to repeat over and over again as she sat with the children the words of some old cradle song, murmured by nature, "I am guarding you — I am your support," but at other times suddenly and unexpectedly, especially when her mind raised itself slightly from the task actually in hand, had no such kindly meaning, but like a ghostly roll of drums remorselessly beat the measure of life, made one think of the destruction of the island and its engulfment in the sea, and warned her whose day had slipped past in one quick doing after another that it was all ephemeral as a rainbow — this sound which had been obscured and concealed under the other sounds suddenly thundered hollow in her ears and made her look up with an impulse of terror. (15–16)

Theism and atheism are framed here as divergent interpretations of aesthetic experience. In the first, the world is a music that seems to speak, in a similar way that beauty spoke to Septimus, of the world's hospitality to human being — "I am guarding you, I am your support." This feeling is a moral and aesthetic anthropomorphism: the "measure" of the waves discloses the presence of divine wisdom in the ordering of the world. But this anthropomorphism is associated with a childish mental state: it is a "cradle song," and Mrs. Ramsay is particularly susceptible to it when she sits "with the children." The language owes something to the critique of religious anthropomorphism — familiar in Nietzsche and especially in Freud — that connects the imagination of consolatory divinity with the infancy of the race (hence its prevalence among "primitives") and psychological immaturity in the individual. When Mrs. Ramsay looks up from "the task at hand"—her tasks are typically motherly acts of consolation[82]— her anthropomorphism collapses. The waves are not heard as supportive speech but the sound of a "ghostly roll of drums." There is a sense in which beautiful sounds operate as that same kind of "golden mesh" that "obscures" and "conceals" a more "hollow" sound worthy of "terror." To hear this latter sound is to relinquish religious anthropomorphisms and grow up. Though Woolf does not refer to it in these terms, this is the truth of the atheistic sublime exposing the duplicitousness of the beautiful. (I discuss Woolf's understanding of the sublime and its relation to religion later in the chapter.) The beautiful is reconfigured in the image of the "rainbow" that yields to sublime terror, an image suggestive of both ephemerality and an obsolete metaphysics: in the biblical tradition the rainbow is a sign to Noah of God's gracious disposition toward the world.

This is not the only moment in which Mrs. Ramsay struggles with her intuition of the world as a religio-aesthetic order. I discussed, in the introduction, Mrs. Ramsay's adventures as a "wedge-shaped core of darkness" (62). Her encounter with the "stroke" of the lighthouse (the same stroke Lily will paint at the end of the novel) is an experience of beauty, a moment "of triumph *over* life when things came together in this peace, this rest, this eternity" (63, emphasis added). "She was beautiful," she thinks, "like that light." There is something about this light, however, that causes her to think: "It will end, it will end, she said. It will come, it will come, when suddenly she added, 'We are in the hands of the Lord'" (63). Here Mrs. Ramsay experiences an eschatological quality in beauty. This beauty possesses an incomprehensible *promise*—we do not know what this "it" that "will come" is—but it is a promise of "peace" and something like "eternity" that "come together" for Mrs. Ramsay in this mental space. This is "beauty," as Theodor Adorno writes, "perceived both as authoritatively binding and as something incomprehensible that questioningly awaits its solution." The longing Mrs. Ramsay feels is what he has described as "the longing for what beauty promises but never unveils." But it is nonetheless, as Adorno says, an *authoritative* promise: "As they [beautiful things] draw to a close with the same radiance and peacefulness with which they began, they emanate that everything is not lost, that things may yet turn out."[83]

I have quoted Adorno because he is one of the most compelling modern theorists of eschatological beauty, or beauty as a sign of possible justice. For Adorno, who (though a non-theist) proposes a negative or "inverse theology," the meaning of "God" *is* this possibility.[84] For Mrs. Ramsay, this eschatological dimension of beauty is both irresistible—religious language comes upon her without her permission—but also, I noted in the introduction, a "trap."[85] Just as the sound of the waves turned from consolatory speech to "remorseless" drums earlier, the light, which was, moments before, beautiful, becomes, after Mrs. Ramsay's purification of the "lie," "the pitiless, the remorseless" (65). Instead of resting in this sublime terror, however, she projects beauty back onto the world—indeed, onto these same waves—through what Nietzsche understood to be magical subjectivity:

> [S]he had known happiness, exquisite happiness, intense happiness, and it silvered the rough waves a little more brightly, as daylight faded, and the blue went out of the sea and it rolled in waves of pure lemon which curved and swelled and broke upon the beach and the ecstasy burst in her eyes and waves of pure delight raced over the floor of her mind and she felt, It is enough! It is enough! (65)

Beauty here is completely subjective: the memory of happiness has colored the world, "silvered the rough waves." The de-divination of beauty means that the sublime is the only truthful aesthetic encounter with the world; beauty is not, as Stendhal said, "a promise of happiness" ("la promesse du bonheur") but the projection of happiness. When Mrs. Ramsay thinks, "The lights were rippling and running as if they were drops of silver water held firm in a wind. And all the poverty, all the suffering had turned to that, Mrs. Ramsay thought" (68), it is unclear whether this alchemy occurs inside or outside of the desiring self.

THE BEAUTIFUL VERSUS THE SUBLIME IN "TIME PASSES"

"Life" resists the stasis of beauty in *To the Lighthouse* because it is characterized by tumult, chaos, and blind exuberance. Another way of saying this is that the most truthful aesthetic encounter with life in the novel is the experience of sublimity rather than beauty. Woolf does not use the term "sublime" to indicate a category of aesthetic experience distinct from the beautiful (she most often uses it casually, as a synonym for "exalted"). But it is a useful concept to describe an encounter with the world that consistently undermines, for Woolf, the religious suggestiveness—the hint of harmony and reconciliation, a world obedient to the good—of the experience of beauty. This is because the sublime, as I'm using the term, is a revelation of the resistance of the world to human flourishing. This is not to say that Woolf's sympathetic characters seek or celebrate the sublime. (Some, like Mr. Ramsay, do, and the fact that they are unsympathetic characters is important.) As we have already seen, the sublime comes upon Mrs. Ramsay unawares; it shocks her with a revelation she wishes were not true—that the truth of the world is "suffering, death, the poor" (60).

The term "shock" is, of course, Woolf's own; it describes the initial component of her "moments of being." It is characteristic of Woolf, moreover, to want to resolve the sublime back into what I am calling the beautiful. The shock of her "moments of being" eventually gives way to "a revelation of some order," of "wholeness," and finally the intuition of the world as a work of art.[86] It gives way, therefore, to the harmony characteristic of the beautiful whole. If we can still call it "sublime," it is more like Wordsworth's sublime: the "sense sublime / Of something far more deeply interfused"—the intimation of a spiritual presence unifying appearances. Or it is like a version of the sublime that was once, in a religious cosmology, a modality of, rather than an experience opposed to, beauty: the sublime as "an aspect of beauty itself—the terrible aspect that is the wounding excess of the visible that pierces our everyday defenses."[87] The secular sublime, however, is an experience that undermines all religious pretensions of moral and aesthetic order: it is an intimation of difference rather than reconciliation, tumult rather than harmony, and of the intractable divergence of the human mind and the material world.[88]

"Time Passes" is an elegy for Julia Stephen and those lost in the Great War, but the argument of this section is that "Time Passes" can also be read as an elegy for the beautiful as it is being displaced by the truth of the secular sublime. The sublime gains an unhappy authority for Woolf in these pages because it recognizes what she takes to be the irreversible dissociation of the beautiful and the good. "The beauty of the world," however, will not cease to display its mysterious, importunate, theological suggestiveness (142). "Time Passes" thus articulates the painful dialectic between the desire for religious beauty and the truth of the secular sublime in Woolf's sensibility. Beauty "murmurs" "messages of peace" throughout the section, but these messages can only be heard in a dream-state that softens the harsh edges of both the material and the historical world. But it is finally only a glassy "surface" that obscures the truth of the tumultuous, atheistic darkness that "boils" underneath.[89]

The history of the relation between beauty and the sublime in modernity is simultaneously a history of religion and secularism. The centrality of the beautiful has waned, and the sublime has become the authoritative aesthetic experience. The sublime, however, has been interpreted in two ways: first, as the place where religious emotions (such as awe or the sense of the infinite) have been preserved in a secular age, and second, as evidence of a decline of religious understandings of the world. These are not divergent explanations so much as differing perspectives on the meaning and value of secularization. The sublime *does* mark the decline of religious understandings of the world, yet it has often seemed to preserve religious attitudes precisely because it has tried to make sense of experiences of transcendence in what Thomas Weiskel calls a "naturalistic key."[90] The sublime has been secular insofar as its growing significance is unthinkable without the reality of secularization; it has been religious insofar as secularization has often meant the translation of religious concepts into a naturalistic framework.

The further removed the experience of the sublime has become from its religious sources, the more it has become a distinctly secular experience.[91] While the Romantic sublime was often tied to religious pictures of the world, the sublime in the twentieth century has tended to completely eliminate the residues from those sources. In Kant, for instance, the initial "displeasure" of the sublime—the revelation of our inadequacy and insignificance as *natural* creatures—eventually yields a sense of what he calls our "supersensible destiny," a realization that we are called to a higher spiritual life according to the dictates of morality and reason.[92] The sublime is only an "abyss" for us as natural creatures, not as rational and spiritual creatures made in the image of God, who is rational spirit. The fact that we are able to take pleasure in the sublime's disclosure of our physical insignificance is actually evidence that our physical limits are not the basic or final truth about us. Thus Stevens in "A High-Toned Old Christian Woman" (discussed in the introduction) derisively figures Kant's position as "disaffected flagellants. . . . Proud of such novelties of the sublime," who "[t]ake the moral law and make a nave of it / And from the nave build haunted heaven" (*CP*, 47).

Kant's sublime is therefore still framed by a theology of creation. But when the idea of creation is eliminated, one is left with a sublime that emphasizes the radical incommensurability of mind and world. It becomes the intimation not of transcendence but of chaotic immanence; the mind (as principle of order) is either fundamentally alienated from or collapsed and immersed into it. In a religious cosmology—whether oriented by a doctrine of creation or something like mana—the world is instinct with *logos*, or divine wisdom, and the presence of *logos* in the mind allows it to find this wisdom in the world. Once this ontology no longer frames the sublime, it becomes an intuition of the staggering disparity between what the mind desires and what is possible in a world that is material all the way down. This is what Woolf is pointing to when she discusses, in "Poetry, Fiction, and the Future," the "monstrous" emotion that accompanies the realization that "the age of the earth is 3,000,000,000 years; that human life lasts but a second; that the capacity of the human mind is nevertheless boundless." The Romantic sublime often remains anthropomorphic—it assumes that the world is animated by something akin to human spirit—and so it remains religious. But once the anthropomorphic critique becomes more pervasive, the sublime is untethered from a religious cosmology. It becomes an intimation of the primordial chaos or conflict at the heart of things and is pleasurable either as we identify ourselves with the exuberance of this chaos or as we enjoy the absolute freedom of our mind in light of the fact that it owes the physical world nothing.

Jean-François Lyotard, who understands himself to be radicalizing Kant's theory of the sublime by pushing it to its logical conclusion, explains why the elevation of the sublime means the end of the beautiful, and why this also means that this aesthetic feeling excludes the good:

> Kant writes that the sublime is a *Geistegefühl*, a sentiment of the mind, whereas the beautiful is a sentiment that proceeds from a "fit" between nature and mind, i.e., when transcribed into the Kantian economy of faculties, between the imagination and the understanding. This marriage or at least, this betrothal proper to the beautiful is broken by the sublime. . . . The *Geistegefühl*, the sentiment of the mind, signifies that the mind is lacking in nature, that nature is lacking for it. It feels only itself. In this way the sublime is none other than the sacrificial announcement of the ethical in the aesthetic field. . . . This heralds the end of an aesthetics of the beautiful, in the name of the final destination of the mind, which is freedom.[93]

The beautiful implies an ontological "fit" between mind and world. In Romanticism, the sublime initially ruptures that fit but eventually establishes a higher one between the mind and the creator of the world or the spirit that animates it. In Lyotard, however, who has completely secularized the sublime, no higher fit is possible. This severs the aesthetic from the ethical because, for Kant, the fit between mind and world is what allows the beautiful to be a symbol of the morally good, since our minds can intuit, in the beautiful, a gracious mind at work ethically in the natural world.

Lyotard reads the sublime incommensurability between mind and world ecstatically as a revelation of the pure freedom of the mind. Woolf, however, finds it far more disturbing even if no less true. It is, as she says, "monstrous." She is, moreover, sensitive to the ways in which the celebration of the freedom of the mind may embed a powerful egotism. For her, this post-religious freedom is often an occasion for masculinist self-regard. Indeed, in *To the Lighthouse*, the atheistic sublime is vitiated by this egotism. Mr. Ramsay is always seeking contexts in which he can bask in the tragic elevation of his discovery that there is no God and that, therefore, the mind can find nothing in the world to mirror its spiritual desires. As Charles Taylor has argued, part of the moral "prestige" of secularism in its stoical mode has been the heroic ethos of responsibility it generates. The disenchanted world throws us back on our own resources; the self is responsible for creating the meanings that no longer reside in a spiritualized external world.[94] Mr. Ramsay takes deep pleasure in this tragic responsibility. In him the sublime becomes a form of post-religious stoicism.[95]

Mr. Ramsay's version of the sublime is the power of the mind to acknowledge its insignificance before the grand indifference of the material world and to bear that acknowledgment with fortitude. But his performance of this sublime is consistently parodied. The young James Ramsay, for instance, "hate[s]" his father precisely for "the exaltation and sublimity of his gestures" (36). (The sublimity of his bearing and his idea of "the sublime" are indistinguishable.) Later in the book, Mr. Ramsay feels that reaching the lighthouse is a victory in which the will's sublime freedom has matched the world's sublime hostility. As they land, "He rose and stood in the bow of the boat, very straight and tall, for all the world, James thought, as if he were saying, 'There is no God'" (207). The comic incongruity between the banality of the achievement and Mr. Ramsay's self-image is evident (though Woolf softens the comedy by investing the episode with narrative significance). Mr. Ramsay likes "to stand on his little ledge facing the dark of human ignorance, how we know nothing and the sea eats away the ground we stand on" (44); his sublime is an awareness of "the waste of the ages and the perishing of the stars" (36) and an acknowledgement that "life is difficult; facts uncompromising . . . our brightest hopes are extinguished, our frail barks founder in darkness" (4). The narrator's presentation of Mr. Ramsay's consciousness emphasizes both its dependence on stale (or perhaps merely shopworn Victorian) images and adjectives ("brightest hopes," "frail barks") and a lack of discrimination (he characteristically refers any minor hardship to the severest of metaphysical conditions). His sublime world is preeminently a sea; he is performing Arnold's "Dover Beach" over and over again, irrespective of the context in which he finds himself. There is a disorganized, breathless eagerness in his sequence of thought: the puzzling grammatical shift from "facing the dark of human knowledge" to "how we know nothing" suggests that Mr. Ramsay is perpetually ready to fire this lament. His sublime is bathetic precisely because Woolf understands that the "moral prestige" of Mr. Ramsay's self-positioning overrides and finally determines what he actually sees and knows. "How we know nothing" recedes before the dignity of what he *does* know—uncompromising "facts"—and what this knowledge refuses—consolation.

What is remarkable about these novelistic efforts at moral psychology is that Woolf largely accepts Mr. Ramsay's picture of the world; the narrative voice registers this same tragic sense of sublimity grounded in the world's indifference to desire. As we have already seen, Mrs. Ramsay has her own moments in which she must "purify" religious "lies" and their aesthetic correlatives out of existence. But Woolf's portrait of Mr. Ramsay complicates our sense of the stability of Woolf's atheistic ontology. Michael Levenson has written that "Woolf's lyricism" raises "the threat of a sentimental attachment to the lyric fragment as a way of avoiding the blank unlovely cosmos"; Woolf herself, he notes, worried in a diary entry that *To the Lighthouse* would be considered "sentimental." Levenson argues that "the novel resists" the "lure" of its own lyric sentimentality through a consistent injection of "irony," understood as an awareness of the gap between the world and the self's exalted descriptions of it. The product of this irony is what Levenson calls a "*chafing* between self and world."[96] I agree with Levenson's assessment, but the example of Mr. Ramsay, whose own lyric sentimentality requires the *exaggeration* of the "blank unlovely cosmos"—his is a sentimental anti-sentimentalism—suggests that this cosmos may not always be a stable agent of irony. Woolf's representation of Mr. Ramsay shows that a description of the cosmos as blank or unlovely can equally become a lyrical subjective projection. It also shows that atheistic models of the sublime can be sponsored by an oppressively masculinist moral ethos; once that ethos is called into question, the sublime is as well.[97] The *lovely* cosmos, moreover, has a good deal of agency in this novel, and the reason it creates ambivalence in Woolf is that this agency seems at times to exist apart from the subject's inner world.

"Time Passes" manifests this ambivalence. The section vacillates between lyrical descriptions of a post-religious sublime as the experience of truth and descriptions of a theologically charged beauty as the end point of desire. The structure of the section reveals a seemingly unending dialectic: the beautiful emerges and beckons, saturated with traces of divine goodness, but these traces dissolve, and the sublime exposes beauty's inefficacy. The beautiful reemerges and recedes four times. "Time Passes" may be an elegy for the beautiful, which is being displaced by the post-religious sublime, but it is also a story of beauty's peculiar resistance to that elegy. An early passage presents what has been lost:

> It seemed now as if, touched by human penitence and all its toil, divine goodness had parted the curtain and displayed behind it, single, distinct, the hare erect; the wave falling; the boat rocking, which, did we deserve them, should be ours always. But alas, divine goodness, twitching the cord, draws the curtain; it does not please him; he covers his treasures in a drench of hail, and so breaks them, so confuses them that it seems impossible that their calm should ever return or that we should ever compose from their fragments a perfect whole or read in the clear pieces the clear words of truth. (127–128)

This is the picture of the world for which Woolf longs. It is a world in which the beautiful—"the hare erect; the wave falling; the boat rocking"—is a charitable gift of "divine goodness" and, as for Septimus, a *language* in which one might read "the clear words of truth."

This "divine goodness" is, of course, ironized; Levenson has called the passage "a parody of Miltonic justification."[98] The punishment is unjust; we do "deserve" the metaphysical stability intuited in beautiful things. But fragmentation reigns. If the sleeper were to come down to the shore to find an answer to his doubts, he would find a night "full of wind and destruction," a place where the sea "tosses itself and breaks itself." Mr. Ramsay's sea is characterized principally by its effects on the embattled self (as it watches its ground recede or its "frail bark" fail); this is a sea—seen, as everything else is in "Time Passes," without a presiding subjectivity—that tosses and breaks "itself." In such a scene,

> [N]o image with semblance of serving and divine promptitude comes readily to hand bringing the night to order and making the world reflect the compass of the soul. . . . Almost it would appear that it is useless in such confusion to ask the night those questions as a what, and why, and wherefore, which tempt the sleeper from his bed to seek an answer. (128)

The sentiment of the beautiful here implies a vision of metaphysical symmetry between self and world, a hope that the order of the world reflects "the compass of the soul." The beautiful would be an "image with semblance of serving" in that it would be a sign of creation's hospitableness. But the world is sublime "confusion"; it is not answerable to the self's compass. We know this because, among other reasons, Mrs. Ramsay's death is a parenthesis in the world's narrative.

Yet Woolf cannot dispose of the intimations of beauty. They reappear almost immediately in the stillness the storm has left behind: "So loveliness reigned, and stillness, and together made the shape of loveliness itself, a form from which life had parted" (129). This loveliness brings with it, once more, the "strange intimation[s]" that the abstract sleeper and the concrete Mr. Ramsay, stretching out his arms in the night for a dead wife, cannot decipher:

> [T]here came to the wakeful, the hopeful, walking the beach, stirring the pool, imaginations of the strangest kind . . . of cliff, sea, cloud and sky brought purposely together to assemble outwardly the scattered parts of the vision within. In those mirrors, the minds of men, in those pools of uneasy water, in which clouds for ever turn and shadows form, dreams persisted, and it was impossible to resist the strange intimation which every gull, flower, tree, man and woman, and the white earth itself seemed to declare (but if

questioned at once withdraw) that good triumphs, happiness prevails, order rules; or to resist the extraordinary stimulus to range hither and thither in search of some absolute good, some crystal of intensity, remote from the known pleasures and familiar virtues, something alien to the processes of domestic life, single, hard, bright, like a diamond in the sand, which would render the possessor secure. (132)

The best way to read this extraordinary passage is to juxtapose it with an equally extraordinary passage from Simone Weil:

Beauty is the only finality here below. As Kant said very aptly, it is a finality which involves no objective. A beautiful thing involves no good except itself, in its totality, as it appears to us. We are drawn toward it without knowing what to ask of it. It offers us its own existence. We do not desire anything else, we possess it, and yet we still desire something. We do not in the least know what it is. We want to get behind beauty, but it is only a surface. It is like a mirror that sends us back our own desire for goodness. It is a sphinx, an enigma, a mystery which is painfully tantalizing. We should like to feed upon it but it is merely something to look at; it appears only from a certain distance. . . . It is because beauty has no end in view that it constitutes the only finality here below. For here below there are no ends.[99]

Weil takes Kant's characterization of beauty—"purposiveness without purpose"— and renders it metaphysical. Beauty afflicts, she writes, because it is the coalescence of the necessary and the good, or, put another way, of "necessity" and "finality"; it is composed both of a sense that things have to be this way (necessity) and that this way is good. "The absence of finality is the reign of necessity" (113), and necessity—one thing after another, the brute movement of things—is the prevailing drift of the world. It is the force that is indifferent to desire and under which we suffer as finite, embodied creatures. We desire the good, the purposeful, the "final," but we cannot find it in the world because necessity, rather than finality, reigns. This is why beauty is painful even while it delights: it *seems* final, but we cannot comprehend what the nature of that finality might be; we do not know "what to ask of it." It is, therefore, the only phenomenon in the world that suggests finality and necessity might be integrated, that subjection to necessity is not absolute. Kant was not exactly right, Weil suggests, to say that we don't "desire" the beautiful (Kant claims that the true perception of beauty is "disinterested"). Rather, it is simply that we don't know what we desire. We know we don't desire the beautiful object as such. Desire is oriented toward something behind it that is inaccessible to the mind.

It stirs the understanding without satisfying it. But this stirring is understood as a religious mystery: an intimation of the divine good that is possible but presently untouchable.

In Woolf's passage, too, beauty is a "mirror" (the image has displaced the "compass"). It generates "strange intimations" that throw us back into our own "minds" and galvanizes our "search for some absolute good." But the relation between interior desire and exterior object is ambiguous in Woolf's lines. The water is both object and metaphor: pools are "stirred" by the observer but also are images for the mind. The beautiful—the "white earth" with its gulls, flowers, and people—"declares" the good, but, as Weil says, only at a distance (for Woolf, "if questioned at once" it "withdraw[s]"). Woolf, however, relegates the entire experience to a kind of "dream" life, which may be synonymous with the life of the mind itself. Beauty—"the shape of loveliness"—is finally a "form from which life has parted." This is an extraordinary formulation: it divests beauty of any ontological bearing. Beauty is in some sense dead; it is not full-ness but emptiness. Yet beauty promises resurrection, a return of the life its form has exiled. Lily later imagines a moment in which "beauty would roll itself up; the space would fill; those empty flourishes would form into shape; if they shouted loud enough Mrs. Ramsay would return" (180). The negative space framed by Mr. Ramsay's outstretched arms (which "remained empty") and the death framed by the figure of Woolf's parentheses might be filled.

This hope, however, is undermined just as it was a few pages before. There it was followed by the parenthetical disruption of Mrs. Ramsay's death; here it is followed by the parenthetical disruption of Prue Ramsay's death in childbirth. Andrew Ramsay's death in the Great War follows a few lines later. Yet even here, with the experience of beauty so chastened by the appalling sublimity of the war's exploding shells, another divine bounty follows. It is received with hesitation and uneasiness:

> At that season those who had gone down to pace the beach and ask of the sea and sky what message they reported or what vision they affirmed had to con-sider among the usual tokens of divine bounty—the sunset on the sea, the pallor at dawn, the moon rising, fishing-boats against the moon, and chil-dren making mud-pies and pelting each other with handfuls of grass, some-thing out of harmony with this jocundity and this serenity. There was the silent apparition of an ashen-coloured ship for instance, come, gone; there was a purplish stain upon the bland surface of the sea as if something had boiled and bled, invisibly, beneath. This intrusion into a scene calculated to stir the most sublime reflections and lead to the most comfortable conclu-sions stayed their pacing. It was difficult blandly to overlook them; to abolish

their significance in the landscape; to continue, as one walked by the sea, to marvel how beauty outside mirrored beauty within. (133–134)

Woolf's use of the word "sublime" here is casual and pejorative: "sublime reflections" are actually generated by beauty—the tokens of divine bounty. They are more like the sentiments of theological design. But such "reflections" threaten to give way, in this passage, to a modern, secular sublime that discloses an ontology of violence or tumult: "something out of harmony." The "mirror" of beauty is demoted to mere "surface glassiness" that hides the truer, "nobler powers" that "sleep beneath"—that which, in the passage just quoted, "boils" and "bleeds" in "silence." These powers are the "flood," "the profusion of darkness" (126), and the "gigantic chaos" (134)—what Neville, in *The Waves*, calls "illimitable chaos" and "formless imbecility," or what Bernard calls "the "undifferentiated chaos of life" and the "undifferentiated forces" (TW, 226, 249, 255). The real is dark formlessness, not the radiance of form. When the narrator then says, "beauty offers her lures, has her consolations"—belief in the reciprocity of "beauty outside" and "beauty within" is a *temptation*—the ontology of beauty has been entirely undermined. Beauty is not now the "radiance" of being but the specious shine of its surface. It is no longer a mirror that announces a relation between mind and world but a mirror in which the self sees its own preposterous desires, or a piece of glass that deflects light so as to distort the observer's vision.

Read in this way, the passage seems to complete the post-religious displacement of the beautiful by the sublime. But the persistence of the sentiment of the beautiful does not quite permit this conclusion. Indeed, the narrator notes that the "stillness and brightness of the day"—of the "violets" and "daffodils"—"were as strange as the chaos and tumult of the night." Beauty is not mere consolation; there is something "strange" about it—its harmonious presence is just as astonishing in the tumult of the world as the tumult of the world is to human desire (135). The peculiarity of the beautiful here is precisely its revelation of a peace that is possible but never actualized, of a necessity not always at odds with the good. The grammar of "Time Passes" is thus threaded with the subjunctive—with things that "might" or "could" become the case.

Indeed, though time in "Time Passes" is constantly disrupted by decomposition, and though a sublime ontology of violence and dissonance seems to overwhelm the appearance of the beautiful, the section nevertheless closes with the murmur of the "beauty of the world," which seems to be a "message of peace" (141). Lily Briscoe is back in the house. She has become one of the sleepers, and she listens in her bed: "Through the open window the voice of the beauty of the world came murmuring, too softly to hear exactly what it said,—but what mattered if the meaning were plain?" This beauty seems, moreover, to coincide with truth. It still seems to confirm, through its authoritative radiance, what is merely a dream: the message it murmurs promises "never to break [the shore's] sleep any more, to lull it rather more deeply to rest, and whatever the dreamers dreamt holily, dreamt wisely, to *confirm*" (142, emphasis added). Beauty would confirm, through its material radiance, dreams characterized by holiness and wisdom—religious dreams. But these are still dreams. If they "preferred sleeping," the "voice might resume" with a song that would console the sleepers with the unreality of dream life. It might say, "why not accept this, be content with this, acquiesce and resign" (142). The desirability of this resignation is accentuated by a figure of the "measure" of the waves "soothing" the sleepers, just as their "measure" had provided anthropomorphic comfort to Mrs. Ramsay earlier. But like Mrs. Ramsay, Lily must purge religious consolation out of exis-tence. And so "Time Passes" closes with an image of Lily waking to a feeling of danger—a sublime intuition of the wildness of being—that galvanizes the will to refuse beauty's calm theological whisper. Faith in beauty would evade this danger. The metaphor used to describe Lily's wakening from the dark "folds" of this voice returns the reader to a classic setting of the sublime, which is Mr. Ramsay's preferred setting: "She clutched at her blankets as a faller clutches at the turf on the edge of a cliff. Her eyes opened wide" (143). As in Stevens, where day opposes "the trash of sleep," here truth is wakefulness: day "broke the veil on their eyes" (143).

Woolf still feels the authority of the sublime because it is, for her, the post-religious sentiment par excellence. Yet it is possible that this "day," this waking life, is the arena of beauty itself. There is a difficulty in the passage. While the "beauty of the world" seems essentially soporific, there is a moment before its message of passivity and resignation in which it asks the sleepers to awaken. Beauty's voice "entreat[s] the sleepers" to "come down to the beach itself"— which would involve, presumably, waking out of the dream. (Septimus found "harmony . . . drawing" him "towards *life*," rather than away from it, just as "before waking . . . the sleeper feels himself drawing to the shores of *life*" [*MD*, 69, emphasis added].) It would then disclose a "night" that is not "chaos and tumult," as it has been throughout the section, but a "night flowing down in purple; his head crowned; his sceptre jewelled; and how in his eyes a child might look" (142). It is almost as if the harmony of beauty and the terror of the sublime are united here in the image of night as a king who makes order possible and is attentive to the innocence of a child yet is terrible in his glory—the word used in the passage is "splendour." Here then is a brief glimpse of a possible reconciliation between the dream of religious beauty and the secular truth of the sublime. But this reconciliation quickly breaks, and beauty counsels, once again, the soothing resignation of the dream life of sleep. This brief moment suggests that Woolf is uncomfortable assigning a final ontological legitimacy to experiences of either the beautiful or the sublime: she is suspicious of the beautiful insofar as it promises a peace it cannot ensure, suspicious of the sublime insofar as it cannot account for the "strange" moments of harmony and joy.

BEAUTY, MIRACLE, AND MYSTERY

Auden wrote of Woolf: "what she felt and expressed with the most intense passion was a mystical, religious vision of life."[100] The sentence preserves the relation between two concepts many readers have wanted to segregate. The desire is understandable. In a letter to her sister, Woolf said of T. S. Eliot's conversion, "I was really shocked. A corpse would seem more credible to me than he is. I mean, there's something obscene in a living person sitting by the fire and believing in God."[101] In *Mrs. Dalloway*, "religion" is a name for the domestication of mystery. When a suspected royal is spotted in a car early in the novel, whispers proliferate, and the narrative voice intervenes: "the spirit of religion was abroad with her eyes bandaged tight and her lips gaping wide" (14). "Mystery" is yoked to "authority"; the former is the self-sanctioning obscurity of the latter. The figure of religion is thus blind but garrulous ("lips gaping wide"); everyone is piously murmuring about a power they cannot see.

Yet "mystery" is also a critical word in what is perhaps the defining passage of the novel. Here "mystery" is dissociated from rather than implicated in "religion":

> Love and religion! thought Clarissa, going back in the drawing room, tingling all over. How detestable, how detestable they are! . . . The cruelest things in the world, she thought, seeing them clumsy, hot, domineering, hypocritical, eavesdropping, jealous, infinitely cruel and unscrupulous, dressed in a mackintosh coat, on the landing; love and religion. Had she ever tried to convert any one herself? Did she not wish everybody merely to be themselves? And she watched out of the window the old lady opposite climbing upstairs. Let her climb upstairs if she wanted to; let her stop; then let her, as Clarissa had often seen her, gain her bedroom, part her curtains, and disappear again into the background. . . . There was something solemn in it—but love and religion would destroy that, whatever it was, the privacy of the soul. . . . Why creeds and prayers and mackintoshes? when, thought Clarissa, that's the miracle, that's the mystery; that old lady, she meant,

whom she could see going from chest of drawers to dressing-table. She could still see her. And the supreme mystery which Kilman might say she had solved, or Peter might say he had solved, but Clarissa didn't believe either of them had the ghost of an idea of solving, was simply this: here was one room; there another. Did religion solve that, or love? (126–127)

For Clarissa, both religion and love are characterized by a will to possess. Yeats preferred the pagan gods to the monotheistic God because in the pagan cosmos, "Man, too, remains separate. He does not surrender his soul. He keeps his privacy" (*TP*, 487). In Woolf too, "religion" violates the soul's integrity by violating its "privacy." Metaphysically, "God" is a principle of transparency that requires a self always potentially exposed and known. Ethically, both "religion" and "love" are forms of "conversion"; they do not "let" the other—"let her climb," "let her stop," "let her . . . gain"—persist in her otherness. Clarissa, however, is satisfied merely to observe the woman's external movement; she does not speculate on her interiority.

Yet Clarissa uses religious language to criticize religion. The "miracle" or "mystery" that religion cannot touch is "simply this: here was one room; there another." We can link this sentiment to Lily Briscoe's similar line of thought near the end of *To the Lighthouse*: "One wanted, she thought, dipping her brush deliberately, to be on a level with ordinary experience, to feel simply that's a chair, that's a table, and yet at the same time, It's a miracle, it's an ecstasy" (202). "Here was one room; there another" partakes of two overlapping mysteries. The first is the sheer gratuitousness and contingency of both rooms. Like the chair and table, the mere fact of their "ordinary" existence is extraordinary. It is important that the sense of wonder attending this existence cannot be explained by the familiar drama of sensory experience. We typically understand wonder as an emotion occasioned by the advent of the surprising or unprecedented. For this reason Philip Fisher has argued that "wonder" and "the ordinary" are incompatible. Following Wittgenstein in the *Brown Notebook* and Heidegger's analysis of tools, he suggests that the ordinary can only appear to consciousness when the latter encounters some "defect," "change," or unexpected failure in the ordinary.[102]

There are no distinguishing features of Woolf's chair, table, or rooms that might evoke wonder. The mystery resides in their mere being; indeed, it is somehow amplified by the recognition of their ordinariness.[103] Fisher notes that for Wittgenstein, "there can be no 'feeling of the ordinary.'" But Wittgenstein carved out a meaningful affective space for a sense of wonder that was not bound to the comparative procedures on which it typically depended: "It is not *how* things are in the world that is mystical, but *that* it exists."[104] He developed this idea—of an "experience" of what he called "absolute value"—in a later "Lecture on Ethics":

> I believe the best way of describing it is to say that when I have it *I wonder at the existence of the world*. And I am then inclined to use such phrases as "how extraordinary that anything should exist" or "how extraordinary that the world should exist." I will mention another experience straight away which I also know and which others of you might be acquainted with: it is, what one might call, the experience of feeling *absolutely* safe. I mean the state of mind in which one is inclined to say "I am safe, nothing can injure me whatever happens."[105]

Wittgenstein observes that in every other imaginable experience of wonder, "I wonder at something being the case which I *could* conceive *not* to be the case," whereas one cannot conceive of the world as not existing. He further suggests that "the verbal expression which we give to these experiences is nonsense."[106] Yet the experience is incontrovertibly real; its inexpressibility is evidence not of its nonsense but of its "absoluteness." In *To the Lighthouse*, Lily's struggle to capture this sort of experience is a struggle "to say not one thing, but everything" (178). But "everything" by definition cannot be expressed, for there is no vantage point from which to grasp it; the meaning or "value" of the miraculous contingency of "everything" lies, as Wittgenstein says, "outside the world."[107]

"Miracle" derives from the Latin *miraculum*—object of wonder—and in its theological sense suggests an event that cannot be exhausted by appeals to natural causation—i.e., anything *in* the world. Thus Wittgenstein wants to "describe the experience of wondering at the existence of the world by saying: it is the experience of seeing the world as a miracle."[108] For Woolf, too, the object of wonder—"mystery"—is linked to its character as "miracle" ("that's the miracle, that's the mystery"). In Woolf, the sense of "miracle" expands from that which challenges imaginative assimilation to that which describes the gratuitousness of being. For Richard Dalloway, "thinking of the War" in its sublime destructiveness "was a miracle," but moments later he uses the term to describe a condition less transparently sublime: "his own life was a miracle; let him make no mistake about it" (*MD*, 115, 117). For Lily, "miracle" names the perpetually shifting and unpredictable ground of human endeavor: "Was there no safety? No learning by heart of the ways of the world? No guide, no shelter, but all was miracle, and leaping from the pinnacle of a tower into the air?" (*TL*, 180). This sense of miracle as danger ("it was very, very dangerous to live even one day") is magnified by the mysterious facticity of what has been given combined with an awareness that it might not have been: "[Richard] repeated that it was a miracle that he should have married Clarissa" (*MD*, 117, emphasis added). But in the miracle of the two rooms at the close of *Mrs. Dalloway* and the miracle of the table and chair near the end of *To the Lighthouse,* the sense of insecurity and groundlessness is combined with a sense of positive gratuitousness; things might not have been, but it is good that they are. The sublime aspect of "miracle" is incorporated into the "mystery" that so often attends beauty: the "strange . . . stillness and . . . brightness of the day" and "strange intimation" of "Time Passes" or the "mysterious" character of "beauty anyhow" for Peter Walsh.

I said that there were two overlapping mysteries in the phrase, "Here was one room; there another." If the first involves the gratuitousness of their very existence, the second is the distance between them. The sense of contingency is translated into the experience of the perceiving subject, from *the* world to *my* world. There are other things out there that persist without reference to Clarissa's immediate concerns. As we have seen, Woolf understands this otherness as a form of "privacy"; the mystery is violated when one tries to possess or convert it in love or creed. Indeed, the condition for the perception of this mystery is the solitude of both subject and object (both Clarissa and the old woman are alone in their rooms). The privacy of the soul is something discovered in the experience of otherness as the mysterious aura of that otherness. But one's own privacy of soul is also the condition required to *contact* that otherness. The soul confirms an inviolable privacy in the other reality from the space of its own privacy.

Yet this solitude, and the ethical imperative that attends it, threatens to imprison. This is what happens for Septimus in both the narrator's and Clarissa's understanding of his suicide. For Septimus, the violation of privacy is crystallized in the "musts" of Holmes and Bradshaw, who do not "let" Septimus be as Clarissa lets the old woman be: " 'Must, 'must,' why 'must'?" (143). His suicidal cry—"I'll give it to you!"—is an act of freedom. In a serious gesture of feigned submission, he takes his life out of the hands of the psychiatrists by preempting their endgame: dominion over his body and soul. But Clarissa, as I noted above, also understands his death as an attempt to "communicate": "Death was an attempt to communicate; people feeling the impossibility of reaching the centre which, mystically, evaded them; closeness drew apart; rapture faded, one was alone. There was an embrace in death" (180). Solitude here is figured as the isolation that is the shadow of inviolability. And the desire to "communicate" implies an instability in the very privacy he is preserving in his act of self-annihilation. This final form of communication can only be achieved by obliterating one's own privacy through the obliteration of the personal identity that made it possible. The cry is an act of freedom, but it is also an act of self-emptying, an attempt to reach the "centre" by dispensing with the integrity of otherness altogether.

As the aura of the gratuitousness of being and the loveliness of distance, "mystery" is nearly indistinguishable from beauty in Woolf's writing. "There is this mystery about people when they leave us," thinks Rhoda in *The Waves*. "When Mrs. Lambert passes, she makes the daisy change; and everything runs like streaks of fire" (45). Septimus's suicide is an attempt to traverse the distance that makes beauty and mystery possible. Just as Septimus thought he had deciphered the meanings that beauty hides in its distance, his death marks a desire to communicate with the sensible goodness of the world—"Life was good. The sun hot. He did not want to die"—that will not make its meanings plain. When Clarissa says that his death "made her feel the beauty; made her feel the fun," the distance that marks the beautiful is eclipsed, for in *Mrs. Dalloway*, as I have argued, beauty is closer to vital energy, to that which bubbles under and courses through, than to that which appears at a distance.

Distance is a pervasive concern in the final sections of *To the Lighthouse*. Lily's reflections are structured by both spatial and temporal distance; she is looking out at the sea and toward the lighthouse, tracing Mr. Ramsay's boat, and struggling to approach the figure of the dead Mrs. Ramsay in her imagination. Looking at the "sea without a stain on it"—the sublime "purplish stain" of "Time Passes" has vanished, though it is perhaps still present in the "triangular purple shape" on her canvas (*TL*, 52)—she thinks, "Distance had an extraordinary power; they had been swallowed up in it, she felt, they were gone for ever, they had become part of the nature of things. It was so calm; it was so quiet" (188). This distant stillness is, as I have argued, an abiding quality of the beautiful in the novel: the "distance they have sailed," Cam thinks from the boat (mirroring Lily's thoughts), gives the "peaceful . . . the composed look" (166). Soon after, Lily thinks, "[Mr. Ramsay] and the children seemed to be swallowed up in that blue, that distance" (191). But the stillness and remoteness of the beautiful horizon eventually yields a sense of participation in that distance: "One glided, one shook one's sails (there was a good deal of movement in the bay, boats were starting off) between things, beyond things. Empty it was not, but full to the brim. She seemed to be standing up to the lips in some substance, to move and float and sink in it, yes, for these waters were unfathomably deep" (192).

This fullness marks a turn, for "emptiness" has been Lily's adversary throughout her final reflections. The emotions that resist linguistic articulation are for her modes of emptiness: "how could one express in words these emotions of the body? express that emptiness there?" (178). The "ghost, air, nothingness" of Mrs. Ramsay envelops the entire scene: "Suddenly, the empty drawing-room steps, the frill of the chair inside, the puppy tumbling on the terrace, the whole wave and whisper of the garden became like curves and arabesques flourishing round a centre of complete emptiness" (179). Beauty seems a mask for emptiness; pleasing lines ("curves and arabesques") obscure an emptiness they only pretend to shape. Yet Lily imagines that if she and Mr. Carmichael—"beings from whom nothing should be hid"—demanded an explanation of life, "beauty would roll itself up; the space would fill; those empty flourishes would form into shape; if they shouted loud enough Mrs. Ramsay would return" (180). This is a further, eschatological beauty: beauty that has "roll[ed] itself up" and exchanged "emptiness" for "shape." It is figured as resurrection—Mrs. Ramsay's return—just as Septimus's "beauty was everywhere" is accompanied by the return of his dead friend, Evans.

Lily never secures the "meaning" that she seeks in "the beauty of the world" (whose "message" is not "plain") or in the beauty of Mrs. Ramsay. She wants to reach something behind that beauty; she calls that something "the meaning of life" (161). "Is the beauty of this world enough," Woolf asks in her essay on Montaigne, "or is there, elsewhere, some explanation of the mystery?"[109] Because of this inaccessibility, beauty continues to be figured as a mask (Mrs. Ramsay's "cover of beauty") or as an epistemological impediment ("One wanted fifty pairs of eyes to see" Mrs. Ramsay, one of which must be "stone cold to her beauty" [177]). But when Lily finally experiences distance as fullness rather than emptiness ("empty it was not, but full to the brim") she has a "feeling of completeness" (192). Whereas Clarissa Dalloway understands "love" as a violation of distance, Lily thinks of this full distance as a form of love: "she must be in love with the place." Indeed, "[S]o much depends, she thought, upon distance . . . her feeling for Mr. Ramsay changed as he sailed further and further across the bay." Distance has become a space of intimacy in which one "glided . . . between things, beyond things" (191–192). This experience of distance as beauty approaches a theological perspective, for theologically "beauty," as David Hart has written, "is the true form of . . . distance, constituting it, as the grammar of difference. This presence of distance within the beautiful, as primordially the *effect* of beauty, provides the essential logic of theological aesthetics: one that does not interpret all distance as an original absence, or as the distance of differentiation's heterogeneous and violent forces" (18). When Lily experiences distance as a fullness in which the desire it evokes can "glide" rather than mourn the inaccessibility of its object, she relinquishes the "old horror": "to want and want and not to have" (202). To encounter beauty is to have and not to have simultaneously, to experience a desire, as Simone Weil writes, that is both satisfied and unsatisfied.

Lily also relinquishes the demand for transparent meaning. She laments that her "great revelation had never come" (161), and it still has not come at the novel's close. If the final line in Lily's painting is the lighthouse, we know that the lighthouse is not a "meaning," for it is not "simply one thing" (208): "I meant *nothing* by The Lighthouse," Woolf wrote. "One has to have a central line down the middle of the book to hold the design together."[110] Like the "golden haze" of Minta's beauty (also described as "the miracle") and the "golden mesh" of beauty's "deceptiveness" earlier in the novel, the lighthouse beyond her painting has "melted away in a blue haze" (208). The steps remain "empty," and her canvas is "blurred." The line merely holds things together. Lily's stroke is thus aligned with the work of Mrs. Ramsay, who also "bring[s]" things "together," "str[ikes]" them "into stability," says, "Life stand still here," and makes it appear that "[i]n the midst of chaos there was shape" (161). In this sense the secular artist has assimilated the vocation of the God who in the act of creation gives chaos form. Painting should, for Lily, secure beauty in a manner that Woolf's secular world of flux and formlessness cannot: "Beautiful and bright it should be on the surface, feathery and evanescent, one colour melting into another like the colours on a butterfly's wing; but beneath the fabric must be clamped together with bolts of iron. It was to be a thing you could ruffle with your breath; and a thing you could not dislodge with a team of horses" (171). The beauty in "Time Passes" appears and withdraws; its surfaces misrepresent the world's true amoral bearing. Lily's painting would somehow anchor its own bright "surface" so securely that its beauty cannot be "dislodge[d]."

We are tempted to characterize Lily as a modernist artist-hero or a priest of the "religion of art." But has the thing that is made accomplished something not subject to the grievances leveled against the given? The painting delivers stillness and shape by "holding" things "together," yet the "stillness" and "shape of loveliness" found in life is repeatedly censured as "a form from which life has parted" (129), and the "penalty" of "beauty" is that it is too "complete," that "[i]t stilled life, froze it" (177). Lily has her "vision," but we also know, as she thinks, "Phrases came. Visions came. Beautiful pictures. Beautiful phrases." The melancholy of art, Adorno writes, is that "it achieves an unreal reconciliation at the price of a real reconciliation. All that art can do is grieve for the sacrifice it makes, which, in its powerlessness, is art itself."[111] Lily's painting is an act of mourning for Mrs. Ramsay; the reconciliation it achieves is potent but may be "unreal."[112] The painting merely prefigures the hope that drives the novel—a hope it grants articulacy yet refuses to entertain. The hope is that "beauty" might "roll itself up," that the radiance of surfaces might trace their own curve until they achieve the ontological density that characterizes what Woolf calls "life." That radiant density would be "single, hard, bright, like a diamond in the sand, which would render the possessor secure" (132). Woolf cannot decide whether the "strange intimation" generated by the open-ended finality of beauty is "lure" and "consolation" or an experience approaching "knowledge." The theology latent in her mysticism tells her it is "half way to truth"; her atheism tells her that there is no second half. But in Lily's experience of distance as beautiful fullness rather than absence or sheer inaccessibility—in her experience of distance as the element of love—there is a hint, neither certain nor emphatic, that creation, as God's primordial act of self-distancing and "letting be," might have a creator.

3

"HOMER IS MY EXAMPLE": YEATS, PAGANISM, AND THE EMOTIONS

There are a number of ways to figure the boundaries between religion and secularity in modernism. Stevens juxtaposes the theologically determined Christian with the unencumbered, self-legislating agent who is, in the language of "Sunday Morning," "unsponsored, free" (CP, 56). One can also, like Stevens, pit the claims of "nature" against the "supernatural": "the great poems of heaven and hell have been written and the great poem of the earth remains to be written" (730). Joyce's *Portrait* juxtaposes the dogmatic, ecclesial priest with the "priest of the eternal imagination" who "transmut[es] the daily bread of experience into the radiant body of everliving life."[1] The broader intellectual culture often framed the transition more simplistically, as the displacement of superstitious, infantilizing piety by an enlightened reason capable of remaking the world, as the vertiginous loss of moral order after Darwin, or as the discovery of a new, progressive order, hidden in the logic of evolutionary science.

Yeats imagines the fault line differently. His choice is not between "religion" (understood as a singular, coherent genre) and secular humanism, but between rival visions of the sacred. Yeats has different names for the fault line: Oedipus and Christ, Homer and von Hügel, Michael Angelo and Saint Catherine of Genoa, Cuchulain and Patrick, "antithetical" and "primary," self and soul. These names can be generalized into broader distinctions: hero versus ascetic; pre-Axial versus Axial;[2] and pagan versus Christian, where the former is understood as the world of Homer, the Greek tragedians, and by analogy the world of Irish myth, rather than as the philosophical tradition that begins with Plato. For Yeats, these two models of the sacred are only "secularized" according to historical context. "What if," he asks in *A Vision*, "every two thousand and odd years something happens in the world to make one sacred, the other secular; one wise, the other foolish; one fair, the other foul; one divine, the other devilish?"[3]

Yeats is unclear about the "something" that "happens"; if we take him at his word, the phases of the moon are a major determining factor. But the testimony of *A Vision*, like all of Yeats's forays into cosmological history, is rhetorical rather than historical. Its descriptions of the momentous shifts in religious thought and feeling are useful primarily for the tension they distill and the way they evaluate that tension. *A Vision* suggests that the principal conflict for Yeats is between the "antithetical," pagan constellation of values and the "primary," Christian one. The former, which obeys "immanent power," is "expressive, hierarchical, multiple, masculine, harsh," and "surgical." The latter, which appeals to "transcendent power," is "dogmatic, levelling, unifying, feminine, humane" and makes "peace its means and end" (AV, 263). A preference for the pagan constellation is built into the system: though "antithetical" paganism and its mutations are ostensibly a "phase" in the cosmology, the fact that the cosmology is itself built on antitheses means that the antithetical, rather than the "primary," *is* ontologically primary; the fact that the system is cyclical rather than eschatological or linear means that it is structurally tilted toward a pagan view of history.[4]

The aim of *A Vision* is not, therefore, to explain history but to elaborate Yeats's fundamental affirmation: "Homer is my example and his unchristened heart."[5] That line, which concludes the disputation of his great poem "Vacillation," signals the affiliation that governs Yeats's struggle to disentangle himself from both the Christian asceticism that continued to fascinate him and the secular humanism that, following Nietzsche, Yeats took to be a continuation of the "ascetic ideal" rather than a break from it. He understood his entire poetic career as a reiteration of this basic problem: "The swordsman throughout repudiates the saint," he writes of his work, "but not without vacillation."[6]

I argue in this chapter that Yeats's reclamation of a pagan ethos for his poetry, and his ambivalence toward the Christianity against which it is defined, is most conspicuous in his portrait of the emotions and the ontological backdrop that give them definition. A conviction embedded in this argument is that Yeats's rehabilitation of pagan emotions and a pagan ontology, and not his occultism, Gnosticism, or supernaturalism, is the chief axis on which his mature religious imagination turns. Yeats's occultism is symptomatic, reactionary, and unwittingly entangled in the secularism it opposes; his Gnosticism, understood as a secret philosophical and poetic tradition, is too syncretic to achieve coherence and credibility; and his supernaturalism is principally a theory of the sublime converted into an account of historical rupture. Whereas all of these heterodox elements have an otherworldly bearing, what I am calling Yeats's paganism is distinctly worldly and thus consistent with secularism's dedication to immanence. But because Yeats refuses any final distinction between nature and the supernatural ("Natural and supernatural with the selfsame ring are wed," says Ribh, his Druidic theological persona [*CPY*, 284]), he departs from familiar modes of the secular. While the later Yeats values power, the body, and the aggressive will, these remain enchanted. They are "caught up," as Leda's body is in his famous poem, in forces that are both immanent and divine, for his "transcendent" world is no different from this one. Yeats's poetry thus seeks to facilitate the work he saw cosmic history already undertaking: a rehabilitation of the "secular" as "sacred" force.

Yeats's early poetry of otherworldly enchantment is sentimental. (Woolf was pleased to discover that "the years" had "dried up the Celtic mists, . . . braced the nerves and sharpened the senses of this particular poet.")[7] It was, he complained in a letter, "a flight into fairy land, from the real world, and a summons to that flight" (*LY*, 63). But the turn to the "real world" in his twentieth-century poetry does not mark, as it does with Stevens, a return to the "first idea," the new beginning of secular perception divested of mythical or theological entanglements. Nor is it characterized by a resigned acknowledgment that the world is best described in terms of a pitiless material science that the imagination must console. For Yeats the real is not synonymous with the secular. He intuitively believed what many philosophers and historians would soon be arguing in theory or historical narrative: that the various ideological forms secularism has taken are often modifications of Christianity rather than departures from it. "The Incarnation," Yeats writes, "involved modern science and modern efficiency and also the modern lyric feeling which give body to the most spiritual emotions. It produced a solidification of all things that grew from the individual will."[8] The implication is that what Eliot called "the impossible / Union of spheres" in the Incarnation (the Word made flesh) does not, as one might think, render the flesh sacramental, but leads instead to science's mechanistic, "efficien[t]" manipulations of the physical world. Yeats also suggests that Christianity, which might seem to unify spirit and matter, paradoxically disembeds the self from the world as the true scene of passion by linking its depth—experienced as "spiritual emotio[n]"—to a transcendent order where its higher good resides. "Individual will" is "solidified" in this isolation because its drama is not determined by the world but by forces that are only discernable inwardly. This shift eventually permits the will to determine instrumentally its own ends rather than to be driven by passion.[9]

In *The Human Condition*, Hannah Arendt observed that secular modernity had not, as many assumed, "thrown" human beings "back upon this world but upon *themselves*."[10] Max Weber had argued similarly that the "ultimate and most sublime values" had, in modernity, "retreated" into the domain of "personal human relations."[11] For Yeats this modernity, in continuity with the Christian culture that preceded it, exaggerates the personal, inward dimension of the self. The Christian elevation of inwardness and all the values that spring from it ("individualism," "sincerity," and "self-realization" are among the terms he uses) are magnified in secular culture.[12] Yeats understood his poetry as a struggle to subvert the sovereignty of these values. "All my life," he wrote in a late letter, "I have tried to get rid of modern subjectivity" (*LY*, 892).

This subjectivity, according to Yeats, emphasizes the merely personal self—the self "that sits down to breakfast".[13] Christianity both validates this self as the site where the personal God is preeminently known and demands that it be emptied and transformed; in Romanticism, at least in its Wordsworthian and Whitmanian currents, it is the mysterious and authoritative source of feeling and sympathy. "I would find myself and not an image," says *Hic* in "Ego Dominus Tuus," but *Ille* protests: "That is our modern hope and by its light / We have lit upon the gentle, sensitive mind, / And lost the old nonchalance of the hand" (*CPY*, 160). This modern subjectivity is still informed by the asceticism that founded it—"Dante's hollow face," in *Ille*'s image—because the subject seeks an inner purity of self-knowledge and feeling to emancipate it from the identity formed in what Yeats calls "the mirror of malicious eyes." This genealogical entanglement is evident in a passage from Yeats's *Autobiographies*:

> I now know that there are men who cannot possess "Unity of Being," who must not seek it or express it—and who, so far from seeking an anti-self, a Mask that delineates a being in all things the opposite of their natural state, can but seek the suppression of the anti-self, till the natural state alone remains. These are those who must seek no image of desire, but await that which lies beyond their mind—unities not of the mind, but unities of Nature, unities of God—the man of science, the moralist, the politician, Saint Simeon Stylites upon his pillar, Saint Anthony in his cavern, all whose preoccupation is to seem nothing; to hollow their hearts till they are void and without form, to summon a creator by revealing chaos, to become the lamp for another's wick and oil; and indeed it may be that it has been for their guidance in a very special sense that the "perfectly proportioned human body" suffered crucifixion. For them Mask and Image are of necessity morbid, turning their eyes upon themselves. . . . [T]hey are indeed of those who can but ask, "Have I behaved as well as So-and-so?" "Am I a good man according to the commandments?" or, "Do I realize my own nothingness before God?" "Have my experiments and observations excluded the personal factor with sufficient rigor?"[14]

These lines reveal Yeats's sympathy with Nietzsche's account of the "ascetic ideal," the spiritual program perfected by Christianity that, according to Nietzsche, wrecked the beauty and power—"the nonchalance," in Yeats's terms—of the aristocratic warrior ethos.[15] Secular modernity, Nietzsche suggests, has merely redistributed the ascetic ideal; representative gestures include Kant's categorical imperative and empirical science, both of which exclude the creative dimension of "perspective" by subjecting their wills to universalizing strictures that exclude, in Yeats's language, "the personal factor." For Yeats, too, the "moralist" and the "man of science" are indistinguishable from "Saint Simeon Stylites" and "Saint Anthony"; all pursue *kenosis* and erect a series of external commandments they write onto that "empty" self.

Paradoxically, however, the exclusion of the personal factor is underwritten by an image of the universe that has been personalized:

> [S]uch men must cast all Masks away and fly the Image, till that Image, transfigured because of their cruelties of self-abasement, becomes itself some Image or epitome of the whole natural or supernatural world, and itself pursues. The wholeness of the supernatural world can only express itself in personal form, because it has no epitome but man, nor can the Hound of Heaven fling itself into any but an empty heart. (A, 201)

The "Image" that was evaded by the ascetic returns, "transfigured" into a picture of the "whole" world, which, because it has passed through the self's depths and is exclusively concerned with its moral, epistemological, or affective purity, "can only express itself in personal form"—that is, a form drawn from an image of the self's "inner" life. Yeats thus shares Stevens's mistrust of both Christianity's anthropomorphic God and the epitomizing "man" of what is sometimes called "secular humanism," for both involve an exaggeration of the significance of the individual and depend on an ontology that is monistic and moral. All modes of asceticism—spiritual, political, scientific—posit, according to Yeats, a "whole" world rather than a world that is, as Yeats insists, "a bundle of fragments" (A, 163).

For Yeats, antithetical paganism provides the countermeasure to the Christian character of "modern subjectivity" by reimagining both world and self. Yeats insists on a world that is not only plural, but also agonistic. It is a world where, as Weber put it, "different gods struggle with each other, now and for all times to come."[16] "My mind," Yeats writes, "had been full of Blake from boyhood up and I saw the world as a conflict—Spectre and Emanation—and could distinguish between a contrary and a negation" (AV, 72). But Yeats ignored the radical Christian elements in Blake's thought ("the Religion of

Jesus, Forgiveness of Sin, can never be the cause of a war"), and he modifies Blake's "energy is eternal delight"[17] into *"will* or energy is eternal delight" (*LE*, 247). The distinction is important: will is an agent that presses its particular claims against others. Yeats's conflict is war, not Blake's progression of contraries, and is thus more closely linked with Nietzsche and Heraclitus: "It was," Yeats writes with approval in *A Vision*, "the Discord or War that Heraclitus called 'God of all and Father of all, some it has made gods and some men, some bond and some free,' and I recall that Love and War came from the eggs of Leda" (*AV*, 67).

This conflict is not the result of a primordial Fall and so not subject to redemption, as in Christian theology (a framework still operative in Blake).[18] Nor can it be framed in a liberal-progressive narrative as atavistic instinct being gradually domesticated by reason, or in an antinomian vision of peaceable desire liberated from the corrosive effects of social institutions and codes. Those visions of peace are, as Yeats says of Shelley's vision of justice in *Prometheus Unbound*, "vague propagandistic emotion." Shelley "lacked the Vision of Evil, could not conceive of the world as a continual conflict" (*AV*, 144). This "evil," as Yeats understands it, is not the opposite of "the good" or "justice"; it cannot be read in moral terms as a condition to be lamented, eradicated, or transcended. For Yeats, any vision of moral transcendence, located in either God or the future, leads to an unfortunate state where men are "stirred into a frenzy of anxiety and so to moral transformation." "Heaven itself," Yeats writes, "transformation finished, must appear so vague and motionless that it seems but a concession to human weakness" (274). The end of moral transformation would be stasis; no conflict, no life.[19] If there is such a thing as Heaven, it is, as Martin says in Yeats's play *The Unicorn from the Stars*, merely the prolongation and amplification of the world's conflict: "Heaven is not what we have believed it to be. It is not quiet, it is not singing and making music, and all strife at an end. I have seen it, I have been there. The lover still loves, but with a greater passion, and the rider still rides, but the horse goes like the wind and leaps the ridges, and the battle goes on always, always. That is the joy of heaven, continual battle." Its only music is "the sound of the swords, the sound of the clashing of the swords!"[20]

The second and, for this chapter, most important implication of Yeats's pagan vision is the way it structures emotion. Yeats seeks nothing less than a full rehabilitation of the "passions," those pre-ethical movements of the will that are distinguished from "vague propagandist emotion" and the inwardness of "modern lyric feeling" by their aggression and impersonality. The later poetry in particular extols passions that have been traditionally condemned or disciplined by ascetic and therapeutic philosophies and remain suspect in Romantic and Victorian literary cultures. "My poetry," Yeats writes in a letter, "comes from rage or lust" (*LY*, 871). These aggressive passions both require and reinforce Yeats's agonistic ontology because they are oppositional in nature: they depend on what Yeats called "a struggle against an immovable [object]" ("On the Boiler," *LE*, 247) or what Philip Fisher, in his book *The Vehement Passions*, has described as "[t]he collision of the will with its limits."[21] A world that issues from or is oriented toward a nonviolent, transcendent domain would be a world where conflict is only partial and provisional; adopting its perspective would permit either a monistic vision, where the world could be seen as an ordered "whole," or a dualistic vision, where the world might be realigned with its transcendent source. But the passions need a world, as Fisher says, "that is not continuous or harmonized; that is, a world that is not from end to end the same ordered whole. A substance encounters difference only in being blocked or impeded."[22] Like Stevens, who begins, in "A High-Toned Old Christian Woman," with "bawdiness" and projects from that central disposition an entire secular worldview ("a masque / Beyond the planets"), Yeats starts from the felt authority of the passions and projects his own distinctly pagan imaginary replete with the ontological postulates needed to secure this authority.

The eclipse of the idea of a *cosmos*—and of the *logos* through which mind encountered the rationality of that *cosmos*—was, as many scholars have noted, a crucial development in the making of modern secularity.[23] To imagine a new, pagan secularity, Yeats reaches back to a world before *logos*. This world doesn't suffer from the modern neutralization of nature and the disengaged, "buffered self" (as Charles Taylor characterized it) that accompanies it (a self that no longer discovers rationality *in* but can only impose its meanings *on* the world).[24] Yeats's passionate self, by contrast, is always engaged with the world because this world is understood as *agon* rather than *logos*. For Yeats, even those post-Homeric philosophies that view the world as infused by "thought" are already preparing the way for the moralized world of Christianity:

> Even before Plato that collective image of man dear to Stoic and Epicurean alike, the moral double of bronze or marble athlete, had been invoked by Anaxagoras when he declared that thought and not the warring opposites created the world. At that sentence the heroic life, passionate fragmentary man, all that had been imagined by great poets and sculptors began to pass away, and instead of seeking noble antagonists, imagination moved towards the divine man and the ridiculous devil. Now must sages lure men away from the arms of women because in those arms man becomes a fragment; and all is ready for revelation. (AV, 272)

Yeats's passions require a model of self that does not subject itself to or appropriate a totalizing moral or theological view. The passionate self must therefore be a "fragmentary" self. By this Yeats does not mean that the self is like a piece of a puzzle seeking a pattern or, in Aristophanes's image from Plato's *Symposium*, an egg divided by a hair seeking its missing half. Its fragmentariness is an awareness of a boundary or limit in the figure of a "noble antagonist," the collision with which permits the self a knowledge of its own identity.[25] For Yeats in "Under Ben Bulben," when "a man is fighting mad / Something drops from eyes long blind / He completes his partial mind" (*CPY*, 326). Self-knowledge does not occur through descent *into* the self but when the self, at the highest pitch of violent passion, crashes against its antagonist, yielding what Fisher calls "self-identical" or "undivided being." The *self* is fragmentary, but that very fragmentariness is the condition for the amplification of the passions, and the *state* of passion is a state of provisional completion, which Yeats calls joy: "Will or energy is eternal delight," Yeats writes, and "when [the will's] limit is reached it may become pure, aimless joy, though the man, the shade, still mourns his lost object" (*LE*, 247).[26]

Weber thought that an agonistic ontology could be imagined as a space of warring gods. For Yeats, the gods are indistinguishable from the emotions.[27] Several early essays develop this identification. "Moods," he writes, "are the labourers and messengers of . . . the gods of ancient days still dwelling on their secret Olympus."[28] Or, "The great Passions are angels of God" (*EE*, 145). "The Symbolism of Poetry" refers to "certain disembodied powers, whose footsteps over our hearts we call emotions"; the powerful "emotion" evoked by great poetry is equivalent to "the god it calls among us" (116). To call the emotions gods is to experience their gravity and revelatory power with such intensity that they cannot be merely personal; they find their origin in something beyond the empirical self. As such they are not events that belong to an "inner" space, as modern theories of emotion tend to assume, but the visitations or incarnations of external forces flooding the self.

Inner, "spiritual emotio[n]" may belong to God, but the passions, which are by nature reactive, belong to the gods: "I go inward to God," Yeats affirms, "outward to the gods."[29] The gods are part of a repository of archetypal emotions that the empirical self absorbs as it becomes impassioned:

> I know now that revelation is from the self, but from that age-long memoried self . . . and that genius is a crisis that joins that buried self for certain moments to our trivial daily mind. There are, indeed, personifying spirits that we had best call but Gates and Gate-keepers, because through their dramatic power they bring our souls to crisis, to Mask and Image, caring not

a straw whether we be Juliet going to her wedding, or Cleopatra to her death; for in their eyes nothing has weight but passion. . . . They have but one purpose, to bring their chosen man to the greatest obstacle he may confront without despair. (A, 216–217)

These "Gates and Gatekeepers" are best understood as tragic dramatists. As gates they are transitive emotional possibilities; as gatekeepers they arrange conflicts that facilitate the expansion of these emotions. Their providence isn't moral or teleological: "in their eyes nothing has weight but passion."

What they seek, in fact, is a repetition of their own energies. In Yeats's play *The Resurrection*, the "Greek" juxtaposes the Homeric vision of the gods to the "self-abasement" demanded by both Christ and Dionysius:

When the goddess came to Achilles in the battle she did not interfere with his soul, she took him by his yellow hair. . . . [The gods] can be discovered by contemplation, in their faces a high keen joy like the cry of a bat, and the man who lives heroically gives them the only earthly body that they covet. He, as it were, copies their gestures and their acts. What seems their indifference is but their eternal possession of themselves. Man, too, remains separate. He does not surrender his soul. He keeps his privacy. *(TP, 487)*

These gods do not penetrate the interior domain of the will and reorder it. Rather, they facilitate the will's amplification. Their engagement is violent but tactful, Athena taking Achilles by the hair. This paradigm is the pagan alternative to the Incarnation and its "spiritual emotions." If the Christian incarnation is *kenosis*, God's voluntary self-emptying in assuming human flesh, these gods demand dramatic repetition of their own life: the passionate hero "gives them the only earthly body that they covet." The gods are pure images of the passions,[30] and to impassion the self is to put on the mask of a god, to "cop[y] their gestures and their acts."[31]

Yeats's gods are not so much objects of belief as postulates of the passionate self, the necessary cosmic frame without which it cannot operate. In this sense Yeats is a sort of self-conscious, Feuerbachian secularist. The gods are valued for their subjective and imaginative utility; their actual existence is a matter of indifference. While Yeats in certain moods complains, like Stevens, of "[a]ll those things whereof / Man makes a superhuman / Mirror-resembling dream" ("The Tower," CPY, 199), he is less willing to view that complaint as an epistemological critique, in light of which one should keep one eye firmly on (secular) reality while allowing the anthropomorphic imagination its play. Both Stevens and Woolf worried about the legitimacy of anthropomorphic projection, but Yeats does not acknowledge any space, purified of subjectivity, in which one might step back from the world and encounter it apart from the *agon*. The four questions asked by the singer at the end of Yeats's last play, *The Death of Cuchulain*, raise the question of subjective projection only in order to redirect it:

> Are those things that men adore and loathe
> Their sole reality?
> What stood in the Post Office
> With Pearse and Connolly?
> What comes out of the mountain
> Where men first shed their blood?
> Who thought Cuchulain till it seemed
> He stood where they had stood?
>
> (*TP*, 554)

The first confesses the classic secular fear of a radical subjectivism: all metaphysical framing of "reality" may be nothing but the fantastical projection of passion onto a cosmos that is otherwise neutral. But the succeeding questions override the first by suggesting that the experience of passion simply *is* the experience of participating in the lives of these god-heroes. "*What* stood," "*What* comes"—the phrases point to mysterious but incontrovertible presences attending acts of passion: Pearse and Connolly in the Easter Uprising or the mythical scene of sacrifice on the mountain. The gods are not first conceptualized and then harnessed for action. The two events occur simultaneously: Cuchulain is not "thought" until the actor generates his very presence through passion, until "it seemed / He stood where they had stood." Passion at a certain pitch of intensity simply cannot, for Yeats, belong to the "trivial" self. It must be thought of as repeating a "supernatural" drama known intuitively in the repository of the "memoried" or "buried" self.

I have been suggesting that Yeats's religious "beliefs" (that he held such beliefs is uncertain) are less interesting than the impact his understanding of the sacred has on his vision of the emotional life. Yeats is never more radical than in his almost indiscriminate valorization and ultimate divinization of the passions. In classical Christian theology, the passions are, Thomas Dixon has argued, "dangerous," "unruly," and potentially "disobedient" movements of the lower (nonrational) portion of the will. Christian theologians elevate the "affections" over the "passions"; the conflict is not between reason and emotion as such, but between reasonable affection and unruly passion.[32] Post-Socratic philosophy tended to be equally suspicious of undisciplined passion: the Stoic ideal is *apatheia*, Plato's tripartite division of the soul elevates reason above spiritedness and appetite, and for Aristotle, being good is synonymous with having the *right* emotions.[33] Wordsworth's Romanticism is indebted to eighteenth-century theories of the "moral sentiments"; when poetry is "emotion recollected in tranquility," those emotions are subjected to critical investigation and judgment in the process of its making.[34] Andrew Stauffer has recently shown how Blake and Shelley—Yeats's chosen Romantic ancestors—tried to rework the passion of anger in a culture where the chaos of political revolution had rendered it suspect. Yet even they were only able to do so by deemphasizing its link to "rage" and aligning it with the sentiment of justice.[35]

For Yeats, the passions ignore this sentiment and crowd out those "affections" that are characteristically associated with moral feeling. In *A Vision*, Walt Whitman is dismissed because he wanted his "emotions" to be "healthy and intelligible"; he preferred "casual loves and affections" and wanted to "clear the intellect of *antithetical* emotions." He overemphasized the "affections" because he was "blinded by hot morality and a very good heart" (AV, 113–114). Christ, Yeats says, converted erotic strife into pity: "We say of Him because His sacrifice was voluntary that He was love itself, and yet that part of Him which made Christendom was not love but pity." But for Yeats, "Fragment delights in fragment and seeks possession, not service; whereas the Good Samaritan discovers himself in the likeness of another, covered with sores and abandoned by thieves upon the roadside, and in that other serves himself. The opposites are gone; he does not need his Lazarus; they do not die the other's life, live the other's death" (275).[36]

This passage reveals an ambiguity in Yeats's account of the passions. The English words "passion" and "passivity" both derive from the Latin *passio*, a word that denotes a suffering to which one is subjected. In ancient philosophy and theology, passion is dangerous precisely because it is characterized by a loss of self-possession; it is passive rather than active. For Yeats, erotic love arises from the self's fragmentary nature, from the lack of complete self-possession that renders it capable of being *moved*, or from what he calls "need": Christ's pity is not "love" because he does not "need his Lazarus." Yet the ferocity of this need eventually converts erotic passion into an expression of power, for its aim is "possession" rather than "service." The "opposite" is always an "opponent," as Yeats says in his 1930 diary: "All that our opponent expresses must be shown for a part of our greater expression, that he may become our thrall—be 'enthralled' as they say. Yet our whole is not his whole and he may break away and enthrall us in his turn, and there arise between us a struggle like that of the sexes. All life is such a struggle."[37]

Yeats abhors, however, what he calls "passive suffering." It is not, he wrote, "a theme for poetry" (LE, 199). The self is impassioned because it is capable of being (passively) moved irrespective of its will, yet for Yeats passion becomes the supreme activity *of* the will, an expression of its drive to possess that which has moved it. The will is enlarged by persisting in that drive when the object or antagonist refuses to be "enthralled." Yeats thinks of this persistence as a form of the very self-possession absent at the origin of passion. Thus the impassioned state that he admires most contains an element of indifference, for to escape the condition of "passive suffering" it must disavow dependence on the object that first moved it. Yeats thus wanted to write poems, he says in "The Fisherman," "as cold / And passionate as the dawn" (*CPY*, 149).

Yeats, then, paradoxically adds a Stoic component to a model of the passions that expressly refuses Stoic moralization. His ideal heroes, he writes, "labour for their objects, and yet . . . *desire whatever happens*, being at the same instant predestinate and free" (*A*, 217).[38] This paradoxical logic is exemplified in "An Irish Airman Foresees His Death," which imagines its hero as motivated not by any empirical attachment but by the knowledge that "will or energy is eternal delight":

> Those that I fight I do not hate,
> Those that I guard I do not love . . .
>
> . . . Nor law, nor duty bade me fight,
> Nor public men, nor cheering crowds,
> A lonely impulse of delight
> Drove to this tumult in the clouds.
>
> (*CPY*, 135)

The airman is simultaneously "cold" and "passionate." He is secure in the solitude of his "lonely impulse," isolated by the boundaries of his aircraft and its distance from other objects in the skyscape,[39] and indifferent to the consequences of his enterprise for either himself or his people: "No likely end could bring them loss / Or leave them happier than before" (135). Yet his indifference is not *apatheia* but a state analogous to that found in "Leda and the Swan," where Zeus's "indifferent beak" is conjoined with his passionate rapture. This indifference is passion so reduced to its primary ontological element—"will or energy"—that it no longer needs an opposing object to move or amplify it. It is will experiencing itself as self-generated.

"Christ does not need his Lazarus," writes Yeats, which is why his love is mere pity. But Yeats's play *Calvary*, a reimagining of the scene of the crucifixion, centers on figures who do not need Christ. The play focuses, in fact, on what Yeats calls "self-sufficiency," which is yoked, like the airman's, to a passionate "loneliness": "I have used my bird-symbolism in these songs to increase the objective loneliness of Christ by contrasting it with a loneliness, opposite in kind, that unlike His can be, whether joyous or sorrowful, sufficient to itself" (*TP*, 696). It is easy to overlook the strangeness of these claims: they pair loneliness, the very concept of which suggests lack or absence, with self-sufficiency. Joy and sorrow, too, seem to require susceptibility to external influence. The choral refrain of the play—"Christ has not died for the white heron"—juxtaposes a bird whose aesthetic dignity depends on its self-sufficient isolation with Christ's "spiritual" isolation on the cross. The play thus sets the image of the heron against a theology that presupposes precisely what Yeats insists its emotional ethics denies: an anthropology of need and a sense of moral and metaphysical insufficiency, the acknowledgment of which creates the context in which a concept like "salvation" becomes intelligible.

This theological need, however, differs from that of fragments for their opposites. The heron itself, figure of lonely self-sufficiency, is fragmented as the play unfolds. The cry of Christ's mockers is like the sound of "a flute of bone / Taken from a heron's thigh, / A heron crazed by the moon" (*TP*, 330). The women surrounding Christ are emblems not of passionate need but of what the German theologian Friedrich Schleiermacher considered the foundational religious emotion, the "sense of absolute dependence."[40] "Martha and those three Marys," the choral musician says, "live but in His love":

> Take but his love away,
> Their love becomes a feather
> Of eagle, swan or gull,
> Or a drowned heron's feather
> Tossed hither and thither
> Upon the bitter spray
> And the moon at the full.
>
> (332)

When the source that sustains their dependence is removed, their "love" becomes passive, subject completely to the bitterness of change. Here, as in the image of the flute, the heron's self-sufficiency does not exclude it from becoming subject to the ultimate sign of passivity—death—and the fragmentation that inevitably follows. The heron can become "crazed" without loss of self-possession, to the extent that its frenzy seems generated by its own all-powerful center. As Judas says, the scene of his planned betrayal was dominated by a lone heron, "So full of itself that it seemed terrified" (333). The heron is Judas's image for his own freedom, his will's divergence from what only appears to be, in the New Testament version of the narrative, the tight providential ordering of his action.

This remarkable mixture of passionate passivity and secular autonomy and freedom is what distinguishes Yeats's pagan yet post-Christian emotional land-scape from that of Homer. As Bernard Williams has said, "the world we actually have is so significantly shaped by Christianity" that "it will never be correct to see Christianity . . . as merely the longest and most painful route from paganism to paganism."⁴¹ The Homer who is Yeats's example could never have imagined, for instance, that Yeats would draw the three governing principles for his passionate poetics from Kant, the philosophical culmination of the Protestant self. "I would found literature," he writes in his 1930 journal,

> [O]n the three things which Kant thought we must postulate to make life livable—Freedom, God, Immortality. The fading of these three before "Bacon, Newton, Locke" has made literature decadent. Because Freedom is gone we have Stendhal's "mirror dawdling down a lane"; because God has gone we have realism, the accidental, because Immortality is gone we can no longer write those tragedies which have always seemed to me alone legit-imate—those that are a joy to the man who dies.⁴²

Collectively these three postulates seem to undermine the logic of the Homeric world that forms the representative backdrop for passion: while tragic passion is amplified by impersonal forces overwhelming the intentional self, Yeats insists on freedom; if Homer's underworld of shades suggests absolute loss unmiti-gated by hope of eschatological transformation, Yeats insists on immortality; while even Homer's gods are subject to fate, Yeats insists on God.

Yeats's tragic world, then, is not that of modern naturalism, where anony-mous and often ignominious material forces, like those reflected in Stendhal's "mirror dawdling down a lane," are ultimately responsible for human action. Yeats despises the "pale victims of modern fiction" who are only acted *upon* (*LY*, 827). Nor is his tragedy a matter of "accident," as in, for example, Hardy's fiction, where, as Terry Eagleton puts it, "things are tragic not because they are ruled by a pitiless Law but precisely because they are not."⁴³ Hardy's godless world is "a world of clashing, angled, and decentered life forms" because things there are "provisional, selective, unfinished"⁴⁴—in Yeats's language, "acci-dental." In place of accident Yeats envisions something he calls "God's chance." His notes to *Calvary* establish a fictional Arab poet who, after losing his home, wife, and child to robbers and murderers, writes three "songs of joy" based in this principle: "Some worship His Choice; that is easy; to know that He has willed for some unknown purpose all that happens is pleasant; but I have spent my life in worshipping His Chance, and that moment when I understand the immensity of His Chance is the moment when I am nearest Him" (*TP*, 697).

This worship of chance is what allows Yeats's passionate personae to preserve their sense of freedom. They desire both their object and the forces that prevent them from ever obtaining it; again, they "labour for their objects, and yet . . . desire whatever happens, being at the same instant predestinate and free." As the soldiers in *Calvary* say, who play at dice "carved," like the flute of heron bone, "[o]ut of an old sheep's thigh at Ephesus," "Whatever happens is the best" (334).

By refusing to adopt a transcendent vantage point from which one might criticize the present world of experience as inadequate or unjust, Yeats, like Stevens, radicalizes the secular dedication to immanence. "God's chance" does not establish the world's dependence on a transcendent source; rather, it divinizes the secular world itself as the proper object of worship. But Yeats achieves this radical immanence at the expense of a particular mode of secular materialism: the natural and social science that emphasize the determined character of human existence. He preserves the will's freedom not to escape the strictures of determining force but to imagine them as *desideratum*. For Yeats, as Stevens writes in "Esthétique du Mal," the true secularity of "tragedy" is not the elevation of accident over providence but a conviction that "under every no / Lay a passion for yes that had never been broken" (*CP*, 282).

JOY, REMORSE, AND HATE IN A POST-CHRISTIAN FRAMEWORK

The passions typically displace spiritual affections and moral sentiments in Yeats's work. They achieve their dignity, as I have argued, within a distinctively pagan landscape. But the term that competes with "passion" for greatest prominence in Yeats's lexicon is "joy," an emotion that owes its own distinction in Western culture to its centrality in the New Testament and the broader Christian tradition. Joy for Yeats is not simply one emotion among others; it is the condition for the possibility of all intense emotions and the underlying energy found in all of them. "Let us have no emotions," Yeats writes in a letter, "in which there is not an athletic joy" (*LY*, 435). Thus even emotions outside the spectrum of happiness—grief, rage, even hate—take on, in Yeats's work, a joyous character. "Indignation is a kind of joy," he writes. "We who are joyous need not be afraid to denounce."[45] Yet Yeats supports this commendation of aggressive joy with a quotation from the Dutch Christian mystic John of Ruysbroeck, who almost certainly does not mean what Yeats does by "joy": "I must rejoice, I must rejoice without ceasing, though the whole world shudder at my joy" (876).

What follows is an attempt to understand the meaning of joy—its phenomenology, its ontological basis, and the anthropology it assumes—in Yeats's poetry. Yeats, I argue, can only elucidate this meaning through a dialogue with the Christian tradition that he so often resists. His great poem "Vacillation," a meditation on the question that concludes the first section—"What is joy?"—is also the poem in which Yeats dramatizes his most sustained dialogue with Christianity. The poem attempts to answer this question by negotiating its avowals and disavowals of that tradition and articulating its alternatives to it. In my reading of "Vacillation," as well as "Lapis Lazuli" and "Dialogue of Self and Soul," I hope to emphasize the ethical dangers that attend Yeats's desire to purge modern, secular subjectivity of its Christian sources, for his understanding of pagan joy replaces the unsettling demands of the "ought" and the potential "remorse" and self-division that accompany it with a vision of the will's mastery and domination. Just as the internal "ought" is extinguished, so is the external: because the joyful self desires "whatever happens," it circumvents the demands of justice and welcomes catastrophe. Yeats's "will" enjoys every power but ethical agency; neither the secular humanist imperative to mend the world through historical action nor the Christian imperative to redeem both world and self survives Yeats's *amor fati*. Yet Yeats's own vacillations—he is never quite finished with Christian spirituality—suggest the limits of paganism as a template for a viable secular ethos.

The fact that Yeats frames joy as a question suggests that it is not a subrational emotional state without cognitive freight; it is, rather, a response to a particular kind of knowledge. The interpretation of this knowledge has, in the West, been largely theological. As Adam Potkay has argued, it is Christianity rather than pagan antiquity that established the importance of joy in the affective life.[46] The eudaimonistic ethics of antiquity treated joy with suspicion precisely for the same reason that it admonished discipline of the passions: "Hellenistic and Latin philosophy opposes human flourishing to those joys in relation to which we are passive. . . . Happiness, insofar as it harkens back to ancient eudaimonism, is opposed to the loss of self that is always, to some degree, involved in joy" (3). By contrast, the New Testament, with its spirituality of transformative self-loss, speaks of joy some 173 times (30). This joy is conceived as a participation in God's reality through "connection, penetration, and fusion" with and by Him; it is a "fullness" that saturates a self that has been emptied through suffering and voluntary asceticism (31). Human joy is made possible by the boundlessness of God's own joy, and it recognizes that its power, because it is dependent on that source, is "gratuitous" rather than "the result of individual agency" (10). Thus, as Potkay notes, "In Greek, joy (*chara*) is etymologically connected to and not clearly distinguished from 'grace' (*charis*), the gift that is freely given" (12). Simone Weil, writing out of the Christian mystical tradition, insists that the self disappears entirely in the experience of joy: "No 'I' obtrudes itself in the fullness of joy. . . . Joy is the consciousness of that which is not me *qua* human being."[47]

There are passages in Yeats's writing that entirely invert this model. His joy is not passive but active: "Joy is of the will which does things, which overcomes obstacles, which is victorious."[48] If for Weil joy decenters the self, for Yeats it depends on self-appraisal and dominance: "all that is less than we are should stir us to some joy, for pure joy masters and impregnates" (*EE*, 184).[49] As we have already seen, because joy is the energy that drives passion to exert its will, its visibility increases when that will is impeded: "when [the will's] limit is reached it may become pure, aimless joy, though the man, the shade, still mourns his lost object." Yeats admired the distinction his father made in a letter between "personal" pleasure and "impersonal" joy (*LY*, 587), and the picture here is of joy as the sheer ecstasy of the will discharging itself, to the point that, while the personal "man" is still conscious of the "object" his passion was denied, the will is aware of an absolute fullness that has no particular ends, no "aims."

These reflections provide the basis for what Yeats calls, in his later poetry, "tragic joy."[50] The concept can be traced to Nietzsche's influence.[51] In Nietzsche's early work, *The Birth of Tragedy*, "Dionysian" joy surfaces when the "Apollonian" principle of individuation collapses and the primal undercurrent of an eternally creative and eternally destructive energy intoxicates those experiencing it: "under the influence of the narcotic potion hymned by all primitive men and peoples, or in the powerful approach of spring, joyfully penetrating the whole of nature, those Dionysic urges are awakened, and as they grow more intense, subjectivity becomes a complete forgetting of self."[52] For Nietzsche, the destruction of the heroic individual in tragic drama yields not pity or terror but joy, because the hero returns to the "primal Oneness" that made his passion possible in the first place. In this tragic state "pain is experienced as joy . . . jubilation tears tormented cries from the breast. At the moment of supreme joy we hear the scream of horror."[53]

Yeats's motive for composing "Vacillation," however, was not to elaborate on Nietzsche but to exorcise the influence that Baron Friedrich von Hügel, a major British theologian of the early twentieth century, was exerting on him.[54] Yeats was impressed by von Hügel's massive *The Mystical Element of Religion*, which he read sometime in the late 1920s or early 1930s. Yeats had just written his "Crazy Jane" poems, the power of which is inseparable from their blasphemy. In December of 1931, he wrote to Olivia Shakespear that he had started work on "a longish poem called 'Wisdom' in the attempt to shake off 'Crazy Jane,' and I begin to think I shall take to religion unless you save me from it" (*LY*, 788). That poem, which would become "Vacillation," attempts to "shake off" the spiritual temptation—"becom[ing] a Christian man," in the words of the poem—that confronted him in the dialectical swing away from Crazy Jane. By the end of the poem the speaker has announced, "So get you gone, Von Hügel, though with blessings on your / head" (*CPY*, 253).

Joy is an animating term in von Hügel's study. "Suffering and sacrifice," he writes, represent the "one way to joy and possession."[55] In Christianity, von Hügel says, suffering is not passive but "the highest form of action, a divinely potent means of satisfaction, recovery, and enlargement for the soul . . . with . . . its immense capacity for joy in self-donation" (1:27). If suffering is an experience of unsatisfied desire, it can become the "means" to a "satisfaction" that circum-vents desire's immediate objects. That unsatisfied satisfaction is called "joy," which is known when suffering becomes "self-donation," an activity in which the self, emptied in voluntary self-giving, is in turn "enlarge[d]" when what it has given returns to it through the life of another. The self's boundaries are thus simultaneously penetrated and expanded. This "joy, different from all mere pleasure, ever accompanies this reconquest of our true self and our re-donation of it to its true source" (1:262). Von Hügel understands this process not as the indiscriminate blending of the individual into the impersonal One but as the "increasing elevation of the moral personality," which "involves that constant death to self, that perpetual conversion, that unification and peace in and through a continuous inner self-estrangement and conflict, which is the very breath and joy of the religious life" (1:76). The principle of individuation is not, therefore, overthrown; the personal self is amplified even as all those acquisitive and appetitive features of the individual *qua* individual—a being, in other words, that understands itself as a center in competition with other centers— recede. The "source" that activates this transformation of the self is God, known preeminently in metaphors of fire and light: the "One God Who is the Fire of Pain and the Light of Joy to souls" (2:218).

Yeats almost certainly has these metaphors in mind in the first section of "Vacillation":

Between extremities
Man runs his course;
A brand, or flaming breath,
Comes to destroy
All those antinomies
Of day and night;

The body calls it death,
The heart remorse.
But if these be right
What is joy?

(CPY, 250)

The challenge when reading this section is to understand how the lines that
precede the question precipitate it. "Extremities," like "antinomies," are those
nodes of opposition that structure the passions, and in doing so structure all of
life. Thus Yeats writes, in "Per Amica Silentia Lunae," "There are two realities,
the terrestrial and the condition of fire. All power is from the terrestrial condition, for there all opposites meet and there only is the extreme of choice
possible, full freedom. And there the heterogeneous is, and evil, for evil is the
strain one upon another of opposites; but in the condition of fire all is music
and all rest" (LE, 25). "Extremities" mark this terrestrial condition, which is a
state of heterogeneity rather than purity or singularity. Without extremities
there is no power, for as Nietzsche writes in the notebooks collected as *The Will
to Power*, "The will to power can manifest itself only against resistances; therefore it seeks that which resists it."[56]

The "condition of fire" announces the end of opposition. The "brand, or
flaming breath" consumes those "antinomies." "The body calls it death"
because fire is the end of striving; the condition of fire is "all rest." For Yeats
this means the end of the impassioned self. For von Hügel the "fire of pain"
and "light of joy" do not abolish striving, for he internalizes the antinomies:
the strife is between elements inside the self, and pain and joy are the
products of the ongoing struggle in which the forces of grace seek to master
recalcitrant desire. "Remorse" is Yeats's term for this internal self-division. The
"heart" calls the "flaming breath" "remorse" because it introduces an absolute
spiritual perspective—what Yeats, in *Autobiographies*, calls an "infinite blinding
beam" (A, 372)—that judges the passions not by their energy but by their consequence.

"Remorse"—the term is ubiquitous in Yeats—is an ongoing problem for
Yeats's vision of the passions.[57] In an early theater review he quotes with approval
the characterization of remorse as an "impure passion"; his late plays *The Words
upon the Window-Pane* and *Purgatory* imagine "remorse" as a purgatorial condition in which "spirit re-lives not the pain of death but some passionate or tragic
moment of life."[58] As such it is a dark parody of passion itself, the template of
which, as I have argued, is the repetition or "re-liv[ing]" of the god's own
passions. The passion of remorse is impure because its object is behind rather
than in front of it. The impassioned self cannot exploit remorse as it exploits

resistance, for it has no access to an opponent that is internal rather than external and which is buffered by layers of time.

Nor can remorse be assimilated to the passions of grief or sorrow,[59] which mourn a lost object, because the object is oneself, and it is overwhelmingly *there*, as the lines dramatizing remorse in the fifth section of the poem announce:

> Things said or done long years ago,
> Or things I did not do or say
> But thought that I might say or do,
> Weigh me down, and not a day
> But something is recalled,
> My conscience or my vanity appalled.
> (CPY, 251)

Remorse can only arise from a perspective that approaches the eternity of "flame." It sees the whole life, as it were, from a disembodied perspective outside that life, and it forms its measurements and judgments not in the eruptive moments of passion but in the interstices of those moments. Thus in *Autobiographies* Yeats calls remorse "a strangely abstract judgment," which divides the self into a series of "isolated" moments; under its power "[w]e are never a unity, a personality to ourselves" (A, 372). Such division is evident in these lines, where the "I" is fragmented into a chaotic volley of verbs that move from past to conditional past, presence to absence: said, done, not said, not done, might say, might do, and the "thought" that exists both in the past and the present.[60] All this "I" can do, syntactically, is repeat itself in different formulations of the same basic words. For Schopenhauer, the fact that the remorseful subject continues to understand itself as a unity even within this awareness of division—"remorse" (*die Reue*) is a knowledge that these past acts *belong* to the self—marks the beginning of the very phenomenon of responsibility and thus moral freedom.[61] But for Yeats, remorse is not a beginning but an impediment.

The body "calls" the flaming breath "death," the heart "remorse"; the two are brought together in the "appalled" of section V. The ambiguity of "calls" suggests that we are not dealing with definitions but names thrown at an experience, and the final question challenges these interpretations directly: "If these be right / What is joy?" "Be right" is linked to "call," which means that the question does not ask, as has often been assumed, how do we find joy in the face of death and remorse?[62] Rather, the implication is that the "brand, or flaming breath" might be "call[ed]" something *better*: not death or remorse but joy. And the fact that there could be a third term that better accounts for the phenomenon suggests that the structure of joy is somehow analogous to those other conditions. Here there is potential agreement with von Hügel, for whom the consuming fire of God produces both the heat of pain and the light of joy.

But whereas von Hügel links joy with self-emptying and transcendent fullness, the stanza is uncomfortable with the collapse of the antinomies that necessarily accompanies that process. Yet "joy" characteristically involves, as Potkay has argued, some kind of self-loss, some infiltration of an external energy, which is why Yeats links it to the "flaming breath" in the first place. "Death" is loss of the vital self, "remorse" a loss of the self's unity achieved in passion. Joy too requires self-loss, but the poet wonders whether its energy might remain "terrestrial" rather than transcendent. In other words, joy might be the state that circumvents the impasse of binary thinking: *either* the descent of a purifying fire that obliterates the oppositions necessary to life *or* a ruthless immanence in which partial selves war with other parts rather than lose themselves through participation in a whole.

The second section builds on this possibility:

> A tree there is that from its topmost bough
> Is half all glittering flame and half all green
> Abounding foliage moistened with the dew;
> And half is half and yet is all the scene;
> And half and half consume when they renew,
> And he that Attis' image hangs between
> That staring fury and the blind lush leaf
> May know not what he knows, but knows not grief.
>
> (CPY, 250)

The tree is an image of a conflagration that does not "destroy," as the flaming breath does, what it "consume[s]." Thus the paradoxical "half all"s invite us to contemplate not a tree divided into two compartments but a state of life in which organic growth ("green abounding foliage") and devouring fire ("glittering flame") are indistinguishable. Both "consume when they renew." The "antinomies" of the first section are stubbornly preserved—"half is half"—but also subsumed into a broader perspective: half "is," in its resolute halfness, "all the scene." In the language of "Per Amica Silentia Lunae," the "condition of fire" is no longer "all music and all rest"; it is no longer *all* anything, and certainly not rest, for consumption is the movement of renewal.

The referent for the tree shifts, at the end of the stanza, from the mythological stories collected in the Welsh *Mabinogion* to the myth and ritual surrounding Attis, which Yeats most likely knew from Frazer's *The Golden Bough*. Attis, in the version Frazer recounts, castrated himself, died, and transformed into a pine tree. In the Roman context, the ritual celebrating the death and resurrection of Attis was called, according to Frazer, "the Festival of Joy."[63] But it involved, in the cultivation of a rapture of "excitement" that left its celebrants "insensible to pain," a ritual of frenzied self-mutilation, the blood from which was used to nourish the "sacred tree." For Yeats, the repetition of that ritual — "he that Attis' image hangs" — produces an expulsion of "grief." This state yields an access to some truth that, as Yeats will later say, can be embodied but not known: he "[m]ay know not what he knows, but knows not grief."

A "Festival of Joy," then, though the state is closer to ecstasy. As Potkay has argued, ecstasy traditionally differs from joy insofar as it moves from self-loss to complete "self-absenting." In Greek *ekstasis* ("standing elsewhere") meant "insanity" or "bewilderment," and these terms reflect both Yeats's confused "know[ing]" and the frenzy of Frazer's "scene."[64] This knowing is really a mode of ecstatic *forgetting*, which is why the "green abundant foliage" becomes, in the next section, "Lethean foliage" in which the self is "caught." The renunciatory voice of the third section counsels disentanglement: "No longer in Lethean foliage caught / Begin the preparation for your death." In doing so it shifts the ground of joy from intoxicated self-loss to the will:

> Test every work of intellect or faith
> And everything that your own hands have wrought,
> And call those works extravagance of breath
> That are not suited for such men as come
> Proud, open-eyed and laughing to the tomb.
>
> (250)

By retooling the words used in the first section, this voice usurps the agency of the flaming breath. "Breath" has become "extravagance," an expendable commodity. "Call" is now an imperative, an act of will, rather than the heart or body's passive interpretation of their own consumption. Thus what seems like renunciation is actually the work of a present will so abundant that it can relinquish what it previously willed. It treats its own past, its works of intellect or faith, with disdain rather than remorse. Its joy is the gaiety of pride.

The next section presents yet another model of joy, which diverges from both the Dionysian practice of hanging Attis's image on the tree and the joyful disdain of the preceding sections:

> My fiftieth year had come and gone,
> I sat, a solitary man,
> In a crowded London shop,

An open book and empty cup
On the marble table-top.

While on the shop and street I gazed
My body of a sudden blazed;
And twenty minutes more or less
It seemed, so great my happiness,
That I was blessèd and could bless.

(251)

The verse is based on an experience Yeats describes in "Per Amica Silentia Lunae":

> At certain moments, always unforeseen, I become happy, most commonly when at hazard I have opened some book of verse. Sometimes it is my own verse when, instead of discovering new technical flaws, I read with all the excitement of the first writing. Perhaps I am sitting in some crowded restaurant, the open book beside me, or closed, my excitement having overbrimmed the page. I look at the strangers near as if I had known them all my life, and it seems strange that I cannot speak to them: everything fills me with affection, I have no longer any fears or any needs. . . . It may be an hour before the mood passes, but latterly I seem to understand that I enter upon it the moment I cease to hate. (*LE*, 31)

The joy in these lines and their prose source is not an activity of the victorious will, for it is unforeseen and passive, nor is it linked to the ecstasy of the flaming tree and ritual effigies. "It seemed, so great my happiness, / That I was blessèd and could bless": here is the link Potkay establishes between joy (*chara*) and grace (*charis*). The graceful energy is so abundant that it overflows: the act of receiving ("I was blessèd") is simultaneously the capacity to give ("could bless").[65] The happiness is attended by images of receptivity rather than will: the book is "open" and the cup is "empty."

This "happiness" requires as its condition that the self cease to "hate." But hate is yet another state that for Yeats is subject to the vacillation between pagan and Christian, swordsman and saint. Conceptually, the modern English word "hate" already embeds a moral reading of the passions of anger or rage. Anger is a visitation, an eruption, but when anger is called hate an ongoing psychological condition is implied. Hate in this sense is a poison that festers and corrodes over a period of time. Yeats distinguishes hate from "indignation" in the letter commending the joy of denunciation and derides the former as a form of "passive suffering." By this he means that hate arises from a position of weakness; in that it is like Nietzsche's *ressentiment*. The letter further suggests that hate is, unlike anger, uniquely susceptible to ideological framings.[66] Fisher has written that anger's natural scope is " '*my* world,' as opposed to '*the* world.' "[67] In this light the conversion of anger into hate can, for Yeats, also be understood as the improper universalizing of anger based on an ideological conviction, whether reactionary or progressive; thus nationalism, Marxism, and other ways of framing *the* world may generate hatred. Just as hatred conceptualized as a disorder of self requires a moralized reading of the psyche, the universalization of anger into hate requires an ethical reading of the world as inadequately just. Both, for Yeats, are the secular legacy of a Christianity (and its prologues in Platonism and Stoicism) that moralized self and world.[68]

Yet elsewhere, and especially later in his career, Yeats flaunts the word "hate," luxuriating in its ethical harshness so as to scandalize both Christian and secular ethical cultures. In his "Introduction" to his work, he writes, "Nor do people hate as we do in whom that past is always alive; there are moments when hatred poisons my life and I accuse myself of effeminacy because I have not given it adequate expression. It is not enough to put it into the mouth of a rambling peasant poet" (*LE*, 210). Hate from this perspective poisons only when it is not discharged, when it remains "passive" instead of finding active expression. This Yeats seeks a hate that is "antithetical" rather than "primary": "Antithetical men are, like Landor, violent in themselves because they hate all that impedes their personality, but are in their intellect . . . gentle, whereas *primary* men whose hatreds are impersonal are violent in their intellect but gentle in themselves, as doubtless Robespierre was gentle" (AV, 84–85). Ideological hate is impersonal in the sense that it is theoretical; it is constituted by an intellectual resistance to life as it is given. But antithetical hate is passionate because it involves the will colliding with that which "impedes" it. It does not sterilize but enlarges the self.

Yeats said that "Vacillation" was an attempt to shake off Crazy Jane, and the Crazy Jane poems articulate this antithetical violence. Yeats says in A *Vision* that "sexual love" may be founded on "spiritual hate," and "Crazy Jane Grown Old Looks at the Dancers" enacts this vision.[69] Jane, watching two dancers, does not balk when she suspects one dancer may kill the other, for "[e]yes under eyelids did so gleam": "They had all that had their hate: / *Love is like the lion's tooth.*" (*CPY*, 260). In "Ribh Considers Christian Love Insufficient," the Druidic theologian refuses the orthodox Christian vision of *agape* or *caritas*:

> Why should I seek for love or study it?
> It is of God and passes human wit;
> I study hatred with great diligence,
> For that's a passion in my own control,

A sort of besom that can clear the soul
Of everything that is not mind or sense.
                    (286)

As in "Under Ben Bulben," where mind, to know itself, must "gro[w] tense / With some sort of violence," here hate serves as a purification that operates internally rather than descending, in the case of "Isaiah's coal" or the "flaming breath," from an external agent. For Ribh, hate is apophatic, a blasphemous version of the *via negativa* as conceived in the negative theological tradition: "Hatred of God may bring the soul to God" (286).

The state of joyful blessedness dramatized in section V of "Vacillation" is thus situated uncomfortably in the proximity Yeats allowed it to hold between the poetics of hatred in the prior Crazy Jane poems and the later *Supernatural Songs*. It should not be read, then, as the episode that definitively dramatizes the poem's early question: "What is joy?" It is a moment of vacillation that turns away from the swordsman and toward the saint, for it demands a marginalization of the will, a cultivation of emptiness and receptivity as the disciplines necessary to inaugurate participation in a higher fullness. This model of joy dissolves boundaries rather than accentuating them in the activity of passionate conflict. Neither does the poem endorse Nietzsche's Dionysian obliteration of the individual. In *The Resurrection*, written around the same time, Dionysian rituals are linked to Christian self-loss, the need to "sacrifice everything that the divine suffering might, as it were, descend into one's mind and soul and make them pure" (*TP*, 485). In the same way, though without the moral orientation, Dionysian worshippers "imitate women that they may attain in worship a woman's self-abandonment. . . . Such people suffer terribly and seek forgetfulness in monstrous ceremonies" (486).[70] If "joy is of the will," as Yeats says, the willful self cannot be so obliterated.

If the poem is drawn to the Dionysian joy in which the individuated will collapses into a broader ontological will that knows only the indiscriminate, impersonal play of creation and destruction, Yeats adds a key element: an image of the individual will capable of willing its own perishability. In the sixth section, which follows the portrait of remorse, the "I" recedes, for the "I" is always too entangled in "responsibility." What remains is the will of history and myth:

A rivery field spread out below,
An odour of the new-mown hay
In his nostrils, the great lord of Chou
Cried, casting off the mountain snow,
'Let all things pass away.'

Wheels by milk-white asses drawn
Where Babylon or Nineveh
Rose; some conquerors drew rein
And cried to battle-weary men,
'Let all things pass away.'
(CPY, 251–252)

The cry approaches but finally outmaneuvers the voice of Ecclesiastes. It is not "all things pass away" but "*Let* all things pass away." The cry is not lamentation but affirmation, even permission: the gesture of assent is equally a fantasy that the will controls that to which it is assenting. It is one part battle rhetoric: the will to conquer is the will to make some things pass away. But the lines, framed by a perspective that contemplates the rise and fall of empires, asks us to imagine that the conqueror's line already contains as foreknowledge what the scene knows as the past. The cry embeds an assent to the knowledge that the empire "some conquerors" have not yet established will equally pass; their will to destroy is but one strand of a larger will that is going to destroy their creation. It is this knowledge that allows the complete identification of the local will with the larger one.

This identification is, in the later Yeats, the fulcrum of joy. "Let all things pass away" aligns the private will with the violently creative ontological will; in saying yes to the latter the private will says yes to itself. In doing so it signals its participation in a prodigious creative action capable of overwhelming it. But this does not require self-loss, in either the Christian or the Dionysian version. Rather, the self is overwhelmed precisely at the apex of its passionate striving, when it is most fully itself. Just as passion is amplified by the resistance of its desired object, joy expands, not at the moment but just before the moment the self is destroyed. Destruction becomes a test of joy's authenticity and its capacity for excess. The proud self comes "laughing to the tomb" because its joy is not dependent on anything the "body of fate"—Yeats's term for the "sum of fact . . . as it affects a particular man" (AV, 82)—gives or withholds; its own death is merely an occasion to prove its own excessive, self-sufficient vitality. This is why the conqueror's knowledge is motivation rather than resignation. The conquest assimilates even more power in the realization that whatever it establishes will also pass. Motivation purifies itself of all worldly acquisitiveness—the accomplishment of this or that military goal—and so becomes what Yeats calls "pure, aimless joy."

This is the "tragic joy" imagined in one of Yeats's most powerful and troubling poems, "Lapis Lazuli." The joy it describes bears some similarity to the ecstasy of aesthetic affirmation present in Woolf's *Mrs. Dalloway*, where the terror and death "in the middle of my party" (*MD*, 179) is subsumed into the party's affirmative buoyancy. But in Woolf there is no element of will or ego and no love of conflict; Yeats had little interest in describing "the world seen without a self" (*TW*, 287). Notable commentators such as Harold Bloom have confessed their uneasiness in reading this poem,[71] but its radical assertions entirely obey the ontology of conflict that underwrites all of Yeats's "modern" poetry. The context for the poem includes the mounting political crisis in Europe in the mid-1930s; Hitler had just annexed the Rhineland, and Mussolini was bombing Abyssinia with mustard gas. But Yeats had fastidious convictions about the ways in which politics should infiltrate literature. In 1928, he wrote a letter to Sean O'Casey explaining his rejection of O'Casey's *The Silver Tassie* for the Abbey Theatre:

> The mere greatness of the world war has thwarted you; it has refused to become mere background, and obtrudes itself upon the stage as so much dead wood that will not burn with the dramatic fire. Dramatic action is a fire that must burn up everything but itself. . . . Among the things that dramatic action must burn up are the author's opinions; while he is writing he has no business to know anything that is not a portion of that action. (*LY*, 741)

He returned to this same issue later in his journal:

> The war, as O'Casey has conceived it is an equivalent for those primary qualities brought down by Berkeley's secret society, it stands outside the characters, it is not part of their expression, it is that very attempt denounced by Mallarmé to build as if with brick and mortar within the pages of a book. The English critics feel differently, to them a theme that "bulks largely in the news" gives dignity to human nature, even raises it to international importance. We on the other hand are certain that nothing can give dignity to human nature but the character and energy of its expression. We do not even ask that it shall have dignity so long as it can burn away all that is not itself.[72]

At first we may think that we know what Yeats is saying: political opinion has no place in literature as either rhetoric or theory. What matters is the integrity of dramatic action and the power of character; these don't need to be artificially inflated by parading them into a grand historical context. But there is a slippage here between Yeats's philosophy of literature and his ontology. This becomes audible in the repeated use of the word "mere," which simultaneously evokes diminishment and singularity. The "mere" greatness of the war suggests that its *only* meaningful quality is its greatness; it should only be evaluated aesthetically, in terms of its immensity and power. As such it should become, in a work of art, "mere background"—a quantum of force against which character defines itself, the historical particularly of which is a matter of indifference.[73]

War is the "background" of "Lapis Lazuli" but also the theme. And in this poem no distinction can be made between war as a historical event that may or may not enter a poem (under whatever conditions it *should* enter) and war as the ontological "background" of life outside of the poem, toward which the poem points:

> I have heard that hysterical women say
> They are sick of the palette and fiddle-bow,
> Of poets that are always gay,
> For everybody knows or else should know
> That if nothing drastic is done
> Aeroplane and Zeppelin will come out,
> Pitch like King Billy bomb-balls in
> Until the town lie beaten flat.
>
> All perform their tragic play,
> There struts Hamlet, there is Lear,
> That's Ophelia, that Cordelia;
> Yet they, should the last scene be there,
> The great stage curtain about to drop,
> If worthy their prominent part in the play,
> Do not break up their lines to weep.
> They know that Hamlet and Lear are gay;
> Gaiety transfiguring all that dread.
> All men have aimed at, found and lost;
> Black out; Heaven blazing into the head:
> Tragedy wrought to its uttermost.
> Though Hamlet rambles and Lear rages,
> And all the drop scenes drop at once
> Upon a hundred thousand stages,
> It cannot grow by an inch or an ounce.

(CPY, 294)

The dramatic framing of the work of art is reaching out into the world and figuring *it*. Our response to war should derive from the best metaphor we have for understanding life: "All perform their tragic play." The comprehensiveness of the metaphor yields astonishing identifications: the "pitch[ing]" of "King Billy bomb-balls" is linked to "[t]he great stage curtain about to drop" and "all the drop scenes drop at once"; "Black out; Heaven blazing into the head" evokes not only the extinguishing of stage lights but the strategic blackouts in London during the Great War to escape the destruction caused by zeppelin raids. (Yeats lived in London for periods of the war.) Both identifications erase the distinction between art and life.

The poem is not suggesting that war is "tragic," in either the casual or Aristotelean sense of that term. The former would presume that there is an order of life that is not tragic, the latter that our primary response should be distress or pity. But in the poem's vision, war is only one particularly visible manifestation of life conceived as tragic drama. This is why, in the poem's terms, no matter how many "drop scenes" appear on innumerable "stages," and by implication, how many bombs are dropping, "[i]t" — tragedy — "cannot grow by an inch or an ounce," because the whole is comprehensively tragic. To receive the tidings of war as "hysterical women" do — to believe that something "drastic" must "be done" to prevent it — is to mistake war for an exceptional condition. But "[a]ll men," the poem insists, "have aimed at, found and lost." That is the comprehensive tragic reality. War merely accelerates that process. "The innocent and beautiful," as Yeats writes in "In Memory of Eva Gore-Booth and Con Markievicz," "[h]ave no enemy but time" (233).

But the passion at stake here is joy, not anger. Or rather, it is "rage" that has so completely consolidated and directed the self's energies (just as the play *King Lear* is consolidated into "Lear rages") that they become "gaiety." Harold Bloom and David Bromwich have asked what evidence we have that "Hamlet and Lear are gay," and of course we have none.[74] This is mere assertion, as are the lines "All things fall and are built again, / And those that build them again are gay." Bloom juxtaposes to this a passage from Nehemiah: "Then I said unto them, Ye see the distress we are now in, how Jerusalem lieth waste, and the gates thereof are burned with fire: come, and let us build up the wall of Jerusalem, that we be no more a reproach."[75] The accent of judgment and humiliation is never lost in Nehemiah. And this is why Yeats, as he accentuates his agonistic ontology at the expense of any Christian or secular vision of responsibility, judgment, and mourning, falters when trying "to hold in a single thought reality and justice" (AV, 25). We have already mistaken the meaning of this famous line if we assume that "justice" means the inauguration of that which "should be" in relation to what "is" — "reality." As Hazel Adams has argued, Yeatsian "justice" is drawn from Anaximander; it means the proper balance of warring opposites rather than the harmony of differences.[76]

Yeats is not inclined, as Woolf was, to fold self-criticism into his aesthetic affirmations of violence. (Recall her resistance to Cobden-Sanderson's suggestion that "Englishmen and Germans blowing each other's heads off in the trenches . . . were conspiring 'to create the great emotions,' " or her mistrust of weaving the bombing "aeroplanes" into the "harmony" of the gramophone in *Between the Acts*.) And Yeats refuses to make the distinction between Necessity and History so important to Auden's later Christian (and secular) poetics. History, according to Auden, is the element of freedom and responsibility, transgression and justice, and should not be conflated with the fateful processes of Nature. Yeats's tragic vision collapses history into natural necessity, which means no distinction can be drawn between war as a historical event and conflict and loss as ontological conditions. He wants to convert all Homeric grief into Homeric joy—what he called the "abounding glittering jet" of "life's own self-delight" in Homer's poetry (200)—and in doing so he converts the fatefully inevitable into the fatefully desirable. There can be no justice within the logic of tragic joy, then, because justice, like remorse, requires a distinction between *is* and *ought*, and tries to wrangle the former into conformity with the latter. The outrageous piety of tragic joy refuses to blaspheme the forces of annihilation by suggesting that either they or the self negotiating them should have done otherwise. Yeats has no place for Lear's "I have ta'en / Too little care of this!" or for the idea that tragic rage could become an experience of exposure, which might in turn become an imperative for justice: "Expose thyself to feel what wretches feel, / That thou mayst shake the superflux to them, / And show the heavens more just."[77] Yeats wants a Lear, in other words, without remorse.[78]

It is easier to affirm tragic joy from a broad, ontological perspective, to climb, like Yeats's "men" at the end of "Lapis Lazuli," to a mountaintop, call for "mournful melodies," and "stare" on "all the tragic scene" (295). "Their ancient, glittering eyes are gay," but their gaiety may not be Lear's. Yeats wrote, in a letter describing the gift of the carving that appeared in the poem, that it modeled "[t]he heroic cry in the midst of despair. But no, I am wrong, the cast has its solutions always and therefore knows nothing of tragedy. It is we, not the east, that must raise the heroic cry" (*LY*, 837). Their gaiety, then, may be ascetic gaiety—the Buddha's smiling levity—achieved through the "solutions" that provide them access to transcendence. For Yeats this Eastern ascetic, like the Christian "saint," has "renounced Experience itself" by becoming a detached spectator perched on a mountaintop.

Tragic joy, then, must be earned from the inside rather than the outside, from the actor's rather than the spectator's position. But this requires not only the abstract affirmation of the world in its violent splendor but also the affirmation of the history of one's own life as the world has detailed it. Nietzsche saw this and formulated his doctrine of eternal return, which is not so much a metaphysical theory as a test of the will's joyful abundance. In *The Gay Science,* Nietzsche devises this test:

> What, if some day or night a demon were to steal after you into your loneliest loneliness and say to you: "This life as you now live it and have lived it, you will have to live once more and innumerable times more; and there will be nothing new in it, but every pain and every joy and every thought and sigh and everything inutterably small or great in your life will have to return to you, all in the same succession and sequence—even this spider and this moonlight between the trees, and even this moment and I myself. The eternal hourglass of existence is turned upside down again and again, and you with it, speck of dust!"
>
> Would you not throw yourself down and gnash your teeth and curse the demon who spoke thus? Or have you once experienced a tremendous moment when you would have answered him: "You are a god and never have I heard anything more divine" . . . [H]ow well disposed would you have to become to yourself and to life *to crave nothing more fervently* than this ultimate eternal confirmation and seal?[79]

Nietzsche would later call this "the highest formula of affirmation that can possibly be attained," the expression of "the *affirmative* pathos *par excellence.*"[80] Here the impulse to theodicy is usurped and converted into a test of the will. It is a kind of affirmative parody of Leibniz's "best of all possible worlds," now de-moralized and untethered from God's providential agency. Only the will can say, "And it was good." To will the eternal repetition of every detail of one's life is to internalize the workings of fortune, or, in Zarathustra's language, to "recreate all 'it was' into a 'thus I willed it.'"[81]

Nietzsche's test is implicit in Yeats's great poem "Dialogue of Self and Soul," which manifests the difficult alternation between ascetic transcendence and pagan immanence that we saw in "Vacillation." It is not truly a dialogue. Soul asks questions and engages Self directly, but Self does not condescend to respond. His tactic, rather, is to use Soul's images and terms against him, by either transvaluing them, so that what seems undesirable becomes desirable, or by appropriating them to accomplish Soul's ends passionately rather than ascetically. Soul travels the negative way of ascent, out of thought and into what Henry Vaughan called "the deep but dazzling darkness" in God. It does not propose a conversation but a spiritual practice: "I summon you to the winding ancient stair," to the "steep ascent" toward "that quarter where all thought is done: / Who can distinguish darkness from the soul?" (CPY, 234). Self matches antiquity with antiquity; his chosen image is not the winding stair but "Sato's ancient blade," emblematical, as Soul complains, "of love and war" (235).

As in "Vacillation," where "Soul," seeking "Isaiah's" purifying "coal," is "struck dumb by the simplicity of fire," the very logic of Soul's negative way evacuates the authority of language, rendering him speechless:

Such fullness in that quarter overflows
And falls into the basin of the mind
That man is stricken deaf and dumb and blind,
For intellect no longer knows
Is from *Ought*, or *Knower* from the *Known*—
That is to say, ascends to Heaven;
Only the dead can be forgiven;
But when I think of that my tongue's a stone.

(235)

"Consciousness is conflict," Yeats wrote, and without the oppositions of is and ought, knower and known, intellect is extinguished.[82] "Fullness" becomes hard to distinguish from emptiness; everything is no-thing. (This is implicit in the pause required by the line break in the draft: "And knowing everything knows nought / of the 'is' & of the 'ought.'")[83] But Self doesn't denounce the project of unifying is and ought or knower and known. Rather, he wants "Unity of Being" instead of ascent to nonbeing, which is the only way Yeats can finally conceptualize ascetic spirituality. The "dancer" in Yeats's poetry accomplishes this in her provisional way, but Self's final monologue proposes a way to render this unity absolute:

My Self. A living man is blind and drinks his drop.
    What matter if the ditches are impure?
    What matter if I live it all once more?
    Endure that toil of growing up;
    The ignominy of boyhood; the distress
    Of boyhood changing into man;
    The unfinished man and his pain
    Brought face to face with his own clumsiness . . .

. . . I am content to live it all again
    And yet again, if it be life to pitch
    Into the frog-spawn of a blind man's ditch,
    A blind man battering blind men;
    Or into that most fecund ditch of all,
    The folly that man does
    Or must suffer, if he woos
    A proud woman not kindred of his soul.

I am content to follow to its source
Every event in action or in thought;
Measure the lot; forgive myself the lot!
When such as I cast out remorse
So great a sweetness flows into the breast
We must laugh and we must sing,
We are blest by everything,
Everything we look upon is blest.

(235–236)

Self refuses the constraint of dumbness but accepts Soul's "blindness." Blindness undergoes, however, an aggressive transvaluation: it is no longer Soul's restorative darkness but a condition of confusion and collision. Oedipus's blindness is the model. As John Jones writes, blindness is the paradigmatic metaphysical state for the Sophocles that Yeats admired and translated: "All men . . . are teleologically blind."[84] If blindness can be redeemed, it will not be through Soul's beatific vision — "that is to say, ascends to heaven" — but through the "Black out; Heaven blazing into the head" of "Lapis Lazuli."

Yet the casual diction — "A living man is blind and drinks his drop" — strips that model of any unearned tragic dignity it might assume through the association. Nietzsche's test is audible here — "I am content to live it all again / And yet again," and the demands of the test are made plain. To will this repetition requires one to assent to all the "ignominy," shame, and "impur[ity]" it will bring in its train. Even "fecundity," a word that evokes the abundance of a world that, in the language of "Vacillation," "consumes what it renews," is charged with repugnance. The generative principle is imaged as "frog-spawn," not as the "great-rooted blossomer" of "Among School Children" (217).

This means that the heroic act of joyful affirmation has to assimilate the nonheroic, or everything that is closer to comedy or farce than tragedy. "Passive suffering is not a theme for poetry," but Self chronicles this suffering — puberty, social humiliation, romantic "folly" — in all its passive "clumsiness." The inclusion of all these ignominious ingredients, however, positions the will to overcome much more than a presently immovable object. If "joy is of the will . . . which overcomes obstacles," there is no more intractable obstacle than the shame of past experience. Thus the will moves backward in imagination and consents to "live it all again."

In doing so the will accomplishes through passion what for Soul can only be accomplished ascetically. One's life, as Kierkegaard said, can only become an object of knowledge when one is no longer its subject. But here, in Soul's language yet without its means, the "knower" becomes identical with the "known"—Self knows its past life while simultaneously willing it forward again and again. "Ought" collapses into "is," not in a New Jerusalem where there is no gap between justice and reality, but in the self's refusal to believe that life would have been better had it been different. Yet Self cannot completely extricate itself from the ascetic imagination. The poem, as I have argued, allows Soul to frame both the terms of abjection (what Stevens would call "poverty") and the salvation demanded by it. The "crime of birth and death," the rhetoric of sacred purity ("consecrated blade"), the gaps between "is" and "ought" and "knower" and "known," the imagery of blindness, and the necessity of "forgiveness"—Self accepts these terms as points of embarkation. If Stevens proposed three modes of secularization—the adaptation, substitution, and elimination of theological concepts—it might seem that this poem employs all three as it fashions pagan means to accomplish essentially ascetic ends. But Yeats seeks a sacred secularity; thus, at his most aggressive, he struggles toward what Nietzsche calls "transvaluation," where values once derided as "secular" or "worldly" are rehabilitated. The "soldier's right" to "commit the crime" of birth and death "once more" becomes a new affirmation as the rhetoric of criminality is absorbed and inverted.

But the affirmation is not as aggressive as it might seem. Self's final monologue relinquishes the martial rhetoric of its earlier lines. For Nietzsche, eternal return marked a complete victory over what he called the "moral interpretation of . . . existence"[85]—the tyranny of *ought* over *is*—disseminated by Christianity. Yeats remains within the Christian dispensation. Nietzsche's will to repeat is a refusal to subject the world to the moral criteria invented by the unhappy self, but for Yeats the will to repeat requires a will to "forgive."[86] The poem thus returns us to the scene of "remorse," that moral impediment to the flow of joyful becoming. What is being repeated, then, is not merely one's life as detailed by fortune, but also as detailed by one's own compromised responsibility.

There is also a tension between the joy generated by the will and the source assigned to joy in the final stanza. On the one hand, "[j]oy is of the will," and without its comprehensive affirmation everything would remain as it appears to the Soul: impurity, the "crime of birth and death." It is also the will, paradoxically, that assumes the prerogative to "forgive" and "cast out remorse." On the other hand, the state of blessedness is syntactically passive, just as it is in "Vacillation"; this is not Oedipus who, as Yeats says, changed kingdoms "according to his blessing and cursing" (AV, 29). "We *must* laugh and we *must* sing" suggests an irresistible external force, and the final chiasmus ("We are blessed by everything; / Everything we look upon is blessed") leaves the speaker, as Helen Vendler has noted, "a receiver, rather than a source, of the great sweetness which has flowed into his breast."[87] We are back to the incongruity in "Vacillation" between a model of joy as an experience of self-emptying and external grace and joy as an act of the will. Thus in the very poem where Yeats is developing the most aggressively Nietzschean modes of tragic affirmation, he remains dependent on a Christian imagination of forgiveness and grace that yields the community and reciprocity embodied in the circularity of the final chiasmus.

THE ONTOLOGY OF CONFLICT AND
THE AMBIVALENCE OF VIOLENCE

Edward Said characterized the "secular attitude" as "a sense of history and of human production."[88] He meant that secular consciousness is particularly attuned to the ways human beings build their own historical existence; it looks for causes and explanations in economic, social, and political motives and activity rather than in spiritual or religious agencies or forces. The "secular attitude" is therefore a distinctly ethical attitude insofar as it holds humans responsible for the history they build, and since it discards concepts such as Fate or Providence, it invests them with the agency to change this history. I discuss this "sense" at length in my chapter on Auden, who contends that Western secularism shares this attitude with the Judaism and Christianity out of which it arose. I mention it here to emphasize its gradual diminishment in "Nineteen Hundred and Nineteen," a poem that, by its very title, is invested in a specific history. The poem is exemplary because it dramatizes the tension between Said's "sense" of history and another "secular attitude": the affirmation of immanence. Both are this-worldly rather than other-worldly imperatives. In "Nineteen Hundred and Nineteen," the will to say "yes" to the generative force of the world—irrespective of the potentially violent form it takes—is a will to resist the ascetic temptations of spiritual and moral transcendence. Yet this very affirmation steadily rehabilitates the sense of fatefulness the secular view of history means to renounce. The poem expresses moral outrage. But such outrage requires an understanding of human beings as responsible historical agents, and historical agency in this (ostensibly historical) poem is perpetually subsumed into a deeper ontological current of conflictual "will and energy." The poem vacillates between outrage and the exhilarating possibility of "riding" this current.

"Nineteen Hundred and Nineteen" is Yeats's most powerful political poem. It is also, perhaps, his most disingenuous. Michael Wood, who dedicated a beautiful book to the poem, has heard in the first line—"Many ingenious lovely

things are gone"—a specter of "ingenuous." This ingenuousness is characterized as a credulity that has taken a semblance of reality. The poem thus develops
its derisive analogy between public attachment to civic ideals and childish
attachment to "pretty toys" because "[t]he rule of law, lack of corruption, habits
of justice, a society informed by mature public opinion. . . . We didn't have
them, only their simulacra; we had only the illusion of having them."[89] The
mockery of the early sections of the poem exposes this social blindness and self-
satisfaction, and Yeats numbers himself among the deceived.

This reading of ingenuousness is only plausible, however, if one assumes
that Yeats is particularly concerned with the moral gap between ideals and realities. But this assumption partakes of the very distinction between ought and is
that Yeats has struggled to collapse. I want to suggest, on the contrary, that the
early sections of the poem are most remarkable not for the ingenuousness they
deride, but for the strange disingenuousness of Yeats's identification with the
humiliated progressive whose hopes have been exposed as fantastical. What is
most noticeable in the first section is the unusual context for some of Yeats's
favored words:

> We too had many pretty toys when young;
> A law indifferent to blame or praise,
> To bribe or threat; habits that made old wrong
> Melt down, as it were wax in the sun's rays;
> Public opinion ripening for so long
> We thought it would outlive all future days.
> O what fine thought we had because we thought
> That the worst rogues and rascals had died out.
>
> (*CPY*, 207)

"Habit" usually evokes in Yeats nothing so abstractly republican as what Wood
calls "habits of justice"; rather, it is linked to aristocratic ceremoniousness or
peasant custom. So, in "A Prayer for My Daughter," also written in 1919, Yeats
famously hopes her future bridegroom will "bring her to a house / Where all's
accustomed, ceremonious," for "How but in custom and ceremony / Are innocence and beauty born?" (190). In his journal, he complains of the difficulty of
writing a national literature because the modern nation is global and bureau-
cratic rather than organic, and thus there is no "organism of habit—a race held
together by folk tradition" because "thought old enough to be a habit cannot
face modern life."[90] Indeed, nothing opposes habit for Yeats so much as
"opinion," a form of knowledge that is, unlike habit, inorganic, highly mediated, ideological, disembodied, and capricious. In "Prayer," Yeats would "let"

his daughter "think opinions are accursed," and "Michael Robartes and the Dancer," also roughly contemporary with "Nineteen," begins with the assertion that "[o]pinion is not worth a rush" (175).

Because these terms are incongruously yoked to the rhetoric of a progressive political vision, Yeats's affiliation with the "we" of this poem is suspect. His attachment to "ingenious lovely things" is uncontroversial, but we are unfamiliar with any Yeats who expected the progressive elimination of deviancy ("we thought / the worst rogues and rascals had died out") or who ever, as the fourth stanza has it, "pieced our thought into philosophy, / And planned to bring the world under a rule." Such piecing is disparaged in Yeats, as in *A Vision*, when he complains that Plato brings an end to all "antithetical" religion when he "thinks all things into a Unity" and, as the "First Christian," prepares the way for Christ, who discloses "[a] *primary* dispensation looking beyond itself towards a transcendent power that is dogmatic, leveling, unifying, feminine, humane, peace its means and end" (AV, 263). Condescension toward the "leveling," democratic quality of Christianity is evident in the "ingenious lovely things" that "seemed sheer miracle to the multitude": this multitude does not partake in the creation of loveliness but can only stand in passive awe before it. And when Yeats asks in the third stanza, "What matter that no cannon had been turned / Into a ploughshare?" the mockery springs not from the conviction that the culture's institutions have not conformed to its governing religious images, but from the speciousness of the images themselves. In Isaiah's eschatological vision, "[H]e shall judge among the nations, and shall rebuke many people: and they shall beat their swords into plowshares, and their spears into pruning hooks: nation shall not lift up sword against nation, neither shall they learn war anymore." But this sentiment, with "peace its means and end" (AV, 238), cannot possibly belong to Yeats; recall that in Martin's vision of heaven in *The Unicorn from the Stars*, the only music is the "sound of the clashing of the swords!" A discarded line from "The Circus Animals' Desertion," though written twenty years later— "cannon is the god and father of all"—has little room for ploughshares.[91] I do not want to depreciate one of the great modern political poems by suggesting that Yeats is fabricating emotions or insist that the voice of a particular poem cannot take on the persona of a mood that has become ubiquitous in the setting out of which it is being written. It is better to proceed by observing that there is an ambivalence *beneath* the derision as to which terms within the argument shall be allowed the decisive traction. In any case, the poem begins with a secular, liberal vision in which the forces of civility and justice are seen to be gradually eliminating violence from the world, yet this is the very violence that occasions the poem, and a violence Yeats has come to believe is necessary to his poetry.

Wood says, with precision, that the poem "tells two stories, the first about loss, the second about the folly of believing we ever had what we think we have lost."⁹² I think that the poem also yields two stories about violence. The first is that violence is to be dreaded as an affront to human flourishing, and thus is to be evaluated morally (and by implication, politically): it is enacted *in history* by agents infused with a responsibility that can be assumed or disavowed. (The importance of the "historical" element is elaborated in the chapter on Auden.) Yeats's attachment to that perspective, then, is not disingenuous but a residue of Christian conviction ("peace its means and end"), or of the liberal-progressive hope that borrows from Christian eschatology. When this perspective governs the poem, violence is particularized. It happens in a singular moment of history, "now"—"Now the days are dragon-ridden"—and to particular people, known to the poet and his friends—"a drunken soldiery / Can leave the mother, murdered at her door, / To crawl in her own blood."⁹³

The second story, however, abstracts violence into a cosmological force. In this story, violence is an intractable condition of being, or better, a condition of *becoming,* for which *being,* imaged aesthetically as the "mighty monuments" that cannot "stand," is the spurious philosophical dream. If violence is "evil," it is so only in the sense that Shelley, who lacked the "Vision of Evil," could not admit: he "could not conceive of the world as a continual conflict" (AV, 144). Even apocalyptic violence in Yeats is subsumed back into this ontological structure because the apocalyptic energies that would usher in something new are merely periodic; they do not truly harbor, as "Nineteen" proposes, "a rage / To end all things" but deliver, as *A Vision* makes clear, a return to the "antithetical," pagan mode of existence rather than the "primary," Christian mode. Because reality *is* antithetical—"Discord or War" is the "God of all and father of all"—and because the "primary" (the vision of transcendent good and peaceableness) is itself the antithetical mode *to* the antithetical, apocalyptic violence is not a final transformation of the world by a transcendent power but the disclosure, through its native means, of the world as it really is: a site of unending conflict.

Because conflict is the element, for Yeats, in which emotion and action become existentially valuable, a question emerges that frames the major tension of his apocalyptic poems: if conflict is the most venerable element in Yeats's ontology, what finally distinguishes the desirable violence of "Under Ben Bulben" ("Even the wisest man grows tense / With some sort of violence / Before he can accomplish fate" [CPY, 326]) or the "greatness" and "self-delight" of the "bitter and violent" men of "Meditations in a Time of Civil War" from the "incendiary or bigot" that would "burn that stump on the Acropolis" in "Nineteen Hundred and Nineteen" or the "rage-driven, rage-tormented, and rage-hungry troop" that "plung[e] towards nothing" in "Meditations" (200, 205)?[94] Good violence appears to be aristocratic, heroic, creative, and passionate, whereas bad violence is mass or lower-class, ideological, and destructive. But in Yeats's apocalyptic scenarios these criteria are blurred. In "The Second Coming" the "worst" are full of "passionate intensity"; in "Meditations" the "rage-driven" troop is honored with Homeric epithets and partakes of the passion that ennobles Yeats's Lear and Oedipus, and the will to destroy is affirmed by the words of the "conqueror" in "Vacillation": "let all things pass away." In "Nineteen Hundred and Nineteen" the distinctions are blurred in the poem's fluctuating emotional responses to the scene of violence, which shift from lamentation and moral indignation to an intoxicating awareness that historical violence is merely one repugnant conduit for those sublimely violent ontological forces that have been masked by the Christian or liberal narrative. This mood of apocalyptic excitement is not, I want to emphasize, mere pleasure in the spectacle of mayhem but a kind of joy at the prospect of absorbing this ontological power, just as Leda, in Yeats's famous poem, "put on" Zeus's "power" even as she submitted to his violence (214). "Nineteen Hundred and Nineteen," then, betrays a fundamental ambivalence about the violence it apparently abhors because it belongs to the circuitry of a world Yeats venerates.

This is evident in the mesmerizing second section, where the binary between chaotic violence and the fragility of aesthetic creation is displaced by a vision of aesthetic creation coalescing *with* that violence:

> When Loie Fuller's Chinese dancers enwound
> A shining web, a floating ribbon of cloth,
> It seemed that a dragon of air
> Had fallen among dancers, had whirled them round
> Or hurried them off on its own furious path;
> So the Platonic Year
> Whirls out new right and wrong,
> Whirls in the old instead;
> All men are dancers and their tread
> Goes to the barbarous clangour of a gong.
>
> (208)

The image of the dancer in Yeats's work manifests, as Frank Kermode showed in *Romantic Image*, that "Unity of Being" he so persistently sought. One "cannot tell the dancer from the dance" because the dance "reconciles antithetical movements: the division of soul and body, form and matter, life and death, artist and audience."[95] To these we might add, following Kermode, intention and performance, meaning and form. "Man can embody truth but he cannot know it," Yeats wrote in one of his last letters (*LY*, 922), and the dance is one of those embodiments. It figures that immanent paradise where the ignominy of being "composite" (as Michael Robartes puts it) is thrown off (*CPY*, 176).

This broader context for the dance makes its inclusion in "Nineteen Hundred and Nineteen" all the more startling. The poem, after all, is about the dissolution of the very "Unity of Being" that depends on what Yeats calls "Unity of Culture." "Nor did I understand," he writes in *Autobiographies*, "how little that Unity, however wisely sought, is possible without a Unity of Culture" and how the latter is, given the nature of modernity, "no longer possible at all" (*A*, 268). In the poem, this dissolution is effected by the violent abstraction of a nationalist ideology that would bully its meanings into historical form rather than remember the organic unity of ancient "habits," which embody the unity of culture as the dancer embodies the unity of being. So what kind of dance is this? The attention to Fuller's performance does not focus, as we might expect, on the bodies of the dancers but on their instruments. For Yeats, the virtue of the dance is that it appears, as Kermode notes, "self-begotten,"[96] but these instruments—"the ribbon[s] of cloth"—generate a spectacle in which the dancers *seem* conditioned, or passively "whirled," by the force of the "dragon of air." This opens onto the imagination of a cosmologically determining force— "the Platonic Year"—that similarly makes persons into tractable bodies obedient to external force. Yeats's "wind" is Stevens's "river"; like Stevens's ferryman in "The River of Rivers in Connecticut," the dancers cannot "bend against" the "propelling force" of this current of becoming (*CP*, 451). To arrive at this picture, however, the lines must mask their own activity. "Enwound" requires an object, but the object given—"a shining web"—is merely another image of the act of enwinding. The implication is that the dancers are themselves enwound, trapped in the web, even though their movements are required to create these effects. The distinction between the human agents and the magically reified force ("a dragon of air") is collapsed.

But dancing can never be passive. Even if it is directed by the dragon of air or, moments later, by the "barbarous clang of a gong," it still requires creative movement. This movement must be understood in relation to the lines the "dragon of air" recalls—"Now days are dragon-ridden, the nightmare / Rides upon sleep." There "ridden," in addition to the meaning of harassed or over-whelmed, points back to its literal sense: the dragon rides the days as the night-mare rides upon sleep. But in the second section the dance itself has become a kind of "ride," a patterned movement absorbing the whirling dragon that set them in motion; if the dragon rides the days, they ride the dragon. The dance cannot change the ultimate direction of this whirling, which carves "its own furious path," but it can concentrate its power and beauty. Passivity becomes passion. The dance figures an experience of being simultaneously overwhelmed and galvanized by a Dionysian energy that is ethically indifferent—it "whirl[s] out" both "right *and* wrong"—and makes no distinction between the "old" and the "new" because it is always both old and new; it is a force that indiscriminately makes new forms and then collapses them into its eternal state of monstrous creativity. Barbarity has been displaced from a particular historical moment—"a drunken soldiery"—onto an ontological register: the "barbarous clang" is merely the music of the energy of becoming, like the "music" of the "clashing of swords" that Martin hears in his heaven in *The Unicorn from the Stars*. With that displacement, the whole logic of aesthetic creation has shifted: it is no longer "master-work of intellect or hand," establishing its timeless *being* against the corrosive force of time, but a dance of *becoming* that absorbs the energy of the dragon's whirl.

That the dance is equally a ride becomes clearer in the transfiguration of the image of the swan in the following section. The image is initially ascetic. The cultivated casualness of the reference—"some moralist or mythological poet," "some Platonist"—suggests that this isn't an influence but a point of resistance. The sensibility of the image is composite, and Yeats uses another version of it in "The Tower," but the main source is likely Plato's *Phaedo* (*On the Soul*), the book that recounts the serenity of Socrates's death. Socrates compares himself to a swan, telling Simmias that swans do not sing lamentations at their death but rather sing more beautifully than ever because they, like Socrates, "are departing into the presence of the god whose servants they are."[97] The swan with which Yeats begins, then, is an image of the soul's flight out of the confused intricacies of the world ("the labyrinth he has made / In art or politics"), into a state of solitude uncomplicated by the soul's worldly entanglements—a heaven of pure moral simplicity.

The speaker, however, is only satisfied by the swan image "if a troubled mirror show it"

> Before that brief gleam of its life be gone,
> An image of its state;
> The wings half spread for flight,
> The breast thrust out in pride
> Whether to play, or to ride
> Those winds that clamour of approaching night.
>   (CPY, 208)

These lines convert vertical ascent into aesthetic "play"; the swan does not fly but "ride[s]." This is not Plato's swan but an image analogous to the disguised Zeus ravaging Leda, which already performs what it produces: Leda's eggs, out of which come "Love" and "War" (AV, 288). The image evokes pure frozen activity ("wings half spread") rather than the purifying stasis of death. As such it both crystallizes and produces passion: "The swan has leaped into the desolate heaven: / That image can bring wildness, bring a rage / To end all things, to end / What my laborious life imagined." The rage, like the dance, is a self-unifying "wildness"; it dismantles "Adam's Curse," that humiliating gap between labor and creation that the aesthetic artifact struggles to mask. It mirrors the rage that Yeats finds in Oedipus, which he juxtaposes to Christ's "abstract" compassion: "He raged against his sons, and this rage was noble, not from some general idea . . . but because it seemed to contain all life." And like that of Oedipus, this "rage / To end all things" is apocalyptic, self-unifying, and finally sacred: "He knew nothing but his mind, and yet because he spoke that mind possessed it and kingdoms changed according to his blessing and cursing. Delphi, that rock at earth's navel, spoke through him" (AV, 28). Rage paradoxically affirms the secular world—"earth's navel"—by refusing to deny and transcend it. As an expression of the world's resistance to human desire, rage is a modality of the same feeling that generates ascetic discontent, but it does not take a position over against the world; rather, the center of the world "sp[eaks] through" it.

The wind that the swan rides coalesces, in the final section of the poem, into a kind of opaque revelation:

Violence upon the roads: violence of horses;
Some few have handsome riders, are garlanded
On delicate sensitive ear or tossing mane,
But wearied running round and round in their courses
All break and vanish, and evil gathers head:
Herodias' daughters have returned again,
A sudden blast of dusty wind and after
Thunder of feet, tumult of images,
Their purpose in the labyrinth of the wind;
And should some crazy hand dare touch a daughter
All turn with amorous cries, or angry cries,
According to the wind, for all are blind.

(CPY, 210)

This wind brings passionate gods, "Herodias' daughters," who are figures of the wind borrowed from Yeats's earlier poetry, which in turn borrows from Irish myth. Yeats notes of "The Hosting of the Sidhe," the opening poem of *The*

Wind in the Reeds, "The gods of ancient Ireland . . . still ride the country as of old. Sidhe is also Gaelic for wind, and certainly the Sidhe have much to do with the wind. They journey in whirling wind, the winds that were called the dance of the daughters of Herodias in the Middle Ages, Herodias doubtless taking the place of some old goddess" (454). The poem is worth quoting in full given its connection to "Nineteen Hundred and Nineteen":

> The host is riding from Knocknarea
> And over the grave of Clooth-na-Bare;
> Caolite tossing his burning hair,
> And Niamh calling *Away, come away:*
> *Empty your heart of its mortal dream.*
> *The winds awaken, the leaves whirl round,*
> *Our cheeks are pale, our hair is unbound,*
> *Our breasts are heaving, our eyes are agleam,*
> *Our arms are waving, our lips are apart;*
> *And if any gaze on our rushing band,*
> *We come between him and the deed of his hand,*
> *We come between him and the hope of his heart.*
> The host is rushing 'twixt night and day,
> And where is there hope or deed as fair?
> Caolite tossing his burning hair,
> And Niamh calling, *Away, come away.*
>
> (55)

The early poem is a summons to flight ("*away, come away*"), a summons compelled by observations similar to those in "Nineteen Hundred and Nineteen": the power of these wind-gods will bring both action ("*the deed of his hand*") and aspiration ("*the hope of his heart*") to grief, just as in "Nineteen Hundred and Nineteen" they wreck everything "my laborious life had imagined." The wind in the early poem seduces, in the later poem it devastates; in both it is invested with a power knowable aesthetically. This is explicit in "Hosting" ("where is there hope or deed as fair?"), implicit in "Nineteen Hundred and Nineteen" (the sublime "dragon of air"). The summons to flight in "Hosting" is a call to cast off "mortal dream" and "rid[e]" with the "host" hovering over the world. In "Nineteen Hundred and Nineteen," the wind-gods are not figures of euphoric immortality hovering above the world of experience, more dreamlike than "mortal dream"; they are the very principle of reality, figurations of the world's violent motion, which "gathe[r] head" at its center rather than on its occult margins. Dreams are razed ("O but we dreamed to mend / Whatever mischief seemed / To afflict mankind"), not by a higher transcendence but by a darker, secular immanence. The effects of this immanent force are encountered everywhere: the winds evoked in the early poem "are called the dance of the daughters of Herodias," but in the later "all men are dancers."

The transfigured residues of "The Hosting of the Sidhe" in "Nineteen Hundred and Nineteen" reflect the broader shifts in Yeats's paganism in the first decades of the twentieth century: it is rinsed of sentimentality and otherworldliness, i.e., rendered more "secular." But the more immanent and the more ontological these divine forces become, the more unsettling they are to the reader, for it is hard to discern whether the principal emotion they evoke is horror or longing, or whether the action they quicken is resistance or play. What we know for sure is Yeats's eye is on them rather than on their particular historical manifestations. In the final section history again gives way to cosmology. The first line, as it meets the eye in isolation—"Violence upon the roads: violence of horses"—is terrifying because it infuses objects that orient and familiarize (roads and horses) with abstraction (what kind of violence?), anonymity (which roads?), and agential confusion (are there riders?). The speaker initially reaches for categories of martial and aesthetic power to render the "violence" intelligible— "Some few have handsome riders, are garlanded / On delicate sensitive ear or tossing mane"—but the attempt at a stable portrait is overwhelmed and scrambled ("All break and vanish"), then yields to a broader violence behind it: the return of Herodias's daughters, a sign of "evil gather[ing] head."

But what sort of evil is this? In "The Hosting" the dance of the daughters is power and beauty superseding worldly deed and aspiration; in "Nineteen" it is an image of directionless violence. It may be that these associations coalesce. "Thunder of feet" links the "violence of horses" to the dance of the daughters. We hear of "their purpose," but as Michael Wood has noted, the syntax surrounding this is slyly confusing: do the "blast," "thunder," and "tumult" collectively constitute their obscure purpose, or is it manifest "after" they pass? Is the purpose malicious or revelatory? Regardless, says Wood, there is "the naming of a purpose when purpose can't really be identified."[98] At the very least, "purpose" has been divested of theological and certainly moral direction, for the daughters, like Oedipus and the "Self" of "Dialogue," are "blind." The only "purpose" they reveal is that there are two modalities to the world: love and war. Their dance is composed of this opposition: if some "crazy hand" reaches for them, their response is either "amorous" or "angry," "according to the wind," which is arbitrary in its whirling.

This arbitrariness may be the sign of an underlying "indifference," a refusal to submit passionate activity to empirical motive, as in Yeats's portrait, in

A *Vision*, of Salomé, the most famous of Herodias's daughters. There Yeats writes, "When I think of the moment before revelation I think of Salomé—she, too, delicately tinted or maybe mahogany dark—dancing before Herod and receiving the Prophet's head in her indifferent hands, and wonder if what seems to us decadence was not in reality the exaltation of the muscular flesh and of civilisation perfectly achieved" (AV, 273). There is an astonishing link, then, between the "barbarous clangour" of "Nineteen" and "civilization perfectly achieved," as if the barbarous act of calling for John the Baptist's head were a manifestation of the dancer's high indifference, which is characterized in *Resurrection* as the gods' "eternal possession of themselves," and which is visible, as I have argued, in Yeats's airman. The moral dualism preached by "the Prophet" cannot touch the gratuitous self-possession of the dance.

But the final section of "Nineteen" discloses a horror that cannot submit to this passionate suspension of the ethical. Yeats speculates, in his notes on "The Hosting of the Sidhe," that the association of Herodias's daughters with the wind was a substitution for "some old goddess" in "the Middle Ages," and this layering of New Testament narrative and Irish myth generates an ethical ambivalence. The theological figuration of the dancing daughters inevitably embeds the outrage implicit in the New Testament account of Salomé's dance, where it is an aesthetic seduction that precipitates a moral disaster. Yeats knew, moreover, that Herodias was widely considered a supernatural witch-leader in medieval Europe, and he had heard the stories of witch processions on the evening of the religious feast of St. John the Baptist.[99]

Why does this matter? The mood of the entire last section depends on the evocation of witchcraft. It is a rare moment in Yeats: the world of Irish folk belief and occult practice is summoned not as a stronghold of enchantment against the acids of modernity, or as a resource for gnostic systems, but as the domain of illicit passion as we know it from Christian rhetoric. "Evil gathers head" conjures the demonic rather than the daemonic; this is a "Vision of Evil" with more ethical charge than the conception of the "world as continual conflict." The stunning final lines confirm this vision of occult evil:

> But now wind drops, dust settles; thereupon
> There lurches past, his great eyes without thought
> Under the shadow of stupid straw-pale locks,
> That insolent fiend Robert Artisson
> To whom the love-lorn Lady Kyteler brought
> Bronzed peacock feathers, red combs of her cocks.
>
>   (CPY, 210)

These characters are known in the annals of witchcraft. The historical Lady Kyteler was a high-born Irishwoman condemned as a witch in 1324. "That insolent fiend Robert Artisson" was her incubus, and as such should have been her servant, but he seduced her into his service. There is a cautionary tale latent in this image with an unmistakable class dimension, though it is often ignored by critics.[100]

Just as the occult surfaces, in this section, as danger rather than as gnosis, Artisson is a travesty of distinctly Yeatsian virtues. He is mindless—his "great eyes" protrude "without thought" from "[u]nder the shadow of stupid straw-pale locks." That may seem simple enough, but Yeats's paganism consistently opposes what it takes to be the tyranny of mind in the primary, Christian dispensation, which "declared that thought and not the warring opposites created the world." In "The Statues," Pythagoras's sculptures are praised for their "empty eyeballs," which "knew that knowledge increases unreality," and in the prose draft for the poem Yeats writes, "empty faces . . . measure Pythagorean perfection . . . only that which is incapable of show is infinite in passion."[101] Michael Robartes, speaking to his dancer, insists that "God, in portioning wine and bread" gave man "His mere body" rather than "His thought"; he admonishes her to "banish every thought" in order to "[l]ive in uncomposite blessedness" (176). Artisson approaches this aesthetic condition as its moral negative. His "insolence" is a half step away from the willful audacity that Yeats admires in his tragic heroes, and his "lurch[ing]" is the most purposeful activity in a poem where persons are otherwise moved by the wind. He emerges, in fact, out of the only stillness of the poem: "wind drops; dust settles." Out of this silence, like Caesar's in "Long-legged Fly" but without his dignity, his "eyes" are "fixed upon nothing" (339).

Just as Artisson's mindlessness cannot be assimilated to Yeats's thoughtless dancer, the poem cannot finally subsume the evil gathering head into the vision of the world as continual conflict. "Nineteen Hundred and Nineteen" still needs the abstract, primary "mind" and the moral thought that waits, in the language from *Autobiographies* quoted at the beginning of this chapter, for that which lies "beyond." Yeats never, in fact, ceases to oscillate back toward that mind. He knows that passionate "play" in the whirl of ontological violence can be characterized in another way: losing one's mind in the mob. When his "rage-driven" troop cries, in "Meditations," for "Vengeance," he is caught up in their cry: "I, my wits astray / Because of all that senseless tumult, all but cried / For vengeance" (206). This is "tumult" on the ground. Its senselessness can't be seen from the "tumult in the clouds" that his airman seeks, or while riding the "dragon of air."

George Orwell said of Auden's "Spain 1937," "Mr. Auden's brand of amor-
alism is only possible if you are somewhere else when the trigger is pulled."[102]
Yeats never counseled, as Auden did, "the necessary murder" (*EA*, 425). Yet
there is a sense in which his ontology of conflict is always "somewhere else,"
and when it takes shape in history he is appalled by its form. At these moments,
in the language of "Meditations," "eyes that rage has brightened, arms it has
made lean, / Give place to an indifferent multitude, / Give place to brazen
hawks" (*CPY*, 206). Yeats's own vocabulary turns against him: here is the historical reality of passionate "indifference" as mythologized in Zeus, Salomé, or the
airman, and "rage" divested of mind-unifying brightness. While it is a testament
to Yeats's generosity that he can "change" a "drunken, vainglorious lout" into a
tragic hero in "Easter, 1916" (181), it is, perhaps, a testament to the honesty of his
"gentle, sensitive," and critical "mind"—the very half-Christian, half-secular
mind scorned in "Ego Dominus Tuus"—that he can dramatize the incongruity
between the passionate violence that seduced his imagination and the corrosive
violence that appears in the actual world.

One of Yeats's greatest last poems leaves us, in fact, with a scene of violence
that cannot be assimilated to joyful conflict. "Man and the Echo" is tormented
by the question of who pulled the trigger:

> Did that play of mine send out
> Certain men the English shot?
> Did words of mine put too great strain
> On that woman's reeling brain?
> Could my spoken words have checked
> That whereby a house lay wrecked?

> (345)

These questions, as representative anxieties within "[a]ll that I have said
and done," return the reader to the "remorse" of both "Vacillation" and
"Dialogue of Self and Soul." But the measure taken to contest remorse in
those poems—the joyful willing of "whatever happens"—meets resistance
here. The man asks his echo: "O rocky voice, / Shall we in that great night
rejoice?," but the poem ends abruptly with an event that cannot be subsumed
into tragic joy:

> Up there some hawk or owl has struck
> Dropping out of sky or rock
> A stricken rabbit is crying out
> And its cry distracts my thought.

> (346)

No pity is acknowledged; we are left with the simple dissonance of a violent detail that "distracts" the will to affirm.

"Some hawk or owl," not the ascetic swan of "[s]ome moralist or mytholog-ical poet" or "[s]ome Platonist." Only "empty heart[s]" project, Yeats says, as the Platonists and Christians do, a moral world that lies "beyond their minds." But Yeats, even in moments when he is defending passion's mask, seems to acknowl-edge that this mask is motivated by something beyond it:

> I think that all happiness depends on the energy to assume the mask of some other self; that all joyous or creative life is a rebirth as something not oneself, something which has no memory and is created in a moment and perpetu-ally renewed. We put on a grotesque or solemn face to hide us from the ter-rors of judgment, invent an imaginative Saturnalia where one forgets reality, a game like that of a child, where one loses the infinite pain of self-realization. Perhaps all the sins and energies of the world are but its flight from an infi-nite blinding beam. (A, 372)

The battle against "modern subjectivity" and its Christian prototype is muddied here; the mask only creates because it first evades a psychological truth. And what it evades is not, as Nietzsche thought, the meaninglessness of existence as revealed by modern science,[103] but the "terrors of judgment" experienced in the "infinite blinding beam." "Self-realization" is less a contin-gent value of modern subjectivity, more an inescapable knowledge of moral answerability. This is perhaps the only passage in Yeats where "sin" is paired with "energy."

If "Man and the Echo" acknowledges a violence outside the affirmations of tragic joy, another late poem, "The Circus Animals' Desertion," chastens the passionate subjectivity in which it is based by acknowledging its basis in self-"flight." The confessional subjectivity of "The Circus Animals' Desertion" could not be more Christian; the poem removes the mask and exposes Yeats's pagan myths to the infinite blinding beam. It reimagines the poet's own mythic landscape as precisely a child's "game"—a grubby "Saturnalia" populated by circus animals—and understands these fantastical projections as forms of self-evasion that in another context would be called idolatry: "Players and painted stage took all my love / And not those things they were emblems of" (CPY, 347). The mask, Yeats says, counters the judgments of remorse by having "no memory," and the poem condenses this operation into a formula: "Character isolated by a deed / To engross the present and dominate memory" (347). But nothing is dominated in the poem. "Overmastering persons," Yeats wrote, "tur[n] from a mirror to meditation on a mask," but this poem, like Auden's late poetry, turns back to the mirror. Yeats discarded the Heraclitan image in the draft—"Cannon is the god and father of all"—and the sensibility of tragic joy ("bitter and gay is the heroic mood," says Yeats) is splintered into the passive "embittered heart" and its martial fantasies: "vain gaiety, vain battle, vain repose" (347). The poem leaves the reader instead with a sharply divergent, Augustinian image of the force that fathers the earthly city: "the foul rag and bone shop of the heart" (348).[104] The saint repudiates the swordsman, but not without vacillation.

4

"THE POWER TO ENCHANT THAT COMES FROM DISILLUSION": W. H. AUDEN'S ANTI-MAGICAL POETICS

Wallace Stevens makes an anonymous appearance in W. H. Auden's "In Praise of Limestone" (1947). The limestone landscape, the speaker says, "calls into question"

> All the Great Powers assume; it disturbs our rights. The poet,
>   Admired for his earnest habit of calling
> The sun the sun, his mind Puzzle, is made uneasy
>   By these marble statues which so obviously doubt
> His antimythological myth . . .[1]

"The poet" is Stevens. The lines were recycled and modified from an unpublished comic lyric, "Miss God on Mr. Stevens," originally scribbled in the margins of Auden's copy of Stevens's *Transport to Summer.*[2]

Auden's quarrel with Stevens presupposes their mutual attentiveness to what Stevens calls the "not ourselves" and to the boundary between the human and the inhuman. Like Stevens, Auden accepts that there is an ontological gap between what "Esthétique du Mal" (a poem in the collection Auden read) describes as "our being" and "our world." These terms map onto what Auden calls the "historical" and "natural" elements of human experience. Both suppose that religious experience is generated from the encounter with this gap. For Auden, however, the immanent, immediate experience of the world Stevens struggles to capture in his tautological speech—calling "the sun the sun"—is impossible. Language is always already lifting material phenomena into a web of meaning; all landscapes are, as Auden titled one of his poems, *paysage moralisé.* Stevens, according to Auden, calls his mind "Puzzle" because he cannot place it within the immanent order of things; he finds it peculiar that this mind should generate desires that do not have material satisfactions. But in Auden's poem natural limestone is fashioned without puzzlement into "marble statue." The material world is receptive to the mind's interventions.

Stevens's puzzlement generates his "antimythological myth," a project of self-conscious fiction making meant to replace naïve participation in obsolete myth. Stevens preserves myth, however, both because he tells a story of a fall into secular self-consciousness ("before we were wholly human and knew ourselves")[3] and because he creates a new myth of the mind's solitary responsibility. Auden's limestone doubts Stevens's myth because it emphasizes the intractably composite nature of human beings. Limestone marginalizes the sublime experiences (of "saints" and "Caesars") that Auden discusses earlier in the poem, experiences that derive from the mind's encounter with the most severe, least human landscapes: the "granite wastes" and the "oceans." It does not permit an account of the human/inhuman divide, exaggerated by the modern sublime, as a strict opposition. Auden suggests, wrongly, that Stevens's poetry ignores the truths of finitude and embodiment. But he is right that Stevens often understands the human relation to the inhuman in terms of an either/or, which is why Stevens's poetry can, on the one hand, dive into material immanence at the expense of human personhood and language and, on the other, speak of the mind as a lonely anomaly that has to persist in its imaginative, anthropomorphic projections to sustain itself in a mythologically impoverished world. In Auden's terminology, Stevens can both call "the sun the sun" by dwelling in the sheer material givenness of a demythologized world and also create a "myth" in which the mind must look to itself for spiritual survival in light of its ontologically puzzling character.

For Auden, the unquestionable ontological tension between infinity and finitude is neither a hierarchical binary nor an impassible divide. Human being is, *pace* Yeats's Michael Robartes ("blessed souls are not composite") paradoxically both composite and dualistic. As body, the self is constituted by impersonal material forces; it belongs to a world of "masses, identical relations and recurrent events" describable in terms of mechanism and number. But as person, the self also belongs to a "world of faces, analogical relations and singular events, describable only in terms of speech." These divergent models of description are simultaneously incommensurable and equally valid; they are, Auden writes in "The Virgin and the Dynamo," "*The Two Real Worlds*."[4] For Stevens, only the world of masses is fundamentally real. The human is, ontologically speaking, an accident, or, in Auden's gloss, a "Puzzle." Auden refuses to privilege either element.

The material world does not, in Auden, submit to the logic of human desire. But the "indifference" of a disenchanted world is for Auden only one feature of its broader gratuitousness. This gratuitousness is the source of the pleasure it bestows (experienced as surprise and gift) and of what "Limestone" calls its "reproach." The material world "disturbs our rights," both in its otherness and in its reminder that we are constituted by this otherness. In Auden's *The Sea and the Mirror* Alonso admonishes Ferdinand to consider how that constitutive otherness might invert one's subject position: he is to attend to "The sunburnt superficial kingdom / Where a king is an object" (*CPA*, 416). Like Stevens, Auden looks to the disenchanting force of secularism as a reminder that the world resists the desires that belong to us as persons. But he refuses to disenchant the human person as such. While in Stevens, secularism can never quite achieve its promise—the elimination of the religious dualisms that supposedly alienate us from the world—in Auden secularism is useful for its power to distinguish between the "historical" (the unique element of human person-hood) and the "natural" (the repeatable element of material life). Moreover, in what only seems a paradox, in Auden secularism is understood within a larger theological perspective that prevents it from reducing the transcendent dimensions of human experience to configurations of material energy.[5] Auden's thinking is thus characterized by an *affirmative dualism*, in the sense that both aspects of human being—the personal and the material—are given equal rights and endowed with two distinct logics that cannot be collapsed into each other.[6]

For the mature Auden, all attempts to eliminate this ontological gap are experiments in "magic." In a magical ontology, the distinction between the order of the person and the order of the impersonal world breaks down. A magical world, unlike the world disenchanted by the instrumental mind, is full of secret sympathies and correspondences. A characteristic malaise of the secular self derives from what Charles Taylor has described as its "buffered," "disengaged" quality.[7] Its interior activity seems to be the only locus of value, for the de-anthropomorphized world outside is conceived as value-neutral matter. The enchanted self was a "porous" self. It enjoyed open passage between symbolically charged external events and internal response; "meaning" emerged from this intercourse rather than from subjective projection. Modern magical thinking, for Auden, wants to make the self porous again. It seeks a world in which no distinction can be made between human desire and the energies that animate the world. Magic is a reaction to the characteristic ailments of modernity that are based in this distinction. Charles Baudelaire defined the modern poet as someone who could break down these distinctions and so mitigate the ailments, who could create a "suggestive magic" between the self and the world:

"What is the modern conception of Art? To create a suggestive magic including at the same time the subject and object, the world outside the artist and the artist himself." Auden took this as a representative statement of modern poetics, and struggled against it throughout his career.[8]

Auden understood how powerful the modern desire was—and is—to re-enchant the world. He considered the pervasiveness of magical thinking in modernism both intelligible and attractive as a response to the contradictions of both modern life and material existence more generally. It satisfied a host of ontological and aesthetic desires: the desire for an end to the dualisms that seemed to sever spirit from body (Yeats's "blessed souls are not composite"), thought from sensation (Eliot's "the dissociation of sensibility"),[9] subject from external world (Rilke's "Oh disobedient world / So full of refusal");[10] for a renewed sense of participation and at-home-ness in that world (Stevens's "the world is not our own"); and for a new poetics that placed poetic modes of thinking at the center of life as a whole and saw such thinking as a form of participation in a comprehensive magico-religious cosmos. But Auden also saw magical thinking as symptomatic of a number of social and psychological problems, some particular to modern social conditions, some products of the difficulties of embodiment as such. "A fascination with the 'occult,'" he wrote, "with astrology, spiritualism, magic, and the like, is generally, I suspect, a symptom of social alienation."[11] Insofar as poetry tried to diagnose and cure that alienation, moreover, it was tempted by those occult responses, particularly because new research in the anthropology of religion suggested that poetry had emerged out of magic ritual.[12]

There is a moment in Auden's 1944 poem *The Sea and the Mirror* that brings together the various strands he isolates in magical thinking. Prospero (as in Shakespeare's *The Tempest*) has "abjured" his magic and accounts for its origins in his personal history:

> When I woke into my life, a sobbing dwarf
> Whom giants served only as they pleased, I was not what I seemed;
>   Beyond their busy backs I made a magic
> To ride away from a father's imperfect justice,
>   Take vengeance on the Romans for their grammar,
> Usurp the popular earth and blot for ever
>   The gross insult of being a mere one among many:
> Now, Ariel, I am that I am, your late and lonely master,
>   Who knows now what magic is:—the power to enchant
> That comes from disillusion. . . .

(CPA, 405)

For the chastened Prospero, magic is first of all a response to the alienating incongruity between the inner and outer life that emerges in self-consciousness: "When I woke into my life." Human beings do not coincide with themselves. It is possible to "seem" rather than seamlessly "be," or as Prospero says, "I was not what I seemed." The subject can always elude its present material context by positing a negative gap between its internal identity and outer performance. The powers of the world do not "serve" the young Prospero as he expects, so his magic is also a method for overcoming the frustration of the ego. It is a response to the "imperfect justice" of both "father" and "earth," a resistance to the subjection implicit in human finitude. Alex Owen has argued that "fin-de-siècle occultism" was not so much a reaction to as a continuation of the instrumental rationality characteristic of modern subjects and institutions; it was "characterized by the will to know and control the natural world."[13] Prospero acknowledges such motives: his magic, in its very attempt to overcome the alienation of self from world, refuses to acknowledge the otherness of that world. "Popular earth" emphasizes the material world's universal, democratic quality—the laws of the earth and of the body are realities to which humans are equally subjected. Magic seeks to "usurp the popular earth," both historically, in its elite, esoteric dimension, and ontologically, in the sense that it is, as Auden wrote elsewhere, "an attempt to make free with necessities."[14]

"Popular" has a political valence as well: Prospero declines to be "a mere one among many." "Usurp" suggests a desire to arrogate power, and indeed, Auden says of the orphic model of the poet as magician: "Orpheus who moved stones is the archetype, not of the poet, but of Goebbels" (P, 2:350). Lastly, because original, mystical naming is a form of occult power, Prospero's magic refuses the constraints of "grammar," which make the subjective appropriation of language, and the expression and understanding language makes possible, dependent on ignominious historical and social forces that transcend the speaker ("Roman" rule). As we will see, magic has been conceived as a form of resistance to the rationalized, "secular" project of empire, and the imperialism of "Roman" grammar is here linked to Auden's reflection on this problem in For the Time Being.

Prospero suggests that magic is not, as some have thought, an attempt to reinstate a noninstrumental relation between self and material world through re-enchantment, but a way of making the world submit to the self. Modern magic is a "power to enchant" that does not overcome, but actually stems from, modern "disillusion," or the psychological dimension of disenchantment. It is characterized by a number of interrelated motivations: (1) a response to the alienation of self from material life, including the life of the body; (2) an attempt to overcome the ontological dualisms and contradictions inherent in human existence, which often take on, especially in modernity, this quality of alienation; (3) a refusal to acknowledge the otherness of the world, because otherness is mistaken for alienation; (4) a technique for mitigating the ego's inability to abide the realities of human finitude and the opposing desires of other egos; 5) a desire to make language mystically efficacious in the material world; and 6) a form of resistance to the instrumentalism of secular imperialism. All of these dimensions of magic find their origin in the problems of alienation and dualism.

MAGIC, "CIVILIZATION," AND SECULAR IMPERIALISM

Prospero wants to take vengeance on the Romans. I discussed in the introduction the problem of contemporary critics who celebrate magic and occultism as a mode of resistance to various cultural hegemonies, particularly in colonial contexts. Gauri Viswanathan, Helen Sword, Christopher Bracken, and Randall Styers all argue, as Styers has written, that the "subversive passions" of magic "ha[ve] proved a potent medium with which to contest the hegemonic social structures and norms of modernity."[15] These contentions begin with a criticism of the implicitly triumphalist narratives of much early anthropology of religion, for which magic was conceived as primitive religion, and both magic and religion as primitive (and now obsolete) Western science. R. G. Collingwood (whom Auden admired) and Ludwig Wittgenstein laid the philosophical ground for this critique many years ago.[16] But critics who celebrate magic tend to conflate the need to contest secular Western norms with a wholesale delegitimization of Western science and rarely investigate the normative implications of the occult attitudes that ostensibly liberate the subject.[17]

The fundamental difference between Auden and the contemporary celebrants of magical thinking is this: the critics believe that to subvert the hierarchies one must eliminate the dualisms. According to this line of thought, to draw a significant distinction between, for instance, reason and instinct is to devalue the body. Magical thinking therefore tends toward a monism that collapses all binaries. Auden, however, maintains that one can eliminate the hierarchies without eliminating certain dualisms. Indeed, he believes that there is an essential dualism—between history and nature—that is critical to the modern (Christian *and* secular) sense of historical responsibility and historical critique. For Auden, one must maintain a distinction between the legitimate claims of the human *person*, who is capable of original, historical agency, transformative imagination, and an experience of the unconditional, on the one hand, and, on the other, the legitimate claims of the body and material life, which are the sources of pleasure and happiness but which constrain, limit, and often frustrate experience and agency. History is a personal order; nature is an impersonal order. Neither should be devalued, but they cannot be magically conflated.

Auden knew very well that Enlightenment rationalism harbored imperialist instincts; he dramatized the problem in his Christmas oratorio, *For the Time Being* (1942), published just two years before *The Sea and the Mirror* (1944).[18] In the New Testament, Herod is a pro-Roman Jewish king who slaughters infants in an attempt to prevent Jesus of Nazareth from eventually replacing him as "king of the Jews." In *For the Time Being,* a retelling of the Christmas story in light of midcentury concerns, Auden's Herod is imagined as a secular, liberal, enlightened ruler at the frontiers of empire, exasperated by the recalcitrancy of magical thinking among his subjects. Written during the bleakest period of the Second World War, this portrait of Herod takes a step back from the reality of nationalist barbarism and explores the limits of the liberal perspective that might oppose it. Herod complains (in prose, of course, rather than poetry),

> And what, after all, is the whole Empire, with its few thousand square miles
> on which it is possible to lead the Rational Life, but a tiny patch of light
> compared with those immense areas of barbaric night that surround it on all
> sides, that incoherent wilderness of rage and terror, where Mongolian idiots
> are regarded as sacred and mothers who gave birth to twins are instantly put
> to death, where malaria is treated by yelling, where warriors of superb cour-
> age obey the commands of hysterical female impersonators, where the best
> cuts of meat are reserved for the dead, where, if a white blackbird has been
> seen, no more work may be done that day, where it is firmly believed that the
> world was created by a giant with three heads or that the motions of stars are
> controlled from the liver of a rogue elephant? (*CPA*, 391–392)

Herod's vision of empire is a vision of secular enlightenment securing a place for itself in the world and gradually expunging all forms of magical thinking within its borders. He recognizes, however, that the imperial rationalism he commends is a source of alienation and implies that a turn to the occult as a strategy to overcome disenchantment and assuage ennui is at the very least understandable. In its mania for productively disciplining the body, the so-called rational life has ignored the claims of the senses and the passions, which look to sensual magic as a mode of liberation:

> [S]o many are still homesick for that disorder wherein every passion formerly
> enjoyed a frantic license. Caesar flies to his hunting lodge pursued by ennui;

in the faubourgs of the Capital, Society grows savage, corrupted by silks and
scents, softened by sugar and hot water, made insolent by theatres and attractive slaves; and everywhere, including this province, new prophets spring up
every day to sound the old barbaric note. (392)

Nonetheless, Herod strives to impede the irrationalist reaction with authoritarian social policies:

> I have tried everything. I have prohibited the sale of crystals and ouija-boards;
> I have slapped a heavy tax on playing cards; the courts are empowered to sen-
> tence alchemists to hard labour in the mines; it is a statutory offence to turn
> tables or feel bumps. But nothing is really effective. How can I expect the
> masses to be sensible, when, for instance, to my certain knowledge, the captain
> of my own guard wears an amulet against the Evil Eye, and the richest mer-
> chant in the city consults a medium over every important transaction? (392)

Herod's tactics are appropriate to the liberal state. They operate through an
appeal to economic self-interest (taxation) or through therapeutic re-education
into "reason" (the alchemists must learn to respect the density and inflexibility
of empirical matter through hard labor). And Herod does not, of course, stop
there. He uses state power to ensure that Christ does not become another
rabble-rousing prophet who plays on the fears of a superstitious people. And,
through the genius of statistical, instrumental reason, he kills all the infants he
can find with the expectation that one will be Jesus.

Both Prospero's desire to take revenge on the Romans for their grammar and
Herod's self-conscious linking of imperialism and secular rationality disclose
Auden's awareness of the fact that magical thinking is intelligible as a mode of
resistance to the tyranny of secular empire. Auden, however, insisted that magical
thinking was a symptom of *anomie* and oppression rather than a constructive
response to it. His reading of historians like E. R. Dodds and Charles Cochrane[19]
convinced him that this was true of Rome's decline, and in his poem "The Fall
of Rome" we find a depiction of magic and aesthetic fantasy as disengaged rather
than engaged:

> Private rites of magic send
> The temple prostitutes to sleep;
> All the literati keep
> An imaginary friend.
>
> (CPA, 332)

These lines undermine Yeats's famous "The Second Coming," where cultural
decay is understood in occult perspective. Indeed, instead of turning the poem

into a form of occult condemnation and embattlement, Auden closes "The Fall of Rome" with a picture of a world so different from the human one that it could not possibly be appropriated through sympathetic magic. Nothing in the poem—in a sense, nothing within language as such—prepares the reader for the gratuitous scene of the last stanza:

> Altogether elsewhere, vast
> Herds of reindeer move across
> Miles and miles of golden moss,
> Silently and very fast.
>
> (333)

The power of "altogether elsewhere" resides in the beauty of the scene's indifference to social crisis. These herds of reindeer cannot be incorporated into the historical afflictions of the poem as objects of romantic longing for a non-alienated world. In his early, pre-conversion poem, "The Creatures," animals are examples of what our life will be once we return to the immediacy on the other side of the fall into self-consciousness: they "are our past and our future: the poles between which our desire / unceasingly is discharged" (*EA*, 158). In "The Fall of Rome," by contrast—a poem written in the decade after Auden became a Christian—the beauty of the reindeer chastises the subject through its very otherness, as something that we could not possibly become or possess. The "altogether elsewhere" dismantles all pretensions of possession, subsumption, or appropriation, or any pretensions that magical thinking might rescue us from the debased rationalistic civilization in which, as the poem says, "an unimportant clerk / Writes *I DO NOT LIKE MY WORK* / On a pink official form" (*CPA*, 333).

MAGIC, THE WISH, AND THE OTHERNESS OF THE WORLD

There is a double aspect to Prospero's not being what he seems. On the level of psychology, it is a state of refusing to be what one is—in other words, refusing to accept the current historical and material basis of one's life as the place in which desire and action must begin. Not to be what one seems is an ontological reality that humans must acknowledge, but it can also be a way of evading the truth of the finite context that currently circumscribes the possibilities for the self. Auden therefore makes a distinction between "desire" and "wish." "[A] wish," he writes, "is fantastic; it knows what is the case but refuses to accept it. All wishes, whatever their apparent content, have the same and unvarying

meaning: 'I refuse to be what I am'" (*DH*, 241). "[T]he task of consciousness"—
and that acute mode of consciousness called poetry—is "to translate wish into
desire." To desire, Auden says, is to accept the current state of the self for what
it is, "for the present state of the self is the ground of every desire, and that is
precisely what the wisher rejects" (241). Since magic is, as Auden says, "an
attempt to make free with necessities," wishfulness is the psychological dimension of the pursuit of enchantment. Paradoxically, however, to wish—to refuse
to be what one currently is—is to refuse the reality of "seeming" in human life
(Prospero says "I was not what I seemed"). To assent to being what one is, in
other words, is to assent to *not* being an organic unity.[20]

In a review, Auden described those who "believe in magic" as those "who
expect their wishes to be granted without any effort on their part."[21] In a late
poem, he gives thanks for being daily "[b]eckoned anew to a World / where
wishes alter nothing" (*CPA*, 881). Even in his early work, which Randall Jarrell
said was full of mana, Auden pitted an aesthetic of disenchanted knowledge
against an aesthetic of magical wish; the latter was often dismantled in the
poems. In a 1933 poem he later entitled "Through the Looking Glass"—an allusion to Lewis Carroll's fictive world—the speaker's fantasies about his lover take
place in a "mirror world where Logic is reversed," a world where "what view I
wish for I shall find." In "A Bride in the 30's," it is all too "easy" for the speaker
to "conjure a camera"—the instrument that captures the world as it is—"into a
wishing-rose" (123, 129).[22]

To persist in a wish, for Auden, is to relinquish the ethical task of forgiveness,
which requires an assessment of things as they are. Forgiving acknowledges
what has come to be, though it be painful; wishing seeks to rearrange the world
according to private need. Wishing is ahistorical: it does not accept the irrevers-
ibility of actions and events as they have accumulated in time. Thus in a 1929
poem, the speaker strives toward an emotional state "without wishing and with
forgiving" (*EA*, 39). In "Horae Canonicae," a poem written thirty years later, the
logic of wishing is the same: the speaker, who is complicit in a crime, knows
that he can evade responsibility for it by retreating into "dream," a state in
which he is "without status" and left "[a]mong its unwashed tribes of wishes,"
which have only "a magic cult to propitiate / What happens" (*CPA*, 640–641).[23]

Auden's strategy for disenchanting "the wish" is precisely to attend to "what
happens," or all those features of the world that do not obey the ego or the will.
As in the "altogether elsewhere" that closes "The Fall of Rome," Auden's poetry
develops a discipline of attention that foregrounds the otherness of the material
world and the body that is constituted by that world. As Prospero says, this world
is "popular": the laws of the earth and of the body are impersonal realities that

ignore the aspirations of particular persons. And the truth of finitude is equally a truth of plurality: there are other things out there. For Auden, we relinquish magic by assenting to the inhuman otherness of the world. This does not mean, as it sometimes does in Stevens, that we suspect the value of human person-hood, which seems ontologically anomalous. It simply means that we cultivate an ethical relation to the world in its otherness and look to it as a source of what "Limestone" calls the "reproach" that disciplines the mind's fantasies.[24] According to Auden, magic, in its very search for an end to alienation, para-doxically violates the otherness of the world. The irony of modern magic is that, while it ostensibly resists the instrumental reason that permits the disen-chanted self to dominate the neutral world, it is actually animated by just this drive for domination. The characteristically modern manifestation of magic is the absorption of everything materially "other" back into subjectivity. It can only respond to the estrangement of self from world by absorbing the world into the self.

For the later Auden, the work of Rainer Maria Rilke was representative of this sort of magical poetics in modernism. Adorno, writing of Rilke, puts it this way: Rilke's "cult of things" "belongs to this form of idiosyncrasy, as an attempt to bring the alien objects into subjectively pure expression and dissolve them there—to give their alienness metaphysical credit."[25] Though Auden admired Rilke as a young man, he became suspicious of his work for just this reason. Rilke, who in his *Sonnets to Orpheus* had given the orphic conception of the poet its modern scripture, became Auden's archetype of the magician-poet. The orphic poet seeks the false immediacy of what Auden calls the "magical musical condition," and when he cannot attain it he laments, as Rilke does, "Oh disobe-dient world / So full of refusal."[26] In *The Sea and the Mirror*, Auden's Caliban (the principle of materiality who suffers under Prospero's imperial magic) discusses this condition in his knotty, late Jamesian pastiche:

> How then, we continue to wonder, knowing all this, could you act as if you did not, as if you did not realize that the embarrassing compresence of the absolutely natural, incorrigibly right-handed, and, to any request for co-operation, utterly negative, with the enthusiastically self-effacing would be a simultaneous violation of both worlds, as if you were not perfectly well aware that the magical musical condition, the orphic spell that turns the fierce dumb greedy beasts into grateful guides and oracles who will gladly take one anywhere and tell one everything free of charge, is precisely and simply that of his finite immediate note *not*, under any circumstances, being struck, of its not being tentatively whispered, far less positively banged. (CPA, 429)

The "magical musical condition" is *"not"* one in which Ariel—the aesthetic imagination—strikes his "finite immediate note" in cooperation with the spiritual capacity for negation and "self-effacement." Contrary to its aspirations, the orphic, magico-aesthetic "spell" is not a return to immediacy but an imposition of subjective desire—a desire for obedience—onto the immediate world. This imposition is a "simultaneous violation of both" subject and object "worlds." Like Adorno, Auden characterized this poetic strategy as an attempt to "endow the gratuitous with a magic utility of its own, so that the poet comes to think of himself as the god who creates his subjective universe out of nothing—to him the visible and material universe *is* nothing. Mallarmé, who planned to write the sacred book of a new universal religion, and Rilke with his notion of *Gesang ist Dasein,* are heresiarchs of this type" (DH, 76).[27]

Auden's poetry from 1940 onward insists on the material world's distinct, extra-human logic. He included the human body in this category of things that resist the attempts of human subjectivity to absorb it. This meant that human beings, as bodies, were other even to themselves. For Auden a return to a sense of at-home-ness in the world can never be absolute; nor does it require that the extra-human be absorbed into the human. In his 1942 poem "Canzone," it is material objects, not us, who are "homeless," and we give them a home through love rather than aesthetic appropriation:

> We are created from and with the world
> To suffer with and from it day by day:
> Whether we meet in a majestic world
> Of solid measurements or a dream world
> Of swans and gold, we are required to love
> All homeless objects that require a world.
> Our claim to own our bodies and our world
> Is our catastrophe. What can we know
> But panic and caprice until we know
> Our dreadful appetite demands a world
> Whose order, origin, and purpose will
> Be fluent satisfaction of our will?
>
> (CPA, 330)[28]

The canzone form puts pressure, in this section, on "world," "know," and "will" while permitting subtle distinctions among their sequential iterations. Their grouping here forms an implicit background—an aggressive will to know the world—against which the words will be recast. In the poem's alternate dispensation, knowledge moves inward rather than outward; the epistemological "what can we know" created by the line break unexpectedly takes emotion and disposition ("panic and caprice") rather than "world" as its object. The first "know" is really "experience," and the more difficult knowledge that follows is self-knowledge, an awareness that object-knowledge is distorted by the "demand[s]" of "dreadful appetite."

"World," in fact, is not principally an object to be known because knowledge is entangled in the will's demands. Rather, it is source ("from") and object of relation ("with"). This is the world, which includes "our own bodies," to which we have "no claim." However the mind meets the world—whether in "measurement" or in "dream"—it remains fundamentally other. But this otherness is not alienation. Rather, the human task is to bring "homeless objects" not into subjectivity's magical design but into "*a* world," now understood as a community of relation. The basis of epistemology turns out to be "love," rather than the "will" that masquerades as detached reason. The "world" knowledge seeks is both a separate thing that requires ethical relation and an achievement of that relation.

In his beautiful sonnet, "Objects" (1956), Auden sees the ontological distance of the nonhuman world as a gift and occasion for wonder rather than as a sign of alienation:

All that which lies outside our sort of why,
Those wordless creatures who are there as well,
Remote from mourning yet in sight and cry,
Make time more golden than we meant to tell.

Tearless, their surfaces appear as deep
As any longing we believe we had;
If shapes can so to their own edges keep,
No separation proves a being bad.

There is less grief than wonder on the whole,
Even at sunset, though of course we care
Each time the same old shadow falls across

One Person who is not: somewhere, a soul,
Light in her bestial substance, well aware,
Extols the silence of how soon a loss.

(CPA, 624)

The life of objects takes place "outside our sort of why." Objects resist our demands for narrative, purpose, and meaning—all the accounts bound up with the questions humans put to things. They are "wordless," for these demands belong to the world of speech, and to confuse the order of things and the order of speech is to slip into magical thinking.

The poem implies that the first movement of relation to objects should be a gesture not of knowledge but of acknowledgment: as in Woolf's *Mrs. Dalloway*, where Clarissa encounters the mysterious otherness of the old woman, in Auden's poem these objects are—before they are anything else—"there as well." The gesture has a tautological quality; thereness is already implicit in the objects' grammatical status as subjects. As in Stevens, there is a hesitation to enter the world of poetic analogy, for analogy moves beyond the singularity of objects by lifting them into a linguistic world of relation. The encounter is spatial and perceptual before it is hermeneutical. When meaning enters, moreover, it is ethical before it is symbolic. The objects are *neighbors*—"within sight and cry"—yet "remote" from the life of feeling, the template for which in the poem is "mourning."

The choice of mourning points to a crucial distinction between the human experience of temporality and the way objects inhabit time. The difference is formally inscribed in the poem: objects are always spoken of in the present tense, whereas human subjectivity—the "we"—is constituted historically and can therefore register a past. Selfhood for Auden involves an awareness of time experienced as what Dickinson calls "internal difference." When the poem discusses the human perception of objects, it speaks not only of a past but also of a present relation to that past. This generates a gap of uncertainty between what *was* and *is* thought, believed, or spoken. Objects make "time more golden than *we meant to tell.*" Their surfaces are as deep as "any longing we *believe we had.*" Speech can only point to a value that eludes the circumscription of definite meaning. The lines simultaneously extol the significance of objects in their elusive otherness and insist on the significance of the human difference that can register surprise. Unlike objects, "we" are not self-identical. Our attempts at meaning and self-understanding do not always coincide with truth, and truth does not always coincide with the expression of it. To *mean to tell* implies that there is a gap between intention and expression. To *believe we had* a longing means that we cannot be sure of desire. The grammar itself renders human time-consciousness, and in doing so renders human self-division.

Auden thinks that the distinctly modern attraction to objects is generated by the anxiety created by this self-division.[29] Objects are self-identical. They are all surface, yet in their perfect self-identity their "surfaces" strike us as "deep." This is precisely why we long for them: they are at peace, "tearless," and "remote from mourning." Yet Auden insists that our longing for objects should not become a desire to be like them or appropriate them inwardly. Indeed, the play between their self-identity and their surface quality requires us to reimagine the character of "separation." Magical thinking codes separation as alienation and strives to overcome it by bridging the distance. But the poem suggests that the beautiful self-identity of objects depends on their self-containment: they "to their own edges keep." This keeping creates separation. Yet the fact that this separation is equally beauty and depth means that "[n]o separation proves a being bad." Separation is not estrangement, rather the condition for ethical relationship. Magic would blur all the "edges," but the poem commends respect for edges as the precondition for wonder.

Yet if objects form the sine qua non of wonder, they are "remote" from "grief." Or rather, the repetitive self-identity that belongs to all natural phenomena creates the background against which grief is experienced. "[T]he same old shadow" is juxtaposed to "One Person who is not"—a singular entity who does not (only) belong to, and whose passing is experienced as absence within, the world of positive repetition. Though the wordlessness of objects enfolds in them a value beyond the reach of language, this wordlessness is not "silence," which is for Auden a distinctly human phenomenon. Silence is the presence of an absence. It requires a perceiving subject who is "well aware" and who experiences time as difference rather than repetition, as both fitting and unfitting; one who "[e]xtols the silence of *how soon* a loss."

HISTORY AGAINST MYTHICAL NATURE

"Objects" manifests a characteristic dialectic in Auden's poetry: he articulates the unique life of the human subject even as he celebrates the inhuman otherness of a world that does not answer to that subject. This marks another affinity with Adorno, a critic of both instrumental reason and the magical thinking that operated in its shadow.[30] Like Auden, Adorno insisted that magical practice could not provide a platform of protest against the dominance of rational, instrumental modernity. Adorno and Horkheimer's *Dialectic of Enlightenment* argued that, far from simply dissolving the magical worldview, so-called secular enlightenment had actually reproduced patterns of mythic experience that it supposedly had supplanted. The problem was not that instrumental reason had not completely expunged magical thinking but that such reason was not truly rational. A return to magical thinking in modernity, therefore, was a regression. In his essay "Theses against Occultism," Adorno wrote,

> The tendency to occultism is a symptom of the regression in consciousness. This has lost the power to think the unconditional and to endure the conditional. Instead of defining both, in their unity and difference, by conceptual labor, it mixes them indiscriminately. The unconditional becomes fact, the

conditional an immediate essence. Monotheism is decomposing into a second mythology. "I believe in astrology because I do not believe in God," one
participant in an American socio-psychological investigation answered.
Judicious reason, that had elevated itself to the notion of one God, seems
ensnared in his fall. Spirit is dissociated into spirits and thereby forfeits the
power to recognize that they do not exist. The veiled tendency of society
towards disaster lulls its victims in a false revelation, with a hallucinated phenomenon.[31]

The desire to "think the unconditional and endure the conditional"—and to
maintain an awareness of their difference—is a characteristic aim of Auden's
later poetry. As I have argued, Auden steadily emphasizes the disparity between,
on the one hand, the legitimate claims of the human *person* who is capable of
original, historical agency, and transformative imagination (and so partakes of
the unconditional) and, on the other hand, the legitimate claims of the body
and material life, which are the sources of pleasure and happiness but which
constrain, limit, and often frustrate experience and agency (the reality of the
conditional). Adorno argued that the "platitudinously natural content of the
supernatural message" of occultism "betray[ed] its untruth." Auden echoes this
criticism in his conviction that modern instrumental reason is analogous to
magic in that both seek the manipulation of the material world for *natural* ends:
success and domination.

For Auden, secular reason's most profound insight, and the one most endan-
gered by magical thinking, is the truth of historicity as the unique element
of human being. Edward Said has broadly defined the "secular attitude" as
"a sense of history and of human production."[32] This "sense" is important to
Auden, though he believed secularism did not so much displace Western mono-
theisms as emerge out of them. In both Judaism and Christianity, salvation is
not a negation of history but its ennobling and consummation: Judaism is a
story of God's actions in history on behalf of a people caught up in historical
events; Christianity is a story of God entering history through the Incarnation.[33]
Belief in the Incarnation ("the Word . . . made flesh"), wrote Auden, requires
the further belief that "matter, the natural order, is real and redeemable, not a
shadowy appearance or the cause of evil, and historical time is real and significant, not meaningless or an endless series of cycles."[34] Yeats, by contrast, blamed
the modern stance of "moral indignation" and "uniform law" on the mistaken
"Christian conviction that the soul has but one life to find or lose salvation in";
he preferred what he called "Asiatic courtesy," a kind of *sprezzatura* grounded
in the occult knowledge that this is merely one of many lives.[35] For Yeats, as I
note in chapter 3, the political hopes of modernity are merely a secularization

of the Jewish and Christian idea that history is a theater of salvation. For Auden, to affirm historicity as the crucial element of human personhood requires the distinction that both monotheism and secularism draw between history and nature.

The framework for Auden's criticisms of magic from the historical perspective is most systematically elaborated in an essay that adopts two images famous from Henry Adams's *Education:* "The Virgin and the Dynamo." The burden of the essay (I touched on this at the beginning of the chapter) is to demonstrate the importance of acknowledging that there are two inexorably different worlds of experience that are, nonetheless, equally *real:* on the one hand, "The Natural World of the Dynamo, the world of masses, identical relations and recurrent events"; on the other, "the Historical World of the Virgin, the world of faces, analogical relations and singular events" (*DH*, 61). By calling the natural world the world of the dynamo, Auden insists that one must accept a degree of irreversible disenchantment. The material world may remain value-laden, but it is nonetheless a world that is fundamentally amenable to quantitative description—a world of "masses." Objects can be identical and events repeatable. Stevens writes, "The world is a force, not a presence" (*CP*, 912), and Auden concurs: the dynamo image also suggests that the material world is a world of power or force, not a world of inherent meaning. Unlike Stevens, however, Auden thinks there are *"Two Real Worlds"*; the world of force is only one of them. For Auden, moderns should accept a distinction not so much between fact and value as between *power* and value. Indeed, a significant danger for modern strategies of re-enchantment is that they tend to sacralize force, and in doing so they confuse the historical project of value making with the natural neutrality of power.[36]

Auden insists that the natural world, and the power that stems from it, is impersonal. But this "secular" truth has, for Auden, paradoxically thrown into relief what he takes to be the fundamentally religious dimension of what he calls "the Historical World," a "world of faces, analogical relations, and singular events" (*DH*, 61). This is an irreducible world in which human beings, though subject to natural limits, are not determined by them but are responsible for their own history—first, through the recognition that persons ("faces") are not exhausted by quantitative analysis; second, through the employment of language, which is able to discover nonidentical *relations* among persons and things (it is "analogical," not "identical"); and third, through the understanding of human beings as agents whose actions bring something new into the world (*"singular"* events, unlike the events of nature that are recurrent). The ability to make the distinction between history and nature, Auden thinks, was honed by the disenchanting power of secular science (of which many have complained), and its dissociation of power and value has beneficially undermined the attempts to make force sacred or re-create a magical world.

Auden argues that the failure to distinguish history from nature results in "two chimerical worlds": a magical world and a reductively secular world. The first, the "magical polytheistic world," is "created by the aesthetic illusion which would regard the world of masses as if it were a world of faces. The aesthetic religion says *prayers* to the Dynamo." The second is its mirror image: the world of "mechanized history," which is "created by the scientific illusion which would regard the world of faces as if it were a world of masses. The scientific religion treats the Virgin as a statistic. 'Scientific' politics is animism stood on its head." For Auden, nature has no "face": Venus is a "pagan mask" that creates the animistic illusion that material energy is something other than "an impersonal natural force": *eros*. The converse, however—the assumption that everything can be reduced to number and weight—is equally distorting. It is "animism stood on its head" (62–63).

The distinction between history and nature and the critique of their magical conflation is invoked in numerous later Auden poems. In "Homage to Clio," for example, Clio—the muse of history—is a figure analogous to the "Virgin" in Auden's essay. In the poem, the natural world is the realm of positive identity, a realm uncompromised by the possibility of valuation (and so of negativity) that enters the world in human language. It is therefore a place where "nothing is too big or too small or the Wrong / Color" (*CPA*, 611). But human beings have been brought into a different, historical realm:

> but we, at haphazard
>
> And unseasonably, are brought face to face
>   By ones, Clio, with your silence. After that
> Nothing is easy. We may dream as we wish
>   Of phallic pillar or navel-stone
>
> With twelve nymphs twirling about it, but pictures
>   Are no help: your silence already is there
> Between us and any magical centre
>   Where things are taken in hand.
>
>   (611)

The "magical centre" is the place in which, because no distinction is made between the human and the natural, the world is thought to respond to our religio-aesthetic representations ("phallic pillar and navel-stone"). "[T]hings" can be "taken in hand"—there is an echo here of Yeats's complaint that we have lost "the old-nonchalance of the hand"—because there is no distance from the world: speech and action participate in its logic no less than the seasons do. The world responds to the desire humans would exercise upon it; it conforms to the human intention figured in the grip or touch. But we are confronted by Clio "unseasonably" because in history we break out of the mythical, repetitive rhythm of the seasons; "haphazardly" because historical action is not something that can be predicted by what has come before or by empirical testing; "face to face" and "[b]y ones" because history is the element of distinct individuals rather than entities describable as statistics. This historical world is a realm of "silence" because it is experienced as possibility and expectation; it is the place where there is something to be done that is not already written into the fabric of things.

"Homage to Clio" was written in 1955, but Auden was already, in the mid-1930s, using the history-nature distinction to transform poetic genres.[37] "Autumn Song" (1936) takes, at first glance, the form of a dark nursery rhyme that uses the change of seasons as an occasion for mythic sorrow.[38] It begins,

Now the leaves are falling fast,
Nurse's flowers will not last,
Nurses to their graves are gone,
But the prams go rolling on.
                (CPA, 139)

These lines present a mythic condition: human decay takes place against a natural backdrop of enduring seasonal repetition. Adorno and Horkheimer write, "Like magical rites, myths signify self-repetitive nature, which is the core of the symbolic: a state of being or a process that is presented as eternal, because it incessantly becomes actual once more by being realized in symbolic form."[39] We find this eternal repetition in the poem: as the leaves fall in autumn, the particular "Nurse" becomes "Nurses," and they and the flowers they arrange come to nothing. But behind this shift is the broader condition of cosmic fecundity: the "prams go rolling on." The subsumption of life into life is proper to an enchanted if tragic world: human beings are not narrative, teleological creatures with particular historical trajectories but a part of the unending cosmic repetition of myth.

But as the poem continues, history punctures the mythological background:

Close behind us on our track,
Dead in hundreds cry Alack,
Arms raised stiffly to reprove
In false attitudes of love.

Scrawny through a plundered wood,
Trolls run scolding for their food,
Owl and nightingale are dumb,
And the angel will not come.

Clear, unscaleable, ahead
Rise the Mountains of Instead,
From whose cold cascading streams
None may drink except in dreams.

                    (CPA, 139)

The element of historical evil undermines the assumptions of this background by disenchanting it. In Baudelaire's "Autumn Song," the seasonal decay corresponds ontologically to the reemergence of frigid dispositions in the human self: "Wrath, / Hate, chills and horror, forced and plodding work."[40] In that poem the seasonal change is indistinguishable from these changes in disposition. In Auden's poem, by contrast, the appearance of fascist soldiers ("arms raised stiffly to reprove") and of the historical dead discloses a world that cannot be assimilated into natural sorrow. (Baudelaire's hard and forced labor has become, in Auden's poem, a historical reality.) The enchanted wood cannot account for this historical, human evil or for the freedom that is evil's implicit horizon: that wood has been "plundered"; the "trolls" are hungry and scrawny; the birds are silent. Rilke, whose model of the poet was Orpheus, expected in his *Duino Elegies* a redeeming angel, but Auden's poem rejects that possibility. All that remains are the "Mountains of Instead."[41] The line conjures the enchanted quest narrative in which the hero seeks or passes through the mountains, but the abstract "Instead" is a state of free choice and action; it registers human possibility rather than mythic necessity. There may be no "instead" to counter the decay of nurses and their flowers, but there is for the "Dead" who "cry Alack."

The same disenchantment of genre operates in one of Auden's best-known poems, "Musée des Beaux Arts." Critics have often considered the obvious mythic content of the poem without recognizing that this mythology is undermined by attention to the strictly profane dimension of suffering. The poem, a reflection on several Brueghel paintings, most centrally *Landscape with the Fall of Icarus*, shifts the focus from the mythical grandeur of Icarus's fall to the material context in which that fall occurs:

About suffering they were never wrong,
The Old Masters: how well they understood
Its human position; how it takes place

While someone else is eating or opening a window or just walking
                                                    dully along;
How, when the aged are reverently, passionately waiting
For the miraculous birth, there always must be
Children who did not specially want it to happen, skating
On a pond at the edge of the wood:
They never forgot
That even the dreadful martyrdom must run its course
Anyhow in a corner, some untidy spot
Where the dogs go on with their doggy life and the torturer's horse
Scratches its innocent behind on a tree.

In Brueghel's *Icarus*, for instance: how everything turns away
Quite leisurely from the disaster; the ploughman may
Have heard the splash, the forsaken cry,
But for him it was not an important failure; the sun shone
As it had to on the white legs disappearing into the green
Water; and the expensive delicate ship that must have seen
Something amazing, a boy falling out of the sky,
Had somewhere to get to and sailed calmly on.

                                        (CPA, 179)

In Ovid's *The Metamorphoses*, Icarus's father, Daedalus, is a magician and an alchemist: "He spoke and turned his mind to arts unknown, / And changed the face of nature." His project to liberate himself and his son is, for Ovid, a "transgressive art."[42] Auden's poem would have us remember that a modernist proponent of alchemical poetics, Stephen Dedalus, is his namesake. In *A Portrait of the Artist as a Young Man*, Stephen aims to forge "out of the sluggish matter of the earth a new soaring impalpable imperishable being."[43] Baudelaire claimed something similar of his own poetry: "I have extracted the quintessence of each thing, / You gave me mud and I turned it into gold."[44]

In the original myth, the "transgressive" aspect of alchemy is its *hubris*. This is true both of Daedalus's "art" and also of Icarus, who is told by his father not to fly too high. But hubris is not the interest of Auden's poem; rather, alchemical *poesis* is undermined by an insistence on the recalcitrant otherness of the material world. Alchemy yields to scientific "disenchantment," which insists on the unalterable, mechanistic necessity of natural events. "The sun shone / *As it had to*" on Icarus's disappearing legs. The basic fact about the world is that it "goes on": instinctual animal life, like the horse's itch, persists undisturbed by the tragic elevation characteristic of myth. The tautologous description of the dogs that "go on" with their "doggy life"—as in Stevens's tautology, where things "occur as they occur" — emphasizes the sheer material facticity of natural process.

The attempt to take on the life of birds (as Icarus and Daedalus do) has a unique resonance in Auden's imagination. From early in his career, birds consistently appear in his poems as figures of enchanted, undivided life. In a very early poem from *The Orators*:

> There are some birds in these valleys
> Who flutter round the careless
> With intimate appeal,
> By seeming kindness trained to snaring,
> They feel no falseness.
>
> Under the spell completely
> They circle the can serenely,
> And in the tricky light
> The masked hill has a purer greenness.
> Their flight looks fleeter.
>
> (EA, 89–90)

For Auden, the birds are "under the spell completely" because they obey the natural determinations of instinct. Their flight pattern has a perfect, unalienated rhythm; there is no gap between their desire and their movement (they "feel no falseness").[45] The scene is enchantingly beautiful ("a purer greenness") because, as Simone Weil writes, what has to be (natural necessity coded as instinct) and what is (the performance of the flight) are seamlessly aligned. The birds cannot, like humans, be "careless," for their activity is by definition purposeful. Yet this purpose is not teleological. They "circle" rather than move forward; they are already "serenely" complete ("Our Hunting Fathers" refers to the "*finished* features" of the "creatures" [CPA, 122, emphasis added]). The "intimate appeal" of this bird-life for the human observer is that it generates a fantasy of identity with nature, which is at bottom a desire for self-identity. As Wyndham Lewis wrote in *Time and Western Man*,

> The belief in magic is the sign of man's persuasion of his identity with nature. As he gradually separates himself from nature and becomes a human personality (as he thinks) and as he sees (and then believes) that nature is inhuman and indifferent to him, he no longer believes that he can influence events outside himself, embodied in the objective mechanism over against which he stands.[46]

In a 1929 poem, the fantasy of identification with bird-life is associated with a childish disposition of magical wishfulness, and the poem understands forgiveness as the wish's other:

Without wishing and with forgiving,
To love my life, not as other,
Not as bird's life, not as child's,
"Cannot," I said, "being no child now nor a bird."

(CPA, 47)

The bird imitation of Icarus and Daedalus must therefore be understood in its broader status within Auden's imagination; it betrays a magical desire to reverse the human emergence out of nature's spell.

Auden formally secularizes suffering—and so refuses tragic apotheosis—by employing a technique in which the poem pans out from the individual moment of defeat to the profane context in which the suffering occurs. The poem de-centers Icarus as a locus of suffering by presenting the banal activities that occur alongside his fall, from sailing, plowing, children playing, to the more abstract gerunds that emphasize the unending vibration of activity: eating, opening a window, walking. In doing so, it refuses the metaphysics of tragedy implicit in the myth. Icarus and Daedalus are not exceptional heroes. The perspective is not comic, for it presents real suffering, but it is characterized by what Auden took to be the disenchanting agency of comedy: the material structure of the world here comes into conflict or contradiction with individual intention and will. The poem draws our attention to the constant disparity between human desire and its web of meaning, on the one hand, and the material world's autonomy on the other. Even the gospel narratives do not escape this disenchantment: the "miraculous birth" and the "dreadful martyrdom" of Christ and his followers are equally subjected to a kind of profanation of perspective. Suffering takes place in untidy corners and in view of indifferent spectators. They are seen in what the poem calls their "human position," a position that actually involves a radical de-centering of the human perspective.[47]

Several of Auden's other great poems of the 1930s follow the same procedure of moving from an "enchanted" moment (whether joyous or tragic) to the secular context that makes that moment possible. In "A Summer Night," a poem of 1933 that describes what Auden was later to call his "vision of agape"— an experience of effortless love and concern that took place during a gathering with his fellow schoolteachers on a lawn—the first stanza describes the moment as "enchanted":

Equal with colleagues in a ring
I sit on each calm evening
    Enchanted as the flowers

The opening light draws out of hiding
With all its gradual dove-like pleading,
   Its logic and its powers.

(CPA, 117)

After several stanzas, however, the poem shifts its perspective from this private, communal beatitude to the political arrangements and violence that make that beatitude possible and are necessarily bracketed from consciousness. The poem makes the invisible visible, and in doing so it dissipates the aura the experience carries. He and his colleagues

       do not care to know,
Where Poland draws her Eastern bow,
   What violence is done,
Nor ask what doubtful act allows
Our freedom in this English house,
   Our picnics in the sun.

(118)

The poem refuses to dwell entirely in the serenity of that joyful moment. Auden disenchants it by exposing the secular historical scaffolding in which it is implicated. The experience is by no means negated, however—disenchantment for Auden is not cynicism. Yet neither does Auden quarantine the moment and allow it to occupy a private, sacred space uncontaminated by historical exigency. He does not say, "these delights need no excuse," but rather, "*May* these delights we dread to lose / This privacy, need no excuse / But to that strength belong" (118, emphasis added). Agape is an unforeseen gift, analogous to enchantment and thus "lucky" (117), but in the poem it becomes a task, an ethical achievement that will serve as a line of defense against the encroaching historical "sea" that has overwhelmed their private "river dreams" (118).

    The same secularization of perspective occurs in a more private moment of a few years later, which Auden later entitled "Lullaby."[48] The speaker, who lies in bed with his sleeping lover, again employs the language of enchantment:

Soul and body have no bounds:
To lovers as they lie upon
Her tolerant enchanted slope
In their ordinary swoon,
Grave the vision Venus sends
Of supernatural sympathy,
Universal love and hope;

While an abstract insight wakes
Among the glaciers and the rocks
The hermit's carnal ecstasy.
                    (CPA, 157)

Both the lovers and (more surprisingly) the ascetic are aroused and sustained by
eros, a power that, for the early Auden, under the influence of Freud, was the
fundamental energy animating the world. "Soul and body have no bounds"
because the sympathetic magic of *eros* ("Venus") erases what in "Objects" are the
necessary "edges" of "separation." Both the lovers and the ascetic are provoked,
moreover, to move from the local experience of sensuality to a vision of "universal
love" and "supernatural sympathy." The connection between *eros* and magic
here is critical: if the force that moves both humans and the rest of the material
world is indistinguishable (a more optimistic rendering of Schopenhauer's "will"
and Freud's own concept of *eros*), the world is, according to the magical mind-set,
sympathetic. As Ioan Culianu argued in *Eros and Magic in the Renaissance*, the
capacity for and understanding of magic was, before the scientific revolution,
understood as an achievement of desire, the ascension of *eros* to a certain
potency.[49] Auden is playing with a similar conception here.

As in Auden's other poems of enchantment, however, this one unsettles
the state lately celebrated. The surprising juxtaposition of "tolerant" and
"enchanted" suggests something in magical *eros* that causes political sedation.
That this "tolerance" is not a liberal virtue becomes clearer in the next stanza,
which widens the perspective to the secular horizon on which everything is
not well:

Certainty, fidelity
On the stroke of midnight pass
Like vibrations of a bell
And fashionable madmen raise
Their pedantic boring cry:
Every farthing of the cost,
All the dreaded cards foretell,
Shall be paid, but from this night
Not a whisper, not a thought,
Not a kiss nor look be lost.
                    (CPA, 157)

The secularizing break from the fairy-tale world in which *eros* is omnipotent is
achieved by employing the disenchanting images of those tales themselves:
as in "Cinderella," the stroke of midnight signals that the enchanted again

becomes the ordinary. The world of tarot cards is turned against itself. These cards, familiar to modernism in the poems of Eliot, here speak a language of responsibility and consequence that is alien to their native logic: they foretell that "[e]very farthing of the cost" produced by political irresponsibility and the perversions of fascism ("fashionable madmen") "shall be paid." The future they envision does not depend on occult correspondences; rather, it is a vision of accountability, of the moral consequences entailed by the misuse of moral freedom. For the Auden of the 1930s, the ordinary is historical and political fact.

The final stanza of the poem reads like a prayer for the speaker's lover, but the prayer does not seek a magical rearrangement of material circumstances. Rather, it offers a simple awareness of contingency in the perspective of hope:

> Beauty, midnight, vision dies:
> Let the winds of dawn that blow
> Softly round your dreaming head
> Such a day of welcome show
> Eye and knocking heart may bless,
> Find our mortal world enough;
> Noons of dryness find you fed
> By the involuntary powers,
> Nights of insult let you pass
> Watched by every human love.
>   (157–158)

The "powers" are "involuntary." They are not susceptible to anthropomorphic interpretation and cannot be manipulated. The speaker's "let"s are imperatives that call attention to their own impotence; they are not so much demands as hopes. Human agency finds its power, rather, in assent and care. In times of abundance we may "bless"; in times of privation we must "watch." Neither action involves a state of control. "Find you fed" suggests passive awareness of an achievement in which the self had no hand. But there is another, active "find" that is closer to affirmation: the beloved must "[f]ind our mortal world enough."

MAGIC AND THE SECULAR CRITIQUE
OF MYSTIFICATION

As the foregoing poems suggest, Auden understood secular historicism as a form of critique. In many of these poems this perspective is applied to private experience. But Auden also endorsed a concern familiar since the

Enlightenment: the demystification of social structures that have been invested with magical being. The secularist in this mode is a genealogist digging for the forgotten human, material origins of institutions and ideas. In his book *The Magic of the State*, the anthropologist Michael Taussig has rearticulated the secular moral perspective that strives to show how social structures are actually the creations of human beings: "Take the case of God, the economy, and the state, abstract entities we credit with Being, species of things awesome with life-force of their own, transcendent over mere mortals. Clearly they are fetishes, invented wholes of materialised artifice into whose woeful insufficiency of being we have placed soul stuff. Hence the big S of the State. Hence its magic of attraction and repulsion."[50] Auden's poetry inherits this perspective, though, as I have noted, he thinks that the historicist aspect of secularism has a religious history. (The secular critique of mystification is analogous to the theological critique of idolatry, and the ground for the critique of idolatry is the transcendence of God or the impossibility of locating God within the powers of the world.) Auden was thus capable of describing the power that seemed to petrify unjust social arrangements as "magic." This is the undercurrent of his picture of Marx in the British Library in his 1939 "New Year Letter":

> As he explored the muttering tomb
> Of a museum reading room,
> The Dagon of the General Will
> Fell in convulsions and lay still;
> The tempting Contract of the rich
> Revealed as an abnormal witch,
> Fled with a shriek, for as he spoke
> The justifying magic broke.
> (CPA, 215)[51]

Dagon was a near-eastern god of agriculture and grain who required sacrifice to ensure productivity. Marx here is the enlightened, D(r)agon-slaying scholar who deconstructs the "justifying magic" and exposes it for what it is: a "contract" (a representative act of the modern liberal self) among rich persons. Under his reasonable gaze the "muttering tomb"—a macabre supernatural force—becomes the reading room at the British Library (an institution that, among other things, secularizes religious artifacts by turning them into objects of knowledge) where Marx researched his great works on capital and political economy. The muttering voices of that tomb are clarified by becoming secular records, histories that document the human processes by which the justifying magic took shape.

Marx is not Auden's only hero of secular disenchantment. Just as Marx slew the "Dagon of the General Will," Freud, in Auden's great elegy, unsettles the "Generalized Life":

> No wonder the ancient cultures of conceit
> in his technique of unsettlement foresaw
>   the fall of princes, the collapse of
>   their lucrative patterns of frustration:
>
> if he succeeded, why, the Generalised Life
> would become impossible, the monolith
>   of State be broken and prevented
>   the co-operation of avengers.
>
>   (CPA, 274)

Freud demystifies the magic power of these capital-lettered entities. If Marx "explored the muttering tomb" and exposed its occult secrets to historical light, Freud descended into the dark, enchanted underworld to shine a different version of the same light:

>   he went his way
> down among the lost people like Dante, down
>   to the stinking fosse where the injured
>   lead the ugly life of the rejected.
>
>   (274)

Instead of examining the damnation of the "injured," like Dante, Freud seeks to anatomize their ugliness. His rational vision gives them, and the characters of their dreams, real, not shadowy identities: the "shades" around Freud all wait "to enter / The bright circle of his recognition." If images of light permeate the poem, this is because it is a poem in praise of Enlightenment in the secular tradition. So much, the elegy tells us, has been "revealed by his undiscouraged shining." At the same time, however, Freud's status as a modern Dante, who was taking the path of the Jesus who "descended into hell," indicates Auden's conviction that secular enlightenment can have a religious frame. The prayer that closes "New Year Letter" finds no cleavage between Christian iconography and the imperatives of enlightenment: "O Dove of science and of light . . . / . . . point our knowledge on its way."

With these heroes,[52] Auden consistently claims that we must accept the experience of *cultural* disenchantment, as in "New Year Letter":

> However we decide to act,
> Decision must accept the fact

That the machine has now destroyed
The local customs we enjoyed,
Replaced the bonds of blood and nation
By personal confederation.
No longer can we learn our good
From chances of a neighborhood . . .

(238)

In these lines Auden opposes the re-enchantment of politics that he saw in the blood-mysticism and occultism of the Nazis, and closer to home in the works of Yeats and Lawrence. He does not, like the Futurists, celebrate the machine, but he accepts it as a force that has permanently transformed social relations. What the so-called pagans and primitivists do not see, Auden claims, is that their return to immediacy is poisoned by a rationalized, instrumental focus on the will; their sacred paroxysms of exuberant destruction are actually "the refined / Creation of machines and mind." Indeed, what he sees is a new *theology* of the daemonic, the mana-like sub-personal force that is worshiped as an immanent god:

The cities we abandon fall
To nothing primitive at all;
This lust in action to destroy
Is not the pure instinctive joy
Of animals, but the refined
Creation of machines and mind,
As out of Europe comes a Voice,
Compelling all to make their choice,
A theologian who denies
What more than twenty centuries
Of Europe have assumed to be
The basis of civility,
Our evil *Daimon* to express
In all its ugly nakedness
What none before dared say aloud,
The metaphysics of the Crowd,
The Immanent Imperative
By which the lost and injured live
In mechanised societies
Where natural intuition dies . . .

(225)

Freud's rational voice had descended to the underworld of the "lost" and the "injured." He sought to illuminate the unconscious, not to celebrate its creative darkness. Fascism sought such creative darkness in the crowd, that locus of sub-personal energy in which individual beings manifest their injury.[53] As we will see, Auden was closely attuned to the relations between fascism and neopagan occultism.[54]

THE LIMITS OF THE IMAGE AND THE DANCE

I have argued that the fascination with magic in modernism is closely connected to an anxiety over the mutual alienation of mind and body. This anxiety takes the form of a widespread reaction against instrumental reason, a form of thinking from which the body is excluded, for it, along with all other material objects, is conceived as so much neutral, passive matter to be manipu-lated by the mind. Magical thinking does not understand mental and material realities as different in kind but only as different in degree. Sharp distinctions between human and inhuman, personhood and animal being, are not drawn. Rather, the world is infused with secret sympathies between mind and material object, spirit and body.

Many familiar categories in Romantic and modernist poetics are aimed at resolving the estrangements and disintegrations between self and world that magic once mitigated. The category of the "aesthetic" emerged largely as a remedy for alienation. It sought to bridge what were felt to be the ever-widening gaps between spirit and matter, thought and sensuous experience, moral reason and animal instinct, permanence and change, infinity and finitude. The "aesthetic" is, as Terry Eagleton has argued, a "dream of reconciliation—of individuals woven into intimate unity with no detriment to their specificity, of an abstract totality suffused with all the flesh-and-blood reality of the individual being."[55] Aesthetic experience would end human estrangement from the world without sacrificing the rationality, objectivity, and moral abstraction that helped produce that estrangement.[56] In *Romantic Image*, Frank Kermode showed how the "image" in modernism—a preoccupation it inherited from Romanticism—served as a quasi-religious agent of reconciliation between soul and body. The image is a poetic device that is equally intellectual and sensuous, a product of both thought and feeling. Through it, "form and matter are coterminous, inseparable; of a detachable meaning there is no trace. In Art, as in dance, 'the body is the soul.'" For Yeats, the "victory" of the image is that it accom-plishes the magical reconciliation of interior and exterior: "the victory is an intellectual daily recreation of all that exterior fate snatches away."[57] According to D. H. Lawrence, the "uncritical ancient *felt* his images," whereas the rationalism of modern anthropology of religion has turned the experiential dynamism of the image into a form of cheap symbolism, where the material image merely "stands for" some abstract meaning.[58]

As a reconciliation of inner and outer, the poetic image was supposed to rectify what Yeats called the lost "Unity of Being" and to renovate the state eclipsed through what Eliot called the "dissociation of sensibility." It may be remarked that both of these problems are synonymous with "disenchantment," which was accompanied by a shift from what Charles Taylor calls a "porous" self to a "buffered" self.[59] Yeats's, Eliot's, and Lawrence's hope that a new poetics of the image could return self and culture to those desired states was a hope that the aesthetic could accomplish religious or magical reconciliations. This was one function of the "religion of art."

Auden's struggle to prevent art from becoming magic led him to oppose these basic modernist passions. The image sought to make thought *concrete*, but for Auden such a task could only be accomplished by items that are already concrete: only "flowers think / Theirs concretely in scent-colors" (*CPA*, 801). As Auden's sardonic line makes plain, the doctrine of the image is organicist: it counters the enervating abstraction of the mind, and the mind's presumption of autonomy, for it comes into being through an organic process. The mind does not impose its will-to-form on the material world but guides it according to its internal logic of growth and development. This is why the tree was such an important image for both Romantics and modernists. Yeats's "Vacillation"— discussed in chapter 3—asks, "What is joy?" and answers with the image of a tree that is "half all glittering flame and half all green." The final stanza of his famous "Among School Children" also evokes the tree as that which overcomes the duality produced by the ascetic rationalism of modernity:

> Labour is blossoming or dancing where
> The body is not bruised to pleasure soul,
> Nor beauty born out of its own despair,
> Nor blear-eyed wisdom out of midnight oil.
> O chestnut tree, great rooted blossomer,
> Are you the leaf, the blossom, or the bole?
> O body swayed to music, O brightening glance,
> How can we know the dancer from the dance?
>   (*CPY*, 217)

For Auden, this vision of the enchanted return to a prelapsarian unity of being is impossible. The ideology of organicism is, for him, an attempt to erase the distinction between the logic of human personhood and the vitality of organic life.

Auden is almost certainly thinking of Yeats's trees in his late poem "Reflections in a Forest":

> But trees are trees, an elm or oak
> Already both outside and in,
> And cannot, therefore, counsel folk
> Who have their unity to win.
>
> Turn all tree-signals into speech,
> And what comes out is a command:
> "Keep running if you want to reach
> The point of knowing where you stand."
> . . . .
> My chance of growing would be slim,
> Were I with wooden honesty
> To show my hand or heart to Him
> Who will, if I should lose, be Me.
>
> Our race would not have gotten far,
> Had we not learned to bluff it out
> And look more certain than we are
> Of what our motion is about . . .
>
> (CPA, 670)

Auden's singsong rhyme scheme formally undermines the seriousness of Yeats's "great rooted blossomer." Because humans have their "unity to win," they cannot imitate the aesthetic unity of oaks and elms, which suffer no friction between their inner and outer lives; a tree's form is a perfect expression or performance of its "interior" being. The poem also plays on another constitutive power of the organic image: its ability to reconcile stillness and motion, being and becoming. As Kermode writes, "The Image is to be all movement, yet with a kind of stillness. She lacks separable intellectual content; her meanings, as the intellect receives them, must constantly be changing."[60] This is precisely how Auden translates his "tree-signals": "running" and "where you stand" are one; they exist at a "point" of perfect self-knowledge that is equally action. Yeats's tree and dancer integrate knowing and being in performances that efface all distinction between what they are and what they do. Auden's humans, however, have to "bluff it out." Their performance is closer to play-acting. We "*look* more certain than we *are*" — our external surfaces and internal being do not coincide — about the meaning of our "motion."[61]

Auden's comic tone does not just undermine the religious aspiration toward unity of being; it also discloses an ontological truth. The comic "wooden honesty," and his employment of "would" as an internal slant rhyme—an imperfect rhyme—with "wooden" exemplifies any pun's reliance on disunity, for the very possibility of a pun on "would" and "wood" is ensured by the fact that a single material sound can have two divergent, "interior" meanings. Moreover, that divergence is itself exemplary of the ontological divergence between human personhood and other organic life. Wood is an organic object, but the subjunctive mood that "would" projects is a distinctly human and nonorganic state: it reveals a possibility that may not coincide with actuality, a potential non-coincidence between internal intention and a material exterior. "Would" implies a possible negative, and the negative, which, as Heidegger notes, only exists in human language, is the ground for meaningful human difference, as an earlier stanza suggests:

For who can quarrel without terms
For Not or Never, who can raise
Objections when what one affirms
Is necessarily the case?

(669)

Human being is the only being in which something is not necessarily the case.[62]

Trees were not the only images of magical unity that Auden parodied. He also probes the limits of the modernist image of the dance. Yeats's "Among School Children" is again a touchstone here. In the early twentieth century, anthropologists of religion saw dance as a representative practice of the sacred. The Cambridge anthropologist Jane Harrison wrote, "Throughout the whole world, the primitive man in the magico-religious age danced where we would pray or worship."[63] In his strange book *The Dance of Life*, Havelock Ellis claimed, "Dancing is the primitive expression alike of religion and of love—of religion from the earliest human times and of love from a period long anterior to the coming of man. . . . Dancing is a magical operation for the attainment of real and important ends of every kind."[64] Gerardus Van Der Leeuw, a Dutch phenomenologist of religion who wrote his great work on the relationship between religion and aesthetics, spoke of the religious dimension of dance in terms very similar to those that interested modernist poetics: "To understand the psychology of the dance and to see at the same time its connection with religion we must look upon its rhythm as motion and response, the seizing of life and the discarding of life. The rhythm unfolds in a double manner. By constraining life, seizing it and limiting it, rhythm gives to life. One can rise from the trivial to the most exalted by saying that rhythm moves the feet, the spirit, the gods. It is the pulse of animal life, the heartbeat of our spiritual life, the movement of the world and the course of the gods. The cosmic meaning of the dance is not a secondary speculation, but has existed from the beginning."[65] The attraction of the dance as a religio-aesthetic state is that it unites the animal and spiritual life, thought and performance; like a modernist poem, its "rhythm gives strength to life" by participating in and channeling cosmic force, infusing motion with sacred significance.

Auden too was attracted to the dance as a state of pagan wholeness in which the aesthetic and the religious are indistinguishable. But Auden made a habit of probing aesthetic desires for their social and psychological implications. In the case of the dance, he suspected that this attraction was closely connected to attitudes desiring a return to a sacred warrior culture. In Yeats this was certainly the case: Robert Gregory, Yeats's exemplary aesthete-warrior, is the masculine counterpart to his dancer. Gregory, a fighter pilot who died in the First World War, attains, through focused, violent action, the unity of being Yeats's dancer also accomplished. In Gregory, "mind and hand were at one, will and desire." (Auden noted in a late essay that the only modern equivalent to the Homeric hero-warrior was the ace fighter pilot, and a pilot serves as the hero of his early poem *The Orators*.)[66] There is a radical expenditure of energy in these states, but that energy is contained and concentrated through aesthetic structuring.

It was just this symmetry between the sacred aesthetics of dance and violence that troubled Auden as his career progressed. In the concluding verse commentary to his 1939 sonnet sequence, *In a Time of War*, he ventriloquizes the fascist promise: "*Violence shall synchronize your movements like a tune*" (EA, 266). Modern war, like the modernist dance, betrays a desire to infuse life with the immediacy of music; it operates as a surrogate sacred. Both seek the synchronization of movement, intention, and meaning. For Auden, integration of motion and meaning is indeed a desirable state, but he insists that we must accept an inexorable degree of duality between our meanings and the matter on which we would impose them. Perfect synchronicity collapses the space in which moral doubt might develop. "Ease" of motion is often a fantasy, as in his poem of the early 1930s, later titled "A Bride in the 30's." The poem begins, "Easily you move, easily your head, / And easily, as through leaves of an album, I'm led / Through the night's delights and the day's impressions." Such ease, however, is an illusion of psychological magic: the speaker is really a conjurer who must project a world of enchantment in order to be with his lover:

Easy for him to find in your face
A pool of silence or a tower of grace,
To conjure a camera into a wishing-rose,
Simple to excite in the air from a glance
Horses, fountains, a side-drum, a trombone,
    The cosmic dance.

                    (CPA, 129)

In the original poem the stanza ended, "and the dance, the dance"—motion is
enchanted through poetic repetition. Auden later changed it to "The cosmic
dance," and the decision underscores an awareness of how the image of the
dance in modernist poetics had been infused with religious desires. But the
accomplishment of this modernized sacred world, where the fairy-tale world of
pools and towers is juxtaposed with cameras and trombones, is too "easy," too
"simple." The poem shifts perspectives, and what Auden later calls "private rites
of magic" are displaced by those more disturbing public rites: fascist political
rallies. Kafka said that "the essence of magic" is to "summons,"[67] and here,

Summoned by such a music from our time,
Such images to sight and audience come
As Vanity cannot dispel or bless,
Hunger and fear in their variations,
Grouped invalids watching movements of birds,
    And single assassins,

Ten desperate million marching by,
Five feet, six feet, seven feet high,
Hitler and Mussolini in their wooing poses . . .

                    (129)

The music of our time, and the movement it synchronizes, is the music of
people marching to a sacred, aestheticized politics. The characteristic modern
dance, the poem suggests, is a military march. (In the later "In Praise of
Limestone," the speaker describes a "band of rivals" climbing the "steep stone
gennels in twos and threes, at times / Arm in arm, but never, thank God, in step"
[540].) The "Vanity" of private magic cannot "dispel" its public twin. Indeed, it
feeds on it like a parasite, for the speaker is among the "[g]rouped invalids
watching movements of birds." As I have argued, birds were signs of integration
for the early Auden; in "O Love, the Interest Itself," they are an image of the very
desire he inherits from the earlier modernists, to make thought concrete: "Inspire
them with such a longing as will make his thought / Alive like patterns a murmu-
ration of starlings / Rising in joy over wolds unwittingly weave" (EA, 118).

In "A Bride in the 30's," the ease of motion and love the speaker desires is depicted in this same movement of birds. As an "invalid" he seeks the reintegration of will and motion, and reintegration is precisely what fascism offers. This invalid magician knows, however, that he hears an amoral music, "The voice of Love saying lightly, brightly, / Be Lubbe, be Hitler, but be my good, / Daily, nightly." This energy of love seeks only adverbs—lightly, brightly, daily, nightly—a *way* of feeling and experiencing that may take place in a moral vacuum, a world of fascist integration. Yet in the last stanza the speaker hears another voice, one that undermines the daemonic version of the sacred: "'Yours the choice to whom the gods awarded / The language of learning, the language of love, / Crooked to move as a money-bug, as a cancer, / Or straight as a dove'" (CPA, 130). The gods here do not possess or inspire but bestow a capacity for motion that may not be perfectly integrated in a rhythmic paroxysm of excess but which may become "straight," a movement toward a goal that only a thinking creature can project.

The questionable coalescence of violence, aesthetics, and enchantment is the theme of Auden's great poem of the early 1950s, "The Shield of Achilles." The setting of the poem is the scene from the *Iliad* where Thetis, Achilles's mother, asks Hephaestus to forge a set of armor for her son. Auden imagines the shield as if, to the horror of Thetis, the images engraved on it were not those of Homeric culture but modern warfare and its social context. For many critics, the juxtaposition serves to dramatize the startling difference between the (attractive) religiously inflected ancient warrior culture of public heroism and the (debased) anonymity of modern violence.[68] But the poem is not interested in a "decline" in the cultural template for violence, and the object of its criticism is not the technological modernity responsible for that decline. The claim of the poem is, rather, that modern violence, now divested of its aesthetic aura, exposes the truth of the nature of force and the problematic intimacy between violence and the sacred that was once masked in ancient warrior culture but can no longer be disguised in modernity. In the terms Auden uses in "The Virgin and the Dynamo," modern warfare as "mechanized history" and ancient warfare as sacralized nature are two sides of the same coin, and each exposes the distortions of the other. The "warrior-hero," wrote Auden in the introduction to his *Greek Reader,* was sacred, "the closest approximation to a god . . . possible to man." (P, 2:363). For Auden this apotheosis is always false: divinity can only move in the opposite, kenotic direction. Indeed, Auden uses Christian theology and "secular" modernity to anchor a critique of the longing (felt so deeply by Yeats, among others) for the old Homeric world of sacred violence. Homer is not Auden's example; secularism should not, he insists, aspire to a new paganism.

The shield, in *The Iliad*, is simultaneously an aesthetic object and a weapon. As such it accomplishes, through the mere fact of its utility, that poetic "Unity of Being" a magical poetics seeks: it is an aesthetic image that has material efficacy in the world. Thetis expects to find representations of the sacred in the shield's artwork:

> She looked over his shoulder
>   For ritual pieties
> White flower-garlanded heifers,
>   Libation and sacrifice,
> But there on the shining metal
>   Where the altar should have been,
> She saw by his flickering forge-light
>   Quite another scene.
>
>   (*CPA*, 597)

Thetis does not find sacred space but an "arbitrary spot" enclosed by "barbed wire." In that spot "bored officials" and "ordinary decent folk" are watching from a distance "[a]s three pale figures were led forth and bound / To three posts driven upright from the ground." The space retains the trappings of the sacred, for it is still a place of sacrifice; it is a modern rendition of the crucifixion of Christ and the two criminals. The psychological energy behind the sacrifice, however, is de-aestheticized, and its brutality is made plain.[69] Auden's poem anticipates René Girard's arguments of a few years later concerning sacrifice and the sacred, and it opposes the host of modern intellectuals who saw in sacrifice the same sacred excess of energy that was also expressed in war.[70]

In using the term "sacred" here I am not arguing that Auden has no place for the sacred in human experience and in poetry. On the contrary, Auden uses the concept to denote that which astonishes the imagination and provokes it into creative response: "The concern of the Primary Imagination, its only concern, is with sacred beings and sacred events" (*DH*, 54). But "The Shield of Achilles" is interested in what Christianity, and, by extension, Western secularism, has done to the imagination's delineation of the sacred. In his essay "Christianity and Art," Auden writes, "To the imagination, the sacred is self-evident," and, analogously, "the godlike or heroic man is self-evident" because the imagination is drawn to the radiance of power (*DH*, 456–467). Christianity subverted the enchanted world by making certain distinctions—for instance, between history and nature—but also by blurring others. According to Auden, Christianity undermined the imagination's ability to distinguish between the sacred and the profane and cling to the former: "The Incarnation, the coming of Christ in the form of a servant who cannot be recognized by the eye of flesh and blood, but only by the eye of faith, puts an end to all claims of the imagination to be the faculty which decides what is truly sacred and what is profane." Christ does not appear as the "godlike and heroic man"—the pagan sacred being—but rather as an ordinary man born to ordinary parents, who goes on to die a humiliating, profane death. And yet Christ is called God. For Auden, this "contradiction between the profane appearance and the sacred assertion is impassible to the imagination" (457). The Christian critique of the pagan, magical sacred is therefore not a critique of the sacred as such but a critique of the identification of the sacred with power and beauty—with extraordinary *natural* success.[71]

In "The Shield of Achilles," Thetis seeks just this kind of power and beauty, but she does not find it:

> She looked over his shoulder
>   For athletes at their games,
> Men and women in a dance
>   Moving their sweet limbs
> Quick, quick, to music,
>   But there on the shining shield
> His hands had set no dancing-floor
>   But a weed-choked field.
>   (CPA, 597)

The synchronized movement of violence can no longer be thought of as music; the dancing-floor has been replaced by a weed-choked field. In that field,

> A ragged urchin, aimless and alone,
>   Loitered about that vacancy; a bird
> Flew up to safety from his well-aimed stone:
>   That girls are raped, that two boys knife a third,
>   Were axioms to him, who'd never heard
> Of any world where promises were kept,
> Or one could weep because another wept.
>   (598)

This is not a portrait of modern degeneracy implicitly juxtaposed with ancient beauty. On the contrary, this scene is the modern equivalent of that ancient world, the disenchantment of which has disclosed its truth. As Auden wrote in the introduction to his *Greek Reader*,

> [T]he assumption of the *Iliad*, as of all early epics, which is so strange to us, is that war is the normal condition of mankind and peace an accidental

breathing space. In the foreground are men locked in battle, killing or being killed, farther off their wives, children and servants waiting anxiously for the outcome, overhead, watching the spectacle with interest and at times interfering, the gods who know neither sorrow nor death, and around them all, indifferent and unchanging, the natural world of sky and sea and earth. That is how things are; that is how they always have been and will be. . . . The world of Homer is unbearably sad because it never transcends the immediate moment; one is happy, one is unhappy, one wins, one loses, finally one dies. That is all. Joy and suffering are simply what one feels at the moment; they have no meaning beyond that; they pass away as they came; they point in no direction; they change nothing. It is a tragic world but a world without guilt for its tragic flaw is not a flaw in human nature, still less a flaw in an individual character, but a flaw in the nature of existence. (P, 2:365–366)

The emphatic, unchangeable "that"s of both the stanza and this prose passage partake of the same metaphysical vision. "*That* girls are raped, *that* two boys knife a third"—these are the same entrenched "that"s that Auden finds in the Greek worldview. "That is how things are; that is how they always have been and will be. . . . That is all." The arbitrariness and anonymity of the modern violence the poem describes—we don't know who these boys and girls are, nor do we know their motives—is more aesthetically unsettling than epic violence. But the structure of Homer's shield and this modern shield are the same; they both present worlds that cannot be different.[72] They both subsume human action into metaphysical necessity: there are no "Mountains of Instead." The sordid arbitrariness of modern violence recasts Homeric necessity by secularizing it; violence is divested of its aesthetic aura.

In the poem, a "world where promises were kept" is only a weak possibility, because a promise is a historical act: it requires a significant sense of both interiority and temporality, a self that takes responsibility for time. Auden, however, describes the aesthetic of Homer's world in entirely spatial terms. The fighting is foregrounded, and its meaning is not evoked temporally, by showing the consequences of past actions for the future, or internally, as the manifestation of interior desires or motives, but as a pure present that achieves perspective only through panning out, from the fighting to the wives, from the wives to the gods, and from the gods to the unchanging natural processes. The fighting is thus not historical in Auden's sense of that term. It is indistinguishable from other forms of natural repetition. The shield, in its spatial juxtaposition of rituals, dances, and games, sets the battle in which it is used in an absolute present; its war is one more instantiation of an infinitely repeatable mythic condition. As Erich

Auerbach writes of Homer, the "procession of phenomena takes place in the foreground—that is, in a local and temporal present which is absolute."[73] Auden, working with remarkably similar insights, demythologizes this world by historicizing it. In Homer's ekphrasis war and death are not and cannot be *out of place*—they exist in aesthetic congruity with the life of dances, games, and harvests. But in Auden's poem, ekphrastic activity restores historical time by translating spatial representation into language and all the subjunctive possibilities language carries.

Critics have also suggested that "Shield" may have been influenced by Simone Weil's essay, "The Iliad, or the Poem of Force."[74] The *Iliad's* main concern, Weil argues, is the overwhelming reality of "force," or "that which makes a thing of anybody who comes under its sway. When exercised to the full, it makes a thing of man in the most literal sense, for it makes him a corpse. There, where someone stood a moment ago, stands no one."[75] In Auden's poem, this same transformation from person to thing takes place: the three crucified "figures" "died as men before their bodies died." But while Auden shares this vision of force, he diverges from Weil at critical junctures. For Auden, as we have seen, one of the troubling characteristics of Greek feeling is that the ontological distinction between personal and impersonal violence is elided: the force that kills Patroclus and Hector is natural. For Weil this is precisely the point: the warriors in Homer can all fall "to the level either of inert matter, which is all passivity, or to the level of blind forces, which are all momentum. This is the final secret of war. This secret the *Iliad* expresses by its similes, by making warriors apparitions of great natural phenomenon: a conflagration, a flood, the wind, ferocious beasts, any and every blind cause of disaster." Indeed, Weil praises the Greeks for their insight concerning the mechanical, natural dimension of revenge: "This retribution, of a geometric strictness, which punishes automatically the abuse of strength, became the principal subject of meditation for the Greeks. . . . We [moderns] are only geometricians in regard to matter."[76]

It is just this naturalizing of human violence—the representation of it in mathematical, mechanical, or natural metaphors—that Auden's poem resists. After his image of the three bound figures, the poem reflects on their situation: "The mass and majesty of this world, all / That carries weight and always weighs the same / Lay in the hands of others" (CPA, 597). As in Weil, force is most palpably disclosed as the impersonal material structure of the world, that which can only be *measured* and which is always uniform (which "carries weight and always weighs the same"). For Auden, however, "majesty"—what in the Homeric context might be called "glory"—is really only a function of the impersonality of force, a quantity rather than a quality. For Auden, the glory that the mastery of force produces is not properly *arête*, nor is it an enchanted, daemonic overtaking of the person. It is simply material force that has a "weight," but, as Auden notes earlier in the poem, no "face." The poem insists that in a human context, force always lies "in the hands" of someone.

Conclusion: Evil and the Adequacy
of the Earth

Auden's poetry shows that the religious and the secular do not have to be at loggerheads. Stevens wanted to write "the great poem of the earth" to rival "the great poems of heaven and hell" (*CP*, 730); "religious" for him was synonymous with "otherworldly," and he thought that a secular poetry could finally engage an earth no longer conceived as a spiritual way station. But the later Auden is unquestionably a poet of the earth. He did not, after converting to Christianity, turn to writing devotional or mystical poetry that strained toward transcendence. He became, rather, more thoroughly a poet of the body than either Stevens, for whom "the world" is principally an object outside the self, or Yeats, for whom the body is only interesting in its moments of ecstasy. For Auden, the theological distinction between God's transcendent reality and Creation emancipates creaturely existence: the material world does not have to supply power, ecstasy, or salvation. When the world is all there is, Stevens and Woolf are moved to ask, "Is it enough?" For Auden, that question draws the world too quickly into the circle of human need. To relinquish one's spiritual demands of the world is to begin to relate ethically to it; its objects and creatures become neighbors, its places neighborhoods.

Auden's "Precious Five," for instance, celebrates the natural life of the senses while expressly circumscribing their access to spiritual meaning. Smell facilitates memory, but the nose can only "[p]oint ... Up the storm beaten slope / From memory to hope / the way you cannot take." The ears are asked to attune themselves to "natural" sound and "dance ... The luck you cannot place"; the hands prosper by "making and giving / To hands you cannot see"; the eyes must "love / Those eyes you cannot be"; and the tongue is to "tel[l] ... The truth She cannot make" (*CPA*, 588–590). If Auden's "cannot"s negate, they

204

also convert the senses' diminished metaphysical authority into a responsibility indistinguishable from an awareness of limit. Each "cannot" is a gesture of assent to that which one had no hand in making and remains epistemologically obscure—as in "Friday's Child," "the analogies are rot / Our senses based belief upon" (676)—but which can be received, returned, and loved. The ears cannot trace the designs of fortune ("luck") but can "dance" when they catch fortuitous confluences of sound; sight cannot attain epistemological certainty ("What sight can never prove") yet can "love" what it sees; the tongue cannot create truth but may bear witness to it ("praise").

The senses no longer dwell in "[t]hat calm enchanted wood, / That grave world" where the nose was "riddle and oracle" or where hands "pulverized the trolls / And carved deep Donts in stone" (587, 589). But by untethering sensory experience from the urgencies of meaning, disenchantment has, the poem suggests, amplified the freedom to dwell without anxiety in what is given. Though the senses are subject to disciplinary imperatives—"Be patient," "Be modest," "Be civil," "Look," "Praise"—obedience to these demands is understood as the condition for meeting a further, liberating imperative: "Be happy" (587–590). The senses can fully *play* in the world only when the self is relieved of responsibility for producing its meaning, or when it assents to

> That singular command
> I do not understand,
> *Bless what there is for being,*
> Which has to be obeyed, for
> What else am I made for,
> Agreeing or Disagreeing?
>   (591)

Sensory happiness involves active responsibility, but this responsibility depends, as in moments of Yeatsian blessing, on an enveloping passivity. For Auden, the experience of blessing and being blessed is identical to the theological sentiment of being "made."

Auden's imperative—"*Bless what there is for being*"—overcomes an anxiety characteristic of Stevens's poetry: "What place in which to be is not enough / To be?" (*CP*, 282). For Auden the primordial religious activity is assent rather than belief. When belief comes first—when the senses ask what they should be "happy *for*"—the problem of evil obtrudes:

> I could (which you cannot)
> Find reasons fast enough
> To face the sky and roar

In anger and despair
At what is going on,
Demanding that it name
Whoever is to blame . . .
                    (CPA, 591)

The command to bless overrides the abstraction of the problem of evil by suggesting that the mysterious contingency and givenness of existence constitute a more fundamental problematic: "Agreeing or Disagreeing" to the provision of one's own being. For Stevens, sheer material existence ("[w]hat place in which to be") seems unable to provide adequate resources for the complexity of human being ("is not enough / To be?"). Yet there is no other resource. This dilemma comprises Stevens's secular version of the problem of evil.

By evil I mean not (only) exceptional human wickedness but the forces in the world, both human and inhuman, that generate suffering. The tension between the benevolent monotheistic God and ubiquity of evil came to be seen, in modernity, as increasingly insoluble to many intellectuals (though as many have noticed, "theodicy"—a term invented by Leibniz in the early eighteenth century to describe the philosophical project of reconciling a good God with evil in the world—is a distinctly modern enterprise). In Hume's *Dialogues Concerning Natural Religion*, Philo, paraphrasing Epicurus, gives the doubt representative form: "Is God willing to prevent evil, but not able? then he is impotent. Is he able, but not willing? then he is malevolent. Is he both able and willing? whence then is evil?"[1] Over a century later, William James wrote of the composition of "Theodicies," "We of the nineteenth century, with our evolutionary theory and our mechanical philosophies, already know too impartially and too well to worship unreservedly any God of whose character [nature] can be seen as an adequate expression."[2] Mrs. Ramsay, as I noted at the beginning of this book, is a representative late Victorian atheist (perhaps only) in her insistence that "God" is incommensurable with "the fact that there is no reason, order, justice: but suffering, death, the poor." When Woolf said of Eliot's conversion that belief in God was "obscene," she, like her character, was drawing on a secular moral feeling that refuses to neutralize the outrage of evil by either understanding it as a product of human failure (sin) or narrating it as an unpleasant moment in the redemption of the world.

But skepticism toward religious claims about evil introduced an unexpected problem for secular modernist aesthetic and moral projects.[3] In its programmatic mode secularism strives, as George Levine writes in his introduction to *The Joy of Secularism*, "to disentangle morality and 'fullness' from the transcendent, to shift attention and emotional investment from the *aldilà* to the here and now." An evaluation accompanies this shift: "This world [is] . . . beautiful and adequate to itself. The earth is room enough—or should be."[4] Similarly Stathis Gourgouris commends the secular idea that "fullness, total plentitude and fulfillment, can be found in the finite and the fragile, in the ephemeral and the mortal, in the uncertain and the passing."[5] Levine's "adequate" and "enough" echo Stevens's repeated search for that which is "adequate" ("On the Adequacy of Landscape") or "enough" ("As if the health of the world might be enough"); Mrs. Ramsay's "It is enough!"; and Neville's objection, in *The Waves*, that for Rhoda and Louis, "It is not enough for them, this ordinary scene."

But this secular affirmation—"enough"—is embattled in Woolf and Stevens. As Hannah Arendt observed, there is a secular problem lodged in the religious concern for theodicy; behind the early modern desire to justify God, she writes, lurked "the suspicion that life as we know it stands in great need of being justified."[6] Mrs. Ramsay resolves the problem of "suffering, death, the poor" only in moments of private ecstasy. Woolf is repeatedly moved to ask the question of "Holburn Viaduct"—"then why?"—when she confronts the incongruity between the world's radiance and the world's suffering. And as I have argued, her intimation of a comprehensive aesthetic order—her "world" as a "work of art"—is closely aligned with the project of theodicy. This very alignment motivates her ambivalent repudiation of the eschatological aura that she discerns in the beautiful. Nietzsche famously claimed, "[I]t is only as an *aesthetic phenomenon* that existence and the world are eternally *justified*."[7] Nietzsche intends "aesthetic" entirely to displace "moral." Though Woolf approaches this view in *Mrs. Dalloway*, beauty in Woolf is rarely an *exclusively* aesthetic criterion: "beauty" is saturated with religious mystery precisely because it is "only two finger's-breadth from goodness."[8] Beauty is not so much a justification in Woolf as a sign of hope, and it cannot be trusted because that hope is illusory. Two finger's-breadth is too much space.

Stevens's phrase in "Esthétique du Mal"—"It seems / As if the health of the world might be enough"—is not quite an affirmation but a potentiality that demands an arduous will to affirm rather than, as in Auden's "Precious Five," assent. Another Stevens poem, "World without Peculiarity," asks, "What good is it that the earth is justified, / That it is complete, that it is an end, / That in itself it is enough?" In so asking it fractures the evaluative position: the world may be "justified" without being "good." Even if we notice the colloquial character of the phrase "What good is it?" the casualness serves to inject an everyday weariness into the metaphysical discussion. Indeed, Nietzsche's dictum aside, it isn't clear what justification entails when severed from moral criteria. Stevens's poem places aesthetics on the evaluative axis before the question even arises:

"The red ripeness of round leaves is thick / With the spices of red summer," but this affirmation cannot stall the question, and the deliberately cloying alliteration and diction suggest that this standard has become desperate.

The poem attacks the question by liquidating the subject position from which it might be asked:

> It is the earth itself that is humanity . . .
> He is the inhuman son and she,
> She is the fateful mother, whom he does not know.
>
> She is the day, the walk of the moon
> Among the breathless spices and, sometimes,
> He too is human and difference disappears
>
> And the poverty of dirt, the thing upon his breast,
> The hating woman, the meaningless place,
> Become a single being, sure and true.
>
> (*CP*, 388)

These lines propose a revolution in the concept of the human. "Human" names a perspective from which judgments of value arise ("What good is it?") and an unfinished identity that trails behind its own projections of desire; it is therefore a state of difference and dissatisfaction. The poem would relinquish this position and award it to "the earth." The earth becomes the arbiter of value; humans are seen as ontologically wayward ("inhuman son") rather than as loci of value that preside in their singularity. The "human" task would no longer be to justify or endorse but rather to assimilate—to become the "human" ("sometimes, / He too is human") of this transvalued inhuman. Such a world would be, the title suggests, a "World without Peculiarity," for the distancing puzzlement experienced in the world's resistance to desire and judgments of value—a puzzlement that generates the sense of evil ("poverty") and the question of theodicy ("justified")—is erased when the human and inhuman collapse into a "single being."

There can be no "secular humanism" when there is no "human." The self of secular humanism is invested with dignity because it is, as in the early Stevens, "unsponsored, free"; it is self-legislating, self-creating, and responsible for the world it makes.[9] But in Stevens, the secular imperative to affirm the immanent world often overwhelms the human itself. The recalcitrance of evil thwarts the will to affirm to the point that evil seems to emerge, not so much from the material world's inadequacy as from the properties of human selfhood. In "Esthétique du Mal," a poem concerned with the secular perception of *mal* ("evil," "wrong," "poverty," "pain"),

The genius of misfortune
Is not a sentimentalist. He is
That evil, that evil in the self, from which
In desperate hallow, rugged gesture, fault
Falls out on everything: the genius of
The mind, which is our being, wrong and wrong,
The genius of the body, which is our world,
Spent in the false engagements of the mind.

(279)

"Evil in the self" is not, as in Christianity, the presence of sin hidden deep within the human subject but a quality of experience produced by merely *having* a self. Yet even here Stevens shares something with the myth of the Fall, which, as Paul Ricoeur has written, is about the "evil infinite of human desire — always something else, always something more. . . . A 'desire' has sprung up, the desire for infinity . . . the infinity of desire itself; it is the desire of desire, taking possession of knowing, of willing, of doing, and of being."[10] In Stevens's lines, evil emerges when the infinite desire constituting our "being" — "the false engagements of the mind" — is projected onto, and frustrated by, the finite "world." The self — what "The Poems of Our Climate" calls "[t]he evilly compounded, vital I" — is that *"from which . . . fault / Falls out on everything."*[11] In this poem and others, Stevens's solution to this problem is to "exile desire / For what is not" (323). To perfect the rejection of otherworldliness, the world must adjudicate the terms of desire; the "inhuman" must adjudicate the terms of the "human." To accomplish this perfect worldliness, however, the self is entangled in a new ascetical project (discipline of desire, loss of self), yet it was impatience with ascetic ideals that motivated world affirmation in the first place.[12]

If Auden's theology of creatureliness emancipates the sensuous, embodied life by limiting the scope of its concern, Stevens's worldliness encumbers the senses with almost salvific agency. When Stevens's poems consider "evil" they consistently counter with "sense." "Esthétique du Mal" concludes its meditation on evil by imagining a world of sense that overcomes evil's unintelligibility:

One might have thought of sight, but who could think
Of what it sees, for all the ill it sees?
Speech found the ear, for all the evil sound,
But the dark italics it could not propound.
And out of what one sees and hears and out
Of what one feels, who could have thought to make
So many selves, so many sensuous worlds

As if the air, the mid-day air, was swarming
With the metaphysical changes that occur,
Merely living as and where we live.

(287)

Speech cannot "propound" the "dark italics" because the world's "ill" cannot be gathered up in meaning; the world is not a text. This ill appears to unsettle even "sight," that mode of sensory encounter that tactically evades the indiscretions of meaning-making poetics throughout Stevens's career. But though the world cannot be read, it can be made ("who could have thought to make"), not as meaning but as sense. The world does not conform to "thought"; this is a consequence of the unintelligibility that, as Susan Neiman has argued, is synonymous with the problem of evil as such.[13] The stanza, however, subtly shifts its perspective on thought: "Who could think" implies philosophical impairment when *facing* evil ("sight"), but "who could have thought to make" registers an autonomous world of sense always already at work before the mind "thought to" intervene, "Merely living as and where we live." We expect a transition in the argument after "propound"—a response to the perplexity measured in the previous lines—yet because this sensory creativity is always moving ahead of thought, the grammar is paratactic: "*And* out of what" rather than the expected "*But* out of what." "But" would announce a solution, a program, yet sight, hearing, and feeling have been making their "sensuous worlds" all along. The poem appeals to a sensuous habitat so affluent that the *questions* generated by evil cannot be sustained: Stevens refuses to impose an interrogative grammar on the interrogative structure of the final sentence.[14] The mind converts questions into metaphysical accounts of evil; sense is always indicative and contains its own "metaphysical changes." Whereas in Auden the senses may evoke ideas and emotions beyond the intelligibility of their domain ("the way you cannot take"), secular paradise for Stevens is a sensory "abundance" that points nowhere, in which "we breathe / An odor *evoking* nothing, absolute" (341, emphasis mine). Yet, as "World without Peculiarity" indicates, this abundance is not always sufficient.

If for Stevens the will to call the world "innocent" (361) demands, at times, an evacuation of the desiring self in which evil originates, Yeats reverses Stevens's problematic: "who will thirst for the metaphysical, who have a parched tongue, if we cannot recover the Vision of Evil?" (A, 251). Evil composes the background and amplifies the desire necessary to maintain exceptional passionate states. The great Romantic writers—Yeats names Wordsworth, Shelley, Emerson, and Whitman—"have become to seem superficial because they lack" this "Vision of

Evil" (200). In *The Prelude* (1805), Wordsworth appeals to "the very world," rather than the displacements of "Utopia," as "the place in which, in the end, / We find our happiness, or not at all."[15] Yeats writes,

> It is natural for a man who believes that man finds his happiness here on earth, or not at all, to make light of the obstacles to that happiness and deny altogether the insuperable obstacles seen by religious philosophy. The strength and weight of Shakespeare, of Villon, of Dante, even of Cervantes, come from their preoccupation with evil. In Shelley, in Ruskin, in Wordsworth, who for all his formal belief was, as Blake saw, a descendent of Rousseau, there is a constant resolution to dwell upon good only; and from this comes their lack of the sense of character, which is defined always by its defects or its incapacity, and their lack of their dramatic sense; for them human nature has lost its antagonist. (*LE*, 42)

The idiosyncrasies of Yeats's pagan secularism are evident in these lines. Though Yeats's instinct to affirm the world is as vigorous as Stevens's ("I am content to live it all again / And yet again"), here as elsewhere he derides secularism in its progressive, eudaemonistic mode ("the Garden City mind") for abandoning the sense of recalcitrant evil demanded by "religious philosophy." Yeats goes on to endorse a syncretic Irish belief—"heathen or Christian"—in "original sin" (43), a sentiment that later finds its way into "Vacillation": "What theme had Homer but original sin?"

But while there are Augustinian moments in Yeats ("the foul rag and bone shop of the heart"), Yeats typically conflates the doctrine of original sin with the doctrines of tragedy. As I argued in chapter 3, "evil" for Yeats is a positive rather than privative force; his most succinct definition of the term is "the strain one upon another of opposites" (25). The sense of evil is valuable principally because it nourishes the "dramatic sense," not because it stimulates introspection and self-transformation or signals dependence on transcendent grace. Stevens has a similar value in mind when he writes, "The death of Satan was a tragedy / For the imagination" (*CP*, 281)—the disappearance of Satan depletes the imagination because the suffering self loses what Yeats calls its "antagonist." Thus in Stevens, as in Yeats, the *historical* "tragedy" of the loss of the religious resources for narrating evil must be displaced by a *metaphysics* of tragedy. Tragedy is an existential need, "a joy," as Yeats says, "to the man who dies." Stevens's hope is that "[t]he tragedy, however, may have begun, / Again, in the imagination's new beginning" (282). This "major" tragedy is the "passion for yes" that overrides the world's "no"—the acknowledgment that we "are spent, / Each one," in "the unalterable necessity / Of being this unalterable animal" (282, 285). Stevens understands this tragic necessity as the force of disenchanted, natural mechanism and the constriction of finitude; Yeats sacralizes necessity—the gods "through their dramatic power . . . bring our souls to crisis"—and views "tragic joy" as a state of self-transcendence in which the self desires both its fugitive object and "whatever happens."

As Auden saw, the danger of the tragic affirmations characteristic of modernist paganism was that they failed to make a distinction between moral evil—the evil enacted in history by responsible beings and the institutions they create—and natural evil. The consequences in Stevens are minor. Though "the genius of misfortune / Is not a sentimentalist," when Stevens tries to subsume historical violence into his meditations on ontological "poverty," the results often are sentimental. We read in canto 7 of "Esthétique du Mal," written during the Second World War,

> How red the rose that is the soldier's wound
> . . . .
> . . . his wound is good because life was.
> No part of him was ever part of death.
> A woman smoothes her forehead with her hand
> And the soldier of time lies calm beneath that stroke.
>   (281)

Here "life," only lately justified by the will, presumes to affirm any of its devastating configurations ("his wound") as "good"; "because" obscures the agency of the will in this prior valuation.

Unlike Stevens, Yeats's imagination is enthralled not so much by "poverty"—the term in Stevens rarely composes a human scene—as by violence. For the later Yeats, conflict is not a philosophical dilemma for the secular or religious mind but an energy that the will can harness. It is the condition for the possibility of the passions. Stevens is not a social poet; when he pushes the secular affirmation of the world to an antihumanistic conclusion he is rarely thinking of the consequences for moral psychology. But Yeats cannot conceive of a human good that isn't measured by its dramatic intensity or of an intensity that does not enlarge itself in conflict. Stevens figures the world as "force" rather than "presence," a flashing, fateful "river that flows nowhere" (911, 451); Yeats, too, like "Homer," finds "it certain" that "out of life's own self-delight spr[ings] / The abounding, glittering jet." In Yeats, however, this jet is also the source of violence, bitterness, and power ("Meditations," *CPY*, 200)—all modes, for Yeats, of "joy." Yeats wants his secular world—secular in that it needs no justification beyond its own "self-delight"—to be organized along Homeric lines, for which, as Auden writes, "war is the normal condition of mankind and peace an accidental breathing space" (*P*, 2:365).

Auden closes this study because he is a powerful critic of this paganism. The later Auden thought that collapsing the distinction between history (the element of personhood) and nature (force or energy) was morally and politically hazardous. He saw National Socialism as a "pagan political religion" (2:172); it subsumed the responsible self of history into the mythical organism of the state. Yeats imagined that the passions were gods, but Auden, following Kierkegaard, believed that the pagan "trust in esthetic immediacy — my feelings are not really *mine* but given me by the gods . . . is destroyed the moment I become aware of possessing a definite continuing self" (2:216). This awareness is a burden — it estranges us from "the magical centre / Where things are taken in hand" (*CPA*, 609) and generates, as Yeats realized, "remorse" — but also a task. It is, for Auden, the element of responsibility, the condition in which both sustained moral action and forgiveness become intelligible. "Paganism had a god of love," Auden writes, "but no god of marriage" (*P*, 2:217).

Secularism has its limits in Auden. "Disenchantment" names for him an ethical project as much as a cultural condition. While Auden was a kind of secularist, he saw a confluence between disengaged scientific rationality and paganism. In "Memorial for the City," a poem written in the aftermath of the Second World War,

> The eyes of the crow and the eye of the camera open
> Onto Homer's world, not ours. First and last
> They magnify earth, the abiding
> Mother of gods and men; if they notice either
> It is only in passing: gods behave, men die,
> Both feel in their own small way, but She
> Does nothing and does not care.
> She alone is seriously there.
>
> (*CPA*, 591)

The crow and the camera — the ancient natural and modern technological ways of seeing — are symmetrical. Under their gaze, human action and even the "behavior" of the gods — Auden claimed that the gods cannot properly be said to *act*[16] — are subsumed into the tragic metaphysical perspective in which the primary reality is natural process. In that perspective, human violence and the violence of time are analogous. A "village is burning," "soldiers fire," "captives are led away": this is "the way things happen" (592). From the perspective of the crow and camera these activities are either anonymous or syntactically passive;

the verbs and gerunds Auden employs evoke a present that is infinitely repeatable. The figures thus become either secular statistics or mythical archetypes. Under these conditions, the emotional and aesthetic response to the world's evil can only be tragic, for both secular science (a science of disengaged observation) and "Homer" view the world's unfolding as necessary and indifferent:

> Plum-blossom falls on the dead the roar of the waterfall covers
> The cries of the whipped and the sighs of the lovers
> And the hard bright light composes
> A meaningless moment into an eternal fact
>
> . . . .
>
> One enjoys glory, one endures shame;
> He may, she must. There is no one to blame.
>
> (CPA, 592)

This is expressly the world of Yeats's "Lapis Lazuli," where

> Every accidental crack or dent
> Seems a water-course or an avalanche,
> Or lofty slope where it still snows
> Though doubtless plum or cherry branch
> Sweetens the little halfway house . . .
>
> (CPY, 295)

Yeats's vision is refused here. For him, "The innocent and beautiful / Have no enemy but time" (233); for Woolf the exploding shell that kills Andrew Ramsay is a mere parenthesis in passing time's broader violence; and for Stevens the soldier at Guadalcanal becomes the "soldier of time" (*CP*, 281). Auden insists that this perspective "lies": "the crime of life is not time." Therefore,

> Our grief is not Greek: As we bury our dead
> We know without knowing there is reason for what we bear,
> That our hurt is not a desertion, that we are to pity
> Neither ourselves nor our city;
> Whoever the searchlights catch, whatever the loudspeakers blare,
> We are not to despair.
>
> (CPA, 592)

Auden's Christianity requires him to disavow the tragic vision so prominent in Yeats, Stevens, and Woolf. "Adam" is still, the poem says, "waiting for his city." In Yeats, "pity" is a perverse moralization of oppositional *eros* and an unheroic concession to human weakness. In Auden it is a failure of accountability: "we" have done this, not life. It is also a failure of hope: "our hurt is not a desertion." But the object of this hope is not an abstract, fleshless heaven (which Stevens can only imagine as a "non-physical . . . paradise" populated by "non-physical people"[*CP*, 286]) but the "City of God" of the poem's epigraph: *"In the self-same point that our soul is made sensual, in the self-same point is the City of God ordained to him without beginning"* (Juliana of Norwich). The basis of this hope is, unexpectedly, the persistence of the flesh: "that is our hope; that we weep and It does not grieve, / That for It the wire and the ruins are not the end: / This is the flesh we are but never would believe" (*CPA*, 595). The body's frailty is coupled with a sense of its impassibility; "It"—Auden's capitalization renders this flesh an anonymous other—endures precisely when we cannot. Its very indifference to the devastation of spirit—its secularity—is also a sign of redemption.

NOTES

INTRODUCTION

1. Virginia Woolf, *To the Lighthouse* (New York: Harcourt, 1981), 63. Hereafter cited in text as *TL*.

2. It is worth remarking that sincerity's authority as a pervasive modern value is linked to Protestant Christianity's configuration of the relations among truth, external world, and an interior self understood to be in some sense pre-linguistic. On sincerity in Protestantism, see Webb Keane, *Christian Moderns: Fetish and Freedom in the Mission Encounter* (Berkeley: University of California Press, 2007), esp. chapter 7.

3. On the character of emotions as tacit interpretations of the world, see Charles Altieri, *The Particulars of Rapture* (Ithaca: Cornell University Press, 2003), and Martha Nussbaum, *Upheavals of Thought* (New York: Cambridge University Press, 2003).

4. Because a reader may object that by "religion" I simply mean "Christianity," or that in using the term "secular" I am mistaking a culture and ideology specific to the West and its Christian history for something normative, I want to say something about my use of these words. There are a number of scholars, who, over the last ten or twenty years, have criticized the concept of "religion" as a coherent genre. These scholars have emphasized the problematic forces, motives, and frameworks that influenced the construction of "religion" as a category, including colonialism, scientism, dubious philosophical universalism, and the conscious or unconscious use of Christian theology (in particular the importance early modern Christianity gave to belief as the paradigmatic religious state) as the template for understanding all other religious cultures and formations. The work of Talal Asad, Tomoko Masuzawa, Jonathan Z. Smith, Saba Mahmood, Timothy Fitzgerald, Peter Harrison, and Brent Nongbri and others has contributed to this critique. In the same way, the term "secular" is now being pluralized, its genealogies investigated, and its Western formulation challenged as the authoritative paradigm for cultures across the world. I am largely sympathetic with these developments and challenges, though I have concerns about the philosophical presuppositions and consequences of many of these arguments. Moreover, I readily

acknowledge that when, say, Wallace Stevens or Virginia Woolf is thinking about "religion," what they have in mind looks more like Christianity than Islam. The problem is that they sometimes mean more than Christianity and sometimes less. Religion for them can suggest any or several of the following: Christianity, asceticism, Platonism, supernaturalism, theodicy, otherworldliness, mysticism, a desire to find a transcendent source of moral or political authority, an understanding of the world as a creation of some kind—even paganism, which is for Stevens and Yeats in particular an attractive ethos within the parameters of secular naturalism. What is more, it could be objected that the term "Christian" would always be in need of further refinement—Protestant? Catholic? Calvinist? Lutheran? Pentecostal?—and in which historical context? Therefore, I will often use the general term "religion" in the hope that it will be clear which aspects of religious thought or feeling I have in mind. My use of the term does not indicate that I think that there is a shared essence among all the traditions commonly called "religious" or that I think of Christianity as a template for all religions, yet it is clear that insofar as Stevens (for instance) resists asceticism he would likely resist many forms of Buddhism, or in resisting transcendent sources of authority (in one poem he compares "God" to the "police") he would equally resist many forms of Islam. Wallace Stevens, *Collected Poetry and Prose* (New York: Library of America, 1997), 120. (All quotations from Stevens, with the exception of his letters and commonplace book, are from this edition and hereafter cited in text as *CP*.) Similarly, I use "secular" as shorthand for the imaginative frame within which Stevens resists or reworks all of the perspectives he thinks of as religious. This is clearly a post-Christian frame. While Stevens certainly does not assent to all of the properties variously attributed to Western secularism (nor is he terribly interested in secularism as a political concept or arrangement), I do not know of a better word than this. Indeed, one of the arguments of this book is that Stevens, like all of my writers, realized secularization could mean a number of things and take a number of shapes, including ones that show significant continuity with religious ideas.

5. José Casanova distinguishes between "secularization," "the secular," and "secularisms" as follows: "secularization" denotes the "empirical-historical patterns of transformation and differentiation" of and in "religious" and "secular" spheres; the "secular" is a category ("theologico-philosophical, legal-political, and cultural-anthropological") that aims to "construct, codify, grasp and experience a realm or reality differentiated from 'the religious'"; "secularisms" refers to secular "world-views (or 'Weltanschauungen') which may be either consciously held and explicitly elaborated into historico-philosophical and normative-ideological state projects, projects of modernity and cultural programs or as an epistemic knowledge regime that may be unreflexively held and phenomenologically assumed as the taken for granted normal structure of modern reality." José Casanova, "Secular, Secularizations, Secularisms," on *The Immanent Frame*, October 25, 2007, http://blogs.ssrc.org/tif/2007/10/25/secular-secularizations-secularisms/. When I refer to "secularization" in this book, however, I am thinking principally of a process and even a *method* through which cultural (philosophical, moral, aesthetic) paradigms break from religion, not something that happens to institutions or the public sphere. Similarly, when using terms like "secular"

and "secularism," I am not here concerned with their "legal-political" dimensions but the ways in which they capture a felt metaphysical or ontological *condition* ("secular") and a worldview and ethos ("secularism").

6. "God is dead; but given the way of men, there may still be caves for thousands of years in which his shadow will be shown.—And we—we still have to vanquish his shadow, too." Friedrich Nietzsche, *The Genealogy of Morals*, trans. Walter Kaufmann (New York: Vintage, 1974), 167.

7. Charles Taylor, *A Secular Age* (Cambridge: Harvard University Press, 2007). Taylor writes, "I mean by this stories of modernity in general, and secularity in particular, which explain them by humans having lost, or sloughed off, or liberated themselves from certain earlier, confining horizons, or illusion, or limitations of knowledge." Instead, he argues, "I will steadily be arguing that Western modernity, including its secularity, is the fruit of new inventions, newly constructed self-understandings and related practices, and can't be explained in terms of perennial features of human life" (22).

8. As Michael Warner, Jonathan VanAntwerpen, and Craig Calhoun put it in their introduction to *Varieties of Secularism in a Secular Age* (Cambridge: Harvard University Press, 2010)—a collection of essays that emerged from a conference on Taylor's book—"The secular is never just the absence of religion, or its privatization, or its waning. It is a cumulatively and dialectically achieved condition" (25). According to Asad, secularism operates as a normative concept that "brings together certain behaviors, knowledges, and sensibilities in modern life." Secularism's "polemical mode," he observes, often requires the use of binaries—"belief and knowledge, reason and imagination, history and fiction, allegory and symbol, natural and supernatural, sacred and profane"—that flatten out the complexity of the conceptual worlds on both the unenlightened and enlightened sides. *Formations of the Secular: Christianity, Islam, Modernity* (Stanford: Stanford University Press, 2003), 25, 23. Taylor has emphasized how what seem to be inevitable or irresistible shifts in knowledge are often underwritten by the moral and aesthetic "prestige" that attends the position of the disengaged, knowing secular subject, who "radiates" a "sense of freedom, power, control, invulnerability" and "dignity" (*Secular Age*, 286). While many modernists share a sense of the inevitability of secularity, they are well aware that part of its power derives from the attractiveness of the dispositions that ground it. Sometimes these dispositions are celebrated (Stevens is exhilarated by the prospect of being "unsponsored, free") and sometimes criticized (Woolf, as we will see, details the at times comic limitations of Mr. Ramsay's attempt to assimilate the prestige of godless dignity).

9. By the term "imaginary" I mean the background worldview and all the normative assumptions that flow from and reinforce it: understandings of selfhood, morality, aesthetics, emotion, the body, etc. It includes the explicit or implicit ontology and metaphysics that shape the worldview, though I treat these categories as what R. G. Collingwood called "absolute presuppositions": they do not have to be theoretically elaborated and they are not *empirically* verifiable. See Collingwood, *An Essay on Metaphysics* (New York: Oxford University Press, 2002). (Auden read Collingwood's book when it appeared in 1940 and repeatedly cited his idea of absolute

presuppositions.) As Giuseppina D'Oro writes, "Collingwood's view is that absolute presuppositions require a different mode of verification. They are verified by assessing whether they are true to the kind of experience or knowledge that they make possible." *Collingwood and the Metaphysics of Experience* (New York: Routledge, 2002), 65. The writers in this study are particularly concerned with the symmetry or asymmetry between, precisely, secular or religious absolute presuppositions and the modes of experience they permit or impede. As Charles Taylor puts it, "The condition of secularity . . . has thus to be described as the possibility or impossibility of certain kinds of experience in our age" (*Secular Age*, 14). Stevens calls the modern poet a "metaphysician in the dark" (*CP*, 219); Stevens, Woolf, Yeats, and Auden are all, in this sense, "metaphysical" writers interested in how things are in the world, the absolute presuppositions we bring to that world, and the implications of those states of affairs for experience. I borrow the term "imaginary" from Charles Taylor in his book *Modern Social Imaginaries* (Durham: Duke University Press, 2006)—which develops Benedict Anderson's language in *Imagined Communities* (New York: Verso, 1993)—though my interest is not primarily "social." Taylor writes, "By social imaginary, I mean something much broader and deeper than the intellectual schemes people may entertain when they think about social reality in a disengaged mode. I am thinking, rather, of the ways people imagine their social existence, how they fit together with others, how things go on between them and their fellows, the expectations that are normally met, and the deeper normative notions and images that underlie these expectations . . . There are important differences between social imaginary and social theory. I adopt the term imaginary . . . because my focus is on the way ordinary people 'imagine' their social surroundings, and this is often not expressed in theoretical terms, but is carried in images, stories, legends" (23). At the same time, Taylor notes, what becomes implicit, almost sensuous, in social imaginaries was often made possible by revolutions in social theories. While my study does not focus on "social" reality, Taylor's "imaginary" fits what I am trying to describe. I assume that literature is a major field in which imaginaries are subjected to refinement, expansion, complication, demolition, or any number of active engagements. Stevens says that "the imagination" comes "always at the end of an era" (*CP*, 656); in modernist literature, the *imagination* is that which comes into conflict with the old *imaginary* in an attempt to forge a new imaginary.

10. This book does not argue that secular modernists are covertly religious. Indeed, I am not primarily concerned with "religious experience" at all, if that term is understood as a discrete genre of human activity focused on the supernatural or a set of ritualized behaviors. Too often that concept works to limit our sense of the ways in which experience is more generally informed by religion. The circumscribing effect of "religious experience" has been generated by two principal forces: the "privatization" of religion that has often accompanied secularization and the desire, as the academic study of religion evolved, to isolate an "essence" of religion grounded in either propositional beliefs about the existence of certain beings or the experience of something called "the sacred." The former relegates religious experience to inner states of belief or faith, while the latter understands it as a response to distinctly "numinous" phenomena. As I have already noted, the boilerplate model of religion generated by these forces has

been heavily criticized in recent years. For this study, however, the trouble with the restriction of religious questions to the domain of "religious experience" is that it obscures the tacit influence that religious (and secular) ideas have on broader areas of experience and reflection. This book, then, is not a study of distinctly "religious" beliefs and practices but an investigation of the impact that religious and secular "imaginaries" have on a range of moral and aesthetic experience. And because these writers have come to suspect that they are incongruously dwelling in competing imaginaries, or in imaginaries that are now seen to depend surreptitiously on the very ones they were meant to replace, their work consistently throws its figurations of subjectivity and experience against metaphysical and ontological backgrounds to investigate their commensurability. On the privatization of religion and its limits, see José Casanova, *Public Religions in the Modern World* (Chicago: University of Chicago Press, 1994). On the instability of the category of the "sacred," see Talal Asad, *Formations of the Secular*, esp. chapter 1; on the construction of religion as an essentialized category and the implicitly Christian template for this essence, see Asad, *Genealogies of Religion* (Baltimore: Johns Hopkins University Press, 1993), chapter 1, and Brent Nongbri, *Before Religion: A History of a Modern Concept* (New Haven: Yale University Press, 2013).

11. Theodore Ziolkowski, *Modes of Faith: Secular Surrogates for Lost Religious Belief* (Chicago: University of Chicago Press, 2007), x.

12. For Matthew Arnold, "Our religion has materialized itself in the fact, in the supposed fact; it has attached its emotion to the fact, and now the fact is failing it. But for poetry the idea is everything; the rest is a world of illusion, of divine illusion. Poetry attaches its emotion to the idea; the idea *is* the fact. The strongest part of our religion today is unconscious poetry." "The Study of Poetry" in *The Complete Prose Works of Matthew Arnold*, vol. 9 (Ann Arbor: University of Michigan Press, 1962), 161. I. A. Richards wrote, "None the less we do not and, at present, cannot order our emotions and attitudes by true statements alone. Nor is there any probability that we ever shall contrive to do so. This is one of the great new dangers to which civilization is exposed. Countless pseudo-statements about God, about the universe, about human nature . . . about the soul, its rank and destiny—pseudo-statements which are the pivotal points in the organization of the mind, vital to its well-being, have suddenly become, for sincere, honest and informed minds, impossible to belief as for centuries they have been believed. . . . The remedy . . . is to cut our pseudo-statements free from that kind of belief which is appropriate to verified statements. . . . [P]oetry conclusively shows, even the most important among our attitudes can be aroused and maintained within any believing of a factual or verifiable order entering in at all." *Poetries and Sciences* (New York: Norton, 1970), 60–62.

13. Clive Bell, *Art* (New York: Capricorn, 1958), 62.

14. For a subtle discussion of how "secularizing is . . . radicalized into psychologizing" in Pater, Arnold, and George Eliot, see Michael Levenson, *A Genealogy of Modernism* (New York: Cambridge University Press, 1984), 9–19. For trenchant criticisms of both Arnold and Pater's aestheticizing, moralizing, and psychologizing of religion, see T. S. Eliot, "Arnold and Pater," in *Selected Essays* (New York: Harcourt, Brace and

World, 1960), 382–393; and Eliot, "Matthew Arnold," in *The Use of Poetry and the Use of Criticism* (Cambridge: Harvard University Press, 1996), 95–112.

15. Michael Levenson has written that modernism belongs to a "culture of metaphysical crisis." This study, which is particularly interested in what Levenson calls "discursive Modernism," seeks to illuminate an important strain of this crisis. Levenson, *Modernism* (New Haven: Yale University Press, 2011), 19.

16. See Immanuel Kant, *Critique of the Power of Judgment*, trans. Paul Guyer and Eric Matthews (New York: Cambridge University Press, 2000), 128–159.

17. *The Critique of Practical Reason*, trans. Mary Gregor (New York: Cambridge University Press, 1997), 133.

18. See Pericles Lewis, *Religious Experience in the Modernist Novel* (New York: Cambridge University Press, 2010); Amy Hungerford, *Postmodern Belief: American Literature and Religion since 1960* (Princeton: Princeton University Press, 2010); and John McClure, *Partial Faiths: Postsecular Fiction in the Age of Pynchon and Morrison* (Athens: University of Georgia Press, 2007).

19. Hungerford, *Postmodern Belief*, xiii–xxi; McClure, *Partial Faiths*, 3, 5.

20. In a trenchant essay on the limits of "post-secularism," Tracy Fessenden similarly notes that most theorists of the post-secular "fit their interventions into the standard template of secularization, in which the hegemony of a once-uniform religious past is broken and dispersed into new forms of agency and the risks and possibilities these entail." As Fessenden argues, the religious past was never so uniform. I agree with Fessenden, moreover, that both McClure and Hungerford tend to affirm the fundamentally "Arnoldian replacement story for literature, in which literature assumes the office of keeping alive the authentic spirituality whose custodianship religion has forfeited." "The Problem of the Postsecular," *American Literary History* 26, no. 1 (January 2014): 163–164. Like Fessenden, I am concerned that post-secularism often seems to depend on an essentialized, ahistorical "sacred," but I worry about this not so much because of the methodological problems the concept of "the sacred" entails for religious studies but because the differences between religious and secular feeling may be elided when they are subsumed under such a concept, and because this focus on the sacred tends to obscure the broader implications of religious and secular paradigms for thought and experience.

21. Lewis, *Religious Experience and the Modernist Novel*, 4–5.

22. Ibid., 5. As Lewis puts it, the modernist novelists, like the social scientists, "conducted their search less for a 'substitute' for religion than for a satisfying *explanation* of such spiritual phenomena" (ibid., emphasis added). For a powerful account of social theory as a secularizing agent, see John Milbank, *Theology and Social Theory* (Cambridge, MA: Blackwell, 1990).

23. See T. E. Hulme, "Romanticism and Classicism," in *Selected Writings* (New York: Routledge, 2003), 71.

24. Charles Taylor, Marcel Gauchet, and others have argued that one feature of modernity often associated with secularity—"disenchantment"—has its origins in the sharper distinction made in monotheistic religions between God's transcendent reality and the world. According to Taylor, in fact, all the "Axial religions" work to "disembed"

social order and moral pursuit from cosmic rhythm. See Taylor, *Secular Age*, and Gauchet, *The Disenchantment of the World*, trans. Oscar Burge (Princeton: Princeton University Press, 1997). On the link between modern secular "individualism" and Christianity, see Louis Dumont, *Essays on Individualism: Modern Ideology in Anthropological Perspective* (Chicago: University of Chicago Press, 1992), 23–60, and Larry Siedentop, *Inventing the Individual: The Origins of Western Liberalism* (Cambridge: Harvard University Press, 2014). In *The Unintended Reformation: How a Religious Revolution Secularized Society* (Cambridge: Harvard University Press, 2012), Brad Gregory argues that the Protestant Reformation unleashed arguments and energies that led to pluralism, possessive individualism, and capitalism. Gregory builds on Max Weber's famous argument about the link between capitalism, this-worldly asceticism, and Lutheran and Calvinist understandings of vocation and election in *The Protestant Ethic and the "Spirit" of Capitalism and Other Writings*, trans. Peter Baehr (New York: Penguin, 2002). For a polemical account of secularism as Christian colonialism, see Gil Andijar's chapter "Secularism," in *Semites: Race, Religion, Literature* (Stanford: Stanford University Press, 2008). Andijar writes, "secularism is a name Christianity gave itself when it invented 'religion,' named its other or others as 'religions'" (48).

25. *The Letters of Wallace Stevens*, ed. Holly Stevens (Berkeley: University of California Press, 1996), 378. Hereafter cited in text as *L*.

26. The classic account of this transformation is Karl Löwith's *Meaning in History: The Theological Implications of the Philosophy of History* (Chicago: University of Chicago Press, 1949). For Löwith, secular doctrines of progress were illegitimate and incoherent because they tried to blend heterogeneous philosophical elements: the Christian eschatological understanding of history, for which meaning is only found in history's consummation, and the modern historiographical imperative, which tries to find meaning in historical facticity as such. Secular interpretations of history appropriated the unique linear conception of history derived from biblical thinking—creation, fall, redemption, consummation—and transformed it into a doctrine of evolutionary progress without the theological framework, while preserving an ungrounded faith that Löwith calls "futurism." Stevens articulates something of this feeling, over a decade before Löwith wrote, in his poem "Owl's Clover," where he complains that Marxists, in taking over the eschatological sensibility, have surreptitiously preserved religious devotion to an eschatological future while eliminating the God who once guaranteed it. For them, "Everything is dead / Except the future" (*CP*, 154). Hans Blumenberg objected to Löwith's characterization of modern philosophy of history as an illegitimate borrowing of theological concepts that were incongruous with its own worldview. While Blumenberg acknowledges that the rhetoric of many Enlightenment progressives is still saturated with the Christian rhetoric of redemption, he argues that modern thinking depends on the "reoccupation" of "answer positions" vacated by theology rather than the "secularization" of theological concepts. See *The Legitimacy of the Modern Age*, trans. Robert Wallace (Cambridge: MIT Press, 1983). On Blumenberg's account of "reoccupation," see Lawrence Dickey, "Blumenberg and Secularization: 'Self-Assertion' and the Problem of a Self-Realizing Teleology in

History," *New German Critique* 41 (Spring–Summer 1987): 151–165. For a sensitive account of the quarrel between Löwith and Blumenberg, see Vincent Pecora, *Secularization and Cultural Criticism* (Chicago: University of Chicago Press, 2006), 57–66.

27. On the persistence of such myths in modern philosophy, see Stephen Mulhall, *Philosophical Myths of the Fall* (Princeton: Princeton University Press, 2005). For an outstanding study of the ongoing importance of Calvinist understandings of fallenness in American literature, see Elisa New, *The Regenerate Lyric: Theology and Innovation in American Poetry* (New York: Cambridge University Press, 1993).

28. M. H. Abrams, *Natural Supernaturalism: Tradition and Revolution in Romantic Literature* (New York: Norton, 1971), 13.

29. Stanley Cavell, *The Claim of Reason: Wittgenstein, Skepticism, Morality, and Tragedy* (New York: Oxford University Press, 1969), 470. Some contemporary thinkers still see, and celebrate, what they take to be the Romantic translation of religion into aesthetics. Mark C. Taylor, for instance, views this translation as religion's discovery of the philosophical truth about itself in "secular" terms (the secular being a new "mode" of religion). The "translation" of theological categories can be understood as their distillation and fulfillment in a secular framework, through a sort of Hegelian *Aufhebung*. Taylor assumes that secularism is a development within theology itself (via Nominalist and Protestant conceptions of subjectivity and understandings of transcendence). From this perspective, it doesn't really matter whether one speaks of secularism or religion, for secularism is to be understood as a positive development within (Western) religion itself. Taylor calls secularity a *"religious* phenomenon—indeed, religion as it has developed in the West has always harbored secularity, and secularity covertly continues the religious agenda." *After God* (Chicago: University of Chicago Press, 2007), 132. The problem with Mark Taylor's perspective is that his definitions of religion and secularism have become so abstract that they are almost useless. If everything is equally religious and secular, there seems little point in using either term. See also Vincent Pecora, who has argued that in Adorno's aesthetic thought, "secularism itself becomes the paradoxical path to a more profound, because more rational, sense of the religious than had ever existed before" (*Secularization and Cultural Criticism*, 20).

30. For a trenchant investigation of the use of unifying "fictions" in the twentieth century to replace doctrine and myth, see Frank Kermode, *The Sense of an Ending* (New York: Oxford University Press, 2000). One religious category absent from this study is "myth"; the best treatment of its importance in modern literature is Michael Bell's *Literature, Modernity, and Myth: Belief and Responsibility in the Twentieth Century* (New York: Cambridge University Press, 1997). For Bell, "Mythopoeia is the underlying metaphysic of much modernist literature" (2). Myth (like Stevens's "supreme fiction") is a modern strategy for structuring worldviews that are both generalized (metaphysical) and consciously inventive and relative. Though self-conscious, myth is not, Bell writes, entirely arbitrary: "mythopoeia" involves a "recognition of" the "inevitability" of "an implicit world of background values and commitments which reason cannot encompass" (22). These values are initially known through a primordial aesthetic feeling; "myth" is aesthetics articulated metaphysically (23). In this sense, myth

is yet another form of Romantic secularization under the auspices of "substitution," yet one that taps into earlier stages of human culture and consciousness.

31. On the attempt to replace religion with culture, see Terry Eagleton, *Culture and the Death of God* (New Haven: Yale University Press, 2014).

32. Ludwig Feuerbach, *The Essence of Christianity*, trans. George Eliot (New York: Harper, 1957), 27.

33. *The Collected Works of W. B. Yeats*, vol. 2, *The Plays*, ed. David Clark and Rosalind Clark (New York: Scribner, 2001), 487.

34. W. H. Auden, *The Dyer's Hand* (New York: Vintage, 1989), 456–457.

35. Blumenberg, *Legitimacy of the Modern Age*, 441.

36. Friedrich Nietzsche, *Human, All Too Human*, trans. R. J. Hollingdale (New York: Cambridge University Press, 1996), 26.

37. Nietzsche writes, "I am afraid that we are not rid of God because we still have faith in grammar." *Twilight of the Idols and the Antichrist*, trans. R. J. Hollingdale (New York: Penguin, 1990), 27. For Foucault's criticisms of the "theologizing of man," see Jeremy Carrette, *Foucault and Religion* (New York: Routledge, 2000), 79–81. Giorgio Agamben makes an interesting distinction between *secularization* and what he calls *profanation*: "[We] must distinguish between secularization and profanation. Secularization is a form of repression. It leaves intact the forces it deals with by simply moving them from one place to another. Thus the political secularization of theological concepts (the transcendence of God as a paradigm of sovereign power) does nothing but displace the heavenly monarch onto an earthly monarchy, leaving its power intact. . . . Profanation, however, neutralizes what it profanes. Once profaned, that which was unavailable and separate loses its aura and is returned to use." *Profanations*, trans. Jeff Fort (New York: Zone Books, 2007), 77. Agamben, then, is a critic of the idea of secularization as the *displacement* of religious powers onto worldly agents, and thus a critic of the idea of "substitution."

38. See Michel Foucault, *History of Sexuality: An Introduction*, trans. Robert Hurley (New York: Vintage, 1990), 34–35, 53–73, and Jean-Luc Nancy, *Dis-enclosure: The Deconstruction of Christianity*, trans. Bettina Bergo, Gabriel Malenfant, and Michael B. Smith (New York: Fordham University Press, 2008). John Dewey provides another, slightly less radical, version of this argument. Wallace Stevens read and commended a 1942 essay of Dewey's in the *Partisan Review*, "Anti-Naturalism in Extremis." In it, Dewey presses his readers to rid themselves of their corrupt supernatural "inheritance" in the domains of language and intersubjectivity: "Students of [the philosophy of language] . . . who regard themselves as antimetaphysical scientific positivists, nevertheless write as if words consisted of an 'inner' private, mentalistic core or substance and an 'outer' physical shell by means of which a 'subjective' intrinsically incommunicable somehow gets conveyed 'trans-subjectively'! And they appear quite unaware of the extranatural origin and status of the postulate. Until naturalists have definitely applied their own principles, methods, and procedures to formulation of such topics as mind, consciousness, self, person, value, and so forth, they will be at a serious and regrettable disadvantage." *The Essential Dewey*, ed. Thomas Alexander and Larry Hickman (Bloomington: Indiana University Press, 1998), 1:164. Later in the essay

Dewey provides another example of what he takes to be the wrongheaded religious conception of the person: "On the political side we usually fail to note that so-called laissez-faire individualism, with its extreme separatism and isolationism of human beings from one another, is in fact a secularized version of the inheritance of the supernatural soul, the latter having intrinsic connection only with God" (170). Dewey insists, then, that secular, naturalistic formulations of everything from the "self" to "value" must discard the religious formulations that belong to an outmoded metaphysical conception of the world. It should be noted, however, that Dewey's account of Christian conceptions of "person" or "soul" are not representative of the Christian theological tradition. At best they apply to Platonized versions of Christian theology, but it's hard to imagine that even a Christian Platonist like Augustine would accept an account of the soul as separate and isolated given doctrines of the church as a spiritual community materially grounded in the "body of Christ." Nietzsche, too, exaggerates the "otherworldly" character of Christianity in his famous description of Christianity as "Platonism for the 'people.'" *Beyond Good and Evil*, trans. Judith Norman (New York: Cambridge University Press, 2002), 4.

39. Hulme, "Romanticism and Classicism," 71. Hulme is a critic of what I call "adaptation" in part because he thinks, unlike the eliminationists, that there are immutable "instincts": "The instincts that find their right and proper outlet in religion must come out in some other way. You don't believe in God, so you begin to believe that man is a god. You don't believe in Heaven, so you begin to believe in a heaven on earth. In other words, you get romanticism. The concepts that are right and proper in their own sphere are spread over, and so mess up, falsify and blur the clear outlines of human experience. It is like pouring a pot of treacle over the dinner table. Romanticism then, and this is the best definition I can give of it, is spilt religion" (71).

40. George Santayana, *Egotism in German Philosophy* (New York: Hackett, 1970), 12–13.

41. Eliot, *Selected Essays*, 433.

42. Eliot further insisted that mere disbelief on the level of propositional assent did not disqualify one from being accounted a Christian. In his well-known review of Bertrand Russell's *Why I Am Not a Christian*, Eliot suggested that Russell, on the evidence of the emotional constitution and moral sensibility displayed in the manifesto, was, in fact, a Christian. He is, Eliot wrote, "essentially a low Churchman," and his "Non-Christianity is essentially a variety of Low Church sentiment." Eliot again sounds the (inverted) eliminationist note by arguing that for a Western modern, disentangling oneself from Christianity was enormously difficult; modes of secularism like "Atheism" are "often merely a variety of Christianity." ("Non-Christianity" signals grammatically the broader dependence.) Eliot continues, "[O]ne only ceases to be a Christian by being something else definite: a Buddhist, a Mohammedan, a Brahmin." "Why Mr. Russell Is a Christian," *Criterion* 6, no. 2 (August 1927): 179. Thus Eliot, as Jeffrey Perl has written, maintained that "Joyce, Russell, Baudelaire, Nietzsche, and Voltaire were Christians, an undeniable part of Christendom and the indispensable product of its religion." *Skepticism and Modern Enmity: Before and After Eliot* (Baltimore: Johns Hopkins University Press, 1989), 63. This is not a triumphalist claim; it must be viewed through the lens of Eliot's complex understanding of skepticism, tradition,

convention, and culture. Perl's *Skepticism and Modern Enmity* is the best study of this understanding.

43. *The English Auden: Poems, Essays, and Dramatic Writings, 1927–1939* (London: Faber and Faber, 1973), 342. Hereafter cited in text as *EA*.

44. See Auden, *The Prolific and the Devourer,* in *The Complete Works of W. H. Auden,* vol. 2, *Prose, 1939–1948,* ed. Edward Mendelson (Princeton: Princeton University Press, 2002), esp. 424–439.

45. Quoted in Edward Mendelson, *Early Auden* (New York: Vintage, 1981), 326.

46. Auden, *Prolific,* 431.

47. As Mendelson puts it, Auden in "September 1939" is writing of love "under the aspect of necessity"; by aligning love with the "Hunger that has no choice," he was again appealing to the idea of a "necessary History" that attracted him throughout the 1930s (*Early Auden,* 327). This "necessary History"—a history that irresistibly moves in a perfectionist direction—is a version of the secularized theologies of history that Karl Löwith found so incoherent in *Meaning in History.*

48. Auden, *Prolific,* 448.

49. Quoted in Michael North, *Reading 1922* (New York: Oxford University Press, 2001), 3. The claim is pure rhetoric; Joyce's novel entails nothing of the sort. On the importance of Catholic thought and practice for Joyce's fiction (irrespective of his private belief), see Robert Boyle, *James Joyce's Pauline Vision* (Carbondale: Southern Illinois Press, 1978), and Mary Lowe-Evans, *Catholic Nostalgia in Joyce and Company* (Gainesville: University of Florida Press, 2008). See also Gert Lernout, *Help My Unbelief: James Joyce and Religion* (New York: Continuum, 2010). Pound also wrote, "Christian theology is a jungle"; one implication of that image is that there may be no clear path out of it once one finds oneself in it. (Pound recommended the "axe" of the *Ta Hio*—Confucius's "Great Learning.") Ezra Pound, "Immediate Need in Confucius," in *Selected Essays* (New York: New Directions, 1973), 78.

50. Virginia Woolf, *Mr. Bennett and Mrs. Brown* (London: Hogarth Press, 1924), 4.

51. On the continuities among Romantic, Victorian, and Modernist poetics, see Frank Kermode, *Romantic Image* (New York: Routledge, 2002); Carol Christ, *Victorian and Modernist Poetics* (Chicago: University of Chicago Press, 1984); and George Bornstein, *Transformations of Romanticism in Eliot, Yeats, and Stevens* (Chicago: University of Chicago Press, 1973).

52. For an account of the major paradigms of secularization in the nineteenth century, see Henry Chadwick, *The Secularization of the European Mind in the Nineteenth Century* (New York: Cambridge University Press, 1975).

53. The term "self-assertion" is Hans Blumenberg's. Blumenberg is a powerful defender of the Enlightenment, though he is also a critic of how Enlightenment "scientism" overreached rhetorically by infusing the real gains of its scientific philosophy with eschatological, world-correcting pretensions. By "self-assertion" he means a more moderate understanding of reason that recognizes its own limits (*Legitimacy of the Modern Age,* 58, 97). One must also clearly distinguish among enlightenments; the German Enlightenment was typically more sympathetic to religion, and thus keener to preserve theological terms even as they were being secularized. And even the

English and French enlightenments retained, as Carl Becker's classic, if limited, study argued, eschatological visions. See *The Heavenly City in the Eighteenth-Century Philosophers* (New Haven: Yale University Press, 1932).

54. Such reductions are most acute in the forms of naturalist realism that preceded modernism. One might think of Émile Zola's claim, "[O]ne and the same determinism must govern the stone in the road and the brain of man." "The Experimental Novel," in *Documents of Modern Literary Realism*, ed. George J. Becker (Princeton: Princeton University Press, 1963), 171.

55. See Charles Taylor, *Sources of the Self* (Cambridge: Harvard University Press, 1989); Caroline Walker Bynum, *The Resurrection of the Body in Western Christianity, 200–1336* (New York: Columbia University Press, 1995) and *Christian Materiality: An Essay on Religion in Late Medieval Europe* (Cambridge: Zone Press, 2011); and Thomas Pfau, *Minding the Modern: Human Agency, Intellectual Traditions, and Responsible Knowledge* (Notre Dame: University of Notre Dame Press, 2013).

56. This tension can be traced back, as Michael Buckley has shown, to the "central paradox of the Enlightenment": "The philosophes urged a gospel of unhampered liberty, a gospel that should have had a telling effect on private morality and on social structures. At the same time, often within the same exhortations, they formulated a rigorously mechanical doctrine of nature and human being enclosed within this nature. Every form of nature, each of its movements and resultant organizations, emerged necessarily, completely determined by the interaction of its particles and by the iron rule of their invariant laws. The rhetoric of human freedom registered a sharp, if unnoticed, dissonance with this undeviating causal determinacy." *At the Origins of Modern Atheism* (New Haven: Yale University Press, 1987), 274. In *The Future of an Illusion*, Freud appeals to *his* god—Logos, or scientific reason—and insists that this god "will fulfill whichever of these wishes nature outside us allows, but he will do it very gradually, only in the unforeseeable future, and for a new generation of men. He promises no compensation for us, who suffer grievously from life. On the way to this distant goal your religious doctrines will have to be discarded, no matter whether the first attempts fail, or whether the first substitutes prove to be untenable. You know why: in the long run nothing can withstand reason and experience, and the contradiction which religion offers to both is all too palpable. Even purified religious ideas cannot escape this fate, so long as they try to preserve anything of the consolation of religion." *The Future of an Illusion*, trans. James Strachey (New York: Norton, 1975), 54. Here, as elsewhere, Freud insists on the stoical dignity of the man of science, who refuses all false consolation in the face of the natural necessity (*Ananke*) that inevitably generates suffering. The "substitutive" satisfactions that the scientific Logos may one day develop will be at best modestly effective, for the pressures of the erotic and death drives are, as *Civilization and Its Discontents*, trans. James Strachey (New York: Norton, 2010), argues, perpetually at "loggerheads" with "reality": "There can be no doubt about [the pleasure principle's psychic dominance], and yet its programme is at loggerheads with the whole world. . . . There is no possibility of its being carried through; all the regulations of the universe run counter to it" (43). But human dignity can be preserved by facing this truth and refusing any "delusional remoulding of reality" (51).

57. "Science as a Vocation," in *From Max Weber: Essays in Sociology*, trans. and ed. H. H. Gerth and C. Wright Mills (New York: Oxford University Press, 1958), 147.

58. *The Collected Works of W. B. Yeats*, vol. 3, *Autobiographies*, ed. William H. O'Donnell and Douglas N. Archibald (New York: Scribner, 1999), 201.

59. While it might seem strange to associate a certain mode of secularism with a term that evokes polytheism, I hope in what follows to defend my use of this term. And I am not the only scholar to link secularism to paganism. Peter Gay's first volume on the Enlightenment is titled "The Rise of Modern Paganism." See *The Enlightenment: The Rise of Modern Paganism* (New York: Norton, 1977). Stathis Gourgouris mentions, somewhat in passing, a "pagan cosmology" as "a possible source of resignification of the secular in the modern world." *Lessons in Secular Criticism* (New York: Fordham University Press, 2013), 23.

60. Nietzsche's most comprehensive account and criticism of ascetic ideals is found in his *Genealogy of Morals*.

61. James Joyce, *Ulysses* (New York: Vintage, 1986), 7.

62. James Joyce, *The Critical Writings* (Ithaca: Cornell University Press, 1989), 204–205. Joyce maintained that Wilde was still a crypto-Catholic; his abiding concern was actually "sin." For an excellent investigation of the decadents' attraction to Catholicism, see Ellis Hanson's *Decadence and Catholicism* (Ithaca: Cornell University Press, 1998).

63. Williams has written, "It is beguiling to dream about a history in which it was not true that Christianity, in Nietzsche's words, 'robbed us of the harvest of the culture of the ancient world.' . . . As things turned out, the world we actually have is so significantly shaped by Christianity" that "[i]t will never be correct to see Christianity . . . as merely the longest and most painful route from paganism to paganism." Bernard Williams, *Shame and Necessity* (Berkeley: University of California Press, 1993), 12.

64. W. H. Auden, *Collected Poems* (New York: Vintage, 1991), 591. Emphasis added.

65. Taylor, *Secular Age*, 369.

66. Virginia Woolf, *The Common Reader* (New York: Harcourt, 1953), 38.

67. Pericles Lewis has made a similar observation. Woolf's novels, he writes, "frequently envision a classical, pagan alternative to Christian monotheism" (*Religious Experience and the Modernist Novel*, 145).

68. Taylor, *Secular Age*, 369.

69. For Karl Jaspers's argument, see *Vom Ursprung und Zeil der Geschichte* (Zurich: Artemis, 1949). On the return to concept of an Axial Age, see Charles Taylor, *Secular Age*, 146ff; Robert Bellah, *Religion in Human Evolution: From the Paleolithic to the Axial Age* (Cambridge: Harvard University Press, 2011), esp. the second half of the book; and the essays in *The Axial Age and Its Consequences*, ed. Robert Bellah and Hans Joas (Cambridge: Harvard University Press, 2012).

70. I do not mean to suggest that asceticism is necessarily linked to aspirations toward transcendence. Both Geoffrey Harpham and Tyler Roberts have shown that there are persistent ascetic elements in two of the great modern philosophers of immanence: Nietzsche and Foucault. See Harpham, *The Ascetic Imperative in Culture and Criticism* (Chicago: University of Chicago Press, 1992), esp. chapter 4: "Philosophy

and Resistance to Asceticism"; and Roberts, *Contesting Spirit: Nietzsche, Affirmation, Religion* (Princeton: Princeton University Press, 1998), esp. chapter 3: "Nietzsche's Asceticism." Nonetheless, Gavin Flood, *The Ascetic Self: Subjectivity, Memory and Tradition* (New York: Cambridge University Press, 2004), has emphasized that ascetic spirituality is difficult to maintain in the absence of a religious "cosmos"—a world viewed as a transcendent moral and aesthetic order—that the self appropriates internally and writes onto the body. A number of intellectual historians have argued that the secular, modern worldview was made possible by a transition from the conceptualization of the world as "cosmos" to a conceptualization of the world as "nature." See Rémi Brague, *The Wisdom of the World: The Human Experience of the Universe in Western Thought*, trans. Teresa Fagan (Chicago: University of Chicago Press, 2003), and Louis Dupré, *Passage to Modernity* (New Haven: Yale University Press, 1993). When "cosmos" (moral order) is eclipsed and replaced by "nature" (material process) as the absolute background of human experience, ascetic practice is disoriented. At the same time, writers like Yeats, Stevens, and Woolf are motivated to conform the self to a new, depersonalized "cosmos," understood now not as moral order but creative material power. (I argue in the chapter on Woolf that she is in many ways in search of a cosmos; she sees an aesthetic order that can never quite become the moral order she hopes to find.) One finds, then, a similar persistence of asceticism even in what I am calling modernist paganism, but because the cosmos being "imitated" is known as morally indifferent, immanent force rather than transcendent moral order, the subjectivity characteristic of this asceticism is often radically de-Christianized.

71. D. H. Lawrence, *Apocalypse* (New York: Viking, 1989), 42. William Connolly, responding to Charles Taylor, has tried to extend, complicate, and affirm the power of what he calls "immanent naturalism": "In a world of becoming, emergent formations are often irreducible to patterns of efficient causality or simple probability, and they never conform to an intrinsic purpose or long cycles of recurrence. Becoming occurs in part through periodic intersections between different force fields, as neural, viral, bacterial, geological, climatic, species, and civilizational force fields set on different tiers of chrono-time infect (or disrupt, charge, invade, etc.) each other, in part through the periodic emergence of new and surprising capacities for autopoesis when such collisions occur, and in part through the patterns of reverberation back and forth between these collisions and capacities during fateful periods of accelerated disequilibrium." Connolly objects to Taylor's portrayal of immanent naturalism as particularly tempted by the violence and conflict of these "collisions": immanent naturalists "who follow in the wake of Nietzsche," he says, are not "transfixed by violence . . . nor are they tempted profoundly by it." See "Belief, Spirituality and Time," in Warner, VanAntwerpen, and Calhoun, *Varieties of Secularism*, 129, 133. The testimony of literary modernism, however—particularly the work of Yeats and Lawrence—does suggest that immanent naturalism can be particularly seduced by an ontology of conflict, especially when that naturalism is re-enchanted. On agonism as a political implication of immanence, see Chantal Mouffe, *Agonism: Thinking the World Politically* (New York: Verso, 2013). Stevens wrote in his "Adagia," "the world is a force, not a presence" (*CP*, 911); Mouffe writes, "The main problem with liberal rationalism is that it deploys

a logic of the social based on an essentialist conception of 'being as presence.' . . . It cannot recognize that there can only be an identity when it is constructed as difference, and that any social objectivity is constituted through acts of power" (4). Against the liberal picture of pluralism "struggling" toward consensus, she insists that "antagonism" is an inescapable ingredient of "agonism." The animating metaphors of Nietzsche and Foucault (the latter audible in Mouffe's "deploying") are equally agonistic and often martial. Foucault rejects "analyses couched in terms of the symbolic field or the domain of signifying structures" and proposes instead "a recourse to analyses in terms of the relations of force, strategic developments and tactics. Here I believe one's point of reference should not be the great model of language and signs, but to that of war and battle. The history which bears and determines us has the form of a war rather than that of a language: relations of power, not relations of meaning. History has no 'meaning,' though this is not to say that it is absurd or incoherent. On the contrary, it is intelligible and should be susceptible of analysis down to the smallest detail—but this in accordance with the intelligibility of struggles, of strategies and tactics. Neither the dialectic, as logic of contradictions, nor semiotics, as the structure of communication, can account for the intrinsic intelligibility of conflicts." *Power/Knowledge* (New York: Pantheon, 1980), 114. On agonism in Nietzsche, see Christa Davis Acampora, *Contesting Nietzsche* (Chicago: University of Chicago Press, 2013). Whether the agonism that emerges from ontologies of difference (or what Yeats would call "opposites") and conflict inevitably venerates *violence* is a difficult question, but when war becomes the dominant metaphor for life, agonistic thinkers certainly struggle to venerate peace.

72. See Jane Bennett's account of Weberian disenchantment in *The Enchantment of Modern Life: Attachments, Crossings, and Ethics* (Princeton: Princeton University Press, 2001), 57–65, and *The Joy of Secularism*, ed. George Levine (Princeton: Princeton University Press, 2011). For a defense of Weber's interpretation of both disenchantment and the "Protestant Ethic," see Philip Gorski, *The Protestant Ethic Revisited* (Philadelphia: Temple University Press, 2011).

73. Weber, "Science as a Vocation," 147–148.

74. The German philosopher Odo Marquard, an heir of Blumenberg, makes a similar historical claim, but his response is celebratory rather than anxious. What he calls the *"disenchanted return of polytheism"* is an opportunity for the individual to achieve a new freedom. While certain modernists like Yeats (see chapter 3) are suspicious of models of the individualized, "inner" self precisely because of their Christian origins, Marquard tells a different story: monotheistic cultures "discovered" individuality as a form of inwardness only in order to carve out a space protected from the tyranny of a "single God," a "single salvation plan," and the "total service" and obedience demanded by this picture. *Farewell to Matters of Principle*, trans. Robert M. Wallace and Susan Bernstein (New York: Oxford University Press, 1989), 102.

75. I am not suggesting that this has been true for all historical configurations of Christianity, only that it has been, for most Christian theologians, implicit in the doctrine of Creation, which views the world as good (just), true (intelligible), and beautiful (ordered). This unity is of course compromised in Christian theology by the Fall.

For twentieth- and twenty-first-century affirmations of this unity, see Hans Urs von Balthasar, *The Glory of the Lord: A Theological Aesthetics*, trans. Erasmo Leiva-Merikakis (San Francisco: Ignatius, 1998), esp. vol. 1, *Seeing the Form*; and David Bentley Hart, *The Beauty of the Infinite: An Aesthetics of Christian Truth* (Grand Rapids, MI: Eerdmans, 2004). Weber himself notes that the Bible sometimes envisions a gap between beauty and sacrality: he cites the twenty-first Psalm and the 53rd chapter of the book of Isaiah. In the latter the "suffering servant," taken by Christians as a prefiguration of Christ, "hath no form or comeliness . . . no beauty that we should desire him." But the rhetorical burden of that passage is to insist on the divergence of the redemptive figure from expected cultural models of dignity and charisma. So St. Augustine writes, "Wherefore then He had no form nor comeliness? Because Christ crucified is both to the Jews a stumbling-block; and to the Greeks foolishness. But wherefore had He comeliness even upon the Cross? Because the foolishness of God is wiser than men; and the weakness of God is stronger than men. To us, however, now that we are believers, let the Bridegroom, wheresoever He is, appear beautiful." *Expositions on the Book of Psalms* vol. 2, trans. John Henry Parker (London: Oxford, 1848), 229–230. In the same way, Nietzsche's famous "aristocratic equation" from the *Genealogy of Morals* (good = noble = powerful = beautiful = fortunate) does not contradict Weber's observation but does serve to limit the scope of all the categories, in the sense that one knows the value of a thing through its power and wills to call it both good and beautiful.

76. Jean Toomer, *Cane* (New York: Norton, 2011), 83.
77. The theologian John Milbank has called this an "ontology of violence." See *Theology and Social Theory*, esp. 278–321. Milbank uses this concept polemically by juxtaposing it to a superior, theological "ontology of peace," but I use the concept descriptively. Normative concerns do emerge, however, especially in the chapter on Yeats, where Yeats's imagination of a pagan, conflictual ontology is closely linked to an ethos of aggression.
78. W. B. Yeats, *A Vision* (New York: Collier, 1977), 67.
79. Yeats, *Autobiographies*, 243.
80. George Santayana, *The Realm of Spirit* (New York: Scribner, 1940), 88.
81. Woolf doesn't follow Yeats or Lawrence in venerating intersubjective conflict, but there are other examples beyond these writers. In Marinetti's "The Founding and Manifesto of Futurism" (1909), we can see how the ontology of conflict is converted into an aesthetics and an ethos: "1) We intend to sing the love of danger, the habit of energy and fearlessness. . . . 7) Except in struggle, there is no more beauty. No work without an aggressive character can be a masterpiece. Poetry must be conceived as a violent attack on unknown forces, to reduce and prostrate them before man." From *Manifesto: A Century of Isms*, ed. Mary Ann Caws (Lincoln: University of Nebraska Press, 2001), 187.
82. D. H. Lawrence, *The Man Who Died*, in *The Selected Short Stories of D. H. Lawrence* (New York: Modern Library, 1999), 459, 462.
83. Weber, "Science as a Vocation," 148.
84. Ibid., 148, 149.

85. This ontology often has far-reaching consequences for modernist understandings of the self and its ethical life. Nietzsche complained the English Victorian novel preserved the moral ethos associated with a God it disavowed: "G. Eliot—They are rid of the Christian God and now believe all the more firmly that they must cling to Christian morality." *Twilight of the Idols*, 80. Modernist writing, however, often derides Christian virtues like agape and its secular analogues, sympathy or pity, which were celebrated in Romantic writing from Rousseau to Whitman. Ezra Pound's Canto XXX reverses Chaucer's "Thus I am slayn sith that Pite is ded" by imagining a pagan Artemis who complains, "Nothing is now clean slayne" *because* of "pity": "Pity causeth the forests to fail, / Pity slayeth my nymphs." *The Cantos of Ezra Pound* (New York: New Directions, 1996), 147. In D. H. Lawrence's short companion poems, "Retort to Whitman" and "Retort to Jesus" (*Selected Poetry* [New York: Penguin, 1986], 223), the critique of sympathy is a part of a comprehensive rejection of Christian love (Jesus) and its secular modifications (Whitman):

RETORT TO WHITMAN

And he who walks a mile full of false sympathy walks to the funeral of the whole human race.

RETORT TO JESUS

And whoever forces himself to love anybody begets a murderer in his own heart.

Both Christian love and secular sympathy tend to understand the human person as a locus of irreducible value. Emile Durkheim argued that if it were possible to speak of a "religion" of secular modernity, it was based on the sacralization of this person: "The human person, whose definition serves as the touchstone according to which good must be distinguished from evil, is considered as sacred, in what one might call the ritual sense of the word. It has something of that transcendental majesty which the churches of all times have given to their gods. It is conceived as being invested with that mysterious property which creates an empty space around holy objects, which keeps them away from profane contacts and which draws them away from ordinary life. And it is exactly this feature which induces the respect of which it is the object." "Individualism and the Intellectuals," in *Durkheim on Religion*, ed. W. S. F. Pickering (London: Routledge, 1975), 61. For Durkheim, this exaltation of the human person was not generated by "an egoistic cult of the self" but by "sympathy for all that is human, a wider pity for all sufferings, for all human miseries, a more ardent desire to combat and alleviate them, a greater thirst for justice" (64). Durkheim thought that the personal God and internalized spirituality of Christianity prepared the ground for this modern sacralization: "Christianity expressed in an inward faith, in the personal conviction of the individual, the essential condition of godliness. . . . The very centre of the moral life was thus transferred from outside to within and the individual was set up as the sovereign judge of his own conduct having no other accounts to render than those to himself and to his God" (68). More recently, Jürgen Habermas has argued, "In the West, Christianity not only fulfilled the cognitive initial conditions for modern *structures* of consciousness; it also demanded a range of *motivations. . . .* For the normative self-understanding of modernity, Christianity has functioned as more than just a precursor or a catalyst. Universalistic egalitarianism, from which sprang the ideals of freedom and a collective life in solidarity, the autonomous conduct of life and emancipation, and the individual morality of conscience, human rights and democracy, is the direct legacy of the Judaic ethic of justice and the Christian ethic of love." *Religion and Rationality: Essay on Reason, God, and Modernity,* ed. Eduardo Mendieta (Cambridge: MIT Press, 2002), 148–149. But the pagan strain of modernism resists this high valuation of the person, which remains pronounced in contemporary secular cultures. The impersonal intensity of the world overwhelms the claims of persons. When Pound's Artemis protests, "Pity befouleth April, / Pity is the root and spring," the play of her grammar suggests that personal emotion has usurped the ontological centrality of the world's own process: it is the "root and spring" of pollution precisely because it has taken over April's proper role as "root and spring." In *The Man Who Died,* D. H. Lawrence uses "personal" as a slight: his "man" (the anonymous risen Christ) is disgusted by the "little, personal body" and the "little personal life" of his peasant host. His "Madeleine" (a figure of Mary Magdalene) is startled by her disillusioned Messiah's "greater indifference to the personal issue" (*Man Who Died,* 458, 462).

86. Wallace Stevens, *Sur Plusieurs Beaux Sujets: Wallace Stevens's Commonplace Book* (Stanford: Stanford University Press, 1989), 33.

87. *The Collected Works of W. B. Yeats,* vol. 5, *Later Essays,* ed. William O'Donnell (New York: Scribner, 1994), 356.

88. Ralph Waldo Emerson, *Nature and Selected Essays* (New York: Penguin, 2003), 48. Emerson explains, "It is not words only that are emblematic; it is things which are emblematic. Every natural fact is a symbol of some spiritual fact. Every appearance in nature corresponds to some state of the mind. . . . [T]he blue sky in which the private earth is buried, the sky with its eternal calm, and full of everlasting orbs, is the type of Reason. That which intellectually considered we call Reason, considered in relation to nature, we call Spirit" (49).

89. William Wordsworth, preface to *The Excursion,* lines 65–68.

90. Georges Poulet, *The Metamorphoses of the Circle,* trans. Carley Dawson and Elliott Coleman (Baltimore: Johns Hopkins University Press, 1966), 95, 101.

91. W. B. Yeats, *A Vision* (New York: Collier, 1977), 272.

92. *Biographia Literaria,* in *Samuel Taylor Coleridge: A Critical Edition of the Major Works,* ed. H. J. Jackson (New York: Oxford University Press, 1985), 313.

93. "The Noble Rider and the Sound of Words," in *CP,* 665.

94. The details of this critique are elaborated in chapter 1.

95. J. Hillis Miller puts it this way in his classic study: "This vanishing of the gods, leaving a barren man in a barren land, is the basis of all Stevens' thought and poetry. His version of the death of the gods coincides with a radical transformation in the way man sees the world. What had been a warm home takes on a look of hardness and emptiness, like the walls, floors, and banisters of a vacant house." *Poets of Reality* (Cambridge: Harvard University Press, 1965), 219. Stevens's poems reenact the scene

of the death or disappearance of the gods over and over. In "Sunday Morning," the earliest of these, after reflecting on the incompatibility of the idea of paradise and the fact of temporality, a pious woman comes to the conclusion that "The tomb in Palestine / Is not the porch of spirits lingering," but a grave in which Jesus's body rotted (*CP*, 56). In "The Man With the Blue Guitar," the guitarist thinks, "Poetry / Exceeding music must take the place of empty heaven and its hymns" (136–137). In "The Greenest Continent," "The Heaven of Europe is empty, like a Schloss / Abandoned because of taxes" (158). In "Esthetique du Mal," "The death of Satan was a tragedy / For the imagination" (281). In "Notes Toward a Supreme Fiction," "The death of one god is the death of all" (329). As we near the end of the *Collected Poems*—say, in "The Auroras of Autumn"—the throne in heaven is still parading its emptiness: "Look at this present throne. What company, / In masks, can choir it with the naked wind?" (358). And still, nearly thirty-five years after the trope first appeared, "An Ordinary Evening in New Haven" reports, "In the genius of summer . . . they blew up / The statue of Jove among the boomy clouds. / It took all day to quiet the sky / And then to refill its emptiness again" (412).

96. See Denis Donoghue, *Speaking of Beauty* (New Haven: Yale University Press, 2004); Elaine Scarry, *On Beauty and Being Just* (Princeton: Princeton University Press, 2001); Roger Scruton, *Beauty: A Very Short Introduction* (New York: Oxford University Press, 2011); Arthur Danto, *The Abuse of Beauty: Aesthetics and the Concept of Art* (Chicago: Open Court, 2003); and Alexander Nehamas, *Only a Promise of Happiness: The Place of Beauty in a World of Art* (Princeton: Princeton University Press, 2007).

97. See Philip Fisher, *The Vehement Passions* (Princeton: Princeton University Press, 2002); Charles Altieri, *The Particulars of Rapture* (Ithaca: Cornell University Press, 2003); Martha Nussbaum, *Upheavals of Thought* (New York: Cambridge University Press, 2003); Sianne Ngai, *Ugly Feelings* (Cambridge: Harvard University Press, 2005); and Thomas Dixon, *From Passions to Emotions: The Creation of a Secular Psychological Category* (New York: Cambridge University Press, 2003). See my extended review of these books, "Human Flourishing and the Sovereignty of Feeling," *Hedgehog Review*, Spring 2010, 33–44.

98. Fisher, *Vehement Passions*, 43.

99. Jenny Franchot, "Invisible Domain: Religion and American Literary Studies," *American Literature* 67, no. 4 (December 1995): 834. Hereafter cited in text.

100. Robert Orsi, *Between Heaven and Earth: The Religious Worlds People Make and the Scholars Who Study Them* (Princeton: Princeton University Press, 2006), 2. While Geertz is not named, his influential discussion of religion as a model "for" and "of" reality is an implicit target. See *The Interpretation of Cultures* (New York: Basic Books, 1973), esp. chapters 5 and 6. I should note that I do not believe, and certainly Geertz never argued, that the primary function of religion is or has ever been to "explain" reality, if that term is understood to imply a comprehensive scientific account of causation. That highly discredited view was implicit in much of the earliest anthropology of religion, which saw religious thinking as a primitive attempt to do what modern Westerns call science.

101. Robert Orsi, "Everyday Miracles: The Study of Lived Religion," in _Lived Religion in America: Toward a History of Practice_, ed. David D. Hall (Princeton: Princeton University Press, 1998), 7.

102. See Hungerford, _Postmodern Belief_; Lawrence Buell, "Religion on the American Mind," _American Literary History_ 19, no. 1 (2007): 32–55; and Michael Warner, "Is Liberalism a Religion?" in _Religion: Beyond a Concept_, ed. Hent de Vries (New York: Fordham University Press, 2008), 610–617.

103. Buell, "Religion on the American Mind," 35.

104. Ibid., 52.

105. _The Collected Poems of W. B. Yeats_, ed. Richard Finneran (New York: Scribner, 1996), 554.

106. Percy Bysshe Shelley, "The Defense of Poetry," in _Shelley's Poetry and Prose_, ed. Donald Reiman and Neil Fraistat (New York: Norton, 2002), 517.

107. See Charles Taylor, _Sources of the Self_ (Cambridge: Harvard University Press, 1989), and "What Is Human Agency?" in _Philosophical Papers_, vol. 1, _Human Language and Agency_ (New York: Cambridge University Press, 1985), 15–44.

108. I take this language from Joanna Brooks, _American Lazarus: Religion and the Rise of African-American and Native American Literatures_ (New York: Oxford University Press, 2007). Brooks is interested, she says, in the "adapting, politicizing, and indigenizing" of "mainline religious discourses" (3). Religious conventions are "strategically adopted" (14). Minority populations "use religion and literature as instruments" (14). I do not deny, of course, that religion can and has been used strategically by marginalized populations, but this language seems entirely to ignore the truth status of religious belief and its capacity to shape the imagination of strategic aims and ends.

109. Ibid., 18.

110. For a powerful critique of the universalizing, liberal model of "strategic" agency (and its subsidiary concepts of "resistance" and "submission") implicit in discussions surrounding feminism and Islam, see Saba Mahmood, _The Politics of Piety: The Islamic Revival and the Feminist Subject_ (Princeton: Princeton University Press, 2005), esp. 5–17.

111. For a forceful but controversial account of how sociology has gradually displaced theology by appropriating its narrative agency, see Milbank, _Theology and Social Theory_.

112. See, for instance, Gauri Viswanathan, "Secularism in the Framework of Heterodoxy," _PMLA_ 123, no. 2 (March 2008): 466–476; Christopher Bracken, _Magical Criticism: The Recourse to Savage Philosophy_ (Chicago: University of Chicago Press, 2007); Helen Sword, _Ghostwriting Modernism_ (Ithaca: Cornell University Press, 2002); Randall Styers, _Making Magic: Religion, Magic, and Science in the Modern World_ (New York: Oxford University Press, 2004); and Simon During, _Modern Enchantments: The Cultural Power of Secular Magic_ (Cambridge: Harvard University Press, 2002).

113. Sword, _Ghostwriting Modernism_, 9.

114. Gauri Viswanathan, "Spectrality's Secret Sharers: Occultism as (Post)Colonial Affect," in _Beyond the Black Atlantic_, ed. Walter Goebel and Saskia Schabio (New York: Routledge, 2006), 135, 138. Viswanathan uses "normative" here to mean something like "normalized" or "authorized." But occultism challenges "normative [Western]

conceptions" by proposing its own normative conceptions (of, say, sexuality) in the sense that it proposes an ethos (an account of how it is best to live and behave) that is underwritten by a metaphysics or ontology ("the cyclical evolution of life forms"). The normative force of occultism is what literary discussions of it tend to evade.

115. The claim that occultism implicitly harbors progressive political dispositions is suspect. There is a curious forgetfulness of the fact that, for instance, occult traditions have typically been elitist and hierarchical. They seek and transmit "secret knowledge" available only to the initiated. Max Weber called Gnostics "intellectual aristocrats." *The Sociology of Religion,* trans. Ephraim Fischoff (London: Methuen, 1965), 131. Some of the early debates within Christianity between orthodoxy and Gnosticism hinged on issues of hierarchy: Gnostics did not like the fact that the orthodox opened the Eucharist to "ordinary" people. See Phillip Lee, *Against the Protestant Gnostics* (New York: Oxford University Press, 1987), 33–40. Within the specific history of modernism, the examples of Lawrence, Pound, and Yeats—whose pagan occultism is closely connected to aristocratic sentiment or idealizations of the charismatic leader—should serve as reminders that the politics of occultism are ambivalent. And there was a significant link between Nazism and the occult. See Nicholas Goodrich-Clark, *The Occult Roots of Nazism: Secret Aryan Cults and Their Influence on Nazi Ideology* (New York: Tauris Parke, 2003).

1. "THE WORLD WAS PARADISE MALFORMED"

1. Helen Vendler, *Wallace Stevens: Words Chosen out of Desire* (Knoxville: University of Tennessee Press, 1984), 30.

2. Jahan Ramazani, *Poetry of Mourning: The Modern Elegy from Hardy to Heaney* (Chicago: University of Chicago Press, 1994), 131. Eleanor Cook assumes something similar when explaining how Stevens appropriated the French thinker Simone Weil's theological concept of "decreation." She discusses Stevens's practice of "borrowing back of religious terms for secular usage" but does not explain how this borrowing works or whether it is intelligible. For Weil, the term "decreation" signifies a process God underwent in order to make room for creation, and we are to imitate God in passing from the created to the uncreated, renouncing our individual being in order to love God and so be annihilated in the plenitude of his being. For Stevens it means nearly the opposite. It denotes the breakdown of the metaphysical presuppositions that sustained our culture, to the extent that we no longer see them as something given to us from elsewhere but as a product of our own imaginations: "Modern reality is a reality of decreation, in which our revelations are not the revelations of belief, but the precious portents of our own powers" (750). In Weil, decreation annihilates the "I" before the Absolute; in Stevens, decreation swells the "I" by absorbing the Absolute into it. (Stevens seems to have completely misunderstood Weil's thought.) See Cook, "The Decreations of Wallace Stevens," *Wallace Stevens Journal* 4, no. 3/4 (1980): 46–57.

3. Robert Rehder, *Stevens, Williams, Crane, and the Motive for Metaphor* (New York: Palgrave Macmillan, 2005), xxiv.

4. I use the term "early" in the sense that this poem was included in the second of Stevens's seven collections of poetry; Stevens was fifty-five years old at the time of its publication.

5. See Lucretius, *On the Nature of the Universe*, trans. Ronald Melville (New York: Oxford University Press, 1997), book 5, lines 1169–1240.

6. Hume thought that religion developed from basic human anxieties over the unpredictability of "powers" that govern life and the tendency of humans to personify those powers. There is, he writes, a "universal tendency" among humans "to conceive all beings like themselves, and to transfer to every object, those qualities, which with they are familiarly acquainted. . . . We find faces in the moon, armies in the clouds; and by a natural propensity, if not corrected by experience and reflection, ascribe malice and good-will to everything, that hurts and pleases." Quoted in J. Samuel Preus, *Explaining Religion* (New Haven: Yale University Press, 1987), 94. Preus's book is the best history available of the major figures and the intellectual paradigms for "explaining" religion in naturalistic terms.

7. I do not want to collapse the distinction between anthropomorphism and egotism, but Stevens often uses the terms almost interchangeably. Anthropomorphism does not suggest selfishness or excessive self-regard in an individual person, but there is an analogy, for Stevens (as in "Decorations"), between the parochial self-concern of a self or a society and the metaphysical anthropocentrism that both generates and is fostered by anthropomorphism. Moreover, and whether valid or not, Santayana suggested in his *Egotism in German Philosophy* (1916) that German political aggression was strengthened by the anthropocentrism of its philosophy, which, according to the book, understood the external world as so much raw material to be consumed and remade in the self's image. It should be noted, though, that Santayana saw American thought as equally infected by anthropocentrism, as is clear in his "The Genteel Tradition in American Philosophy."

8. "The derivation of religious needs from the infant's helplessness and the longing for the father aroused by it seems to me incontrovertible, especially since the feeling is not simply prolonged from childhood days, but is permanently sustained by fear of the superior power of Fate." Sigmund Freud, *Civilization and Its Discontents*, trans. James Strachey (New York: Norton, 2010), 36.

9. See in particular James Frazer's *The Golden Bough: A New Abridgement*, ed. Robert Fraser (New York: Oxford University Press, 1994). Subsequent anthropologists of religion (and philosophers like Ludwig Wittgenstein) criticized their forebears for their scientistic prejudices, which generated their assumption that religion emerged out of a proto-scientific need to explain the causes of things, like why we have dreams or why it rains at certain times rather than others. In his notes on *The Golden Bough*, Wittgenstein writes, in criticism of James Frazer, "A religious symbol does not rest on any *opinion*. And error belongs only with opinion." *Remarks on Frazer's Golden Bough* (London: Brynmill, 1979), 3. But many, like Mircea Eliade and Clifford Geertz, still felt that religion was "explanatory" in a more general, metaphysical sense: that it was an attempt to give an hermeneutic account of experience as a whole, to produce what Eliade called a "world." Clifford Geertz, *The Interpretation of Cultures* (New York:

Basic Books, 2000); Mircea Eliade, *The Sacred and the Profane* (New York: Harcourt Brace, 1957). Talal Asad, an anthropologist influenced by Foucault, has recently, however, criticized the revisionist mode as well, not for its evolutionist and scientistic prejudices but for its overly Protestant, cognitive model of religion as a "meaning"-producing symbolic system, rather than, as he writes, "a constituting activity in the world," a way of organizing and disciplining power. *Genealogies of Religion* (Baltimore: Johns Hopkins University Press, 1993), 37. For a trenchant defense of Geertz against Asad, see Kevin Schilbrack, "Religion, Models of, and Reality: Are We Through with Geertz?" *Journal of the American Academy of Religion* 73, no. 2 (June 2005): 429–452. According to the anthropological understanding of Stevens's time, once religious "explanations" had been refined by science—by what Freud somewhat ironically called "the god Logos"—religion would become obsolete. As Stevens noted in his essay "The Noble Rider and the Sound of Words," Freud thought that an "education to reality" meant a progression out of the various anthropomorphic illusions that he called religious (*CP*, 651).

10. Tylor summarizes, "It seems as though thinking men, as yet at a low level of culture, were deeply impressed by two groups of biological problems. In the first place, what is it that makes a difference between a living body and a dead one; what causes waking, sleep, trance, disease, death? In the second place, what are those human shapes which appear in dreams and visions? Looking at these two groups of phenomena, the ancient savage philosophers probably made their first step by the obvious inference that every man has two things belonging to him, namely, a life and a phantom as being its image or second self; both, also, are perceived to be things separable from the body. . . . The second step would seem also easy for savages to make, seeing how extremely difficult civilized men have found it to unmake. It is merely to combine the life and the phantom. . . . the result is that well-known conception . . . the personal soul, or spirit." E. B. Tylor, *Religion in Primitive Culture* (London: Peter Smith, 1970), 24ff.

11. Frazer, *Golden Bough*, 155–156, 160.

12. "What is required . . . is to stop courageously at the surface, the fold, the skin, to adore appearance, to believe in forms, tones, words, in the whole Olympus of appearance. Those Greeks were superficial—*out of profundity!*" Nietzsche, *The Gay Science*, trans. Walter Kaufmann (New York: Vintage, 1974), 38.

13. I think it likely that in his resistance to "shadow," Stevens is implicitly opposing the rhetoric of T. S. Eliot in "The Hollow Men." "Shadow" is the word Eliot chooses to describe the sorts of inner divisions that are erased in Stevens's immanent world, in which the distinction between interior and exterior is not, or should not be, seen as metaphysically meaningful:

> Between the emotion
> And the response
> Falls the Shadow
>
> *Life is very long*
>
> Between the desire
> And the spasm

> Between the potency
> And the existence
> Between the essence
> And the descent
> Falls the Shadow

The "Shadow" in Eliot's language suggests an opacity of self attributable to a fall from an original wholeness in God, a fall that has issued in an incongruity between inner and outer experience. It also bears a connotation of "foreshadow." This is why Eliot interpolates the eschatological language of the Lord's Prayer, "Thine is the Kingdom": current experience is a shadow of experience to come, experience that is not yet fulfilled. T. S. Eliot, *The Collected Poems* (New York: Harcourt Brace, 1991), 81–82. As I argue later in this chapter, at its highest pitch, Stevens's secular life of immanence takes place in a pure present: a life without progress, without teleology, and that doesn't desire a future abundance.

14. William James, *The Varieties of Religious Experience* (New York: Modern Library, 2000), 541.

15. James thus preserves a "soft" anthropomorphism. Though he does not believe that the world actively exhibits human qualities, his thinking carries, as David Bromwich has noted of James's *A Pluralistic Universe*, a "vivid suggestion of the world's readiness for the truths we wish to engender upon it." *Skeptical Music* (Chicago: University of Chicago Press, 2000), 74. This was George Santayana's (a thinker who influenced Stevens) basic criticism of James's thinking, which he called—demonstrating the power of the vocabulary of the anthropology of religion—a "new animism": "[Nature's] purposes are not to be static harmonies, self-unfolding destinies, the logic of spirit, the spirit of logic . . . its purposes are to be concrete endeavors, finite efforts of souls living in an environment which they transform and by which they, too, are affected. A spirit, the divine spirit as much as the human, as this new animism conceives it, is a romantic adventurer." *The Genteel Tradition* (Lincoln: University of Nebraska Press, 1998), 57. Insofar as Stevens follows Santayana in completing the criticism of anthropomorphism, he departs from a tradition in Romanticism that conceived the world as incomplete or unfinished, and thus, by nature, open to completion by human action. Hans Blumenberg calls this the principle of "open consistency." *The Legitimacy of the Modern Age*, trans. Robert Wallace (Cambridge: MIT Press, 1983), 215.

16. Nietzsche, *Gay Science*, 168–169.

17. Stevens's speculations concerning the original identity of the poetic and religious impulse were influenced by his encounter (through critical studies) with the Italian philosopher Giambattista Vico. In *The New Science*, Vico argued that for primitive cultures, poetry, metaphysics, and religion were not separate categories, but aspects of the total human encounter with its environment as that encounter is taken up into language. All language was "poetry," all poetry was "imaginative metaphysics" (i.e., religion) and imaginative metaphysics produced the structures of consciousness through which national, cultural, and personal identities were formed. As in later anthropological discourse, Vico thought that religion emerged through imaginative

responses to elusive experiences: "Their poetry was at first divine, because . . . they imagined the causes of the things they felt and wondered at to be gods. . . . Jove was born naturally in poetry as a divine character or imaginative universal . . . the poets founded religion among the gentiles." *The New Science of Giambattista Vico*, trans. Thomas Bergen (Ithaca: Cornell University Press, 1968), 116, 119, 120. For the most thorough account of Vico's influence on Stevens's poetics, see B. J. Leggett, *Wallace Stevens and Poetic Theory* (Chapel Hill: University of North Carolina Press, 1987), chapter 3: "Why It Must Change: Stevens, Vico, and Harold Bloom."

18. Wallace Stevens, *Sur Plusieurs Beaux Sujets: Wallace Stevens's Commonplace Book*, ed. William Bates (Stanford: Stanford University Press, 1989), 107.

19. Matthew Arnold, *Literature and Dogma* (London: Smith, Elder, 1884), 56.

20. The unnamed reference to Eliot in "Extracts" (1940) probably involves a barbed allusion to Eliot's collection of poetry *Old Possum's Book of Practical Cats*, published in 1939.

21. Santayana was a young professor at Harvard when Stevens was an undergraduate, and critics have long noted his influence on Stevens's thinking about poetry, in particular the relation between the imagination and religion. Some critics, like James Longenbach, think Stevens probably wrote an anonymous review of Santayana's *Interpretations of Poetry and Religion* in the *Harvard Advocate* in 1900, his last year at Harvard. See Longenbach, *Wallace Stevens: The Plain Sense of Things* (New York: Oxford University Press, 1991), 18–20.

22. George Santayana, "The Poetry of Barbarism" in *Interpretations of Poetry and Religion*, ed. William Holzberger and Herman Saatkamp (Cambridge: MIT Press, 1989), 129.

23. Storrs's argument was elaborated in the early twentieth century by philosophers of religion like Martin Buber, whose emphasis on the "Thou" derived from a conviction that human love presupposed an orientation toward a person and not a mere object. For Buber, Spinoza's anti-anthropomorphic conception of an impersonal divinity and impersonal love had damaged modern religious thought: "Anthropomorphism always reflects our need to preserve the concrete quality evidenced in the encounter; yet even this need is not its true root: it is in the encounter itself that we are confronted with something compellingly anthropomorphic, something demanding reciprocity, a primary Thou." *The Eclipse of God* (New York: Harper, 1952), 14–15.

24. Stevens, *Sur Plusieurs Beaux Sujets*, 33. Yet even this statement is complicated by the question of whether the relation of love is itself an anthropomorphism. In "An Ordinary Evening in New Haven," Stevens suggests that the "lineaments of earth" are "seen as inamorata" only through "loving fame / Added and added out of a fame-full heart" (*CP*, 413). They can only be loved at a "distance," and only through the self's *additions* to what is already there. In the next canto, one of the scholar's "drafts" of "The Ruler of Reality" reads, "This man abolishes by being himself / That which is not ourselves: the regalia, / The attributions, the plume and helmet-ho" (414). The anthropomorphic "regalia" is "abolished" by the human actually *becoming* the "not ourselves."

25. In his essay "Writing Off the Self," Richard Poirier briefly discusses the antihumanist strands in Stevens's writing, which he too finds anti-religious in bearing. Poirier sees in

Stevens a recurrence of the desire for self-eradication or self-erasure and a quest for modes of experience that do not further any human or religious ends, whether those ends are knowledge or sanctification. He notes that quests for such self-eradication have often been cast in terms of a religious project of purification in the expectation of union with God or a higher Good, but he thinks that in Stevens we are merely asked "to get excited about a future which will be brought about by our own extinction," in which we will be released from what Foucault calls "arrangements of knowledge." *The Renewal of Literature* (New Haven: Yale University Press, 1987), 195. I want to argue that the very pursuit of self-eradication in Stevens is complicated by its religious (especially mystical) heritage, and want to make a more specific claim that the desire for such an evacuation of the human is precipitated by the intellectual crisis over anthropomorphism brought about by the study of religion and exacerbated by Darwinism.

26. The same irony animates "The Course of a Particular," in which the speaker experiences the "cry of the leaves"—an instance of anthropomorphic, pathetic fallacy—yet insists that no anthropomorphic analogy can account for the cry: "It is not a cry of divine attention, / Nor the smoke-drift of puffed out heroes, nor human cry, / It is the cry of leaves that do not transcend themselves" (460).

27. Richard Poirier says of the first section of "Notes Toward a Supreme Fiction," "It is offhandedly suggested that the genesis of the gods is simply an irresistible consequence of the human compulsion to use words" (*Renewal of Literature*, 209).

28. Stevens's complaint is similar to Jean-Luc Nancy's criticisms of the monotheistic legacy, which bestows "a world whose sense is given in the mode of not being given—not yet, and, in a certain respect, never—is a world in which 'sense' itself defies all received and receivable sense." "The Deconstruction of Monotheism," in *Religion: Beyond a Concept*, ed. Hent de Vries (New York: Fordham University Press, 2008), 386.

29. Hans-Georg Gadamer, for instance, has written of the intractably "metaphysical background" of the "concept of the symbol": "It is possible to be led beyond the sensible to the divine. For the world of the senses is not mere nothingness and darkness but the outflowing and reflection of truth. The modern concept of the symbol cannot be understood apart from this gnostic function and its metaphysical background." *Truth and Method*, trans. Joel Weinsheimer and Donald G. Marshall (New York: Continuum, 2000), 73.

30. See, for instance, Michael Benamou, *Wallace Stevens and the Symbolist Imagination* (Princeton: Princeton University Press, 1972). In a very early journal entry (August 1899), Stevens adopts a mystical Symbolist attitude—attributable, perhaps, to the influence of Emerson—that he would find completely anathema two decades later: "I am completely satisfied that behind every physical fact there is a divine force. Don't therefore, look *at* facts, but *through* them" (*L*, 32). Robert Buttel notes that in an early, unpublished poem "Tides," "Stevens, in observing an underlying 'mystic sense' that relates by correspondence the tides and the secretive oceans, was tentatively drawing on the technique as well as mystique of the French Symbolists." *Wallace Stevens: The Making of Harmonium* (Princeton: Princeton University Press, 1967), 54. For a compelling reading of Stevens as an Emersonian determined to loosen the constraints

of the Calvinist imagination, see Elisa New, *The Regenerate Lyric: Theology and Innovation in American Poetry* (New York: Cambridge University Press, 1993), 56–94.

31. Arthur Symons, *The Symbolist Movement in Literature* (New York: Dutton, 1919), 5.

32. Stevens, *Sur Plusieurs Beaux Sujets*, 107.

33. See James, *Varieties of Religious Experience*, 552.

34. Odo Marquard, *In Defense of the Accidental*, trans. Robert M. Wallace (New York: Oxford University Press, 1991), 36.

35. This project is one of many that distance Stevens from his Romantic forebears, who, here as elsewhere, have preserved certain theological dualisms. Though there are affinities in their theories of imagination, the Samuel Taylor Coleridge who lamented the "despotism of the eye" and "the despotism of outward impressions" is nowhere to be found in Stevens (Coleridge quoted in M. H. Abrams, *Natural Supernaturalism: Tradition and Revolution in Romantic Literature* [New York: Norton, 1973], 366). Nor is there a trace of the Wordsworth in *The Prelude* who, when confronting Mont Blanc in its actuality, is "grieved / To have a soulless image on the eye / That had usurped upon a living thought." These are Christian sentiments modified in Romanticism, but the same is true of Judaism. In his book on religion and literature, Harold Bloom has noted how Judaism tends to devalue vision in favor of an interior life of meanings: "A curious sense of interiority marks Jewish thought, as a mode that negates all idolatry, all bondage to the bodily eye." *Ruin the Sacred Truths* (Cambridge: Harvard University Press, 1987), 149.

36. Wolfhart Pannenberg, *Anthropology in Theological Perspective* (New York: Continuum, 1985), 394.

37. Johann Georg Hamann, *Writings on Philosophy and Language*, ed. Kenneth Haynes (New York: Cambridge University Press, 2007), 71. While Hamann is the most creative modern Christian theorist of this picture of language, the idea goes back at least to Augustine in book 15 of his *De trinitate*. For an account of Augustinian theology's impact on Romantic theories of language that continue to frame modern debates, see Charles Taylor's essay "Language and Human Nature," in *Philosophical Papers*, vol. 1, *Human Agency and Language* (New York: Cambridge University Press, 1985), 215–247.

38. David Jarraway, one of the few critics who have written on Stevens and religion in the last decades, seems to misunderstand Stevens's rhetoric of "the eye" and of "sight" even as he quotes "On the Road Home." Jarraway writes, "The eye, of course, is the eye of logic or reason in the Western metaphysical tradition, overlooking the safety and security of stable self-presence, the first-person 'I' on which it plays and with which it equivocates." "Stevens and Belief," in *The Cambridge Companion to Wallace Stevens*, ed. John N. Serio (New York: Cambridge University Press, 2007), 198. Jarraway is right about the role that vision has often played in the Western metaphysical tradition, but this has nothing to do with Stevens's poetry, the highest state in which is often to "see" the world "with the hottest fire of sight" ("Credences of Summer," *CP*, 322). Jarraway claims that the "eye" for Stevens is an image of "logocentrism," whereas in almost every poem in which this image is employed it serves as a force that undermines the authority of speech and reason. It is surprising that Jarraway looks to "On the Road Home" as evidence of the way Stevens's poetry undermines the logocentric religious

and metaphysical tradition but does not see that "The world must be measured by eye" is precisely the line that reinforces the anti-logocentric proposition: "Words are not forms of a single word." Harold Bloom, by contrast, tends to over-spiritualize (rather than over-rationalize) the image of the "eye" in Stevens by reading Stevens through the gnostic lens of Blake and Emerson. He says of a passage in "Notes toward a Supreme Fiction," "[B]oth the seeing and unseeing are *in* the eye, rather than by it, and the implication is the Emersonian-Blakean one that the eye altering would alter all." *Wallace Stevens: The Poems of Our Climate* (Ithaca: Cornell University Press, 1977), 188. For a compelling discussion of the eye's status in Stevens and, more broadly, of Stevens's landscapes, see Bonnie Costello, *Shifting Ground: Reinventing Landscape in Modern American Poetry* (Cambridge: Harvard University Press, 2003), 53–85.

39. *Shelley's Poetry and Prose*, ed. Donald Reiman and Neil Fraistat (New York: Norton, 2002), 512.

40. Paul Ricoeur, *The Rule of Metaphor*, trans. Robert Czerny (Toronto: University of Toronto Press, 1979), 274. For his full argument concerning the relations among analogy, metaphor, and theology, see 272–295.

41. Ralph Waldo Emerson, *Nature and Selected Essays* (New York: Penguin, 2003), 85, 86.

42. Graham Ward, *Cities of God* (New York: Routledge, 2002), ix.

43. Kenneth Burke, *The Rhetoric of Religion* (Berkeley: University of California Press, 1961), 7.

44. Ibid., 24.

45. The very possibility of analogy was often thought to imply a divine ordering of the world. M. H. Abrams held that it was difficult to disentangle eighteenth-century classicist conceptions of analogy and their Romantic modifications from their origins in Renaissance theology: "[T]he divine architect has designed the universe analogically, relating the physical, moral, and spiritual realm by an elaborate system of correspondences." *English Romantic Poets: Modern Essays in Criticism*, ed. M. H. Abrams (New York: Oxford University Press, 1975), 43. While the strict and inflexible hierarchies of such a universe were largely rejected by Romantic theorists, Paul de Man has claimed that half-secularized words such as "affinity" and "sympathy" continued to sustain an "analogical imagination" in which mind was not a chance, epiphenomenal accident of a prior "physical realm" but rather a reality that existed in ontological congruity with that realm. Such congruity presupposed a world that was theologically infused by *logos*. *Blindness and Insight* (Minneapolis: University of Minnesota Press, 1983), 194–196. It is just this congruity that Stevens flatly rejects; indeed, the presupposition of incongruity is one of the most familiar tropes in his poetry. Stevens has often been considered one of the most Romantic of the modernist poets, and in many ways he is, but his rejection of an analogical universe, with all its attendant sympathies and affinities between mind and world, is a major departure from Romantic theory. Such a departure is evidence of Stevens's concern to purify Romanticism of what Abrams considered its theological residue. On Stevens as a neo-Romantic, see Joseph Carroll, *Wallace Stevens's Supreme Fiction: A New Romanticism* (Baton Rouge: Louisiana State University Press, 1987), and George Bornstein, *Transformations of Romanticism in Yeats, Eliot, and Stevens* (Chicago: University of Chicago Press, 1976).

46. This anti-anthropomorphic, tautologous world is one in which "desire for day" is "accomplished" because desire does not have to suffer the religious deferral or expectation that a logic of signs creates. In a world of signs the fulfillment of desire is still something to come, because when objects become signs they cease to be ends. In a tautologous world, where the sun and moon have no symbolic significance beyond their sheer existence, the bodily experience of them as other bodies is sufficient.

47. Friedrich Nietzsche, "On Truth and Lies in an Extra-Moral Sense," in *The Portable Nietzsche*, trans. Walter Kaufmann (New York: Viking, 1954), 42. On the importance of metaphor in Nietzsche's thought, see Sarah Kofman, *Nietzsche and Metaphor*, trans. Duncan Large (Stanford: Stanford University Press, 1993).

48. The best discussion of Stevens's various uses of and reflections on metaphor is Eleanor Cook, *Poetry, Word-Play, and Word-War in Wallace Stevens* (Princeton: Princeton University Press, 1988), 171–188.

49. This second perspective on metaphor is perhaps not so different from the first. The experience of freedom from the "weight of primary noon"—made possible by metaphor—is like a mode of transcendence beyond the painful intensity of the world and the difficulty of existing as a finite particular that must accept the material boundaries of its existence.

50. Martin Heidegger, *The Principle of Reason*, trans. Reginald Lilly (Bloomington: Indiana University Press, 1991), 48.

51. Ricoeur, *Rule of Metaphor*, 280. The criticism also came from materialist philosophies indebted to Marxism. As John Milbank writes, "In primitive times, so these accounts ran, the original sensory reference of language was lost sight of, and metaphoric substitution (or catachresis) necessary for the naming of near objects was falsely extended to the imagining of unreal 'spiritual' objects—for example, the 'breath' of human life became a hypostasized 'soul.' But the objection to this materialistic critique, already voiced by Vico and Herder in the eighteenth century, is that metaphoric substitution is always already involved in every signifying procedure, insofar as every articulation of 'something' in terms of 'something else' necessary for there to be a 'meaning,' involves more than the mere equivalence of a statement to a state of affairs." *Theology and Social Theory* (New York: Blackwell, 1990), 179.

52. For a rich discussion of the complexities of the word "sense" in Stevens, see Bart Eeckhout's chapter "Between the Senses of Sense," in *Wallace Stevens and the Limits of Reading and Writing* (Columbia: University of Missouri Press, 2003), 184–203.

53. What is at stake is not the classic empiricist suspicion that metaphor is a misleading ornamentation of "literal truth" derived from the senses but a fear that metaphor is a way of *losing* experience as such.

54. For a wonderful analysis of how this same problem—the reinscription of the Fall in the very act of trying to discard it—is ubiquitous in modern philosophy, see Stephen Mulhall, *Philosophical Myths of the Fall* (Princeton: Princeton University Press, 2005).

55. Eleanor Cook writes, "As for analogy, in his 1948 essay, 'Effects of Analogy,' it is widened into a general principle of resemblance, governed not by God, but by something Stevens calls a 'discipline of rightness.' I read this as a quiet replacing of the divine in

a Thomistic doctrine of analogy" (*Poetry, Word-Play, and Word-War*, 175). This is true—Stevens never returns to a fully theological "analogy of being"—but I see this essay more as a return to a religious vision of analogy than a break from it, for it revises Stevens's earlier, comprehensive suspicion of analogy as generative of an unacceptable transcendence.

56. James Longenbach has suggested that world politics was on Stevens's mind as he composed the poem; he wrote it when he was commissioned to give the Phi Beta Kappa poem at Harvard's 1945 commencement, which, as Longenbach writes, "would turn out to be a final wartime graduation of conscriptable young men" (*Wallace Stevens*, 282). Longenbach contends, perhaps rightly, that "Description without Place" suffers from a wishful exaggeration of the capacity of poetic speech to remake places, in particular "a place like wartime Germany." I would suggest (to look at Longenbach's concerns from a religious perspective) that one of the dangers of secular apotheosis—where humans, now seen as agents of "the Word," are invested with the capacity to remake the world—is that the world seems excessively malleable. Such apotheosis also exaggerates the ability of the imagination to generate a redeemed world of subjective experience within a material world (a "place") that remains materially unchanged.

57. Wittgenstein, *Remarks on Frazer's Golden Bough*, 4e.

58. Henry James, *The Art of Criticism: Henry James on the Theory and Practice of Fiction*, ed. William Veeder (Chicago: University of Chicago Press, 1986), 279.

2. "TANGLED IN A GOLDEN MESH"

1. Fyodor Dostoevsky, *The Brothers Karamazov*, trans. Richard Pevear and Larissa Volokhonsky (New York: Vintage, 1991), 108.

2. My analysis of Woolf shares something with, but also departs from, Vincent Pecora's fascinating discussion of Woolf and secularism in *Secularization and Cultural Criticism* (Chicago: University of Chicago Press, 1996). Pecora argues that Woolf's secularism (and Bloomsbury's more generally) can be understood as a translation or adaptation of ideas of community and spiritual interiority that originated in the evangelical Clapham community, among whom Woolf numbered her ancestors. Woolf, writes Pecora, "purg[ed] the Clapham Sect of its project for universal conversion and power while preserving its quasi-ecstatic ideal of associated minds, its embrace of a worldly sociality outside of conventional institutions, and the vestiges of its puritanical discomfort with the individual body" (173). Pecora is well aware of the complexities involved in what it means to "translate" religious ideas—his entire study is subtly engaged with this problematic—but nonetheless insists that Woolf "translated the social forms of her family's secularizing religious pilgrimage with great deliberateness" (190). His discussion, however, underplays both the ways in which Woolf dramatizes problems of incommensurability and ambivalence in her own secularizing translations and the ways in which Woolf remains concerned with metaphysical and aesthetic questions that take her well outside a comfortably "secularized religious habitus" (160). This chapter is, of course, about the religious and secular dimensions

of aesthetic experience rather than ideals of sociality and community. Yet I argue that Woolf, far from comfortably naturalizing an older theology, continues to find traces of this theology in experiences she does not want to abandon.

3. "Science as a Vocation," *From Max Weber*, trans. and ed. H. H. Gerth and C. Wright Mills (New York: Oxford University Press, 1958), 146.

4. Friedrich Nietzsche, *The Will to Power*, trans. Walter Kaufmann and R. J. Hollingdale (New York: Vintage, 1968), 435, 424.

5. Yeats suggested that Christianity, at least in its modern, Protestant (and later, secular) form, was responsible for the dissociation Weber observes. In *The Trembling of the Veil* he complained that since Spenser, "certain qualities of beauty, certain forms of sensuous loveliness were separated from all the general purposes of life"; our "images," he writes, "grow in beauty as they grow in sterility," for the major nineteenth-century poets could not unite "aesthetic values" with "moral values." Baudelaire, among other religious decadents, understood the desire galvanized yet unsatisfied by beauty as a desire for a transcendent good—"poetry" and "music," Baudelaire writes, "bear witness" to a "revealed paradise" that can be provisionally possessed in aesthetic experience. Ellis Hanson, *Decadence and Catholicism* (Ithaca: Cornell University Press, 1998), 4. But for Yeats the representative "late" Christian attitude is Bernard of Clairvaux "averting his eyes" from the "Italian Lakes" (*The Collected Works of W. B. Yeats*, vol. 3, *Autobiographies*, ed. William H. O'Donnell and Douglas N. Archibald [New York: Scribner, 1999], 242–243) or Lionel Johnson lamenting that "all the things of beauty burn / With flames of evil ecstasy" (*The Collected Works of W. B. Yeats*, vol. 5, *Later Essays*, ed. William O'Donnell [New York: Scribner, 1994], 133). Beauty for the early Yeats resides exclusively in a mythical past; "loveliness" "has long faded from the world" (*CPY*, 62). The distance embedded in the phenomenon of beauty is temporal rather than spatial; it is "the sweet, far thing" (38).

6. J. M. Bernstein, *The Fate of Art: Aesthetic Alienation from Kant to Derrida and Adorno* (University Park: Pennsylvania State University Press, 1992), 4.

7. He continues, "And even if it was not always the face of *evil*, once its connection with goodness was severed, beauty was still always a *face*, capable of promising one thing and delivering another: a mere surface and for that reason alone morally questionable." Alexander Nehamas, *Only a Promise of Happiness: The Place of Beauty in a World of Art* (Princeton: Princeton University Press, 2007), 9–10. Hans Urs von Balthasar, perhaps the greatest Catholic theologian of the twentieth century, puts it this way: "No longer loved or fostered by religion, beauty is lifted from its face as a mask, and its absence exposes features on that face which threaten to become incomprehensible to man. We no longer dare to believe in beauty and we make of it a mere appearance in order the more easily to dispose of it. . . . The witness borne by Being becomes untrustworthy for the person who can no longer read the language of beauty." *The Glory of the Lord: A Theological Aesthetics*, vol. 1, *Seeing the Form*, trans. Erasmo Leiva-Merikakis (San Francisco: Ignatius, 1998), 18–19.

8. Virginia Woolf, *The Voyage Out* (New York: Penguin, 1992), 5.

9. See G. W. F. Hegel, *Introductory Lectures on Aesthetics*, trans. Bernard Bosanquet (New York: Penguin, 2004).

10. *Samuel Taylor Coleridge: A Critical Edition of the Major Works*, ed. H. J. Jackson (New York: Oxford University Press, 1985), 558.

11. George Santayana, *The Sense of Beauty* (New York: Dover, 1955), 11, 31. Certain recent critics have sought to rehabilitate the reputation of beauty, which has in their view been devastated by political criticisms attacking its gentility, elitism, otherworldliness, and indifference to or complicity in social injustice. Denis Donoghue's compelling book *Speaking of Beauty* (New Haven: Yale University Press, 2003) is perhaps the most sophisticated attempt to rethink beauty's relation to goodness and truth. Elaine Scarry's *On Beauty and Being Just* (Princeton: Princeton University Press, 2011) tries to realign beauty with moral experience, but she focuses primarily on the subjective *effects* of beauty on the beholder. When she attempts to derive ethical principles from beauty's objective qualities, her argument is less compelling: she wants to map Rawls's account of "justice as fairness" onto the classic material characteristics of beauty (symmetry, proportion, harmony) and insist that the latter imply the former.

12. Charles Mauron, *The Nature of Beauty in Art and Literature*, trans. Roger Fry (London: Hogarth Press, 1927), 9.

13. G. E. Moore, *Principia Ethica* (New York: Cambridge University Press, 1994), xxiii. Denis Donoghue has suggested that from its outset, the discipline of aesthetics emphasized psychology rather than ontology: "By the eighteenth century, aesthetics was conducted, however tentatively, as a separate discipline. 'The beautiful' was analyzed apart from 'the true' and 'the good.' But there was no strict agreement on the character of aesthetics, except that most theorists regarded it as a special form of perception and therefore of mainly psychological interest. . . . Shaftesbury, Addison, and Hutcheson in his revisionary mode adumbrated a theory of the aesthetic attitude rather than of the beautiful object, and they recommended the notion of disinterestedness as its main quality, the subjective correlative of what passed in the object for autonomy. It was as if they internalized dissent as the determination to stand aside from worldly purposes. They had a better chance of grounding an aesthetic in the subject, the viewer's attitude, than in any qualities of the objects looked at" (*Speaking of Beauty*, 66–67).

14. *The Essays of Virginia Woolf*, ed. Andrew McNeillie, vol. 4, 1925–1928 (New York: Harcourt, 1994), 77.

15. Ibid., 429, 433.

16. Modernism was famously interested in the ugly and the disgusting. The attempt of modern art to incorporate the ugly and the disgusting begins in French naturalism, receives its most extraordinary spokesperson in Baudelaire, and moves through T. S. Eliot, Wyndham Lewis, Ezra Pound, Picasso, and others. Pound insisted, "the cult of beauty and the delineation of ugliness are not in mutual opposition." T. S. Eliot argued that the "contemplation of the horrid or sordid or disgusting" was "the necessary and negative aspect of the impulse toward the pursuit of beauty." When the journal *New Age* complained about Joyce's *Ulysses* and Wyndham Lewis's *Tarr*, T. S. Eliot responded, "The *New Age* is 'mystified, bewildered, repelled.' That is quite intelligible. *Ulysses* is volatile and heady. *Tarr* is thick and suety, clogging the weak intestine. Both are terrifying. That is the test of a new work of art. . . . But this attractive terror repels the majority of men; they seek the sense of ease which the sensitive man avoids,

and only when they find it do they call anything 'beautiful.'" These quotations are found in Lesley Higgins, *The Modernist Cult of Ugliness* (New York: Palgrave Macmillan, 2002), 132, 140. As Higgins has noted, this preoccupation with the ugly was often a masculinist test of artistic strength: how much ugliness could the writer digest and convert into art? My interest is in the religious and philosophical framework that makes such a test compelling in the first place.

17. Woolf, *Essays*, 4:481–483.
18. *The Complete Shorter Fiction of Virginia Woolf* (New York: Harcourt, 1989), 315. Emphasis added.
19. Woolf, *Essays*, 4:434. Mallarmé wrote a friend that he found the "Nothingness" on the other side of God, and there "found Beauty": "Beauty is all there is—and beauty has only one perfect expression, Poetry." Quoted in Steven Cassedy, *Flight from Eden: The Origins of Modern Literary Criticism and Theory* (Berkeley: University of California Press, 1990), 86–87. Woolf's fiction resists Mallarmé's secular substitutions—God/ Beauty/Poetry—by subjecting the purity of poetic beauty to "the sneer, the contrast, the closeness and complexity of life" (*Essays*, 4:436).
20. Virginia Woolf, *To the Lighthouse* (New York: Harcourt, 1981), 134. Hereafter cited in text as *TL*.
21. Virginia Woolf, *The Waves* (New York: Harcourt, 1959), 133. Hereafter cited in text as *TW*.
22. James Joyce, *A Portrait of the Artist as a Young Man* (New York: Penguin, 2003), 229, 231.
23. James Joyce, *Stephen Hero* (New York: New Directions, 1963), 213.
24. Ibid., 211.
25. In *Portrait of the Artist*, Stephen explicitly rejects aesthetics as "eugenics," or the suggestion that aesthetic feeling can be traced back to the biological urgency of sex. He ridicules the Darwinian proposal that you "admired the great flanks of Venus because you felt she would bear you burly offspring" (226).
26. Jacques Maritain, *Creative Intuition in Art and Poetry* (New York: Meridian, 1957), 124, 127.
27. The epiphanic character of the experience of beauty is also central for Marcel Proust. In *Swann's Way*, the encounter with the hawthorne hedge contains an element of revelation and inexhaustible meaning that cannot be rendered in discursive terms but that nonetheless manifests an "intention" not ascribable to a human subject: "But it was in vain that I lingered beside the hawthorns—breathing in their invisible and unchanging odour, trying to fix it in my mind (which did not know what to do with it), losing it, recapturing it, absorbing myself in the rhythm which disposed the flowers here and there with a youthful light-heartedness and at intervals as unexpected as certain intervals in music—they went on offering me the same charm in inexhaustible profusion, but without letting me delve any more deeply, like those melodies which one can play a hundred times in succession without coming any nearer to their secret. . . . In vain did I make a screen with my hands, the better to concentrate upon the flowers, the feeling they aroused in me remained obscure and vague, struggling and failing to free itself, to float across and become one with them. They themselves

Notes to Page 71

offered me no enlightenment, and I could not call upon any other flowers to satisfy this mysterious longing. . . . [I]t was in no artificial manner, by no device of human fabrication, that the festal intention of these flowers was revealed, but that it was Nature herself who had spontaneously expressed it." *In Search of Lost Time*, vol. 1, *Swann's Way*, trans. C. K. Scott Moncrieff and Terence Kilmartin (New York: Modern Library, 2003), 194–196.

28. Roger Fry, "An Essay in Aesthetics," in *Vision and Design* (Mineola, NY: Dover, 1981), 26.

29. Clive Bell, *Art* (New York: Capricorn, 1958), 28. Theodor Adorno criticizes this general modern tendency to devalue natural beauty by arguing that it is linked to the apotheosis of the human subject and its drive for domination: "Natural beauty vanished from aesthetics as a result of the burgeoning domination of the concept of freedom and human dignity . . . in accordance with this concept nothing in the world is worthy of attention except that for which the autonomous subject has itself to thank. . . . In the experience of nature, dignity reveals itself as the subjective usurpation that degrades what is not subordinate to the subject." He adds that he would like to see a "reorientation of aesthetic theory toward natural beauty." *Aesthetic Theory*, trans. Robert Hullot-Kentor (Minneapolis: University of Minnesota Press, 1997), 62. Adorno's complaint is confirmed by some of the most excessive statements of the Decadents (which are fully aware of their own exaggeration, but still meant seriously). Wilde, for instance, writes, "[T]he more we study art, the less we care for nature. What Art really reveals to us is Nature's lack of design, her curious crudities, her extraordinary monotony, her absolutely unfinished condition." *Complete Works of Oscar Wilde*, vol. 4, *Historical Criticism, Intentions, the Soul of Man*, ed. Josephine M. Guy (Oxford: Oxford University Press, 2007), 73.

30. Christine Froula, *Virginia Woolf and the Bloomsbury Avant-Garde: War, Civilization, Modernity* (New York: Columbia University Press, 2005), 12.

31. Ibid., 14.

32. As Adorno writes, "[E]very part of nature . . . is able to become luminous from within," and this has "little or nothing to do with formal proportion" (*Aesthetic Theory*, 70). Or as Elisa New has written of Marianne Moore in her wonderful study, *The Line's Eye*, beauty in theological tradition (New traces Moore's descent from the aesthetics of Jonathan Edwards) is "intrinsic and structural rather than merely formal." Moore, like Woolf, is astounded not by "some sentimental 'miracle' of creation but rather [by] the blessing of a Being that flows out of itself into form": "That Being should articulate itself at all into measurable extent and palpable texture; that it should acquire color and contour" is, New writes, an engrossing "mystery" to Moore. *The Line's Eye: Poetic Experience, American Sight* (Cambridge: Harvard University Press, 1998), 294. Woolf, too, is engrossed by this mystery—indeed, by this "miracle," a term she repeats in critical moments of her novels—yet unlike Moore and Edwards, she has no recourse to a doctrine of creation that would render the mystery intelligible if incomprehensible.

33. Hans-Georg Gadamer, *The Relevance of the Beautiful*, trans. Nicholas Walker (New York: Cambridge University Press, 1989), 30.

34. Fry, *Vision and Design*, 25.
35. James Wood, *The Broken Estate: Essays on Literature and Belief* (New York: Modern Library, 2000), 117.
36. Moore, *Principia Ethica*, 250.
37. Emily Dalgarno has remarked on "Woolf's constant attention to beauty in her essays and letters" (86). Dalgarno is the only Woolf scholar I've encountered who discusses Woolf's understanding of beauty. Yet I believe it is misleading to argue, as Dalgarno does, that "[i]n *To the Lighthouse* Woolf deconstructs the term 'beauty.'" *Virginia Woolf and the Visible World* (New York: Cambridge University Press, 2001), 84. While the novel is certainly exploring and resisting what Dalgarno calls the Victorian "ideology of feminine beauty" (85), especially in the interplay between Lily Briscoe and Mrs. Ramsay, it does not figure beauty as a merely "ideological phenomenon" peddled by Plato, Keats, and Wordsworth (84–85), even if (as I argue) it has powerful misgivings about the metaphysical status of beauty. Woolf's attraction to metaphysical and theological understandings of beauty was likely reinforced by her early love of Plato. As Dalgarno notes, Woolf read the *Symposium* as a young woman and was taken by Plato's account of the ascent of *eros* from earthly beauty to metaphysical beauty. For Plato, the desire that one feels when confronted with beauty is a metaphysical (or, what is nearly the same, theological) desire. Beauty draws the soul beyond the object that occasioned desire toward a perfect order. The response to beauty, for Plato, is not merely subjective or psychological but grounded in the truth that beauty discloses about reality and what stands behind it; namely, the Good. Feeling for beauty is rooted in our situation as embodied, desiring creatures—our erotic nature—but beauty draws us beyond our pleasure in the immediate object toward an identification with the good metaphysical and theological structure of the world as a whole. The experience of beauty, in this account, always has a meaning that transcends its occasion. Insofar as Woolf cannot resist looking for this meaning, she grapples with beauty as a religious phenomenon. Her early comments on Plato's account of beauty (1907–1909) are recorded on holograph reels in the Berg collection in the New York Public Library. They are partially quoted in Dalgarno (54–55). Woolf says that Socrates's recounting of Diotima's speech "should be read again and again." She summarizes the speech: "[H]e should learn to love the beauty in one form first; then he will perceive that all beauty is related, and he will love the beauty in all forms equally. Then he will love the beauty of the mind above all others. Personal beauty is only a trifle . . . he will contemplate the whole sea of beauty" (54).
38. "Beauty," Hegel writes, "powerless and helpless, hates understanding, because the latter exacts from it what it cannot perform." *The Phenomenology of Mind*, trans. J. B. Baillie (New York: Harper & Row, 1967), 93. Denis Donoghue beautifully glosses this passage: "The beautiful thing holds its secret by allowing us to divine that it has one" (*Speaking of Beauty*, 24).
39. Jorge Luis Borges, "The Wall and Its Books," in *Labyrinths*, ed. Donald A. Yates and James E. Irby (New York: Penguin, 1970), 223, quoted in Donoghue, *Speaking of Beauty*, 71.
40. Virginia Woolf, *Orlando* (New York: Harcourt, 2006), 236.

41. Jacques Maritain, *Creative Intuition in Art and Poetry* (New York: Meridian, 1957), 128.
42. Simone Weil, *First and Last Notebooks*, trans. Richard Rees (New York: Oxford University Press, 1970), 615.
43. Virginia Woolf, *Moments of Being* (New York: Harcourt, 1985), 71.
44. In Woolf's wonderful essay "On Being Ill," pain is the agent that de-centers the self, shocking it out of its habitual perceptions and so allowing it to encounter the beautiful, but the beautiful is then disclosed as the quality of the world that is, paradoxically, indifferent to pain: "This then has been going on all the time without our knowing it!—this incessant making up of shapes and casting them down. . . . [T]his interminable experiment with gold shafts and blue shadows, with veiling the sun and unveiling it, with making rock ramparts and wafting them away—this endless activity, with the waste of Heaven knows how many million horse power of energy, has been left to work its will year in year out. The fact seems to call for comment and indeed for censure. Some one should write to *The Times* about it. Use should be made of it. One should not let this gigantic cinema play perpetually to an empty house. But watch a little longer and another emotion drowns the stirrings of civic ardour. Divinely beautiful it is also divinely heartless. Immeasurable resources are used for some purpose which has nothing to do with human pleasure or human profit. If we were all laid prone, frozen, stiff, the sky would be experimenting with its blues and golds" (*Essays*, 4:321).
45. Virginia Woolf, *Mrs. Dalloway* (New York: Harcourt, 1981), 186. Hereafter cited in text as *MD*.
46. Woolf, *Moments of Being*, 72.
47. In *The Book of God: Secularization and Design in the Romantic Era* (Philadelphia: University of Pennsylvania Press, 2007), Colin Jager has shown how important the idea of design (and its complex, "secularized" developments) was to the Romantic era and its aesthetic thinking. Woolf is, I think, still wrestling with this legacy.
48. Woolf, *Moments of Being*, 72.
49. Ibid., 78.
50. Ann Banfield, *The Phantom Table* (New York: Cambridge University Press, 2007), 60, 78. Emphasis in original.
51. Ibid., 260. This passage from *A Room of One's Own*, for instance, makes it very difficult to understand Woolf's "reality" as a neutral, impersonal domain waiting for the imprint of the human meaning: "What is meant by 'reality'? It would seem to be something very erratic, very undependable—now to be found in a dusty road, now in a scrap of newspaper in the street, now in a daffodil in the sun. It lights up a group in a room and stamps some casual saying. It overwhelms one walking home beneath the stars and makes the silent world more real than the world of speech—and there it is again in an omnibus in the uproar of Picadilly. Sometimes, too, it seems to dwell in shapes too far away for us to discern what their nature is. But whatever it touches, it fixes and makes permanent. That is what remains over when the skin of the day has been cast into the hedge; that is what is left of past time and of our loves and hates." *A Room of One's Own* (New York: Harcourt, 1957), 110. Note that "reality" is close to what Woolf means by "beauty" and especially what I have called "radiance." It "lights up"; it is associated with "permanen[ce]" or what *To the Lighthouse* calls "eternity." "Reality" is

the presence behind appearance that makes those appearances radiant and that gives them significance.

52. I do not have space here for a detailed analysis of the relationship between secularism and modern epistemological frameworks, but Charles Taylor provides a compelling account of how the latter have become constitutive of the former: "At its most blatant this structure operates with a picture of knowing agents as individuals, who build up their understanding of the world through combining and relating, in more and more comprehensive theories, the information which they take in, and which is couched in inner representations. . . . I know the world through my representations. I must grasp the world as fact before I can posit values." *A Secular Age* (Cambridge: Harvard University Press, 2007), 557–558. This model is still widely held, but twentieth-century phenomenology provided a powerful challenge to it by emphasizing the irreducible "background" against which things "show up" for us and have significance *before* we act to disengage ourselves in order to know the world. Taylor emphasizes, moreover, that while secular epistemology generally assumes that the projection of value occurs after the recognition of fact, in reality the establishment of the epistemological model depended on the values it made possible for subjectivity: "Rather what happened is that experience was carved into shape by a powerful theory which posited the primacy of the individual, the neutral, the intra-mental as the locus of certainty. What was driving this theory? Certain 'values,' virtues, excellences: those of the independent, disengaged subject, reflexively controlling his own thought processes. . . . There is an ethic here, of independence, self-control, self-responsibility, of a disengagement which brings control; a stance which requires courage, the refusal of the easy comforts of conformity to authority, of the consolations of an enchanted world, of the surrender to the promptings of the senses. The entire picture, shot through with 'values,' which is meant to emerge out of the careful, objective, presuppositionless scrutiny, is now presented as having been there from the beginning, driving the whole process of 'discovery'" (559–560).

53. Virginia Woolf, *A Writer's Diary*, ed. Leonard Woolf (New York: Harcourt, 1982), 138.

54. Rhoda's famous statement in *The Waves* about squares and oblongs suggests that while art's powerful arrangement of the world is a "triumph," it also has the artificiality of a game and necessarily leaves things out: "There is a square; there is an oblong. The players take the square and place it upon the oblong. They place it very accurately; they make a perfect dwelling place. Very little is left outside. The structure is now visible; what is inchoate is here stated; we are not so various or so mean; we have made oblongs and stood them upon squares. This is our triumph, this is our consolation" (163). While Rhoda suggests that "very little is left outside," the implication is that art cannot make the *world* into a work of art. Rhoda is, moreover, Woolf's character who dwells most in the imagination and lacks an ability to encounter the world outside it.

55. Friedrich Nietzsche, *The Gay Science*, trans. Walter Kaufmann (New York: Vintage, 1974), 168–169. I quoted these lines in chapter 1 to illuminate Stevens's engagements with anthropomorphism and religion more generally, but here they are useful for the more specific purposes of thinking about religion, anthropomorphism, and the category of beauty.

56. On the collapse of these sorts of "anthropomorphic" judgments in modernity, see Rémi Brague, "The End of a World," in *The Wisdom of the World: The Human Experience of the Universe in Western Thought*, trans. Teresa Lavender Fagan (Chicago: University of Chicago Press, 2004).

57. In *Wonder, the Rainbow, and the Aesthetics of Rare Experiences* (Cambridge: Harvard University Press, 1998), Philip Fisher has tried to rehabilitate a sense of "wonder" in beautiful (not sublime) phenomena that nonetheless resists the temptation to find in beauty a religious or metaphysical significance. He thinks we should understand the experience of wonder in the beautiful (as in the experience of the rainbow) as analogous to the secular curiosity that animates the natural sciences. To predicate a "meaning" of an experience of beauty is to "pass beyond the sensory or aesthetic experience, beyond the pleasure in the presence of the object of wonder" (38). His example is the way the rainbow operates in the Jewish and Christian tradition: "In the Bible the rainbow is placed by God in the sky, after the flood, as a sign—that is, as a token or reminder—of his promise never again to destroy the earth with water. . . . This explanation turns it into a sign. It has passed from being an aesthetic object to being a meaningful object, a reminder" (ibid.). As Fisher notes, however, this drive for something like religious meaning in aesthetic experience is not easy to prevent: "The drive within wonder toward curiosity, questioning, and the search for explanation seems to involve no less than the religious move toward sign, history, memory, and meaning, a move away from the aesthetic experience itself, a passage from wonder to thinking" (41). Woolf is, I think, irresistibly driven toward just this kind of "explanation" of certain experiences of beauty that Fisher associates with religious consciousness. This is exactly how she experiences the second stage (after the initial blow) of her "moments of being": the "shock is at once in my case followed by the desire to explain it" (*Moments of Being*, 72).

58. Adorno, *Aesthetic Theory*, 74.

59. Virginia Woolf, *Between the Acts* (New York: Harcourt, 1970), 175.

60. Though Woolf is skeptical, she acknowledges her attraction to Cobden-Sanderson's idea of a "cosmos": "[W]e look on with sympathy, but feel a little chill about the feet and not very clear as to the direction of the road. . . . [Cobden-Sanderson] is neither vapid nor insipid nor wrapped round, as so many idealists tend to become, in comfortable cotton wool" (*Essays* 4:371). The last image, which she also uses to describe "nonbeing" when discussing her "moments of being," links Cobden-Sanderson to her own understanding of the world as a work of art.

61. Woolf, *Between the Acts*, 196.

62. Ibid., 195–196.

63. Ibid., 197.

64. In her biography of Roger Fry, Woolf notes that Fry shied away from a "mystical" interpretation of aesthetic emotion but claims that such emotion is nonetheless characterized by *expectation*: "But if reason must stop short, beyond reason lies reality—if nothing will make him doff his reason, nothing will make him lose his faith. The aesthetic emotion seems to him of supreme importance. But why?—he cannot say. 'One can only say that those who experience it feel it to have a peculiar quality of

'reality,' which makes it a matter of infinite importance in their lives. Any attempt I might make to explain this would probably land me in the depths of mysticism. On the edge of that gulf I stop.' But if it stops it is in the attitude of one who looks forward. We are always left with the sense of something to come." Virginia Woolf, *Roger Fry: A Biography* (New York: Harcourt, Brace, 1940), 229.

65. Santayana, *Sense of Beauty*, 33, 31. Santayana defined beauty this way precisely as an antidote to vague theological conceptions of beauty, or what he called "beauty" as "the manifestation of God to the senses" (7).

66. Later in the novel Neville uses a similar vocabulary of aesthetic "opposition": "Oppose ourselves to this illimitable chaos, said Neville, this formless imbecility" (*TW*, 226).

67. The question of whether beauty is a phenomenon to be experienced in a sheer present or whether it must point beyond itself to some eschatological future is raised again and again in Woolf. In *Between the Acts*, the question arises in an unsaid conversation between William and Isa. Thinking about "the beauty of the visible world," William thinks, "Isn't that enough? . . . Beauty—isn't that enough? But here Isa fidgeted. Her bare brown arms went nervously to her head. She half turned in her seat. 'No, not for us, who've the future,' she seemed to say. The future disturbing our present" (82).

68. Nietzsche, *Gay Science*, 223.

69. Denis Donoghue suggests that Peter takes beauty to be mere "appearance": "What else does Peter Walsh do—or Virginia Woolf, for that matter—than make of beauty a mere appearance? Not necessarily to dispose of it—there is no evidence of that intention. But he is entirely willing to have one parade of appearances replaced by another. He places himself at the point where he can best see the parade, and he enjoys it, but he does not ask that the appearances do anything more than minister to his satisfaction. He does not invoke the true and the good to make, with the beautiful, a triple value more profound than any one of its particles" (*Speaking of Beauty*, 58). While I agree with Donoghue that the true and the good are not invoked, I argue that the beautiful here is given a deeper ontological grounding as something like vital force rather than mere appearance.

70. Indeed, Woolf acknowledges this ambivalence by presuming that "atheism"—or at least the atheism particular to late Victorian and early twentieth-century England—is connected to a certain kind of subjectivism. The narrator's wry description of Peter early in the novel (before the major encounter with beauty) makes this clear: "By conviction an atheist, perhaps, he is taken by surprise with moments of extraordinary exaltation. Nothing exists outside of us except a state of mind, he thinks; a desire for solace, for relief, for something outside these miserable pigmies, these feeble, these ugly, these craven men and women" (57). For Peter, atheism means both a suspicion of "exaltation" as something dangerously mystical and a sense that "nothing exists outside us"—that value is something which only resides in individual human subjects who are isolated both from the world and from each other.

71. The philosopher Jeffrey Stout, in developing an account of distinctly secular, democratic virtues, acknowledges a similar quandary in trying to renovate the virtue of "gratitude" as a form of "piety" for an ethos based loosely on Emersonian self-reliance and moral perfectionism. He calls gratitude "religious": "Suppose we grant, then, that

there is room for gratitude in the self-reliant heart, at the point where self-reliance recognizes its dependence on the natural and social circumstances without which it would be nothing. Is there a place in such gratitude for recognition of an indebtedness that can never wholly be discharged? The Augustinians suspect that the answer is no. Nietzsche is probably the leading modern critic of piety to press this question in a skeptical direction. What worries him about piety is precisely the implication that we owe more to the sources of our existence and progress through life than we could ever repay. This, he thinks, is a debilitating thought, a seed of resentment that cannot be a part of a life that affirms life." *Democracy and Tradition* (Princeton: Princeton University Press, 2004), 38. William Connolly does not acknowledge such a quandary but insists that "immanent naturalists . . . find it important to cultivate and amplify gratitude for being in the world of becoming." "Belief, Spirituality, and Time," in *Varieties of Secularism in a Secular Age*, ed. Michael Warner, Jonathan VanAntwerpen, and Craig Calhoun (Cambridge: Harvard University Press, 2010), 130.

72. *The Collected Essays of Virginia Woolf*, vol. 3, *1919–1924*, ed. Andrew McNeillie (New York: Harcourt, 1994), 159.

73. Clarissa will not appropriate the vocabulary of a Miss Kilman, but Clarissa is closer to a Christian spirit of gratitude for being than is Miss Kilman. The latter is a thoroughly diminished ghost of the Puritan Jonathan Edwards, who, in his writings on religious aesthetics, called this spirit the "benevolence towards being in general" or "consent to being" that is evoked in the feeling of beauty. See "The Beauty of the World," "On Being," and "The Nature of True Virtue" in *A Jonathan Edwards Reader*, ed. John E. Smith et al. (New Haven: Yale University Press, 2003).

74. Many of Woolf's feelings about religion, like her father's, hung on the question of improper consolation. For instance, when she is praising the Greeks in "On Not Knowing Greek," it is because they "do not attempt to mitigate" the "sadness at the back of life." We look to them, she says, when we are tired of "Christianity and its consolations." *The Common Reader* (New York: Harcourt, 1953), 38. Woolf resists Christianity insofar as it is an eschatological religion, a religion of expectation and hope. She therefore resists the potentially eschatological dimension of the beautiful. "Sorrow" is the term Woolf used to describe what Keats saw in the "shadow" of "beauty," yet in *To the Lighthouse* the narrator notes, after everything that has happened in "Time Passes," "beauty offers her lures, has her consolations" (134). The tension here is similar to comments in *A Room of One's Own*: "the beauty of the world. . . . has two edges, one of laughter, one of anguish, cutting the heart asunder" (17). The first edge is beauty seen in its potentially eschatological dimension, the second the pain that is felt when one experiences the radiant peace of the beautiful as something desirable but fundamentally inaccessible. The anguish of beauty is for Woolf the more honest feeling; the laughter is important but tends to lead to dishonesty or illusion, as it does for Septimus, who finds in beauty a "laughing goodness."

75. It is important that Septimus is here associated with "the sleepers" in the "Time Passes" section of *To the Lighthouse*. I discuss this section below.

76. Ernst Bloch, *The Principle of Hope*, vol. 1, trans. Neville Plaice, Stephen Plaice, and Paul Knight (Cambridge: MIT Press, 1995), 215. Emphasis in original.

77. Septimus senses the relation between beauty and good that for Kant was an aesthetic consequence of a creationist theology. As Paul Guyer has noted in his introduction to Kant's *Critique of the Power of Judgment*, for Kant, "[O]ur disinterested affection for beauty prepares us for the non-self-regarding respect and love for mankind that is required of us by morality; that the existence of beauty in nature gives us a hint that nature is hospitable to human morality; and that we can only give content to the idea of a purpose for nature that we are led to by our reflection on the purposiveness of organisms by thinking of human moral development as the ultimate end of nature." Immanuel Kant, *Critique of the Power of Judgment*, trans. Paul Guyer and Eric Matthews (New York: Cambridge University Press, 2000), xxvii. As I have already noted, Gadamer has commented sympathetically about these relations in Kant: "It is certainly not without significance that we find nature beautiful, for it is an ethical experience bordering on the miraculous that beauty should manifest itself in all the fecund power of nature as if she displayed her beauties for us. In Kant a creationist theology stands behind this unique human capacity to encounter natural beauty" (*Relevance of the Beautiful*, 30).

78. Emily Dalgarno has argued that the Keatsian or Romantic quality of Septimus is "part of Woolf's satire of Romantic attitudes. . . . The madness of Septimus suggests less the waste of human potential than this helpless display of the destructive delusions of Romanticism" (*Virginia Woolf and the Visible World*, 75). But Dalgarno also argues that "Woolf shared several fifth-century attitudes [she is linking Woolf's novels to Greek tragedy] towards madness and its special relationship to vision" (74); it seems unlikely that Septimus, who is so closely linked to Clarissa and so sympathetically defended from authoritarian, rationalist psychologists, is the object of "satire." Woolf is drawn to Septimus's mad vision, and if it is finally resisted or recognized as unsustainable, it is with reluctance.

79. See George Bataille, *Theory of Religion*, trans. Robert Hurley (New York: Zone Books, 1992).

80. W. H. Auden, *Collected Poems* (New York: Vintage, 1991), 55.

81. Joyce, *Portrait of the Artist*, 231. Novalis shares Stephen Dedalus's perspective: "Everything beautiful is a *self-illuminated*, perfect individual. . . . That which the external world perceives as quite motionless has the appearance of being quite *at rest*. However much it may change, in relation to the external world it always stays at rest. This principle governs all self-modifications. That is why the beautiful feels so much at rest. Everything beautiful is a *self-illuminated*, perfect individual." Novalis, *Philosophical Writings*, trans. Margaret Stoljar (Albany: SUNY Press, 1997), 41.

82. In his excellent essay "An Agnostic Daughter's Apology: Materialism, Spiritualism, and Ancestry in Woolf's *To the Lighthouse*," *Journal of Modern Literature* 26, no. 2 (Winter 2002–2003): 1–41, Mark Gaipa has pointed out how often the task of resisting religious consolation (which both promises a material reversal of life's pain in heaven and dispenses an immediate emotional consolation in the form of hope) arises in Leslie Stephen's writings on agnosticism and religion. Gaipa suggests that at the heart of Woolf's impatience with Mr. Ramsay is the hypocrisy implicit in the gap between his pronouncements of the need for manly, agnostic courage (now that the bleakness

of his metaphysical situation is transparent) and his absolute emotional dependence on his wife. Mr. Ramsay's displacement of spiritual succor from Christ onto his wife raises, once again, but in a psychological key, interesting questions about how needs and desires are translated and eliminated as they move from religious paradigms to secular ones.

83. Adorno, *Aesthetic Theory*, 71, 73.

84. On Adorno's account of an "inverse theology" and his relation to the negative theological tradition, see Christopher Craig Brittain, *Adorno and Theology* (London: T and T Clark, 2010).

85. There is another moment earlier in the book where Mrs. Ramsay finds herself irritated with the hopefulness that seems to reside in the beautiful. When she remembers one of their former maids, Marie, whose father was dying back in her native Switzerland, she seizes on a line that Marie kept repeating "with tears in her eyes": "The mountains are so beautiful." "At the recollection—how she had stood there, how the girl had said, 'At home the mountains are so beautiful,' and there was no hope, no hope whatsoever, she had a spasm of irritation" (*TL*, 28). The pain and consolation that the girl feels in her memory of the beautiful mountains has an element of what Adorno calls the feeling that "things will turn out yet," combined with the sense that it does not immediately give the peace it promises. Mrs. Ramsay is irritated by the disparity between the fact that, in reality, there is "no hope, no hope whatsoever," and the muted expectation that the girl's memory of beauty makes possible. She would rather see the pain of beauty as the "sorrow" experienced in its "shadow," as Woolf says of the Greeks and Keats, than as a hope of reconciliation that is possible but not actual.

86. Woolf, *Moments of Being*, 72.

87. John Milbank, *Theological Perspectives on God and Beauty* (New York: Continuum, 2003), 3.

88. In his important book *Religious Experience and the Modernist Novel* (New York: Cambridge University Press, 2010), Pericles Lewis has associated Woolf's "moments of being" and her ecstatic mysticism with an interest in the sublime. Insofar as the "sublime" can refer to a mystical shock that pleasurably fragments the perceiving subject— or, as he says, "what transcends the limits of rational self-possession" (160)—I agree that Woolf's mysticism can be described as "sublime." Lewis also connects Woolf to Sappho, who was one of Longinus's examples of sublimity. Along these lines, some feminist critics like Laura Doyle have found in Woolf a distinctly female sublime that would rescue what they take to be the classical sublime's associations with empire and masculinity. See her "Sublime Barbarians in the Narrative of Empire; or, Longinus at Sea in *The Waves*," *Modern Fiction Studies* 42 (1996): 323–347. I argue in what follows that what I am calling the "secular sublime" has often been related to a certain kind of post-religious subjectivity that emphasizes the stoical, masculine will. In general, however—and this is what distinguishes my analysis from that of Lewis and Doyle—I am most interested in what, for Woolf, an aesthetic response like the sublime discloses about the nature of the world as a whole, how what is disclosed affects religious or secular descriptions of that world, and the relation of that disclosure to what is experienced in the beautiful.

89. My analysis of "Time Passes" is sympathetic to that of Mark Gaipa, who argues, "'Time Passes' originates not in war, nor in the death of Mrs. Ramsay, nor even in Woolf's earlier aesthetic theory, but rather in the Victorian crisis of religion—the struggle between religion and science, faith and skepticism—that shook her parents' generation" ("Agnostic's Daughter's Apology," 6). My reading of "Time Passes," however, tries to push the "crisis of religion" beyond its often narrow Victorian coordinates and show how it is simultaneously a crisis of the aesthetic character of the world. Gaipa's account of the centrality of Stephen's ideas and vocabulary for "Time Passes" is germane to my discussion. For instance, a line from Stephen's "Agnostic's Apology" compresses many of the issues at stake in Woolf's understanding of the beautiful and its meaning for her "sleepers": agnostics deny, for instance, the proposition that "the harmony beneath the discords is a reality and not a dream . . . agnostics . . . have not been able to escape into any mystic rapture" (quoted in Gaipa, "Agnostic's Daughter's Apology," 24).

90. In his classic study, *The Romantic Sublime* (Baltimore: Johns Hopkins University Press, 1976), Thomas Weiskel argues, "[I]n the history of literary consciousness the sublime revives as God withdraws from an immediate participation in the experience of men. The secondary or problematic sublime is pervaded by the nostalgia and the uncertainty of minds involuntarily secular. . . . The Romantic sublime was an attempt to revise the meaning of transcendence precisely when the traditional apparatus of sublimation—spiritual, ontological . . . was failing to be exercised or understood." It was a "massive transposition of transcendence into a naturalistic key" (3–4). More recently, Philip Fisher has argued, "The sublime secularized feelings of the infinite and of the relative insignificance of human powers in an attractive way, allowing the modern intellectual to hold onto covert religious feelings under an aesthetic disguise" (*Wonder, the Rainbow*, 2). These two perspectives diverge, not so much as to the meaning of the sublime as to the relationship that secular consciousness should have to the religious consciousness that came before it: for Weiskel (as for Abrams) the sublime marks a legitimate attempt to make sense of the experience of transcendence in a "naturalistic key"; for Fisher the sublime is an illegitimate attempt to smuggle religious feelings into a secular setting.

91. Weiskel thinks that the sublime has dissipated in the twentieth century, but that is largely, I think, because his understanding of it is so focused on its Romantic modes, which are modes of transcendence. The twentieth-century "secular" sublime, however, remains an experience of the ineffable and the overwhelming, but this is no longer an experience of transcendence.

92. "Thus nothing that can be an object of the senses is, considered on this footing, to be called sublime. But just because there is in our imagination a striving to advance to the infinite, while in our reason there lies a claim to absolute totality, as to a real idea, the very inadequacy of our faculty for estimating the magnitude of things of the sensible world awakens the feeling of a supersensible faculty in us." Kant, *Critique of the Power of Judgment*, 134. Later in the *Critique* Kant writes: "Thus the feeling of the sublime in nature is respect for our own vocation"; the sublime "makes intuitable the superiority of the rational vocation of our cognitive faculty over the greatest faculty of

sensibility. . . . Thus the inner perception of the inadequacy of any sensible standard for the estimation of magnitude by reason corresponds with reason's laws, and is a displeasure that arouses the feeling of our supersensible vocation in us, in accordance with which it is purposive and thus a pleasure to find every standard of sensibility inadequate for the ideas of the understanding" (141). Similarly, Roger Scruton writes, "The experience of beauty guides us along this second path: it tells us that we *are* at home in the world, that the world is already ordered in our perceptions as a place fit for the lives of beings like us. But . . . beings like us become at home in the world only by acknowledging our 'fallen' condition. . . . Hence the experience of beauty also points us beyond this world, to a 'kingdom of ends' in which our immortal longings and our desire for perfection are finally answered. As Plato and Kant both saw, therefore, the feeling for beauty is proximate to the religious frame of mind, arising from a humble sense of living with imperfections, while aspiring towards the highest unity with the transcendental." *Beauty: A Very Short Introduction* (New York: Oxford University Press, 2011), 145–146.

93. Jean-François Lyotard, *The Inhuman*, trans. Geoffrey Bennington and Rachel Bowlby (Stanford: Stanford University Press, 1988), 137.

94. Taylor, *Secular Age*, 286, 377–419.

95. In his compelling and comprehensive intellectual history of the sublime, James Kirwan concludes, "The sublime has traditionally been proffered as a certain intuition of the truth of two indemonstrable theses that are themselves assertions of our ability to transcend our worldly condition, either through an absolute potency of the will (Stoicism) or through our intrinsic unworldliness (religion)." *Sublimity* (New York: Routledge, 2004), 165. I think that Mr. Ramsay's version of the secular sublime is actually a modified combination of these two models. According to Mr. Ramsay, we would *like* to believe in our "intrinsic unworldliness," and so rest in the consolations of religion, but we cannot, so we look to our sublime encounters with a godless world precisely to increase "potency of the will," so that *our* spirits can bear a world *without* spirit. Numerous passages from Leslie Stephen's writings reveal this secular stoicism, and Woolf shows how his moments on the cliffs, of tragic exaltation, are an aesthetic spur or "shock" that he seeks to reinforce his sense of the embattled, isolated human will. In his essay, "Dreams and Realities," for instance, he criticizes religious believers and escapists of the "imagination" for "declaring that the sole worthy aim of human effort is to be found in dreamland, instead of amidst the harsh shock of struggling realities." *An Agnostic's Apology and Other Essays* (London: Smith, Elder, 1893), 126. His constant decision to face the "harsh shock of struggling realities" is what I take to be his (narrow) version of the sublime. (The "shock" Stephen feels is so regularized and expected that it is rarely actually a shock; it has nothing of the power and authenticity of Woolf's "shocks.") Stephen praises "a certain fine stoicism, a sturdy, tough-fibered sense of manly duty." In "A Sketch of the Past," Woolf notes her father's predilection for always "cracking up sense and manliness." "Thoroughly masculine . . . feminine delicacy" are two phrases that she remembers as characteristic of his general commentary (*Moments of Being*, 115). Though she does not use the word, she wryly suggests that his travel is always meant to occasion an encounter with the sublime. He would never travel to Italy or Greece because "[g]oing abroad meant

to him going to Switzerland to climb mountains; or going to Switzerland to look at mountains" (ibid.). The repetition with slight variation implies a sardonic perspective on the masculine will and its favored setting.

96. Michael Levenson, *Modernism and the Fate of Individuality* (New York: Cambridge University Press, 1991), 174–175.

97. From the beginning of the modern discourse, the sublime has been coded as masculine and the beautiful as feminine. Edmund Burke argued that "perfection" is not an essential feature of beauty because the highest manifestation of beauty that we know, the beauty of a woman, "almost always carries with it an idea of weakness and imperfection"; "Beauty in distress is much the most affecting beauty." Burke, *A Philosophical Enquiry into the Origin of Our Ideas of the Sublime and the Beautiful* (Notre Dame: University of Notre Dame Press, 1968), 110. The association of the sublime with the masculine will often meant, in the nineteenth century, the demotion of beauty as that which encouraged a feminine passivity in a harmonious world. As Friedrich Schiller writes in his second essay on the sublime, in lines that could easily almost have come from the pen of Leslie Stephen had he been more interested in aesthetic theory: "Away then, with the coddling that is based upon a false understanding and with the frail, unpampered taste that throws a veil over the stern face of necessity and, in order to put itself in a sensuously advantaged position, *lies* about some sort of harmony . . . a harmony of which there are no traces in the real world. On brow after brow cruel fate shows itself to us. There is salvation for us, not in ignorance of the dangers encamped around us. . . . but only in the *acquaintance* with those dangers. To make this acquaintance we are helped along by the terrifying and magnificent spectacle of change destroying everything and re-creating it and then destroying it once again, a spectacle of ruin at times eating slowly away at things, other times suddenly assaulting them." Friedrich Schiller, *Essays*, trans. Daniel Dahlstrom (New York: Continuum, 2001), 83.

98. Levenson, *Modernism and the Fate of Individuality*, 171.

99. Simone Weil, *Waiting for God*, trans. Emma Craufurd (New York: Harper Perennial, 2001), 105.

100. W. H. Auden, *Forewords and Afterwords* (New York: Vintage, 1989), 414. Some critics, like Mark Hussey, have concurred: "Although an ardent atheist, Woolf gradually came to hold what can best be described as a faith, the essential element of which was belief in a 'soul.' Her point of departure is always a simple, but radical wonder in the face of being at all." *The Singing of the Real World: The Philosophy of Virginia Woolf's Fiction* (Columbus: Ohio State University Press, 1986), xv. Later he writes, "Her idea of 'reality' and the soul, can, though, readily be construed as theological" (97). I have been arguing, however, that Woolf's religiosity and secularity do not reside so much in her "beliefs" as in her attachment to a theological interpretation of aesthetic experience. For a good overview of Woolf's relation to the "mystical" currents in her culture, see Julie Kane, "Varieties of Mystical Experience in the Writings of Virginia Woolf," *Twentieth Century Literature* 41, no. 4 (Winter 1995): 328–349.

101. *The Letters of Virginia Woolf*, vol. 3, 1923–1928, ed. Nigel Nicholson and Joanne Trautmann (New York: Harcourt Brace Jovanovich, 1977), 457–458.

102. Fisher, *Wonder, the Rainbow,* 19–20.

103. On Woolf and "the ordinary," see Liesl Olson, *Modernism and the Ordinary* (New York: Oxford University Press, 2009), esp. chapter 2, "Virginia Woolf and the 'Cotton Wool' of Daily Life."

104. Ludwig Wittgenstein, *Tractatus Logico-Philosophicus,* trans. D. F. Pears and B. F. McGuiness (New York: Routledge and Kegan, 1961), 149.

105. Ludwig Wittgenstein, "A Lecture on Ethics," *Philosophical Review* 74 (January 1965): 8.

106. Ibid.

107. "The sense of the world must lie outside the world. In the world everything is as it is, and everything happens as it does happen: *in* it no value exists—and if it did exist, it would have no value. . . . If there is any value that does have value, it must lie outside the whole sphere of what happens and is the case. . . . It must lie outside the world." Wittgenstein, *Tractatus,* 145.

108. Wittgenstein, "Lecture on Ethics," 11. It is difficult to disentangle the "religious" from the "mystical" here. For the experience of the world as miracle, as well as the feeling of absolute safety, Wittgenstein says, "is, I believe, exactly what people were referring to when they said that God had created the world; and the experience of absolute safety has been described by saying that we feel safe in the hands of God" (ibid.). The remarkable symmetry between Wittgenstein and Mrs. Ramsay's language ("we are in the hands of the Lord") suggests that it is hard to disentangle a mystical "feeling" from the theological language in which that feeling has been rendered intelligible. Once again we are confronted with a paradox of Woolf's intimation of a creation that has no creator.

109. Woolf, *Essays,* 4:78–79.

110. Woolf, *Letters,* 3:385.

111. Adorno, *Aesthetic Theory,* 52.

112. The later, Christian Auden argues that literature is only an analogy of reconciliation, not an enactment, and that beauty is the sign of this reconciliation: "Every poem . . . is an attempt to present an analogy to that paradisal state in which Freedom and Law, System and Order are united in harmony. Again, an analogy, not an imitation; the harmony is possible and verbal only; a poem is a natural, not an historical object. . . . [A] poem is beautiful or ugly to the degree that it succeeds or fails in reconciling contradictory feelings in an order of mutual propriety. Every beautiful poem presents an analogy to the forgiveness of sins, an analogy not an imitation, because it is not evil intentions which are repented of and pardoned but contradictory feelings which the poet surrenders to the poem in which they are reconciled. . . . The effect of beauty, therefore, is good to the degree that, through its analogies, the goodness of created existence, the historical fall into unfreedom and disorder, and the possibility of regaining paradise through repentance and forgiveness are recognized. Its effect is evil to the degree that Beauty is taken, not as analogous to but as identical with Goodness, so that the artist regards himself or is regarded by others as God, the pleasure of beauty taken for the joy of Paradise, and the conclusion drawn that, since all is well in art, all is well in history. But all is not well there." *Collected Prose,* vol. 3, *1949–1955,* ed. Edward Mendelson (Princeton: Princeton University Press, 2008), 233.

3. "HOMER IS MY EXAMPLE"

1. James Joyce, *A Portrait of the Artist as a Young Man* (New York: Penguin, 2003), 240.
2. See discussion in introduction.
3. W. B. Yeats, *A Vision* (New York: Collier, 1977), 29. Hereafter cited in text as *AV*.
4. On the difference between pagan and Christian patterning of history, see Karl Löwith's classic study, *Meaning in History: The Theological Implications of the Philosophy of History* (Chicago: University of Chicago Press, 1949).
5. *The Collected Poems of W. B. Yeats*, ed. Richard Finneran (New York: Scribner, 1996), 253. Hereafter cited in text as *CPY*.
6. *The Collected Letters of W. B. Yeats*, ed. Allan Wade (New York: Macmillan, 1955), 798. Hereafter cited in text as *LY*.
7. "Mr. Yeats," in *The Essays of Virginia Woolf*, vol. 4, *1925–1928*, ed. Andrew McNeillie (New York: Harcourt, 1994), 545. Privately Woolf wrote that, while the later Yeats still spoke in terms of occult systems ("in the unconscious soul, in fairies, in magic"), which were "not altogether easy to understand," "I agreed with many of his views; and he is also surprisingly sensible." *The Letters of Virginia Woolf*, vol. 4, *1929–1931*, ed. Nigel Nicolson and Joanne Trautman (New York: Harcourt, 1975), 250. And in a diary entry of 1930 she wrote of a meeting with him: "I was impressed by his directness, his terseness. No fluff & dreaminess." *The Diary of Virginia Woolf*, vol. 3, ed. Anne Olivier Bell and Andrew McNeillie (New York: Harcourt, 1980), 330. The post-Christian vision of the direct, terse, nondreamy Yeats is the concern of this chapter.
8. W. B. Yeats, *Memoirs*, ed. Denis Donoghue (New York: Macmillan, 1972), 166.
9. The claim about modern science (or a version of it) has been persuasively argued by contemporary intellectual historians like Peter Harrison; the link between "modern efficiency" and Protestant Christianity was given classic formulation by Max Weber, and M. H. Abrams and others have demonstrated Romanticism's ("modern lyric feeling's") theological genealogy. See Peter Harrison, *The Bible, Protestantism, and the Rise of Natural Science* (New York: Cambridge University Press, 2001) and *The Fall of Man and the Foundations of Science* (New York: Cambridge University Press, 2009); Max Weber, *The Protestant Ethic and the "Spirit" of Capitalism and Other Writings*, trans. Peter Baehr and Gordon Wells (New York: Penguin, 2002); M. H. Abrams, *Natural Supernaturalism: Tradition and Revolution in Romantic Literature* (New York: Norton, 1973); and, more recently, Terry Eagleton's chapter "Romantics" in *Culture and the Death of God* (New Haven: Yale University Press, 2014).
10. Hannah Arendt, *The Human Condition* (Chicago: University of Chicago Press, 1958), 254. Emphasis added.
11. "Science as a Vocation," in *From Max Weber*, trans. and ed. H. H. Gerth and C. Wright Mills (New York: Oxford University Press, 1958), 154.
12. On the Christian origins of modern individualism, see Louis Dumont, *Essays on Individualism: Modern Ideology in Anthropological Perspective* (Chicago: University of Chicago Press, 1992), 23–60, and Larry Siedentop, *Inventing the Individual: The Origins of Western Liberalism* (Cambridge: Harvard University Press, 2014). On the Christian valuation of interiority, see Phillip Cary, *Augustine's Invention of the Inner*

Self (New York: Oxford University Press, 2000), and Gavin Flood, *The Truth Within: A History of Inwardness in Christianity, Hinduism, and Buddhism* (New York: Oxford University Press, 2013). On the Protestant Christian construction of sincerity, see Webb Keane, *Christian Moderns: Freedom and Fetish in the Mission Encounter* (Berkeley: University of California Press, 2007), esp. 197–222, and Lionel Trilling, *Sincerity and Authenticity* (Cambridge: Harvard University Press, 1970).

13. *The Collected Works of W. B. Yeats*, vol. 5, *Later Essays*, ed. William O'Donnell (New York: Scribner, 1994), 204. Hereafter cited in text as *LE*.

14. *The Collected Works of W. B. Yeats*, vol. 3, *Autobiographies*, ed. William H. O'Donnell and Douglas N. Archibald (New York: Scribner, 1999), 201. Hereafter cited in text as *A*.

15. See Friedrich Nietzsche, *On the Genealogy of Morals* (New York: Vintage, 1969).

16. Weber, "Science as a Vocation," 148.

17. The "Religion of Jesus" passage is from *Jerusalem* (chapter 2, plate 52), in *The Poetry and Prose of William Blake*, ed. David Erdman (New York: Doubleday, 1965), 198. "Energy is Eternal Delight" is from "The Marriage of Heaven and Hell" (plate 4), ibid., 34.

18. Northrop Frye is surely right to insist that a text like "Jerusalem," however heterodox the details, contains "a fall, the struggle of men in a fallen world which is what we usually think of as history, the world's redemption by a divine man in which eternal life and death achieve a simultaneous triumph, and an apocalypse." *Fearful Symmetry: A Study of William Blake* (Princeton: Princeton University Press, 1947), 347. For an excellent study of Blake's elaboration and reworking of the Christian tradition, see Christopher Rowland, *Blake and the Bible* (New Haven: Yale University Press, 2010).

19. In his 1930 diary, Yeats juxtaposes the unifying project of "metaphysics" with conflict: "I am trying to understand why certain metaphysicians whom I have spent years trying to master repel me, why those invisible beings I have learned to trust would turn me from all that is not conflict, that is not from sword in hand." *Explorations* (New York: Collier, 1962), 301.

20. *The Collected Works of W. B. Yeats*, vol. 2, *The Plays*, ed. David Clark and Rosalind Clark (New York: Scribner, 2001), 238, 236. Hereafter cited in text as *TP*.

21. Philip Fisher, *The Vehement Passions* (Princeton: Princeton University Press, 2003), 51.

22. Ibid., 51. This world, in other words, must be tragic. Yeats's model is the Greeks, and as Bernard Williams writes in *Shame and Necessity* (Berkeley: University of California Press, 2008), "Greek Tragedy precisely refuses to present human beings who are ideally in harmony with their world, and has no room for a world that, if it were understood well enough, could instruct us how to be in harmony with it" (164). Harmony, as Williams conceives it, is not so much elusive as undesirable. The world does not yield a *logos* that grounds or pervades it, for harmony is not the "ideal" order of human life. As Yeats puts it, "We begin to live when we have conceived life as tragedy" (A, 127). Only such a conception permits the amplification of the passions.

23. See Rémi Brague, *The Wisdom of the World: The Human Experience of the Universe in Western Thought*; Louis Dupré, *Passage to Modernity*; Charles Taylor, *A Secular Age* (Cambridge: Harvard University Press, 2007); and Pfau, *Minding the Modern*.

24. On the "buffered self," see Taylor, *Secular Age*, esp. 37–42.

25. As Fisher writes of the Homeric image of wave crashing on rock: "The sound of their collision makes each substance known, and it does so because each is now set into a state. The shattering wave, the pounded rock make visible on each side the nature of sea and rock, but they do so at the very moment that each of the two is situationally flooded from without by the differences that occur as each limits the other" (*Vehement Passions*, 51).

26. Undivided being is not the therapeutic antidote to self-division. Fragmentariness is not synonymous with self-division, because a fragment is partial only in respect to other fragments, not to itself. Self-division is dangerous for Yeats because it is traditionally the problematic that generates ascetic religious therapies. Plato's tripartite division of soul sets up the hierarchy in which reason will have to discipline spiritedness and appetite, and St. Paul's famous vision of sin—"For that which I do I allow not: for what I would, that I do not; but what I hate, that I do" (Romans 7:15, KJV)—commends an abandonment of the impotent will to transforming grace.

27. Yeats tends to use the terms "passions" and "emotions" somewhat interchangeably, but in his later writing favors "passion" or "passions"; while "emotion" can, when Yeats yokes the word to certain adjectives ("vague," "spiritual") accrue negative connotations, "passion" is always positive. The best way to think about the relation between the two terms in Yeats is that the passions are a particularly intense, distinctly impersonal, and outward rather than inner-oriented species of emotions. On the intellectual-historical shift from the idea of the "passions" to "emotions" and the changes in moral psychology and worldview that made that shift possible, see Thomas Dixon, *From Passions to Emotions: The Creation of a Secular Psychological Category* (New York: Cambridge University Press, 2003).

28. *The Collected Works of W. B. Yeats*, vol. 4, *Early Essays*, ed. Richard Finneran and George Bornstein (New York: Scribner, 2007), 143. Hereafter cited in text as *EE*.

29. The line is a quotation from Edward Calvert in Yeats's essay "The Tribes of Danu," in *The Collected Works of W. B. Yeats*, vol. 9, *Early Articles and Reviews*, ed. John Frayne and Madeleine Marchaterre (New York: Scribner, 2004), 355.

30. Auden, in his introduction to Kierkegaard's writings, characterizes Kierkegaard's "aesthetic" stage in terms of what Auden calls "the aesthetic religion," which bears a striking resemblance to the "Greek"'s portrait. He too links the Greek gods to the passions: "The experience from which the aesthetic religion starts, the facts which it sets out to overcome, is the experience of the physical weakness of the self in the face of an overwhelmingly powerful not-self. To survive I must act strongly and decisively. What gives me the power to do so? Passion. The aesthetic religion regards the passions not as belonging to the self, but as divine visitations, powers which it must find the means to attract or repel if the self is to survive. . . . Being images of passions, [the gods] themselves are not *in* their passion—Aphrodite is not in love; Mars is not angry." *The Living Thoughts of Kierkegaard*, ed. W. H. Auden (New York: New York Review Books, 1999), xiv–xv. Yeats would not accept Auden's psychologizing (as Fisher says, modern psychology, as heir to Christianity and Stoicism, diminishes the passions by trying to displace their concrete force onto a "'true' biological target"), but his description helps clarify the status of the gods. They are not "in their passions" in the sense that, as gods,

they do not have to contend with finitude and thus have no "immobile objects" to collide with. Rather, they *are* passion: the "high keen joy" of their faces is, as the Greek says, a sign of their "eternal possession of themselves," or, in other words, an imagined state of unchanging passion, which is the state of self-identical being.

31. This is, I think, the best way to understand how Yeats conceptualizes his use of "the mask" in his theory and poetry. As Yeats puts it in *A Vision*, "the *antithetical Mask*" is "a form created by passion to unite us to ourselves" (82). The concept of the mask is, for Yeats, a way to preserve the experience of mythic repetition in a nonheroic, subjective culture and for a poet, who is not a man of action, to create objects of resistance in the mind that do not actually exist in the world. Passion, as I have argued, is a state of self-unification, and the mask, which "unite[s] us to ourselves," is the aesthetic means of accomplishing this. The gods are those forms of passion that the heroic man copies onto his body, and the mask, as the "form created by passion," is the same process looked at from the opposite, or Feuerbachian direction: passion creates the images of the gods which it then imitates. The mask, which Christianity would understand as refusal of spiritual transparency, a way of dividing the self by hiding parts of itself from itself, for Yeats actually (and paradoxically) generates undivided being. Whereas the Christian Auden chooses the "mirror" (see *The Sea and the Mirror*, for instance) as one of his governing poetic images, Yeats chooses the "mask."

32. Dixon, *From Passions to Emotions*, esp. 26–61.

33. Michael Stocker, *Valuing Emotions* (New York: Cambridge University Press, 1996), 1.

34. See Stuart Allen, *Wordsworth and the Passions of Critical Poetics* (London: Palgrave, 2010).

35. Andrew Stauffer, *Anger, Revolution, and Romanticism* (New York: Cambridge, 2009).

36. It's a peculiar alchemy: Yeats, like both Nietzsche and Lawrence, understands Christian *agape*, a concept of self-giving love, as fundamentally narcissistic. In "The Man Who Died," Lawrence's unnamed Christ says to Mary Magdalene: "Neither were your lovers in the past nothing. They were much to you, but you took more than you gave. Then you came to me for salvation from your own excess. And I, in my mission, I too ran to excess. I gave more than I took, and that also is woe and vanity." *The Selected Short Stories of D. H. Lawrence* (New York: Modern Library, 1999), 456. "Love" harbors a will to dominate; it is the apotheosis rather than elimination of need: "the need for excessive giving was in her, and she could not bear to be denied. . . . [T]he flicker of triumph had gleamed in her eyes; the greed of giving" (457).

37. Yeats, *Explorations*, 302.

38. Yeats shares this with Nietzsche, who, as Nuno Nabias has argued, grew closer to Stoic positions in his doctrines of *amor fati* and eternal recurrence after early criticisms of the Stoics. See "Nietzsche and Stoicism," in *Nietzsche and the Metaphysics of Tragedy*, trans. Martin Earl (New York: Continuum, 2006). "Nietzsche knew that this *wanting what was necessary in each happening* was the central pillar of the ethical programme of the philosophy of the Portico and that it was embodied in the maxim 'live in accordance with nature'" (85), emphasis mine.

39. Modris Eksteins notes of air combat in the Great War, "The air ace was the object of limitless envy among infantry, mired in mud and seeming helplessness. Soldiers

looked up from their trenches and saw in the air a purity of combat that the ground war had lost. The 'knights of the sky' were engaged in a conflict in which individual heroism still counted, romantic notions of honor, glory, heroism, and chivalry still intact. Flyers were the 'aristocracy of war.'" Quoted in Fran Brearton, *The Great War in Irish Poetry: W. B. Yeats to Michael Longley* (New York: Oxford University Press, 2003), 58. Brearton's chapter ("W. B. Yeats: Creation from Conflict") provides an outstanding discussion of Yeats's response to the Great War.

40. See Friedrich Schleiermacher, *The Christian Faith*, trans. H. R. Mackintosh and J. S. Stewart (London: T and T Clark, 1999).

41. Williams, *Shame and Necessity*, 12.

42. Yeats, *Explorations*, 332–333.

43. Terry Eagleton, *Sweet Violence: The Idea of the Tragic* (Oxford: Blackwell, 2003), 111.

44. Ibid., 112.

45. He has in mind Swift's "joyous saying": "'When I am told that somebody is my brother Protestant, I remember that the rat is a fellow creature'" (*LY*, 876).

46. Adam Potkay, *The Story of Joy: From the Bible to Late Romanticism* (New York: Cambridge University Press, 2011).

47. Simone Weil, *The Notebooks of Simone Weil*, trans. Arthur Mills (New York: Routledge, 2004), 291.

48. Yeats, *Memoirs*, 152.

49. The quotation adapts Blake: "Joys impregnate. Sorrows bring forth" (*The Marriage of Heaven and Hell*). (I am indebted to David Bromwich for this reference.) But here again, as when Yeats adds "will" to "energy is eternal delight," Yeats adds the accent of mastery.

50. For a powerful reading of tragic joy that understands it as a version of the sublime, see Jahan Ramazani, "Tragic Joy and the Sublime," in *Yeats and the Poetry of Death: Elegy, Self-Elegy, and the Sublime* (New Haven: Yale University Press, 1990).

51. See, on this influence, Michael Valdez Moses, "Nietzsche," in *W. B. Yeats in Context*, ed. David Holdeman and Ben Levitas (New York: Cambridge University Press, 2010), and Otto Bohlman, *Yeats and Nietzsche* (New York: Barnes and Noble, 1982), though this latter study is awkward in the handling of the poems. Denis Donoghue's *William Butler Yeats* (New York: Viking, 1971) is probably the best single short study of Yeats ever published, and Donoghue makes a compelling case that the Nietzschean influence overshadows those of other philosophers like Plotinus and poets like Blake.

52. Nietzsche, *The Birth of Tragedy*, trans. Shaun Whiteside (New York: Penguin, 1994), 17.

53. Ibid., 20. Thus tragic joy, as the early Nietzsche describes it, is structurally akin to Christian joy in the sense that both involve self-loss and the transfiguration of suffering. They differ in the conceptualization of the source: in Nietzsche, the source is the world, that amoral "monster of energy," the power of which is "justified" only "aesthetically." In Christianity joy partakes of a higher good—God's reality—that is known particularly acutely, though certainly not exclusively, in suffering. Suffering in the latter is the means to self-loss and the advent of God; in Nietzsche it is simply one manifestation of a broader creativity, though it is also the means through which the illusion of individuation is dispelled and the indiscriminate jubilation of that creativity known most directly.

54. In the late 1920s and early 1930s Yeats seems to have been particularly attracted to Christianity. In an entry from his 1930 journal where he discusses the life and writing of the Japanese Christian reformer Toyohiko Kagawa, Yeats similarly imagines his own writing as a mode of defense: "I write this paragraph to protect myself against the fascination of Toyohiko Kagawa and his heroic life" (*Explorations*, 328).

55. Friedrich von Hügel, *The Mystical Element of Religion* (New York: Crossroad, 1999), 1:34.

56. Friedrich Nietzsche, *The Will to Power*, trans. Walter Kaufmann and R. J. Hollingdale (New York: Vintage, 1968), 364. For Nietzsche pleasure, like passion, needs "obstacles," or what Yeats calls "immovable objects," to magnify itself: "What is pleasure but: an excitation of the feeling of power by an obstacle—so it swells up" (347).

57. See Peter McDonald, "Yeats and Remorse," in *Serious Poetry: Form and Authority from Yeats to Hill* (New York: Oxford, 2007). McDonald's chapter, however, focuses on "remorse" as a problem for a public poet whose writing potentially galvanized political action, whereas I am primarily interested in it as the wrench in Yeats's imagination of the passions.

58. The line is from Dr. Trench in *The Words* (TP, 470).

59. As Kierkegaard argued in "The Ancient Tragical Motif," the presence of "remorse" generates an ethical absolute that undermines the integrity of the ancient tragic self. His claims overlap with Yeats's resistance to "modern subjectivity": "the ancient world did not have subjectivity fully self-conscious and reflective," and the "individual . . . still rested in the substantial categories of state, family, and destiny." *Either/Or*, trans. Walter Lowrie (Princeton: Princeton University Press, 1971), 141. These categories sustain the fatalism of Greek tragedy; the hero is only partially "guilty" because his guilt-producing deed is as much "suffering" as "action." But the modern subject is "left to himself," and his guilt becomes "ethical." The "deep sorrow" of tragedy is converted into "pain," and "the bitterest pain is remorse," which has an "ethical, not aesthetic reality" (141, 146). Laurel Fulkerson's *No Regrets: Remorse in Classical Antiquity* (New York: Oxford University Press, 2013) argues that for the ancients the emotion of "remorse" was almost always evaluated negatively. Remorse only came to be seen as a moral good with the rise of Christianity, for which it marks the beginning of repentance and self-transformation.

60. The language mirrors the language of the prayer of contrition in the 1662 *Book of Common Prayer*, minus the key omission of "ought": "We have left undone those things which we ought to have done; / And we have done those things which we ought not to have done." Repentance would transfer the heart's remorse back to the body's death. It can be only the emotional prologue to the virtue of repentance, which submits that action or inaction to a transcendent good.

61. See Nuno Nabias's reading of Schopenhauer's *On the Basis of Morality* and Nietzsche's attempt to overcome it in *Nietzsche and the Metaphysics of Tragedy*, 105–115.

62. See, for instance, Vereen M. Bell, *Yeats and the Logic of Formalism* (Columbia: University of Missouri Press, 2006): "The sense, then, of the question 'what is joy?' is that, given the pitiless authority of this arrangement, what could 'joy' really be said to be, assuming that it is achievable in some form in the first place? The answer in the

poem will turn out to be that there is no answer—that, except in sweetly transient moments, joy, grief, and pain, and what Thomas Parkinson describes as 'deathful knowledge,' are so inextricably interwoven that there is no word that describes the state that the word *joy* is otherwise taken to refer to" (162).

63. James Frazer, *The Golden Bough: A New Abridgement,* ed. Robert Fraser (New York: Oxford University Press, 1994), 348.

64. Yeats occasionally used the term "ecstasy," but he seems to have preferred "joy" and only used the former because of its academic gravity: "I shall not be able to use the word joy in my lecture for it would confuse things, I shall have to leave the word 'ecstasy' " (*LY,* 576).

65. Blessing and blessedness are theologically ambivalent states in Yeats. He writes, in a letter, "Our traditions only permit us to bless, for the arts are an extension of the beatitudes." But his beatitudes look little like those from the Sermon on the Mount. He continues: "Blessed be heroic death (Shakespeare's tragedies), blessed be heroic life (Cervantes), blessed be the wise (Balzac)" (*LY,* 832). The Sermon on the Mount is admired in *The Unicorn from the Stars* (a play that presents a peculiar synthesis of the Christian social radicalism of Tolstoy, whom Yeats was reading at the time, as well as Blake's Christian antinomianism, with the pagan warrior ethos) for "the fascination of what's difficult": "You have accused me of upsetting order by my free drinks, and I have showed you that there is more dreadful fermentation in the Sermon on the Mount than in my beer-barrels. Christ thought it in the irresponsibility of His omnipotence" (*TP,* 643). Thus the Sermon, which ostensibly inverts the pagan equation of social power with blessedness, becomes a mood of excess in a man whose power is such that he can enjoy the insouciance of irresponsibility. On blessing in Yeats, see Sean Pryor, *W. B. Yeats, Ezra Pound, and the Poetry of Paradise* (London: Ashgate, 2013), 191–192.

66. "We must set our love and indignation against [the Communist's] pity and hate" (*LY,* 876–877).

67. Fisher, *Vehement Passions,* 175. Emphasis added.

68. Yeats mistrusts passions that have become ideological. Political ideologies, for Yeats, generate hatred for the world because they resent its unmanageability; as the world refuses to conform to the demands of justice, the self tries to carve it up in its own moral image. This is why political and ascetic images so often converge in Yeats. In "Easter, 1916," "Too long a sacrifice / Can make a stone of the heart," which troubles the natural mutations of the "living stream" (*CPY,* 181). In "In Memory of Eva Gore-Booth and Con Markievicz," the dreaming of "some vague Utopia" leaves the passionate body "withered old and skeleton-gaunt, / An image of such politics" (233). Political hate sterilizes the passionate body. "Hatred as a basis of imagination," Yeats complained in his 1909 journal, "helps to dry up the nature and makes the sexual abstinence, so common among young men and women in Ireland, possible. This abstinence reacts in its turn on the imagination, so that we get at last that strange eunuch-like tone and temper" (*A,* 359).

69. Yeats attributes this sentiment to "Blake's old thought," but as Harold Bloom has shown, he completely misunderstands the "moral allegory" of his source: "This 'spiritual Hate,'

as Yeats fails to see, is *not* between men and women, but between Albion and his Sons, or between what man was before his fall, and the Zoas or warring faculties into which he is broken up after his fall." *Yeats* (New York: Oxford University Press, 1970), 404.

70. As Yeats himself suggests in *A Vision* (in a passage I quote at the beginning of this chapter), his paganism is distinctly masculine (antithetical paganism is "masculine, harsh," Christianity is "unifying, feminine"). Here Yeats elaborates: "self-abandonment," a major theme in Christian spirituality, is a woman's work; self-assertion, the stance that for Hans Blumenberg characterizes modern secular attitudes, is a man's. A little further below I discuss "Lapis Lazuli," which derides the "hysterical women" who read the signs of aggression in mid-1930s Europe and Abyssinia with what, in historical retrospect, seems entirely appropriate anxiety. It is worth noting that Celsus, one of the earliest pagan critics of Christianity, contended that the resurrection of Christ was the invention of a "hysterical woman" (Mary Magdalene); Celsus, like the much later Nietzsche, characterized Christianity as a religion of women, slaves, and children. See Margaret MacDonald, *Early Christian Women and Pagan Opinion: The Power of the Hysterical Woman* (New York: Cambridge University Press, 1996). Gender ideology in Yeats is complex, however: "Crazy Jane," who might be characterized as another kind of "hysterical" woman, serves as the mouthpiece for many of Yeats's most cherished sentiments; her antiestablishment feeling and heterodoxy distinguish her from stale, conventional moralism. Marianne DeKoven finds "misogyny" in "A Prayer for My Daughter"—perhaps because Yeats says, "let her think opinions are accursed"—but, as I note in my discussion of "Nineteen Hundred and Nineteen," "opinion" for Yeats figures impoverished, *disembodied*, and merely ideological intellectual activity and is broadly disparaged by him irrespective of gender concerns. (DeKoven notes that many Yeats poems provide "empowering representations" of women.) DeKoven, "Modernism and Gender," in *The Cambridge Companion to Modernism*, ed. Michael Levenson (New York: Cambridge University Press, 1999), 215. The best book on gender in Yeats is Elizabeth Butler Cullingford, *Gender and History in Yeats's Love Poetry* (New York: Cambridge University Press, 1993).

71. See Bloom, *Yeats*, 437–439.

72. Yeats, *Explorations*, 339–340.

73. Yvor Winters noticed a similar use of "mere" in the "mere anarchy" of "The Second Coming." See "The Poetry of W. B. Yeats," *Twentieth-Century Literature* 6, no. 1 (1960): 9.

74. Bloom writes, "The gaiety of Lear is of course non-existent" (*Yeats*, 439). Bromwich writes, "The observation should not be allowed to pass as if its truth were obvious; in an obvious sense, indeed, Hamlet and Lear are anything but joyful . . . it is false to saddle Shakespeare and his characters with such a conceit." "Destruction and the Theory of Happiness in the Poetry of Yeats and Stevens," *Essays in Criticism* 60, no. 2 (2010): 113.

75. Bloom, *Yeats*, 438.

76. Hazard Adams, *The Book of Yeats's Vision* (Ann Arbor: University of Michigan Press, 1995), 34.

77. William Shakespeare, *King Lear*, ed. Stephen Orgel (New York: Penguin, 1999), 73 (3.4.34–38).

78. He also wants, as I have suggested, a Homer without pity. Yeats writes, in an unpublished note to *A Vision*: "Homer was wrong in saying, 'Would that strife might perish from among gods and men.' He did not see that he was praying for the destruction of the universe; for if his prayers were heard all things would pass away." Quoted in Richard Ellmann, *The Identity of Yeats* (New York: Oxford University Press, 1964), 274.

79. Friedrich Nietzsche, *The Gay Science*, trans. Walter Kaufmann (New York: Vintage, 1974), 273–274.

80. Friedrich Nietzsche, *Ecce Homo*, trans. R. J. Hollingdale (New York: Penguin, 2004), 69–70.

81. Friedrich Nietzsche, *Thus Spoke Zarathustra*, trans. Walter Kaufmann (New York: Penguin, 1966), 139.

82. Yeats, *Explorations*, 331.

83. *The Winding Stair: Manuscript Materials*, ed. David Clark (Ithaca: Cornell University Press, 1995), 35.

84. John Jones, *On Aristotle and Greek Tragedy* (New York: Oxford University Press, 1968), 168.

85. Nietzsche, "Attempt at a Self-Criticism," in *Birth of Tragedy*, 8.

86. On the absence of forgiveness in pagan antiquity, see David Konstan, *Before Forgiveness: The Origins of a Moral Idea* (New York: Cambridge University Press, 2010), esp. chapters 2 and 3.

87. Helen Vendler, *Our Secret Discipline: Yeats and Lyric Form* (Cambridge: Harvard University Press, 2007), 315.

88. Edward Said, *The World, the Text, and the Critic* (Cambridge: Harvard University Press, 1983), 290.

89. Michael Wood, *Yeats and Violence* (New York: Oxford University Press, 2010), 38.

90. Yeats, *Memoirs*, 251.

91. Jon Stallworthy, *Between the Lines: Yeats's Poetry in the Making* (New York: Oxford University Press, 1963), 221.

92. Wood, *Yeats and Violence*, 36.

93. The image taken from an event described in Lady Gregory's journal and related to Yeats: "Then Ellen told me it was Malachi Quinn's young wife that had been shot dead—with her child in her arms" (ibid., 20).

94. Nietzsche is up against the same difficulty in *On the Genealogy of Morals* when he works to distinguish the aesthetically admirable will to power, obedient to the "aristocratic equation" ("good = noble = beautiful = happy = loved by the gods" [34]) from the will-to-power of *ressentiment*, which, though it masks its violence in the language of peaceableness is, as Nietzsche reluctantly acknowledges, itself a clever mode of that will.

95. Frank Kermode, *Romantic Image* (New York: Routledge, 2002), 72.

96. Ibid., 102.

97. Plato, *Phaedo*, trans. David Gallop (New York: Oxford, 1993), 37.

98. Woods, *Yeats and Violence*, 206.

99. A. Norman Jeffares, quoting a 1927 study, *The Geography of Witchcraft*, notes that on that night the witches "ride upon certain beasts"; if Yeats knew the particulars of that legend, the "violence of horses" and the "thunder of feet" might be linked to this witch horde. *A New Commentary on the Poems of W. B. Yeats* (Stanford: Stanford University Press, 1984), 234.

100. The gifts Kyteler (the high-born woman) brings Artisson (the low incubus)—"Bronzed peacock feathers, red combs of her cocks"—recall Phidias's grasshoppers and bees, and the suggestion is that the violence done to both sets of animal figures (in the case of Kyteler they are stripped and dismembered) is in part generated by an aristocratic infatuation with the one of the "multitude." Vendler comments on these gifts: "The outrageous obeisance of high-born lady to low incubus is a symbol, for Yeats, of the drivenness of human desire: it will abase itself before its object, it will commit violence for its object" (*Our Secret Discipline*, 76). She thus ignores the class implication of the hierarchy she acknowledges. The "ingenious lovely things" with which the poem begins belong to aristocratic creativity and are thus "sheer miracle to the multitude"; the populist violence the poem laments was inaugurated by the original "dogmatic, leveling, unifying" demand that Yeats, like Nietzsche, attributes to Christianity. Simplistically ideological as this reading might seem, it is clear that the high-born Lady Kyteler mirrors this leveling through an erotic infatuation that should be beneath her dignity. The lines, in their evocation of unsuitable erotic coupling, look forward to the aristocratic disgust over the "filthy modern tide" of "The Statues" and "the base-born products of base beds" of "Under Ben Bulben." Artisson's "eyes without thought" and "stupid strawpale locks" evoke the mindlessness of the modern mob; we might even say that she pays the same penalty for her infatuation that the dying aristocracy pays for the modern nation's democratic infatuation with *l'homme moyen sensuel*.

101. Quoted in Jeffares, *New Commentary*, 412.

102. George Orwell, "Inside the Whale," in *The Collected Essays, Journalism, and Letters of George Orwell*, vol. 1, ed. Sonia Orwell and Ian Angus (New York: Penguin, 1970), 516.

103. See Nietzsche, *Gay Science*, 163, and David Bromwich's compelling use of this passage from Nietzsche, which counsels the dishonesty of art in such a world, for Stevens and Yeats's late poetry in "Destruction and the Theory of Happiness."

104. The line echoes the "valley of the bones" section in Ezekiel 37, as well as Isaiah 64: "But we are all as an unclean thing, and all our righteousnesses are as filthy rags; and we do fade as a leaf; and our iniquities, like the wind, have taken us away." The biblical prophets, rather than Homer, are the presiding spirits of this poem.

4. "THE POWER TO ENCHANT THAT COMES FROM DISILLUSION"

1. W. H. Auden, *Collected Poems* (New York: Vintage, 1991), 542. Hereafter cited in text as *CPA*. All other quotations from the poetry are from *The English Auden: Poems, Essays, and Dramatic Writings, 1927–1939* (Boston: Faber and Faber, 1973). These are cited in text as *EA*.

2. On this poem, see Liesl M. Olson, "Wallace and Wystan, Antimythological Meetings," *W. H. Auden Society Newsletter* 23 (December 2002): 12–23. For two compelling readings of "In Praise of Limestone," see Douglas Mao, "Auden and Son: Environment, Evolution, Exhibition," *Paideuma* 32 (2003): 301–349, and Susannah Young-ah Gottlieb, *Regions of Sorrow: Anxiety and Messianism in Hannah Arendt and W. H. Auden* (Stanford: Stanford University Press, 2003). Mao's reading provides insight into Auden's abiding concern with the ways in which material environments shape the self, and the extent to which this is a good or bad thing; Gottlieb's reading is the most profound account that I know of regarding how the poem thinks about and figures blessedness and forgiveness. (Neither Mao nor Gottlieb mentions the allusion to Stevens.)

3. Wallace Stevens, *Collected Poetry and Prose* (New York: Library of America, 1997), 280.

4. W. H. Auden, *The Dyer's Hand* (New York: Vintage, 1989), 61. Hereafter cited in text as *DH*.

5. For insightful accounts of how Auden's Christian faith (he returned to the Anglican church around 1940) influenced his later poetry and thought, see Alan Jacobs, *What Became of Wystan: Continuity and Change in Auden's Poetry* (Fayetteville: University of Arkansas Press, 1998), and Arthur Kirsch, *Auden and Christianity* (New Haven: Yale University Press, 2005).

6. This is by no means what philosophers call a *substance* dualism. Auden does not think that human being is made up of two different kinds of ontological stuff; this is why I generally refer to the dualism as that between personhood and material world, not mind and body. It is more like a *value* dualism; and yet, as I'm arguing, the dualism is not a value hierarchy but an insistence on value *differentiation*. Because it is *affirmative* it does not create hierarchies. Randall Jarrell is therefore mistaken when he argues that Auden's poetry starting around 1940 stems from an "absolute dualism" betraying the influence of the neo-orthodox concept of God as "wholly other." For this Auden, says Jarrell, only the completely transcendent God is good, and "existence is wholly evil." Jarrell continues, "The whole theological tradition Auden comes at the tail of is essentially a series of adaptations of the dualism of Paul." Jarrell's claim is a willful misunderstanding of both the neo-orthodox theological tradition and the extent to which Auden incorporated neo-orthodox theology into his poetry and thought. *Randall Jarrell on W. H. Auden*, ed. Stephen Burt (New York: Columbia University Press, 2005), 99, 105.

7. Charles Taylor, *A Secular Age* (Cambridge: Harvard University Press, 2007), 37–42, 134–141.

8. He quotes it in his series of lectures entitled *The Enchafed Flood*. W. H. Auden, *Collected Prose*, ed. Edward Mendelson, vol. 3, *1949–1955* (Princeton: Princeton University Press, 2007), 51.

9. T. S. Eliot, "Metaphysical Poets," in *The Sacred Wood and Major Early Essays* (Mineola, NY: Dover, 1998), 127.

10. *Ahead of All Parting: The Selected Poetry and Prose of Rainer Maria Rilke*, trans. Stephen Mitchell (New York: Modern Library, 1995), 114.

11. W. H. Auden, *Forewords and Afterwords* (New York: Vintage, 1989), 44. Auden may also be talking about his earlier self. Randall Jarrell has said of Auden's early poetry,

"The objects of the poems are vaguely tabooish, totemistic, animistic—everything is full of *mana* . . . When we say that some patch of an early poem seems 'magical,' we mean, sometimes, that the effect does not appear to be produced by any of the rhetorical devices we expect to find; that the poem works directly at levels we are not accustomed to verbalize or scrutinize." Jarrell, *On W. H. Auden*, 85–86.

12. In the late nineteenth and early twentieth century, new research in the anthropology and history of religion as well as the history of aesthetics contributed to a heightened level of interest in the genealogy of poetry. Scholars have long noted the importance of one work, Frazer's *The Golden Bough* (briefly discussed in chapter 1), on literary modernism. For an excellent overview of its influence, see John Vickery, *The Literary Impact of the Golden Bough* (Princeton: Princeton University Press, 1973). One consequence of this research was that poets and philosophers came to accept that art emerged out of a sacred framework and only became a discrete practice as societies became more complex and less religiously unified. An awareness of the prehistory of "art" and "poetry" raised questions about its contemporary status and native strengths. Had art been devitalized by an increased distance from its religious sources, or was a secular departure from its origins necessary for its full development? Did art have an inexorable, ontological access to the sacred that needed to be rediscovered in an age of disenchantment? Or was the aura of the sacred an anachronistic fantasy, a residue to be removed? The underlying aesthetic attraction to magical thinking, however, was that it assumed a sympathetic universe of correspondences in which distinctions between human consciousness and the material world were blurred. Poetically speaking, these sympathies could be explored by language, naming, and incantation. Speech in such a universe had real material efficacy: energies could be released, bodies vitalized, power channeled, objects manipulated. Magic took the characteristic processes of poetic thought—association through metaphor and metonymy—and made them characteristics of the entire world. In such a world the modern rift between subject and object was erased. Nearly all modernist poets and philosophers reflected on, and many appealed to, poetry's magical heritage. Baudelaire spoke of his poetry as alchemy, the work of making mud into gold. In his *Divagations*, Mallarmé wrote that magic found a home in poetry because art, unlike political economy, was honest about its origins: "Verse is an incantation! And one cannot deny the similarity between the circle perpetually opening and closing with rhymes and the circles in the grass left by a fairy or magician." *Divagations*, trans. Barbara Johnson (Cambridge: Harvard University Press, 2007), 264. Yeats's magical claims were not relegated to private séances or idiosyncratic philosophies of history but were deeply entrenched in his aesthetics. Numerous writings—*Mythologies* and his essay "Magic" in *Ideas of Good and Evil* are good places to start—connected the symbol-making power of the poet with the power the magician has to evoke the ontological interrelations of all minds and all energies. W. B. Yeats, *Essays and Introductions* (New York: Macmillan, 1961), 28–52. Wyndham Lewis vacillated between thinking of "creative art" as "a spell, a talisman, an incantation," and a "civilized *substitute* for magic." *Time and Western Man* (Boston: Beacon, 1957), 113. Finally, the entire first section of Adorno and Horkheimer's *Dialectic of Enlightenment* (New York: Continuum, 1972) is a

discussion of the relations between art and enchantment, given that "[w]hen language enters history . . . its masters are priests and sorcerers" (20).

13. "As such, the formulation of occult subjectivity was inseparable from the instrumental rationality that Weber argued is intrinsic to the complex social processes of a modern order. In particular, and in common with all magical traditions, fin-de-siècle occultism was characterized by the will to both know and control the natural world." *The Place of Enchantment: British Occultism and the Cult of the Modern* (Chicago: University of Chicago Press, 2007), 14.

14. "Squares and Oblongs" (1947), in W. H. Auden, *Collected Prose*, ed. Edward Mendelson, vol. 2, *1939–1948* (Princeton: Princeton University Press, 2002), 341. The prose volumes in the Princeton *Collected Works of W. H. Auden* series are cited in text hereafter as *P.*

15. Randall Styers, *Making Magic: Religion, Magic and Science in the Modern World* (New York: Oxford University Press, 2004), 16, 20.

16. See Ludwig Wittgenstein, *Remarks on Frazer's Golden Bough* (London: Brynmill, 1979), in which he eviscerates James Frazer's influential account of magic as pseudoscience, and R. J. Collingwood, *The Principles of Art* (New York: Oxford University Press, 1958), in particular the section "Art as Magic" (57–77). Collingwood's arguments about art and magic were influential on Auden.

17. Styers writes, "Fortunately, the world is no more disenchanted than it used to be, machines are not more polished, reasoning is no tighter, and exchanges are not better organized. How can we speak of a 'modern world' when its efficacy depends on idols: money, law, reason, nature, machines, organization, or linguistic structures?. . . . Since the origins of the power of the 'modern world' are misunderstood and efficacy is attributed to things that neither move nor speak, we may speak of magic once again" (226). The rhetoric is peculiar: "fortunately," the world is still enchanted, which means that "modernity" is no more "advanced" than a "primitive," magical world. But the evidence of good fortune is that we still have idols (like money, that classic modern fetish) that are problematically invested with agency—and thus regarded as powers invulnerable to human reflection and intervention—that is not properly theirs. But why is it "fortunate" that we still have idols? The argument suggests that we should reject post-magical rationality because we have our own magical delusions: we know that premodern magic is good because, thank goodness, we are still magical—which means, it turns out, that we are thoroughly deluded. Auden would say, I suspect, that moderns should certainly feel chastened by the fact that they have magical idols of their own. But this should not mean, as Styers suggests, that we should therefore relinquish our capacity to distinguish between magical and human agency.

18. For a critical discussion of the relationship between secularism and colonialism, see Saba Mahmood, "Secularism, Hermeneutics, and Empire: The Politics of Islamic Reformation," *Public Culture* 18, no. 2 (2006): 323–347.

19. Auden concluded a review of Charles Cochrane's *Christianity and Classical Culture* by noting, "Our period is not so unlike the age of Augustine: the planned society, caesarism of thugs or bureaucracies, paideia, scientia, religious persecution are all with us. Nor is there even lacking the possibility of a new Constantinism; letters

have already begun to appear in the press, recommending religious instruction in the schools as a cure for juvenile delinquency; Mr. Cochrane's terrifying description of the 'Christian' empire under Theodosius should discourage such hopes of using Christianity as a spiritual benzedrine for the earthly city" (P, 2:231). The poem is suspicious of "the Cerebrotonic Cato" who extols *paideia* or "the ancient disciplines." Auden's review of Eliot's *Notes Towards the Definition of a Culture* suggests that Eliot has become one of these Catos and Constantinian letter writers (P, 3:97–101).

20. I do not mean to suggest that Auden's acceptance of dualism implies that he does not think of unity as a desirable goal. For Auden, unity, or the coalescence of being and seeming, is an existential project. What he refuses is the premature reconciliation of certain dualism, in particular by taking aesthetic practice to be a mode of such reconciliation. As Auden says in "Reflections in a Forest," which I examine later in this chapter, humans have "their unity to *win*" (emphasis added).

21. Auden, *Forewords and Afterwords*, 200.

22. When a choice is presented between the original versions of Auden's poems of the late 1920s and the 1930s as they appear in *The English Auden* and the revised versions as they appear in the *Collected Poems*, I have typically chosen to quote from the latter. Auden's assault on magical thinking is, as I am arguing, present in much of his early poetry, but it doesn't receive its full philosophical and theological framing until the 1940s. Since the Auden of this chapter is, for the most part, the later Auden, it strikes me that I should refer to the early poems as he came to understand them (and came occasionally to disagree with certain sentiments voiced in them). I also believe, against one current of opinion, that his revisions sometimes (but not always) made his poems better. For the brief lines quoted in this paragraph, the only difference between the two versions is the absence of a comma (in *EA*, the line just quoted reads "what view I wish for, I shall find").

23. Auden was a reader of Freud from early in his life, and his influence is seen in his appropriation of Freud's theory of "the omnipotence of thought." According to Freud, magical thinking (and religion more generally) involves a confusion of thought and world. To believe in magic is to believe that thought has material power and can manipulate events and objects in the world according to desire or fear. See *Totem and Taboo*, trans. James Strachey (New York: Norton, 1950). Auden takes up and modifies this theory in *The Prolific and the Devourer*. The young child, he says, believes in the omnipotence of his "will" and his "sensual desires": "A thing is what I want it to be." The adolescent, however, exchanges this for a belief in the "omnipotence of *intellect*: instead of thought being a creation of desire ... matter is a creation of thought." Auden calls these beliefs "phantasies," and maturity is achieved when one outgrows them and abjures their magical pretensions. The illustrations Auden uses to describe these psychological states come from the gospel stories of Jesus's temptations in the wilderness. Satan first tempts Jesus to "command that these stones be turned into bread." Auden reads Jesus's resistance to this temptation as a critique of the fantasy of the omnipotence of desire and a vindication of the otherness of the world. The second temptation—"If thou be the Son of God, cast thyself down"—is a resistance to the omnipotence of intellect, an awareness that gravity is a force absolutely independent

of him. Jesus's successful resistance to Satan is a renunciation of magic. *The Prolific and the Devourer* (Hopewell, NJ: Ecco, 1981), 47–50.

24. This is why Auden was always attracted to *paysage moralisé*, the most famous instance of which is "In Praise of Limestone." *Paysage moralisé* is not the anthropomorphic projection of human attributes and desires *onto* the landscape but a way of looking at the landscape as a source of moral self-knowledge — or, as "Limestone" says, "reproach" — precisely insofar as its nonhuman logic humbles egoistic pretensions.

25. *The Adorno Reader*, ed. Brian O'Connor (New York: Blackwell, 2000), 214–215.

26. *Ahead of All Parting: The Selected Poetry and Prose of Rainer Maria Rilke*, trans. Stephen Mitchell (New York: Modern Library, 1995), 113.

27. As Erich Heller, a critic Auden often quoted, writes, "Rilke succeeds in concluding an everlasting truce with the anonymous powers on the other side — by appropriating their territory 'inwardly.' Where man knew merely the terror of the monstrous emptiness of the beyond, there is now the peace of 'reiner Bezug,' 'pure relatedness,' which is so pure because no real 'otherness' enters into it." *The Disinherited Mind: Essays on Modern German Literature and Thought* (New York: Harcourt Brace Jovanovich, 1975), 171.

28. An outstanding reading of this poem is found in Gottlieb, *Regions of Sorrow*, 177–182.

29. On this attraction, see Douglas Mao's study, *Solid Objects: Modernism and the Test of Production* (Princeton: Princeton University Press, 1998).

30. For an excellent essay that reveals the remarkable convergence between Auden and Adorno and Horkheimer's understandings of "enlightenment," with regard in particular to the figure of Voltaire, see Susannah Young-ah Gottlieb, "Two Versions of Voltaire: W. H. Auden and the Dialectic of Enlightenment," *PMLA* 120, no. 2 (March 2005): 388–413. Gottlieb argues persuasively that Auden, like Adorno and Horkheimer, was concerned with the new forms of mythological consciousness that emerged in an ostensibly secular era.

31. Theodor Adorno, *The Stars down to Earth* (New York: Routledge, 1994), 172.

32. Edward Said, *The World, the Text, and the Critic* (Cambridge: Harvard University Press, 1983), 290. The essays in Said's book, however, especially "Secular Criticism" and "Religious Criticism," reveal that Said can only conceive of religion as "consolation" for "worldly" disappointment or as mystical obfuscation, a prejudice that derives from the Enlightenment assumption that religion is a form of false explanation. Said believes that religion is where one turns when one despairs of finding in human practices (social, economic, political) the true sources of explanation for what occurs in the world. Religion, he thinks, relishes the inexplicable, "unthinkability, undecidability, and paradox" (291). Auden, however, felt that a dedication to the secular was the legacy of Judaism and Christianity, which are thoroughly invested in historical events. Like Charles Taylor, who has traced the modern elevation of ordinary life to Protestant Christian dispositions concerning the religious significance of life in the world, Auden thought that Christianity created a profound interest in, precisely, "history" and "human production." See Taylor, *Sources of the Self* (Cambridge: Harvard University Press, 1989), 211–284.

33. For an informative essay on Auden's abiding interest in Judaism, including its relation to the Christianity he later embraced, see Beth Ellen Roberts, "W. H. Auden and the Jews," *Journal of Modern Literature* 28, no. 3 (Spring 2005): 87–108.

34. James A. Pike, ed., *Modern Canterbury Pilgrims* (London: Morehouse Gorham, 1956), 38.

35. W. B. Yeats, *Essays and Introductions*, 436.

36. Recent thinkers who have argued, against the Weberian thesis, that modern life really *isn't* disenchanted, have tried to break down precisely this human/inhuman divide, which they take to be a mistake of secular modern consciousness. In *We Have Never Been Modern* (Cambridge: Harvard University Press, 1993), Bruno Latour argues that modernity "creates two entirely distinct ontological zones: that of human beings on the one hand; that of nonhumans on the other"; to recognize that this split is artificial is to be on the road back to enchantment (10). The argument of Jane Bennett's book, *The Enchantment of Modern Life* (Princeton: Princeton University Press, 2001), proceeds along the same lines. Auden insists that this distinction cannot be done without. Again, this does not mean that human being isn't continuous with nonhuman life. In the same breath that he insists on the human-inhuman distinction he gently satirizes gnostic attitudes that would like to preserve an *absolute* ontological distinction, as in "In Praise of Limestone," where he writes of "the fungi / And insects of the jungle, the monstrous forms and lives / With which we have nothing, we like to hope, in common." Later in the same poem the speaker reproaches himself for his desire "[n]ot to lose time, not to get caught, / Not to be left behind, not, please! to resemble / The beasts who repeat themselves" (*CPA*, 541–542).

37. The greatest difficulty Auden encountered in distinguishing the realm of history from nature finally resided, not in the temptation to make nature mythical, but in the temptation to invest history with the sort of "necessity" that only exists in the natural world. "Spain, 1937" closes by distinguishing the time of our responsibility from cosmic and animal time, but then undermines that distinction by insisting that history is a juggernaut indifferent to the concerns of persons existing in it and that works its course irrespective of the actors that ostensibly bring it to pass: "The stars are dead; the animals will not look: / We are left alone with our day, and the time is short and / History to the defeated / May say Alas but cannot help or pardon" (*EA*, 212). Later in his life, Auden spent a good deal of time in his critical prose trying to correct this naturalization of history (see, for example, his review of Albert Camus's *The Rebel*, in *P*, 3:498–502). Edward Mendelson is insightful about how the earlier Auden's attempt to make history a natural force invests it with a kind of magic: "Here History is a tangible force, a *mana* that infuses certain persons and objects with power, while it abandons others to subsist on a debased form of energy instead. As in Fascist or imperialist claims of historical national destiny, History provides a metaphysical excuse to make obeisance to force." *Early Auden* (New York: Farrar, Straus and Giroux, 2000), 309.

38. I should note, however, that I am working with the revised poem as it appears in the *Collected Poems*, not the original as reproduced in *The English Auden*.

39. Adorno and Horkheimer, *Dialectic of Enlightenment*, 17.

40. "[C]olère, / Haine, frissons, horreur, labeur dur et force." Charles Baudelaire, *The Flowers of Evil*, trans. James McGowan (New York: Oxford University Press, 1993), 116.

41. This phrase does not occur in the original version of the poem as it is reproduced in *The English Auden*. There the final lines read: "Cold, impossible, ahead / Lifts the mountain's lovely head / Whose white waterfall could bless / Travellers in their last distress" (*EA*, 159). The decision to replace the concrete, natural mountain image with an abstract ethical possibility is perhaps characteristic of the later Auden.

42. Ovid, *The Metamorphoses*, trans. Charles Martin (New York: Norton, 2004), 270–272.

43. James Joyce, *A Portrait of the Artist as a Young Man* (New York: Penguin, 2003), 183.

44. "Car j'ai de chaque chose extrait la quintessence, / Tu m'as donné ta boue et j'en ai fait de l'or." Charles Baudelaire, *Les fleurs du mal*, 'Projets d'un épilogue pour l'édition de 1861,' vol. 1 of *Oeuvres completes*, ed. Claude Pichois (Paris: Gallimard, Editions de la Pléïade, 1975), 192 (translation mine).

45. In his discussion of "natural beauty," Adorno writes, "Yet something frightening lurks in the song of birds precisely because it is not a song but obeys the spell in which it is enmeshed . . . With regard to its content, the ambiguity of natural beauty has its origin in mythical ambiguity." *Aesthetic Theory*, trans. Robert Hullot-Kentor (Minneapolis: University of Minnesota Press, 1997), 66.

46. Wyndham Lewis, *Time and Western Man* (Boston: Beacon, 1957), 312.

47. Here as elsewhere what I am calling the "secularization" of suffering is equally a kind of Christianization. As Mendelson says of the style of "Museé," "Auden sees in [the poem's insignificant figures of suffering] an example of Christianity's great and enduring transformation of classical rhetoric: its inversion of the principle that the most important subjects require the highest style. If the sufferings of a carpenter turned preacher mattered more to the world than the doom of princes, then the high style, for all its splendor, was a limited instrument, more suitable to the narrow intensities of personal isolation than to the infinite complexities of responsible relationship." *Early Auden*, 363.

48. I am using the revised (*Collected Poems*) version of this poem because I believe the final stanza has been strengthened; those strengths include the change from "the mortal world" to "our mortal world" and the subtle implications of the doubling of "find" when thinking about human agency and natural power (discussed below). For the original version, see *EA*, 207.

49. Ioan Culianu, *Eros and Magic in the Renaissance* (Chicago: University of Chicago Press, 1987). Culianu writes, "Magic is merely eroticism applied, directed, and aroused by its performer" (27). For both Giordano Bruno and Marsilio Ficino, "magic is love" and "love is magic" (87).

50. Michael Taussig, *The Magic of the State* (New York: Routledge, 1997), 3.

51. The eighteenth-century style—the octo-syllabic couplet, and the "Essay on Man" quality—of Auden's "New Year Letter" gives the poem a tone of high reasonableness.

52. Auden's enduring reverence for Marx and Freud raises important questions as to the religious or secular genealogy of what Paul Ricoeur, describing these two and Nietzsche, called the "hermeneutics of suspicion." On the one hand, these figures are secularists who used suspicion to reduce what were thought to be religious "causes"

and sacred structures to their economic or psychological (secular) bases. On the other, the hermeneutic of suspicion has itself a Jewish and Christian origin. Christians are supposed to examine their surface behavior and thought, or the political events in the world, for *spiritual* meanings, and thus they use a disenchanting hermeneutic of suspicion as a religious method. On this issue, see Merold Westphal, *Suspicion and Faith: The Religious Uses of Modern Atheism* (New York: Fordham University Press, 1999). René Girard's work is also an excellent example of this tension. His critique of myth as a subconscious cultural attempt to mask the violence of mimetic rivalry and scapegoating is clearly a hermeneutic of suspicion, but for Girard this suspicion is made possible by theological insight: the biblical insistence that the victims of these practices are actually innocent. See esp. Girard, *I See Satan Fall Like Lightning*, trans. James G. Williams (New York: Orbis, 2001).

53. Carl Jung's thought, for instance, manifests the consequences of sacralizing the unconscious. As Richard Wolin has noted of Jung's relation to Freud, "Jung skips this enlightened disenchantment and . . . seeks the primeval right of the artistic imagination, of religious myths, and precisely in the unconscious." Jung said of Hitler in a letter, "There is no question but that Hitler belongs in the category of the truly mystic medicine man. As somebody commented about him at the last Nuremberg party congress, since the time of Mohammed nothing like it has been seen in this world. This markedly mystic characteristic of Hitler's is what makes him do things which seem to us illogical, inexplicable, curious and unreasonable. . . . So you see, Hitler is a medicine man, a form of spiritual vessel, a demi-deity or, even better a myth." Quoted in Wolin, *The Seduction of Unreason: The Intellectual Romance with Fascism from Nietzsche to Postmodernism* (Princeton: Princeton University Press, 2006), 65, 75. Phillip Rieff's *The Triumph of the Therapeutic: The Uses of Faith after Freud* (Chicago: University of Chicago Press, 1966) provides a powerful account of how figures like Lawrence and Jung sacralized the very unconscious that Freud sought to disenchant. For a less Enlightenment-inflected view of Freud that attends to his mystical dimension, see Yosef Yerushalmi, *Freud's Moses: Judaism Terminable and Interminable* (New Haven: Yale University Press, 1993).

54. Auden wrote in a review of 1940, "[W]e are today confronted by the spectacle, not of a Utilitarian rationalism that dismisses all that cannot be expressed in prose and statistics as silly childish stuff, but by an ecstatic and morbid abdication of the free-willing and individual before the collective and the daemonic. We have become obscene night-worshipers who, having discovered that we cannot live exactly as we will, deny the possibility of willing anything and are content masochistically *to be lived*, a denial that betrays not only us but our daemon itself" (*P*, 2:38).

55. Terry Eagleton, *The Ideology of the Aesthetic* (New York: Blackwell, 1989), 25.

56. Michael Bell writes, "In the nineteenth century, religion and physical science were notoriously in competition for authority, but this apparent antinomy was increasingly dissolved by another order of significance, the realm of the 'aesthetic,' which . . . eventually dislodged the hegemonic claims of both religion and science." *Literature, Modernity, and Myth: Belief and Responsibility in the Twentieth Century* (New York: Cambridge University Press, 1997), 12.

57. Frank Kermode, *Romantic Image* (New York: Routledge, 2002), 11.

58. D. H. Lawrence, *Apocalypse* (New York: Cambridge University Press, 1985), 102.

59. Taylor, *Secular Age*, 37–42, 134–141. Yeats's and Eliot's accounts of dissociation could be understood as historicizations of the Jewish and Christian myths of the Fall.

60. Kermode, *Romantic Image*, 102.

61. In Auden's imaginary, the ability of humans to "frame any feature" of organic beings was initially a great source of anxiety, but later it became the important capacity of humans to *play*. Here the objects are trees, but in much of the poetry they are animals. In a very early poem, this is clearly a disturbing condition:

> Look not too closely, be not over-quick;
> We have no invitation, but we are sick,
> Using the mole's device, the carriage
> Of peacock or rat's desperate courage,
> And we shall only pass you by a trick. (*CPA*, 64)

A 1933 poem, "Our Hunting Fathers," imagines that when our ancestors looked at the creatures, they "[p]itied the limits and the lack / Set in their *finished* features" (*CPA*, 122, emphasis added). They thought their "liberal appetite and powers" were superior, but the poem deflates their expectations. In the first of his *Sonnets from China*, this is an anthropological fact: "[F]inally, there came a childish creature / On whom the years could model any feature, / Fake, as chance fell, a leopard or a dove" (ibid., 184). In the later poetry, this capacity to "fake" and assume multiple identities discloses the freedom of play, which is a freedom from physiological necessity.

62. Auden explicitly objected to organicist aesthetics in his essay on D. H. Lawrence in *The Dyer's Hand*: "Lawrence draws a false analogy between the process of artistic creation and the organic growth of living creatures. . . . Organic growth is a cyclical process; it is just as true to say that the oak is a potential acorn as it is to say the acorn is a potential oak. But the process of writing a poem, of making any art object, is not cyclical but a motion in one direction towards a definite end. . . . A natural object never appears unfinished; if it is an inorganic object like a stone, it is what it has to be, if an organic object like a flower, what it has to be at this moment. But a similar effect—of being what it has to be—can only be achieved in a work of art by much thought, labor and care. The gesture of a ballet dancer, for example, only looks natural when, through long practice, its execution has become 'second nature' to him. That perfect incarnation of life in substance, word in flesh, which in nature is immediate, has in art to be achieved and, in fact, can never be perfectly achieved. In many of Lawrence's poems, the spirit has failed to make itself a fit body to live in, a curious defect in the world of a writer who was so conscious of the value and significance of the body" (*DH*, 283–284). A poem, Auden says, is historical insofar as it moves toward a goal and will not swallow its tail. One also observes in this passage the ambivalence attending Auden's understanding of the status of art in human life. If human life is inexorably historical—if unity and incarnation are *never* perfectly present in it—then a work of art can deceive exactly insofar as it has approached perfection in making possibility and

necessity into actuality (even if that unity was achieved in the aesthetic process). For a trenchant investigation into Auden's shifting views on the theory of poetry, see Lucy MacDiarmid, *Auden's Apologies for Poetry* (Princeton: Princeton University Press, 1990).

63. Quoted in Gerardus Van Der Leeuw, *Sacred and Profane Beauty: The Holy in Life* (New York: Holt, Rinehart and Winston, 1963), 16.

64. Havelock Ellis, *The Dance of Life* (New York: Modern Library, 1929), 35–36.

65. Van Der Leeuw, *Sacred and Profane Beauty*, 27.

66. Roger Caillois and George Bataille, members of the Collège de sociologie, a group of thinkers that held seminars (and apparently pagan rituals) on the possibilities of the sacred in the modern world, argued that war was the great modern repository of the sacred. In his 1939 book *L'homme et le sacré*, Caillois argued that war had taken the place of the festival—which Caillois calls "facsimile, dance, and play" in the catalogue of sacred activities that a society performs. World war is a "kind of total festival" that yields the joy of excess energy and discloses the superabundance of life. *Man and the Sacred*, trans. Meyer Barash (Urbana: University of Illinois Press, 2001), 180.

67. Franz Kafka, "Selections from Diaries, 1911–1923," in *The Basic Kafka* (New York: Simon and Schuster), 262.

68. See, for example, Anthony Hecht's reading of the poem: "But a hero is more or less by definition a very public figure, whose action alters the fate and lives of others. In this poem, the three men who are executed and the abandoned urchin are not martyrs; they are, alas, merely victims. All of this has had the effect of making traditional heroism a thing of the past and greatly diminishing the world of human possibility. Auden's 'The Shield of Achilles' is about that terrible diminishment." *The Hidden Law: The Poetry of W. H. Auden* (Cambridge: Harvard University Press, 1993), 437.

69. In an excellent reading of "Shield of Achilles," Lucy MacDiarmid has argued that the poem "disenchants" art by exposing the gap between what Thetis expects out of art and what she gets (*Auden's Apologies*, 127–133). However, while her reading of the poem emphasizes "disenchantment" as metaphor for the limits of art, my reading concerns ontological disenchantment, in the sense that Auden is desacralizing not only art's aspirations but also its ontological status, as well as desacralizing the warlike Homeric world that is, for Yeats, Nietzsche, and many other modern artists and intellectuals, an object of profound nostalgia.

70. See, for instance, George Bataille, who wanted to reinstate the sacred in modern life: "Glory . . . expresses a movement of senseless frenzy, of measureless expenditure of energy . . . which the fervor of combat presupposes." *Visions of Excess: Selected Writings, 1927–1939*, trans. Alan Stoekl (Minneapolis: University of Minnesota Press, 1985), 204.

71. For more on Auden's aesthetics of the sacred, see Jonathan Hufstader, "Auden's Sacred World," *Essays in Criticism* 59, no. 3 (2009): 234–254.

72. Edward Mendelson makes a related claim: "[Thetis's] world is no less impersonal than its modern counterpart on the shield. Both are places ruled by fate because choice has abdicated into silence. Both are the proper settings for doomed embodiments of

power. . . . Both are settings where cruelty is divorced from conscience." *Later Auden* (New York: Farrar, Straus and Giroux, 1999), 377.

73. Erich Auerbach, *Mimesis*, trans. Willard Trask (Princeton: Princeton University Press, 1959), 7.

74. See Hecht, *Hidden Law*, 429–430, and David Bromwich, *Skeptical Music: Essays on Modern Poetry* (Chicago: University of Chicago Press, 2001), 140.

75. *The Simone Weil Reader*, ed. George Panichas (London: Moyer Bell, 1977), 154–155.

76. Ibid., 164.

CONCLUSION

1. David Hume, *Dialogues Concerning Natural Religion and Natural History of Religion* (New York: Oxford University Press, 1993), 100.

2. William James, "Is Life Worth Living?" in *Pragmatism and Other Writings*, ed. Giles Gunn (New York: Penguin, 2000), 227.

3. As Clifford Geertz argued, for religious thinking there is not merely a problem *of* evil but a problem *about* it: "As a religious problem, the problem of suffering is paradoxically, not how to avoid suffering but how to suffer, how to make of physical pain, personal loss, worldly defeat, or the helpless contemplation of others' agony something bearable, supportable—something, as we say, sufferable. . . . [T]he problem of evil, or perhaps one should say the problem *about* evil, is in essence the same sort of problem of or about bafflement and the problem of or about suffering. The strange opacity of certain empirical events, the dumb senselessness of intense or inexorable pain, and the enigmatic unaccountability of gross iniquity all raise the uncomfortable suspicion that perhaps the world, and hence man's life in the world, has no genuine order at all—no empirical regularity, no emotional form, no moral coherence. And the religious response to this suspicion is in each case the same: the formulation, by means of symbols, of an image of such a genuine order of the world which will account for, and even celebrate, the perceived ambiguities, puzzles, and paradoxes in human experience." "Religion as a Cultural System," in *The Interpretation of Cultures* (New York: Basic Books, 2000), 107–108. We may dissent from Geertz's universalizing claim that the "religious response is . . . in each case the same," but his argument shifts the focus from the abstract metaphysical coherence of concepts of God and evil to the existential encounter with suffering. Religion, for Geertz, facilitates the self's ability to inhabit suffering by organizing it in patterns of narrative and symbolic meaning inscribed in a cosmic order. Secularism does not merely reject the metaphysical coherence of this order; it also confronts the loss of the order as the loss of an existential resource.

4. George Levine, ed., introduction to *The Joy of Secularism* (Princeton: Princeton University Press, 2011), 4, 6.

5. Stathis Gourgouris, *Lessons in Secular Criticism* (New York: Fordham University Press, 2013), 40–41. Gourgouris is attacking here a scholar that he calls "Charles Taylor" but who bears little resemblance to the author of *A Secular Age*. ("Taylor cannot fathom" this "idea.") In his ten-page polemic against Taylor he misreads him at almost every turn: he writes that Taylor says the discourse of psychoanalysis (the

"therapeutic") "at best provides us" with the "'dignity of sin'" (41), whereas in fact Taylor says that the therapeutic has *lost* the "dignity of sin" in replacing the language of good and evil with that of health and "sickness." A *Secular Age* (Cambridge: Harvard University Press, 2007), 619–620. Nowhere does Taylor contend that "believers are blissed out with certainty and fulfillment" (*Lessons in Secular Criticism*, 42); rather, Taylor writes that "believers" are constantly "aware of being very far from the condition of full devotion and giving" that they might hope to attain at the "place of fullness" (*Secular Age*, 8). The whole logic of "fullness" is, according to Taylor, eschatological, now and not yet. (There are other fundamental misreadings.) Gourgouris also reverts to a bizarrely ad hominem attack and presumes that he is acquainted with Taylor's inner life; thus he refers to Taylor's "fear of the tragic" (*Lessons in Secular Criticism*, 42) and his "panic before the obstacle of Nietzsche" (38). Yet Gourgouris's question— "From what position is one authorized to claim that the tragic does not in fact bear fullness?" (42)—is provocative given the concerns of this conclusion. It is true that Taylor is concerned with the ethical dangers of what Gourgouris praises as "tragic amorality"—I have argued in my chapter on Yeats that these dangers are well founded and acknowledged by Yeats himself, who certainly harbored no fear of the tragic. Stevens, Yeats, and Woolf would all assent to the proposition that tragedy can bear dignity, energy, exhilaration, or power, but does it contain "fullness" or, even more strikingly, "total plentitude"? Doesn't that formulation approach self-contradiction? If tragedy is fullness and plentitude, in what sense does it remain tragic? In refusing a too-casual identification of secularity (even tragic secularity) with "total plentitude," the modernist writers in this book confront a resurgent problem of evil that unsettles their secular affirmations. The tension between this affirmation and recalcitrant evil— even when the concept of "evil" undergoes multiple revisions—is the concern of this conclusion.

6. Hannah Arendt, *Lectures on Kant's Political Philosophy* (Chicago: University of Chicago Press, 1982), 24.

7. *Basic Writings of Nietzsche*, trans. Walter Kaufmann (New York: Modern Library, 1992), 52, emphasis in original.

8. *The Essays of Virginia Woolf*, ed. Andrew McNeillie, vol. 4, *1925–1928* (New York: Harcourt, 1994), 77.

9. In his recent defense of secular humanism, the philosopher Philip Kitcher puts it this way: "My version of secularism places humanity at the center of value. It does not need a detour through some dim and remote transcendent. . . . My naturalism conceives us as both creators and loci of value, our work of creation prompted by the exigencies of the human predicament." *Life after Faith: The Case for Secular Humanism* (New Haven: Yale University Press, 2015), 59.

10. Paul Ricoeur, *The Symbolism of Evil*, trans. Emerson Buchanan (Boston: Beacon, 1986), 253–254.

11. The sacred originates here, too: the projection of evil is a gesture of "desperate hallow." The peculiarity of this description is important: conceptions of the sacred (that which is hallowed) are desperate modes of interpreting and engaging the very evil produced by virtue of having a self.

12. One aspect of Stevens's broader effort to affirm the immanent world involves his recognition of and poetic engagement with the diurnal, repetitive character of immanent temporality. For a compelling and often beautiful analysis of Stevens's "diurnal" poetics, see Siobhan Phillips, "The Faithful Mode of Wallace Stevens," chapter 2 of *The Poetics of the Everyday: Creative Repetition in Modern American Verse* (New York: Columbia University Press, 2010). As Phillips's chapter title suggests, Stevens's endeavor to inhabit diurnal time creatively is for him a kind of secular piety.

13. "[T]he problem of evil . . . is fundamentally a problem about the intelligibility of the world as a whole." Susan Neiman, *Evil in Modern Thought* (Princeton: Princeton University Press, 2002), 5, 8.

14. Stevens wrote to John Crowe Ransom of this final stanza: "The last poem ought to end with an interrogation mark, I suppose, but I have punctuated it in such a way as to indicate an abandonment of the question" (*L*, 469).

15. William Wordsworth, *The Prelude*, ed. Jonathan Wordsworth, M. H. Abrams, and Stephen Gill (New York: Norton, 1979), 398.

16. They are, rather, *actors*. Auden assents to Kierkegaard's understanding of "aesthetic religion" as he describes it in his preface to *The Living Thoughts of Kierkegaard* (New York: New York Review of Books, 1952): "[I]n the aesthetic cosmology, the gods are created by nature, ascend to heaven, are human in form, finite in number (like the passions) and interrelated by blood. Being images of passions, they themselves are not *in* their passion—Aphrodite is not in love; Mars is not angry—or, if they do make an appearance of passionate behavior, it is frivolous; like actors, they do not suffer or change" (xv).

BIBLIOGRAPHY

Abrams, M. H., ed. *English Romantic Poets: Modern Essays in Criticism*. New York: Oxford University Press, 1975.

———. *Natural Supernaturalism: Tradition and Revolution in Romantic Literature*. New York: Norton, 1973.

Acampora, Christa Davis. *Contesting Nietzsche*. Chicago: University of Chicago Press, 2013.

Adams, Hazard. *The Book of Yeats's Vision*. Ann Arbor: University of Michigan Press, 1995.

Adorno, Theodor. *The Adorno Reader*. Edited by Brian O'Connor. New York: Blackwell, 2000.

———. *Aesthetic Theory*. Translated by Robert Hullot-Kentor. Minneapolis: University of Minnesota Press, 1997.

———. *The Stars down to Earth*. New York: Routledge, 1994.

Adorno, Theodor, and Max Horkheimer. *Dialectic of Enlightenment*. New York: Continuum, 1972.

Agamben, Giorgio. *Profanations*. Translated by Jeff Fort. New York: Zone Books, 2007.

Allen, Stuart. *Wordsworth and the Passions of Critical Poetics*. London: Palgrave, 2010.

Altieri, Charles. *The Particulars of Rapture*. Ithaca: Cornell University Press, 2003.

Anderson, Benedict. *Imagined Communities*. New York: Verso, 1993.

Andijar, Gil. *Semites: Race, Religion, Literature*. Stanford: Stanford University Press, 2008.

Arendt, Hannah. *The Human Condition*. Chicago: University of Chicago Press, 1958.

———. *Lectures on Kant's Political Philosophy*. Chicago: University of Chicago Press, 1982.

Arnold, Matthew. *The Complete Prose Works of Matthew Arnold*. Edited by R. H. Super. Vol. 9, *English Literature and Irish Politics*. Ann Arbor: University of Michigan Press, 1962.

———. *Literature and Dogma*. London: Smith, Elder, 1884.

Asad, Talal. *Formations of the Secular: Christianity, Islam, Modernity*. Stanford: Stanford University Press, 2003.

———. *Genealogies of Religion*. Baltimore: Johns Hopkins University Press, 1993.

Auden, W. H. *Collected Poems*. New York: Vintage, 1991.

——. *Collected Prose.* Vol. 1, 1926–1938. Edited by Edward Mendelson. Princeton: Princeton University Press, 1996.

——. *Collected Prose.* Vol. 2, 1939–1948. Edited by Edward Mendelson. Princeton: Princeton University Press, 2002.

——. *Collected Prose.* Vol. 3, 1949–1955. Edited by Edward Mendelson. Princeton: Princeton University Press, 2008.

——. *The Dyer's Hand.* New York: Vintage, 1989.

——. *The English Auden.* Edited by Edward Mendelson. Boston: Faber and Faber, 1977.

——. *Essays and Introductions.* New York: Macmillan, 1961.

——. *Forewords and Afterwords.* New York: Vintage, 1989.

——. *Lectures on Shakespeare.* Edited by Arthur Kirsch. Princeton: Princeton University Press, 2000.

——. *The Prolific and the Devourer.* Edited by Edward Mendelson. Hopewell, NJ: Ecco, 1981.

Auerbach, Erich. *Mimesis.* Translated by Willard Trask. Princeton: Princeton University Press, 1959.

Augustine. *Expositions on the Book of Psalms.* Vol. 2. Translated by John Henry Parker. London: Oxford University Press, 1848.

Bakhtin, Mikhail. *Rabelais and His World.* Translated by Helene Iswolsky. Bloomington: Indiana University Press, 1984.

Balthasar, Hans Urs von. *The Glory of the Lord: A Theological Aesthetics.* Vol. 1, *Seeing the Form.* Translated by Erasmo Leiva-Merikakis. San Francisco: Ignatius, 1998.

Banfield, Ann. *The Phantom Table.* New York: Cambridge University Press, 2007.

Barfield, Owen. *Saving the Appearances: A Study in Idolatry.* Hanover: Wesleyan University Press, 1988.

Bataille, George. *Theory of Religion.* Translated by Robert Hurley. New York: Zone Books, 1992.

——. *Visions of Excess: Selected Writings, 1927–1939.* Translated by Alan Stoekl. Minneapolis: University of Minnesota Press, 1885.

Bates, Milton J. *Wallace Stevens: A Mythology of Self.* Berkeley: University of California Press, 1985.

Baudelaire, Charles. *The Flowers of Evil.* Translated by James McGowan. New York: Oxford University Press, 1993.

——. *The Painter of Modern Life and Other Essays.* New York: Phaidon Press, 1995.

Becker, Carl. *The Heavenly City in the Eighteenth-Century Philosophers.* New Haven: Yale University Press, 1932.

Bell, Clive. *Art.* New York: Capricorn, 1958.

Bell, Michael. *Literature, Modernity, and Myth: Belief and Responsibility in the Twentieth Century.* New York: Cambridge University Press, 1997.

Bell, Vereen M. *Yeats and the Logic of Formalism.* Columbia: University of Missouri Press, 2006.

Bellah, Robert. *Religion in Human Evolution: From the Paleolithic to the Axial Age.* Cambridge: Harvard University Press, 2011.

Bellah, Robert, and Hans Joas, eds. *The Axial Age and Its Consequences*. Cambridge: Harvard University Press, 2012.

Benamou, Michael. *Wallace Stevens and the Symbolist Imagination*. Princeton: Princeton University Press, 1972.

Bennett, Jane. *The Enchantment of Modern Life: Attachments, Crossings, and Ethics*. Princeton: Princeton University Press, 2001.

Bergson, Henri. *Laughter: An Essay on the Meaning of the Comic*. Translated by Cloudesty Brereton and Fred Rothwell. New York: Macmillan, 1911.

Bernstein, J. M. *The Fate of Art: Aesthetic Alienation from Kant to Derrida and Adorno*. University Park: Pennsylvania State University Press, 1992.

Bernstein, Richard J. *Radical Evil: A Philosophical Interrogation*. Cambridge: Polity, 2002.

Blake, William. *The Poetry and Prose of William Blake*. Edited by David Erdman. New York: Doubleday, 1965.

Bloch, Ernst. *The Principle of Hope*. Vol. 1. Translated by Neville Plaice, Stephen Plaice, and Paul Knight. Cambridge: MIT Press, 1995.

Bloom, Harold. *Ruin the Sacred Truths*. Cambridge: Harvard University Press, 1987.

———. *Wallace Stevens: The Poems of Our Climate*. Ithaca: Cornell University Press, 1977.

———. *Yeats*. New York: Oxford University Press, 1970.

Blumenberg, Hans. *The Legitimacy of the Modern Age*. Translated by Robert Wallace. Cambridge: MIT Press, 1983.

Bohlman, Otto. *Yeats and Nietzsche*. New York: Barnes and Noble, 1982.

Bonhoeffer, Dietrich. *Letters and Papers from Prison*. Edited by Eberhard Bethge. New York: Macmillan, 1967.

Borges, Jorge Luis. *Labyrinths*. Edited by Donald A. Yates and James E. Irby. New York: Penguin, 1970.

Bornstein, George. *Transformations of Romanticism in Yeats, Eliot, and Stevens*. Chicago: University of Chicago Press, 1976.

Boyle, Robert. *James Joyce's Pauline Vision*. Carbondale: Southern Illinois Press, 1978.

Bracken, Christopher. *Magical Criticism: The Recourse to Savage Philosophy*. Chicago: University of Chicago Press, 2007.

Brague, Rémi. *The Wisdom of the World: The Human Experience of the Universe in Western Thought*. Translated by Teresa Lavender Fagan. Chicago: University of Chicago Press, 2004.

Brearton, Fran. *The Great War in Irish Poetry: W. B. Yeats to Michael Longley*. New York: Oxford University Press, 2003.

Brient, Elizabeth. *The Immanence of the Infinite: Hans Blumenberg and the Threshold to Modernity*. Washington: Catholic University of America Press, 2002.

Brittain, Christopher Craig. *Adorno and Theology*. London: T and T Clark, 2010.

Brogan, Jacqueline. *The Violence Within, the Violence Without: Wallace Stevens and the Emergence of a Revolutionary Poetics*. Athens: University of Georgia Press, 2003.

Bromwich, David. "Destruction and the Theory of Happiness in the Poetry of Yeats and Stevens." *Essays in Criticism* 60, no. 2 (April 2010): 105–128.

———. *Skeptical Music: Essays on Modern Poetry*. Chicago: University of Chicago Press, 2001.

Brooks, Joanna. *American Lazarus: Religion and the Rise of African-American and Native American Literatures*. New York: Oxford University Press, 2007.

Buber, Martin. *The Eclipse of God*. New York: Harper and Brothers, 1952.

Buckley, Michael. *At the Origins of Modern Atheism*. New Haven: Yale University Press, 1987.

Bucknell, Katherine, and Nicholas Jenkins, eds. *Auden Studies*. Vol. 1, *W. H. Auden: "The Map of All My Youth": Early Works, Friends, and Influences*. Oxford: Clarendon, 1990.

———, eds. *Auden Studies*. Vol. 2, *W. H. Auden: "The Language of Learning and the Language of Love": Uncollected Writings; New Interpretations*. Oxford: Clarendon, 1994.

———, eds. *Auden Studies*. Vol. 3, *In Solitude, for Company: W. H. Auden after 1940: Unpublished Prose and Recent Criticism*. Oxford: Clarendon, 1995.

Buell, Lawrence. "Religion on the American Mind." *American Literary History* 19, no. 1 (2007): 32–55.

Burke, Edmund. *A Philosophical Enquiry into the Origin of Our Ideas of the Sublime and the Beautiful*. Notre Dame: University of Notre Dame Press, 1968.

Burke, Kenneth. *The Rhetoric of Religion*. Berkeley: University of California Press, 1961.

Buttel, Robert. *Wallace Stevens: The Making of Harmonium*. Princeton: Princeton University Press, 1967.

Bynum, Caroline Walker. *Christian Materiality: An Essay on Religion in Late Medieval Europe*. Cambridge: Zone Press, 2011.

———. *The Resurrection of the Body in Western Christianity, 200–1336*. New York: Columbia University Press, 1995.

Caillois, Roger. *Man and the Sacred*. Translated by Meyer Barash. Westport, CT: Greenwood Press, 1980.

Calhoun, Craig, Jonathan Vanantwerpen, and Michael Warners, eds. *Varieties of Secularism in a Secular Age*. Cambridge: Harvard University Press, 2010.

Callan, Edward. *Auden: A Carnival of Intellect*. New York: Oxford University Press, 1983.

Carrette, Jeremy. *Foucault and Religion*. New York: Routledge, 2000.

Carroll, Joseph. *Wallace Stevens's Supreme Fiction: A New Romanticism*. Baton Rouge: Louisiana State University Press, 1987.

Cary, Phillip. *Augustine's Invention of the Inner Self*. New York: Oxford University Press, 2000.

Casanova, José. *Public Religions in the Modern World*. Chicago: University of Chicago Press, 1994.

———. "Secular, Secularizations, Secularisms." *The Immanent Frame*, October 25, 2007, http://blogs.ssrc.org/tif/2007/10/25/secular-secularizations-secularisms/.

Cassedy, Steven. *Flight from Eden: The Origins of Modern Literary Criticism and Theory*. Berkeley: University of California Press, 1990.

Cavell, Stanley. *The Claim of Reason: Wittgenstein, Skepticism, Morality, and Tragedy*. New York: Oxford University Press, 1969.

Caws, Mary Ann, ed. *Manifesto: A Century of Isms*. Lincoln: University of Nebraska Press, 2001.

Chadwick, Henry. *The Secularization of the European Mind in the Nineteenth Century*. New York: Cambridge University Press, 1975.

Chai, Leon. *Aestheticism*. New York: Columbia University Press, 1990.

Chakrabarty, Dipesh. *Provincializing Europe: Postcolonial Thought and Historical Difference*. Princeton: Princeton University Press, 2007.

Christ, Carol. *Victorian and Modernist Poetics*. Chicago: University of Chicago Press, 1984.

Clark, T. J. *Farewell to an Idea: Episodes from a History of Modernism*. New Haven: Yale University Press, 1999.

Coleridge, Samuel Taylor. *Samuel Taylor Coleridge: A Critical Edition of the Major Works*. Edited by H. J. Jackson. New York: Oxford University Press, 1985.

Collingwood, R. G. *An Essay on Metaphysics*. New York: Oxford University Press, 2002.

——. *The Principles of Art*. New York: Oxford University Press, 1958.

Connolly, William. "Belief, Spirituality and Time." In *Varieties of Secularism in a Secular Age*, edited by Michael Warner, Jonathan VanAntwerpen, and Craig Calhoun, 126–144. Cambridge: Harvard University Press, 2010.

Cook, Eleanor. "The Decreations of Wallace Stevens." *Wallace Stevens Journal* 4, no. 3/4 (1980): 46–57.

——. *Poetry, Word-Play, and Word-War in Wallace Stevens*. Princeton: Princeton University Press, 1987.

——. *A Reader's Guide to Wallace Stevens*. Princeton: Princeton University Press, 2007.

Costello, Bonnie. *Shifting Ground: Reinventing Landscape in Modern American Poetry*. Cambridge: Harvard University Press, 2003.

Critchley, Simon. *Things Merely Are: Philosophy in the Poetry of Wallace Stevens*. New York: Routledge, 2005.

Culianu, Iaon. *Eros and Magic in the Renaissance*. Chicago: University of Chicago Press, 1987.

Cullingford, Elizabeth Butler. *Gender and History in Yeats's Love Poetry*. New York: Cambridge University Press, 1993.

Dalgarno, Emily. *Virginia Woolf and the Visible World*. New York: Cambridge University Press, 2001.

Danto, Arthur. *The Abuse of Beauty: Aesthetics and the Concept of Art*. New York: Open Court, 2003.

Davenport-Hines, Richard. *Auden*. New York: Pantheon, 1995.

De Man, Paul. *Blindness and Insight*. Minneapolis: University of Minnesota Press, 1983.

Desmond, William. *Art and the Absolute: A Study in Hegel's Aesthetics*. New York: SUNY Press, 1986.

Dewey, John. *The Essential Dewey*. Edited by Thomas Alexander and Larry Hickman. Vol. 1, *Pragmatism, Education, Democracy*. Bloomington: Indiana University Press, 1998.

Dickey, Lawrence. "Blumenberg and Secularization: 'Self-Assertion' and the Problem of a Self-Realizing Teleology in History." *New German Critique* 41 (Spring–Summer 1987): 151–165.

Dixon, Thomas. *From Passions to Emotions: The Creation of a Secular Psychological Category*. New York: Cambridge University Press, 2003.

Donoghue, Denis. *Adam's Curse: Reflections on Religion and Literature*. Notre Dame: University of Notre Dame Press, 2001.

——. *Speaking of Beauty*. New Haven: Yale University Press, 2003.

——. *William Butler Yeats*. New York: Viking, 1971.

Doolittle, Hilda. *Trilogy*. New York: New Directions, 1998.

D'Oro, Giuseppina. *Collingwood and the Metaphysics of Experience*. New York: Routledge, 2002.

Dostoevsky, Fyodor. *The Brothers Karamazov*. Translated by Richard Pevear and Larissa Volokhonsky. New York: Vintage, 1991.

Doyle, Laura. "Sublime Barbarians in the Narrative of Empire; or, Longinus at Sea in *The Waves*." *Modern Fiction Studies* 42 (1996): 323–347.

Dumont, Louis. *Essays on Individualism: Modern Ideology in Anthropological Perspective*. Chicago: University of Chicago Press, 1992.

Dupré, Louis. *Passage to Modernity*. New Haven: Yale University Press, 1993.

During, Simon. *Modern Enchantments: The Cultural Power of Secular Magic*. Cambridge: Harvard University Press, 2002.

Durkheim, Emile. *Durkheim on Religion*. Edited by W. S. F. Pickering. London: Routledge, 1975.

Eagleton, Terry. *Culture and the Death of God*. New Haven: Yale University Press, 2014.

——. *The Ideology of the Aesthetic*. New York: Blackwell, 1989.

——. *Sweet Violence: The Idea of the Tragic*. Oxford: Blackwell, 2003.

Edwards, Jonathan. *A Jonathan Edwards Reader*. Edited by John E. Smith, Harry S. Stout, and Kenneth P. Minkema. New Haven: Yale University Press, 2003.

Eeckhout, Bart. *Wallace Stevens and the Limits of Reading and Writing*. Columbia: University of Missouri Press, 2003.

Eksteins, Modris. *Rites of Spring: The Great War and the Birth of the Modern Age*. New York: Mariner Books, 2000.

Eliade, Mircea. *The Sacred and the Profane*. New York: Harcourt Brace, 1957.

Eliot, T. S. *The Collected Poems*. New York: Harcourt Brace, 1991.

——. *Selected Essays*. New York: Harcourt, Brace and World, 1960.

——. *The Use of Poetry and the Use of Criticism*. Cambridge: Harvard University Press, 1996.

——. "Why Mr. Russell Is a Christian." *Criterion* 6, no. 2 (August 1927): 177–179.

Ellis, Havelock. *The Dance of Life*. New York: Modern Library, 1929.

Ellmann, Richard. *The Identity of Yeats*. New York: Oxford University Press, 1964.

Emerson, Ralph Waldo. *Nature and Selected Essays*. New York: Penguin, 2003.

Fessenden, Tracy. "The Problem of the Postsecular." *American Literary History* 26, no. 1 (January 2014): 154–167.

Feuerbach, Ludwig. *The Essence of Christianity*. Translated by George Eliot. New York: Harper and Row, 1957.

Filreis, Alan. *Wallace Stevens and the Actual World*. Princeton: Princeton University Press, 1991.

Fisher, Philip. *The Vehement Passions*. Princeton: Princeton University Press, 2003.

——. *Wonder, the Rainbow, and the Aesthetics of Rare Experiences*. Cambridge: Harvard University Press, 1998.

Flood, Gavin. *The Ascetic Self: Subjectivity, Memory, and Tradition*. New York: Cambridge University Press, 2004.

——. *The Truth Within: A History of Inwardness in Christianity, Hinduism, and Buddhism*. New York: Oxford University Press, 2013.

Foucault, Michel. *The History of Sexuality: An Introduction*. Translated by Robert Hurley. New York: Vintage, 1990.

——. *The History of Sexuality*. Vol. 2, *The Use of Pleasure*. Translated by Robert Hurley. New York: Vintage, 1990.

——. *The History of Sexuality*. Vol. 3, *The Care of the Self*. Translated by Robert Hurley. New York: Vintage, 1988.

——. *Power/Knowledge*. New York: Pantheon, 1980.

Franchot, Jenny. "Invisible Domain: Religion and American Literary Studies." *American Literature* 67, no. 4 (1995): 833–842.

Frazer, James. *The Golden Bough: A New Abridgement*. Edited by Robert Fraser. New York: Oxford University Press, 1994.

Freud, Sigmund. *Civilization and Its Discontents*. Translated by James Strachey. New York: Norton, 2010.

——. *The Future of an Illusion*. Translated by James Strachey. New York: Norton, 1975.

——. *Totem and Taboo*. Translated by James Strachey. New York: Norton, 1950.

Froula, Christine. *Virginia Woolf and the Bloomsbury Avant-Garde*. New York: Columbia University Press, 2005.

Fry, Roger. *Vision and Design*. Mineola, NY: Dover, 1981.

Frye, Northrop. *Fearful Symmetry: A Study of William Blake*. Princeton: Princeton University Press, 1947.

Fulkerson, Laurel. *No Regrets: Remorse in Classical Antiquity*. New York: Oxford University Press, 2013.

Fuller, John. *W. H. Auden: A Commentary*. Princeton: Princeton University Press, 1998.

Gadamer, Hans-Georg. *The Relevance of the Beautiful*. Translated by Nicholas Walker. New York: Cambridge University Press, 1989.

——. *Truth and Method*. Translated by Joel Weinsheimer and Donald G. Marshall. New York: Continuum, 2000.

Gaipa, Mark. "An Agnostic Daughter's Apology: Materialism, Spiritualism, and Ancestry in Woolf's *To the Lighthouse*." *Journal of Modern Literature* 26, no. 2 (Winter 2002–2003): 1–41.

Gauchet, Marcel. *The Disenchantment of the World*. Translated by Oscar Burge. Princeton: Princeton University Press, 1997.

Gay, Peter. *The Enlightenment: The Rise of Modern Paganism*. New York: Norton, 1977.

Geertz, Clifford. *The Interpretation of Cultures*. New York: Basic Books, 2000.

Girard, René. *I See Satan Fall Like Lightning*. Translated by James G. Williams. New York: Orbis, 2001.

Goodrich-Clark, Nicholas. *The Occult Roots of Nazism: Secret Aryan Cults and Their Influence on Nazi Ideology.* New York: Tauris Parke, 2003.

Gorski, Philip. *The Protestant Ethic Revisited.* Philadelphia: Temple University Press, 2011.

Gourgouris, Stathis. *Lessons in Secular Criticism.* New York: Fordham University Press, 2013.

Gottlieb, Susannah Young-ah. *Regions of Sorrow: Anxiety and Messianism in Hannah Arendt and W. H. Auden.* Stanford: Stanford University Press, 2003.

——. "Two Versions of Voltaire: W. H. Auden and the Dialectic of Enlightenment." *PMLA* 120, no. 2 (March 2005): 388–413.

Graves, Robert. *The White Goddess.* New York: Farrar, Straus and Giroux, 1966.

Gregory, Brad. *The Unintended Reformation: How a Religious Revolution Secularized Society.* Cambridge: Harvard University Press, 2012.

Greenberg, Herbert. *Quest for the Necessary: W. H. Auden and the Dilemma of Divided Consciousness.* Cambridge: Harvard University Press, 1968.

Habermas, Jürgen. *Religion and Rationality: Essay on Reason, God, and Modernity.* Edited by Eduardo Mendieta. Cambridge: MIT Press, 2002.

Hadot, Pierre. *Philosophy as a Way of Life: Spiritual Exercises from Socrates to Foucault.* Oxford: Blackwell, 1995.

Hamann, Johann Georg. *Writings on Philosophy and Language.* Edited by Kenneth Haynes. New York: Cambridge University Press, 2007.

Hanson, Ellis. *Decadence and Catholicism.* Ithaca: Cornell University Press, 1998.

Harpham, Geoffrey Galt. *The Ascetic Imperative in Culture and Criticism.* Chicago: University of Chicago Press, 1987.

Harrison, Peter. *The Bible, Protestantism, and the Rise of Natural Science.* New York: Cambridge University Press, 2001.

——. *The Fall of Man and the Foundations of Science.* New York: Cambridge University Press, 2009.

Hart, David Bentley. *The Beauty of the Infinite: An Aesthetics of Christian Truth.* Grand Rapids, MI: Eerdmans, 2003.

Hecht, Anthony. *The Hidden Law: The Poetry of W. H. Auden.* Cambridge: Harvard University Press, 1993.

Hegel, G. W. F. *Aesthetic Theory.* Translated by Robert Hullot-Kentor. Minneapolis: University of Minnesota Press, 1997.

——. *Introductory Lectures on Aesthetics.* Translated by Bernard Bosanquet. New York: Penguin, 2004.

——. *The Phenomenology of Mind.* Translated by J. B. Baillie. New York: Harper Torchbacks, 1967.

Heidegger, Martin. *The Principle of Reason.* Translated by Reginald Lilly. Bloomington: Indiana University Press, 1991.

Heller, Erich. *The Disinherited Mind: Essays on Modern German Literature and Thought.* New York: Harcourt Brace Jovanovich, 1975.

Higgins, Lesley. *The Modernist Cult of Ugliness.* New York: Palgrave Macmillan, 2002.

Hufstader, Jonathan. "Auden's Sacred World." *Essays in Criticism* 59, no. 3 (2009): 234–254.

Hügel, Friedrich von. *The Mystical Element of Religion*. 2 vols. New York: Crossroad, 1999.

Hulme, T. E. *Selected Writings*. New York: Routledge, 2003.

Hume, David. *Dialogues Concerning Natural Religion and Natural History of Religion*. New York: Oxford University Press, 1993.

Hungerford, Amy. *Postmodern Belief: American Literature and Religion since 1960*. Princeton: Princeton University Press, 2010.

Hussey, Mark. *The Singing of the Real World: The Philosophy of Virginia Woolf's Fiction*. Columbus: Ohio State University Press, 1986.

Izzo, David, ed. *W. H. Auden: A Legacy*. West Cornwall, CT: Locust Hill Press, 2002.

Jacobs, Alan. *What Became of Wystan: Continuity and Change in Auden's Poetry*. Fayetteville: University of Arkansas Press, 1998.

Jager, Colin. *The Book of God: Secularization and Design in the Romantic Era*. Philadelphia: University of Pennsylvania Press, 2007.

James, Henry. *The Art of Criticism: Henry James on the Theory and Practice of Fiction*. Edited by William Veeder. Chicago: University of Chicago Press, 1986.

James, William. *Pragmatism and Other Writings*. Edited by Giles Gunn. New York: Penguin, 2000.

———. *The Varieties of Religious Experience*. New York: Modern Library, 2002.

Jarraway, David R. "Stevens and Belief." In *The Cambridge Companion to Wallace Stevens*, edited by John N. Serio, 193–206. New York: Cambridge University Press, 2007.

———. *Wallace Stevens and the Questions of Belief: Metaphysician in the Dark*. Baton Rouge: Louisiana State University Press, 1993.

Jarrell, Randall. *Randall Jarrell on W. H. Auden*. Edited by Stephen Burt. New York: Columbia University Press, 2005.

Jaspers, Karl. *Vom Ursprung und Zeil der Geschichte*. Zurich: Artemis, 1949.

Jeffares, A. Norman. *A New Commentary on the Poems of W. B. Yeats*. Stanford: Stanford University Press, 1984.

Jenkyns, Richard. *The Victorians and Ancient Greece*. Oxford: Blackwell, 1980.

Jones, John. *On Aristotle and Greek Tragedy*. New York: Cambridge University Press, 1968.

Josipovici, Gabriel. *On Trust: Art and the Temptations of Suspicion*. New Haven: Yale University Press, 1999.

Joyce, James. *The Critical Writings*. Ithaca: Cornell University Press, 1989.

———. *A Portrait of the Artist as a Young Man*. New York: Penguin, 2003.

———. *Stephen Hero*. New York: New Directions, 1963.

———. *Ulysses*. New York: Vintage, 1986.

Kafka, Franz. *The Basic Kafka*. Edited by Eric Heller. New York: Simon and Schuster, 1979.

Kane, Julie. "Varieties of Mystical Experience in the Writings of Virginia Woolf." *Twentieth Century Literature* 41, no. 4 (Winter 1995): 328–349.

Kant, Immanuel. *The Critique of Practical Reason*. Translated by Mary Gregor. Cambridge University Press, 1997.

———. *Critique of the Power of Judgment*. Translated by Paul Guyer and Eric Matthews. New York: Cambridge University Press, 2000.

Keane, Webb. *Christian Moderns: Freedom and Fetish in the Mission Encounter.* Berkeley: University of California Press, 2007.

Kermode, Frank. *Romantic Image.* New York: Routledge, 2002.

———. *The Sense of an Ending.* New York: Oxford University Press, 2000.

Kierkegaard, Soren. *Either/Or.* Translated by Walter Lowrie. Princeton: Princeton University Press, 1971.

———. *The Humor of Kierkegaard: An Anthology.* Edited by Thomas Oden. Princeton: Princeton University Press, 2004.

———. *The Living Thoughts of Kierkegaard.* Edited by W. H. Auden. New York: New York Review Books, 1952.

Kirsch, Arthur. *Auden and Christianity.* New Haven: Yale University Press, 2005.

Kirwin, James. *Sublimity.* New York: Routledge, 2004.

Kitcher, Philip. *Life after Faith: The Case for Secular Humanism.* New Haven: Yale University Press, 2015.

Kohak, Erazim. *The Embers and the Stars: A Philosophical Inquiry into the Moral Sense of Nature.* Chicago: University of Chicago Press, 1984.

Kofman, Sarah. *Nietzsche and Metaphor.* Translated by Duncan Large. Stanford: Stanford University Press, 1993.

Konstan, David. *Before Forgiveness: The Origins of a Moral Idea.* New York: Cambridge University Press, 2010.

Latour, Bruno. *We Have Never Been Modern.* Translated by Catherine Porter. Cambridge: Harvard University Press, 1993.

Lawrence, D. H. *Apocalypse.* New York: Cambridge University Press, 1985.

———. *The Selected Short Stories of D. H. Lawrence.* New York: Modern Library, 1999.

Lee, Phillip. *Against the Protestant Gnostics.* New York: Oxford University Press, 1987.

Lee, Susanna. *A World Abandoned by God: Narrative and Secularism.* Lewisburg, PA: Bucknell University Press, 2006.

Leggett, B. J. *Early Stevens: The Nietzschean Intertext.* Durham, NC: Duke University Press, 1992.

———. *Wallace Stevens and Poetic Theory.* Chapel Hill: University of North Carolina Press, 1987.

Lensing, George. *Wallace Stevens and the Seasons.* Baton Rouge: Louisiana State University Press, 2001.

Lentricchia, Frank. *Modernist Quartet.* New York: Cambridge University Press, 1994.

Lernout, Gert. *Help My Unbelief: James Joyce and Religion.* New York: Continuum, 2010.

Levenson, Michael. *A Genealogy of Modernism.* New York: Cambridge University Press, 1984.

———. *Modernism.* New Haven: Yale University Press, 2011.

———. *Modernism and the Fate of Individuality.* New York: Cambridge University Press, 1991.

Levin, Jonathan. *The Poetics of Transition: Emerson, Pragmatism, and American Literary Modernism.* Durham, NC: Duke University Press, 1999.

Levinas, Emmanuel. *Totality and Infinity.* Translated by Alphonso Lingis. Pittsburgh: Duquesne University Press, 1969.

Levine, George, ed. *The Joy of Secularism*. Princeton: Princeton University Press, 2011.

Levinson, Henry. *Santayana, Pragmatism, and the Spiritual Life*. Chapel Hill: University of North Carolina Press, 1992.

Lewis, Pericles. *Religious Experience in the Modernist Novel*. New York: Cambridge University Press, 2010.

Lewis, Wyndham. *Time and Western Man*. Boston: Beacon, 1957.

Longenbach, James. *Wallace Stevens: The Plain Sense of Things*. New York: Oxford University Press, 1991.

Lowe-Evans, Mary. *Catholic Nostalgia in Joyce and Company*. Gainesville: University of Florida Press, 2008.

Löwith, Karl. *Meaning in History: The Theological Implications of the Philosophy of History*. Chicago: University of Chicago Press, 1949.

Lucretius. *On the Nature of the Universe*. Translated by Ronald Melville. New York: Oxford University Press, 1997.

Lyotard, Jean-Francois. *The Inhuman*. Stanford: Stanford University Press, 1988.

MacDiarmid, Lucy. *Auden's Apologies for Poetry*. Princeton: Princeton University Press, 1990.

MacDonald, Margaret. *Early Christian Women and Pagan Opinion: The Power of the Hysterical Woman*. New York: Cambridge University Press, 1996.

Mahmood, Saba. *The Politics of Piety: The Islamic Revival and the Feminist Subject*. Princeton: Princeton University Press, 2005.

Mallarmé, Stéphane. *Divagations*. Translated by Barbara Johnson. Cambridge: Harvard University Press, 2007.

Mao, Douglas. "Auden and Son: Environment, Evolution, Exhibition." *Paideuma* 32 (2003): 301–349.

——. *Solid Objects: Modernism and the Test of Production*. Princeton: Princeton University Press, 1998.

Maritain, Jacques. *Creative Intuition in Art and Poetry*. New York: Meridian, 1957.

Marquard, Odo. *Farewell to Matters of Principle*. Translated by Robert M. Wallace. New York: Oxford University Press, 1989.

——. *In Defense of the Accidental*. Translated by Robert M. Wallace. New York: Oxford University Press, 1991.

Marx, Karl. *Selected Writings*. Edited by Lawrence H. Simon. New York: Hackett, 1994.

Masuzawa, Tomoko. *In Search of Dreamtime: The Quest for the Origin of Religion*. Chicago: University of Chicago Press, 1993.

——. *Invention of World Religions; or, How European Universalism Was Preserved in the Language of Pluralism*. Chicago: University of Chicago Press, 2005.

Materer, Timothy. *Modernist Alchemy: Poetry and the Occult*. Ithaca: Cornell University Press, 1995.

Mauron, Charles. *Aesthetics and Psychology*. Translated by Roger Fry. London: Hogarth Press, 1935.

——. *The Nature of Beauty in Art and Literature*. Translated by Roger Fry. London: Hogarth Press, 1927.

McClure, John. *Partial Faiths: Postsecular Fiction in the Age of Pynchon and Morrison.* Athens: University of Georgia Press, 2007.

McDonald, Peter. *Serious Poetry: Form and Authority from Yeats to Hill.* New York: Oxford, 2007.

Mendelson, Edward. *Early Auden.* New York: Farrar, Straus and Giroux, 2000.

———. *Later Auden.* New York: Farrar, Straus and Giroux, 1999.

Midgley, Mary. *Beast and Man: The Roots of Human Nature.* New York: Routledge, 1995.

———. *Wickedness: A Philosophical Essay.* New York: Routledge, 1984.

Milbank, John. *Theological Perspectives on God and Beauty.* New York: Continuum, 2003.

———. *Theology and Social Theory.* New York: Blackwell, 1990.

Miller, J. Hillis. *Poets of Reality.* Cambridge: Harvard University Press, 1965.

Monod, Jean-Claude. *Querelle de la sécularisation: Theólogie politique et philosophies de l'histoire de Hegel à Blumenberg.* Paris: Vrin, 2003.

Moore, G. E. *Principia Ethica.* New York: Cambridge University Press, 1994.

Moore, Marianne. *The Complete Prose of Marianne Moore.* New York: Penguin, 1987.

Morris, David. *The Culture of Pain.* Berkeley: University of California Press, 1991.

Moses, Michael Valdez. "Nietzsche." In *W. B. Yeats in Context,* edited by David Holdeman and Ben Levitas, 266–275. New York: Cambridge University Press, 2010.

Mouffe, Chantal. *Agonism: Thinking the World Politically.* New York: Verso, 2013.

Mulhall, Stephen. *Philosophical Myths of the Fall.* Princeton: Princeton University Press, 2005.

Murdoch, Iris. *Metaphysics as a Guide to Morals.* New York: Penguin, 1993.

Mutter, Matthew. "Human Flourishing and the Sovereignty of Feeling." *Hedgehog Review,* Spring 2010, 33–44.

Nabias, Nuno. *Nietzsche and the Metaphysics of Tragedy.* Translated by Martin Earl. New York: Continuum, 2006.

Nancy, Jean-Luc. "The Deconstruction of Monotheism." In *Religion: Beyond a Concept,* edited by Hent de Vries, 380–391. New York: Fordham University Press, 2008.

———. *Dis-enclosure: The Deconstruction of Christianity.* New York: Fordham University Press, 2008.

Nehamas, Alexander. *Only a Promise of Happiness: The Place of Beauty in a World of Art.* Princeton: Princeton University Press, 2007.

Neiman, Susan. *Evil in Modern Thought.* Princeton: Princeton University Press, 2002.

New, Elisa. *The Line's Eye: Poetic Experience, American Sight.* Cambridge: Harvard University Press, 1998.

———. *The Regenerate Lyric: Theology and Innovation in American Poetry.* New York: Cambridge University Press, 1993.

Ngai, Sianne. *Ugly Feelings.* Cambridge: Harvard University Press, 2005.

Nietzsche, Friedrich. *Beyond Good and Evil.* Translated by Judith Norman. New York: Cambridge University Press, 2002.

———. *The Birth of Tragedy.* Translated by Shaun Whiteside. New York: Penguin, 1994.

———. *Ecce Homo.* Translated by R. J. Hollingdale. New York: Penguin, 2004.

———. *The Gay Science.* Translated by Walter Kaufmann. New York: Vintage, 1974.

——. *Human, All Too Human*. Translated by R. J. Hollingdale. New York: Cambridge University Press, 1996.

——. *On the Genealogy of Morals and Ecce Homo*. Translated by Walter Kaufmann. New York: Vintage, 1969.

——. *The Portable Nietzsche*. Translated by Walter Kaufmann. New York: Viking Press, 1954.

——. *Thus Spoke Zarathustra*. Translated by Walter Kaufmann. New York: Penguin, 1966.

——. *Twilight of the Idols and the Antichrist*. Translated by R. J. Hollingdale. New York: Penguin, 1990.

——. *The Will to Power*. Translated by Walter Kaufmann and R. J. Hollingdale. New York: Vintage, 1968.

Nongbri, Brent. *Before Religion: A History of a Modern Concept*. New Haven: Yale University Press, 2013.

North, Michael. *Reading 1922*. New York: Oxford University Press, 2001.

Novalis. *Philosophical Writings*. Translated by Margaret Stoljar. Albany: SUNY Press, 1997.

Nussbaum, Martha. *Upheavals of Thought: The Intelligence of the Emotions*. New York: Cambridge University Press, 2003.

Olson, Liesl. *Modernism and the Ordinary*. New York: Oxford University Press, 2009.

——. "Wallace and Wystan, Antimythological Meetings." *W. H. Auden Society Newsletter* 23 (December 2002): 12–23.

O'Neill, Michael. *The All-Sustaining Air: Romantic Legacies and Renewals in British, American, and Irish Poetry since 1900*. New York: Oxford University Press, 2007.

Orsi, Robert. *Between Heaven and Earth: The Religious Worlds People Make and the Scholars Who Study Them*. Princeton: Princeton University Press, 2006.

——. "Everyday Miracles: The Study of Lived Religion." In *Lived Religion in America: Toward a History of Practice*, edited by David D. Hall, 3–21. Princeton: Princeton University Press, 1998.

Orwell, George. *The Collected Essays, Journalism and Letters of George Orwell*. Vol. 1. Edited by Sonia Orwell and Ian Angus. New York: Penguin, 1970.

Ovid. *The Metamorphoses*. Translated by Charles Martin. New York: Norton, 2004.

Owen, Alex. *The Place of Enchantment: British Occultism and the Cult of the Modern*. Chicago: University of Chicago Press, 2007.

Pannenberg, Wolfhart. *Anthropology in Theological Perspective*. New York: Continuum, 1985.

Pearce, Roy Harvey, and J. Hillis Miller, eds. *The Act of the Mind: Essays on the Poetry of Wallace Stevens*. Baltimore: Johns Hopkins University Press, 1965.

Pecora, Vincent. *Secularization and Cultural Criticism*. Chicago: University of Chicago Press, 2006.

Perl, Jeffrey. *Skepticism and Modern Enmity: Before and After Eliot*. Baltimore: Johns Hopkins University Press, 1989.

Pfau, Thomas. *Minding the Modern: Human Agency, Intellectual Traditions, and Responsible Knowledge*. Notre Dame: University of Notre Dame Press, 2013.

Phillips, Siobhan. *The Poetics of the Everyday: Creative Repetition in Modern American Verse*. New York: Columbia University Press, 2010.

Pike, James A., ed. *Modern Canterbury Pilgrims*. London: Morehouse Gorham, 1956.

Plato. *Phaedo*. Translated by David Gallop. New York: Oxford, 1993.

Poirier, Richard. *The Renewal of Literature*. New Haven: Yale University Press, 1987.

Potkay, Adam. *The Story of Joy: From the Bible to Late Romanticism*. New York: Cambridge University Press, 2011.

Poulet, Georges. *The Metamorphoses of the Circle*. Translated by Carley Dawson and Elliott Coleman. Baltimore: Johns Hopkins University Press, 1966.

Pound, Ezra. *The Cantos of Ezra Pound*. New York: New Directions, 1996.

———. *Selected Essays*. New York: New Directions, 1973.

Preus, J. Samuel. *Explaining Religion*. New Haven: Yale University Press, 1987.

Proust, Marcel. *In Search of Lost Time*. Vol. 1, *Swann's Way*. Translated by C. K. Scott Moncrieff and Terence Kilmartin. Revised by D. J. Enright. New York: Modern Library, 2003.

Pryor, Sean. *W. B. Yeats, Ezra Pound, and the Poetry of Paradise*. London: Ashgate, 2013.

Ramazani, Jahan. *Poetry of Mourning: The Modern Elegy from Hardy to Heaney*. Chicago: University of Chicago Press, 1994.

———. *Yeats and the Poetry of Death: Elegy, Self-Elegy, and the Sublime*. New Haven: Yale University Press, 1990.

Ransom, John Crowe. "Artists, Soldiers, Positivists." *Kenyon Review* 6 (Spring 1944): 276–277.

Rehder, Robert. *Stevens, Williams, Crane, and the Motive for Metaphor*. New York: Palgrave Macmillan, 2005.

Renza, Louis. "Wallace Stevens: Parts of an Autobiography, by Anonymous." *Journal of Modern Literature* 31, no. 3 (Spring 2008): 1–21.

Richards, I. A. *Poetries and Sciences*. New York: Norton, 1970.

Ricoeur, Paul. *Freud and Philosophy*. Translated by Denis Savage. New Haven: Yale University Press, 1970.

———. *The Rule of Metaphor*. Translated by Robert Czerny. Toronto: University of Toronto Press, 1979.

———. *The Symbolism of Evil*. Translated by Emerson Buchanan. Boston: Beacon, 1986.

Riddel, Joseph. *The Clairvoyant Eye: The Poetry and Poetics of Wallace Stevens*. Baton Rouge: Louisiana State University Press, 1965.

Rieff, Philip. *The Triumph of the Therapeutic: The Uses of Faith after Freud*. Chicago: University of Chicago Press, 1966.

Rilke, Rainer Maria. *Ahead of All Parting: The Selected Poetry and Prose of Rainer Maria Rilke*. Translated by Stephen Mitchell. New York: Modern Library, 1995.

Roberts, Beth Ellen. "W. H. Auden and the Jews." *Journal of Modern Literature* 28, no. 3 (Spring 2005): 87–108.

Roberts, Tyler. *Contesting Spirit: Nietzsche, Affirmation, Religion*. Princeton: Princeton University Press, 1998.

Rougement, Denis de. *Love in the Western World*. Translated by Montgomery Belgion. New York: Harper and Row, 1940.

Rowland, Christopher. *Blake and the Bible*. New Haven: Yale University Press, 2010.

Said, Edward. *The World, the Text, and the Critic.* Cambridge: Harvard University Press, 1983.

Santayana, George. *Egotism in German Philosophy.* New York: Haskell House, 1971.

———. *The Genteel Tradition: Nine Essays.* Edited by Douglas L. Wilson. Lincoln: University of Nebraska Press, 1998.

———. *Interpretations of Poetry and Religion.* Edited by William Holzberger and Herman Saatkamp. Cambridge: MIT Press, 1989.

———. *The Last Puritan: A Memoir in the Form of a Novel.* Edited by William Holzberger and Herman Saatkamp. Cambridge: MIT Press, 1994.

———. *Obiter Scripta.* New York: Charles Scribner's Sons, 1936.

———. *The Realm of Spirit.* New York: Scribner, 1940.

———. *The Sense of Beauty.* New York: Dover, 1955.

———. *Skepticism and Animal Faith.* New York: Dover, 1955.

Scarry, Elaine. *The Body in Pain.* New York: Oxford University Press, 1985.

———. *On Beauty and Being Just.* Princeton: Princeton University Press, 2001.

Schilbrack, Kevin. "Religion, Models of, and Reality: Are We Through with Geertz?" *Journal of the American Academy of Religion* 73, no. 2 (June 2005): 429–452.

Schiller, Friedrich. *Essays.* Translated by Daniel Dahlstrom. New York: Continuum, 2001.

Schleiermacher, Frederick. *The Christian Faith.* Translated by H. R. Mackintosh and J. S. Stewart. London: T and T Clark, 1999.

Schopenhauer, Arthur. *The World as Will and Representation.* Translated by E. F. J. Payne. New York: Dover, 1969.

Scruton, Roger. *Beauty: A Very Short Introduction.* New York: Oxford University Press, 2011.

Serio, John N. *The Cambridge Companion to Wallace Stevens.* New York: Cambridge University Press, 2007.

Shakespeare, William. *King Lear.* Edited by Stephen Orgel. New York: Penguin, 1999.

Shaviro, Steven. "That Which Is Always Beginning: Stevens's Poetry of Affirmation." *PMLA* 100, no. 2 (March 1985): 220–233.

Shelley, Percy Bysshe. *Shelley's Poetry and Prose.* Edited by Donald H. Reiman and Neil Fraistat. New York: Norton, 2002.

Siedentop, Larry. *Inventing the Individual: The Origins of Western Liberalism.* Cambridge: Harvard University Press, 2014.

Stallworthy, Jon. *Between the Lines: Yeats's Poetry in the Making.* New York: Oxford University Press, 1963.

Stauffer, Andrew. *Anger, Revolution, and Romanticism.* New York: Cambridge, 2009.

Stephen, Leslie. *An Agnostic's Apology and Other Essays.* London: Smith, Elder, 1893.

Stevens, Wallace. *Collected Poetry and Prose.* Edited by Frank Kermode and Joan Richardson. New York: Library of America, 1997.

———. *Letters of Wallace Stevens.* Edited by Holly Stevens. Berkeley: University of California Press, 1996.

———. *Sur Plusieurs Beaux Sujets: Wallace Stevens's Commonplace Book.* Edited by Milton Bates. Stanford: Stanford University Press, 1989.

Stewart, Susan. *Poetry and the Fate of the Senses*. Chicago: University of Chicago Press, 2002.

Stocker, Michael. *Valuing Emotions*. New York: Cambridge University Press, 1996.

Storrs, Richard. *The Eclipse of God*. New York: Harper, 1952.

Stout, Jeffrey. *Democracy and Tradition*. Princeton: Princeton University Press, 2004.

Surette, Leon. *The Birth of Modernism: Ezra Pound, T. S. Eliot, W. B. Yeats, and the Occult*. Montreal: McGill-Queens University Press, 1993.

Styers, Randall. *Making Magic: Religion, Magic, and Science in the Modern World*. New York: Oxford University Press, 2004.

Sword, Helen. *Ghostwriting Modernism*. Ithaca: Cornell University Press, 2002.

Symons, Arthur. *The Symbolist Movement in Literature*. New York: Dutton, 1919.

Tate, Allen. *Essays of Four Decades*. Wilmington, DE: ISI Books, 1999.

Taussig, Michael. *The Magic of the State*. New York: Routledge, 1997.

Taylor, Charles. *Modern Social Imaginaries*. Durham, NC: Duke University Press, 2006.

——. *Philosophical Papers*. Vol. 1, *Human Agency and Language*. New York: Cambridge University Press, 1985.

——. *Philosophical Papers*. Vol. 2, *Philosophy and the Human Sciences*. New York: Cambridge University Press, 1985.

——. *A Secular Age*. Cambridge: Harvard University Press, 2007.

——. *Sources of the Self*. Cambridge: Harvard University Press, 1989.

Taylor, Mark C. *After God*. Chicago: University of Chicago Press, 2007.

Tillich, Paul. *The Interpretation of History*. Translated by Elsa Rasetzki. New York: Charles Scribner's Sons, 1936.

Toomer, Jean. *Cane*. New York: Norton, 2011.

Trilling, Lionel. *Sincerity and Authenticity*. Cambridge: Harvard University Press, 1970.

Tylor, E. B. *Religion in Primitive Culture*. London: Peter Smith, 1970.

Van Der Leeuw, Gerardus. *Sacred and Profane Beauty: The Holy in Life*. New York: Holt, Rinehart and Winston, 1963.

Vendler, Helen. *On Extended Wings: Wallace Stevens' Longer Poems*. Cambridge: Harvard University Press, 1969.

——. *Our Secret Discipline: Yeats and Lyric Form*. Cambridge: Harvard University Press, 2007.

——. *Wallace Stevens: Words Chosen out of Desire*. Knoxville: University of Tennessee Press, 1984.

Vickery, John. *The Literary Impact of the Golden Bough*. Princeton: Princeton University Press, 1973.

Vico, Giambattista. *The New Science of Giambattista Vico*. Translated by Thomas Bergen. Ithaca: Cornell University Press, 1968.

Viswanathan, Gauri. "Secularism in the Framework of Heterodoxy." *PMLA* 123, no. 2 (March 2008): 466–476.

——. "Spectrality's Secret Sharers: Occultism as (Post)Colonial Affect." In *Beyond the Black Atlantic*, edited by Walter Goebel and Saskia Schabio, 135–146. New York: Routledge, 2006.

Ward, Graham. *Cities of God*. New York: Routledge, 2002.

Warner, Michael. "Is Liberalism a Religion?" In *Religion: Beyond a Concept*, edited by Hent de Vries, 610–617. New York: Fordham University Press, 2008.

Weber, Max. *From Max Weber: Essays in Sociology*. Translated by H. H. Gerth and C. Wright Mills. New York: Oxford University Press, 1958.

——. *The Protestant Ethic and the "Spirit" of Capitalism and Other Writings*. Translated by Peter Baehr and Gordon Wells. New York: Penguin, 2002.

——. *The Sociology of Religion*. Translated by Ephraim Fischoff. London: Methuen, 1965.

Weil, Simone. *First and Last Notebooks*. Translated by Richard Rees. New York: Oxford University Press, 1970.

——. *Gravity and Grace*. Translated by Arthur Wills. Lincoln: University of Nebraska Press, 1997.

——. *The Notebooks of Simone Weil*. Translated by Arthur Mills. New York: Routledge, 2004.

——. *The Simone Weil Reader*. Edited by George Panichas. London: Moyer Bell, 1977.

——. *Waiting for God*. Translated by Emma Craufurd. New York: Harper Perennial, 2001.

Weiskel, Thomas. *The Romantic Sublime*. Baltimore: Johns Hopkins University Press, 1976.

West, Nathanael. *Novels and Other Writings*. New York: Library of America, 1997.

Westphal, Merold. *Suspicion and Faith: The Religious Uses of Modern Atheism*. New York: Fordham University Press, 1999.

Williams, Bernard. *Shame and Necessity*. Berkeley: University of California Press, 1993.

Winters, Yvor. "The Poetry of W. B. Yeats." *Twentieth-Century Literature* 6, no. 1 (April 1960): 3–24.

Wittgenstein, Ludwig. "A Lecture on Ethics." *Philosophical Review* 74 (January 1965): 3–12.

——. *Remarks on Frazer's Golden Bough*. London: Brynmill, 1979.

——. *Tractatus Logico-Philosophicus*. Translated by D. F. Pears and B. F. McGuiness. New York: Routledge and Kegan, 1961.

Wolin, Richard. *The Seduction of Unreason: The Intellectual Romance with Fascism from Nietzsche to Postmodernism*. Princeton: Princeton University Press, 2006.

Wood, James. *The Broken Estate: Essays on Literature and Belief*. New York: Modern Library, 2000.

Wood, Michael. *Yeats and Violence*. New York: Oxford University Press, 2010.

Woodman, Leonora. *Stanza My Stone: Wallace Stevens and the Hermetic Tradition*. West Lafayette, IN: Purdue University Press, 1983.

Woolf, Virginia. *Between the Acts*. New York: Harcourt, 1969.

——. *The Common Reader*. New York: Harcourt, 1953.

——. *The Complete Shorter Fiction of Virginia Woolf*. New York: Harcourt, 1989.

——. *The Diary of Virginia Woolf*. Edited by Anne Olivier Bell and Andrew McNeillie. Vol. 3, 1925–1930. New York: Harcourt, 1980.

——. *The Essays of Virginia Woolf*. Edited by Andrew McNeillie. Vol. 3, 1919–1924. New York: Harcourt, 1988.

——. *The Essays of Virginia Woolf.* Edited by Andrew McNeillie. Vol. 4, 1925–1928. New York: Harcourt, 1994.

——. *The Letters of Virginia Woolf.* Edited by Nigel Nicolson and Joanne Trautmann. Vol. 3, 1923–1928. New York: Harcourt Brace Jovanovich, 1977.

——. *The Letters of Virginia Woolf.* Edited by Nigel Nicolson and Joanne Trautmann. Vol. 4, 1929–1931. New York: Harcourt, 1975.

——. *Moments of Being.* New York: Harcourt, 1985.

——. *Mr. Bennett and Mrs. Brown.* London: Hogarth Press, 1924.

——. *Mrs. Dalloway.* New York: Harcourt, 1981.

——. *Orlando.* New York: Harcourt, 2006.

——. *Roger Fry: A Biography.* New York: Harcourt, Brace, 1940.

——. *A Room of One's Own.* New York: Harcourt, 1957.

——. *To the Lighthouse.* New York: Harcourt, 1981.

——. *The Waves.* New York: Harcourt, 1959.

——. *A Writer's Diary.* Edited by Leonard Woolf. New York: Harcourt, 1982.

——. *The Voyage Out.* New York: Penguin, 1992.

Yeats, W. B. *The Collected Poems of W. B. Yeats.* Edited by Richard Finneran. New York: Scribner, 1996.

——. *The Collected Works of W. B. Yeats.* Vol. 2, *The Plays.* Edited by David Clark and Rosalind Clark. New York: Scribner, 2001.

——. *The Collected Works of W. B. Yeats.* Vol. 3, *Autobiographies.* Edited by William H. O'Donnell and Douglas N. Archibald. New York: Scribner, 1999.

——. *The Collected Works of W. B. Yeats.* Vol. 4, *Early Essays.* Edited by Richard Finneran and George Bornstein. New York: Scribner, 2007.

——. *The Collected Works of W. B. Yeats.* Vol. 5, *Later Essays.* Edited by William O'Donnell. New York: Scribner, 1994.

——. *The Collected Works of W. B. Yeats.* Vol. 9, *Early Articles and Reviews.* Edited by John Frayne and Madeleine Marchaterre. New York: Scribner, 2004.

——. *Essays and Introductions.* New York: Macmillan, 1961.

——. *Explorations.* New York: Collier, 1962.

——. *The Letters of W. B. Yeats.* Edited by Allan Wade. New York: Macmillan, 1955.

——. *Memoirs.* Edited by Denis Donoghue. New York: Macmillan, 1972.

——. *A Vision.* New York: Collier Press, 1977.

——. *The Winding Stair: Manuscript Materials.* Edited by David Clark. Ithaca: Cornell University Press, 1995.

——. *The Yeats Reader.* Edited by Richard J. Finneran. New York: Scribner, 2002.

Yerushalmi, Yosef. *Freud's Moses: Judaism Terminable and Interminable.* New Haven: Yale University Press, 1993.

Ziolkowski, Theodore. *Modes of Faith: Secular Surrogates for Lost Religious Belief.* Chicago: University of Chicago Press, 2007.

Zola, Émile. "The Experimental Novel." In *Documents of Modern Literary Realism,* edited by George J. Becker, 161–197. Princeton: Princeton University Press, 1963.

CREDITS

INDEX

Abrams, M. H., 8, 9, 13
Adams, Hazel, 142
Adams, Henry, 179
adaptation, secular method of, 9, 11–12, 31, 147, 226n39
Adorno, Theodor, 77, 94, 112, 173, 174, 177–178, 181, 250n29, 250n32, 274–275n112
aesthetic, category of, 192
aesthetic creation, logic of, 154
aesthetic experience, 5, 69, 192
aestheticism, 79, 81
aesthetic religion, 285n16
aesthetics, 22; anthropomorphic, 75; emphasizing psychology, 248n13; metaphysics and, 23, 72; organicist, 281n62; religion and, 65
affirmation, 15, 89, 139, 144, 212
agape, 18, 185–186, 266n35
agency, 21, 28, 79; of beauty, 92; causation and, 34; comedy and, 185; of the cosmos, 100; of human beings, 179, 188; of religion, 28; strategic, 236n110; of will, 19, 212; of the world, 73
agonism, 230–231n71
alienation, 9; aesthetic as remedy for, 192–193; magical thinking and, 176–177; rationalism and, 169
amor fati, 83, 86, 129, 266n37
analogical worldview, 42

analogy, 38–39; Auden's hesitation regarding, 176; desirability of, 51; and divine ordering of the world, 244n45; immanence and, 56–57; poetry and, 46; refusal of, 49; religion and, 51; Stevens on, 42–53, 56–57; understanding of, 46
analogy of being, 52
Anaximander, 142
anger, 136–137
animism, 34, 180
anthropocentrism, 16, 34, 21
anthropology: God and, 62; of religion, 43, 168, 193; religious and secular, 14; theology as, 10, 61
anthropomorphism, 22, 33; aesthetic, 36–37, 76–78, 93; critique of, 35–37, 40–42, 240n15; egotism and, 238n7; moral, 77, 93; poetry and, 37–38; projection of, 37; refusal of, 49; religious, 33, 93–94
antinomies, 132, 134
appearance, vs. reality, 75
Aquinas, Thomas, 52, 70
Arendt, Hannah, 116, 207
Aristotle, 123–124
Arnold, Matthew, 4, 10, 12, 16, 39, 99, 221n12
art: beauty and, 71, 92–93; as creation, 112; order achieved by, 75, 253n54; prehistory

religious sense of, 5, 32; in Romantic philosophy, 39–40; secular, 32, 165; shift in, from porous to buffered, 193; symmetry of, with the world, 101
self-consciousness, 9, 167, 171
self-division, 129
selfhood, in Auden, 176
self-identity, desire for, 184
self-knowledge, 121
self-unification, 266n30
sense: and eschatological possibility, 60; making the world, 210; secular paradise and, 210; Stevens on, 53–54
Sense of Beauty, The (Santayana), 66–67
senses, spiritual meaning of, 204–205
separation, ethical relationship and, 177
shadow: beauty and, 81–82; in Eliot, 239–240n13; power of, 73; in Stevens, 17, 18, 35–36
Shelley, Percy Bysshe, 27, 46, 119, 124, 151, 210–211
signs, 42, 245n46
Silver Tassie, The (O'Casey), 140
social identity, 1
social imaginary, 220n
social science, 7–8
social structures, as human creations, 189
social supernaturalism, 8
Sonnets to Orpheus (Rilke), 173
soul, 31–35, 107, 265n25
Spenser, Edmund, 247n5
Spinoza, Baruch, 241n23
spirit, devastation of, 215
spiritualism, 28
spiritual mediums, 28
Stauffer, Andrew, 124
Stendhal, 93, 127
Stephen, Leslie, 75, 76, 260n95
Stephen Hero (Joyce), 70–71
Stevens, Wallace, 2, 3, 4, 8, 21, 22, 29, 50, 105, 116; adopting dietetics of meaning, 44; aestheticist neopaganism in, 17–18; on alienation, 41; on analogy, 42–53, 56–57, 176; anthropomorphism and,

33–42, 37, 122; antihumanist stance of, 241–242n25; anxiety in, 205; Auden on, 163–164; on being a god, 62; chariot in work of, 60; on conflict, 20; critique of religious anthropomorphism, 33, 118; death of God/gods in, 23, 234–235n95; on decreation, 237n2 on desire, 47, 76, 209; desire of, for order, 47–49; on distinction between appearance and reality, 75; on dreams and shadows, 35–36; on egotism, 34; Emerson's influence on, 242–243n30; on eschatology, 59; evil and sense in, 209–210; on experience, 44, 45, 79; on the fall, 55–56; French Symbolism and, 43; on the gods, 10; Heidegger's influence on, 53; on human speech, 54; on the idea of God, 8–9; on idolatry, 45; on imagination, 22, 62; on the impersonal, 21; on instinct for heaven, 47; interest of, in genealogy of religious belief, 54; language and bias toward transcendence, 23; longing for animalistic language, 54; loss of religious faith, in poetics of, 30–31; material immanence in, 164; on metaphor, 53–56; as metaphysical writer, 220n; on "not ourselves," 39, 163; "occurrence" in language of, 49–50; ontology and, 20, 46; otherness in, 173; on paganism, 218n; on poetic impulse, 240–241n17; poetics of tautology and, 33; presupposing incongruity, 244n45; on radical politics, 60; "reality," dedication to, 14–15; reconceiving religion, 61; on relation, 48–49; on religious impulse, 240–241n17; religious language in, as "supreme fiction," 64; resisting asceticism, 218n; Romantics and, 243n35, 244n45; Santayana's